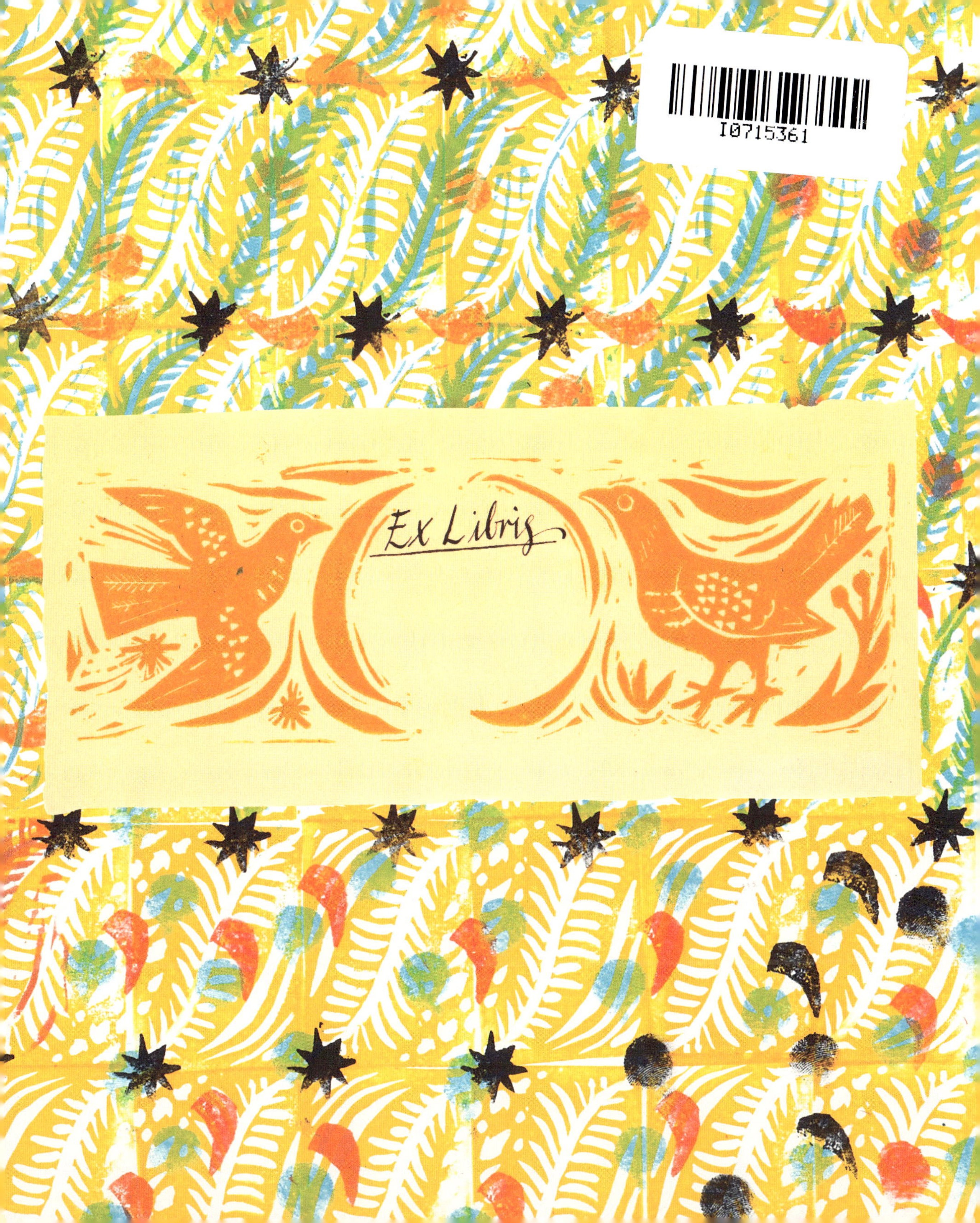
Ex Libris

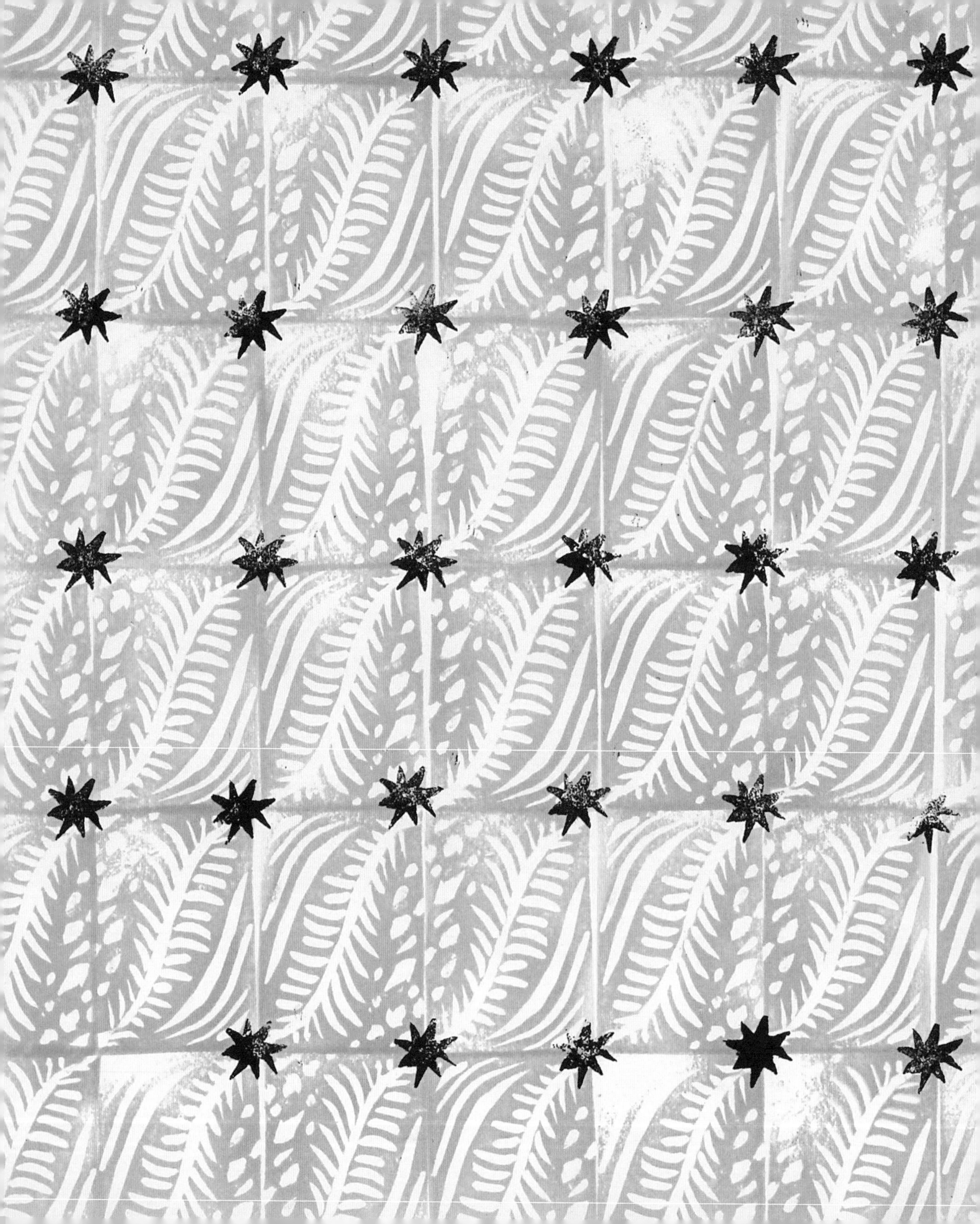

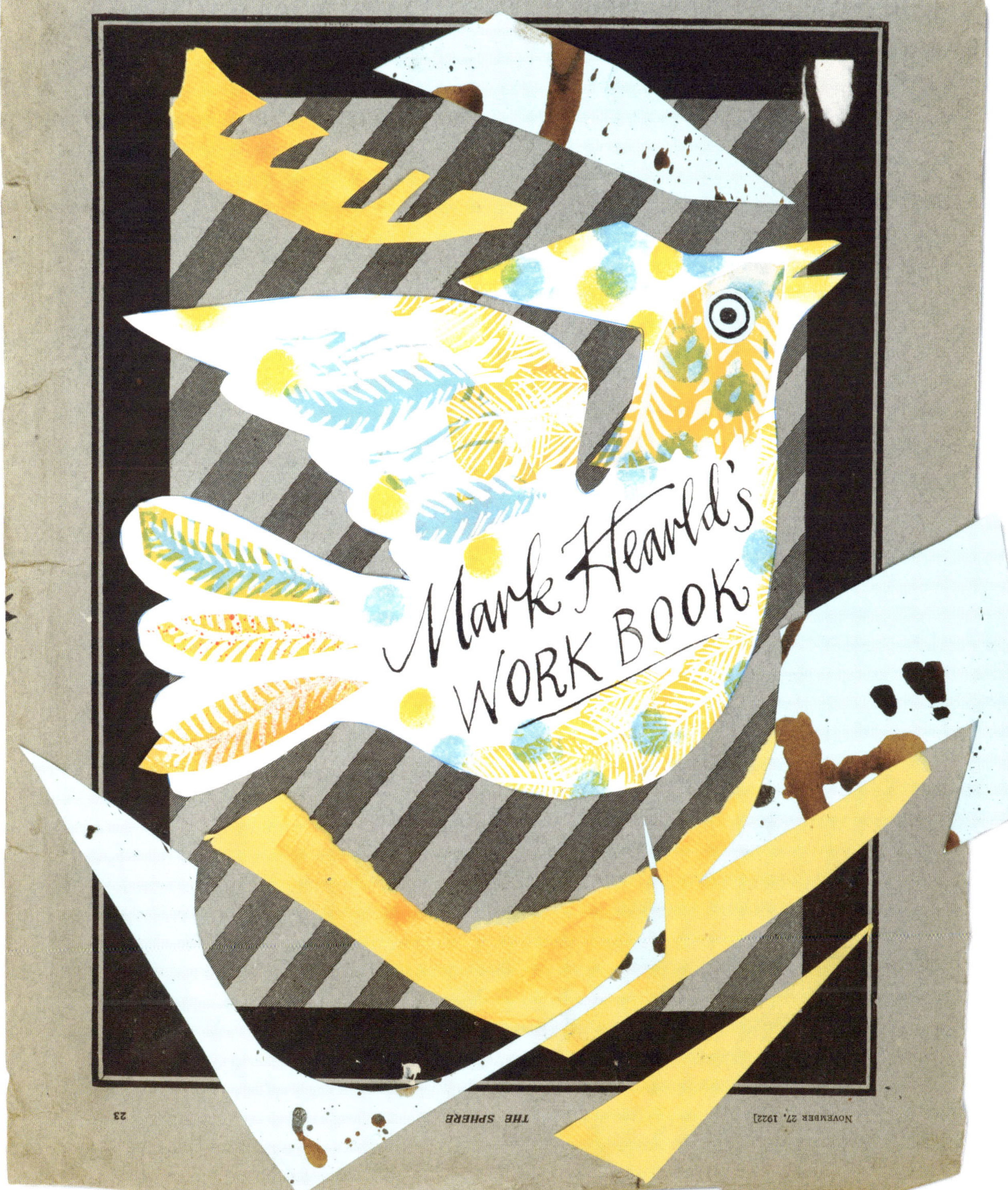

Mark Hearld's
WORK BOOK
23
THE SPHERE
[NOVEMBER 27, 1922]

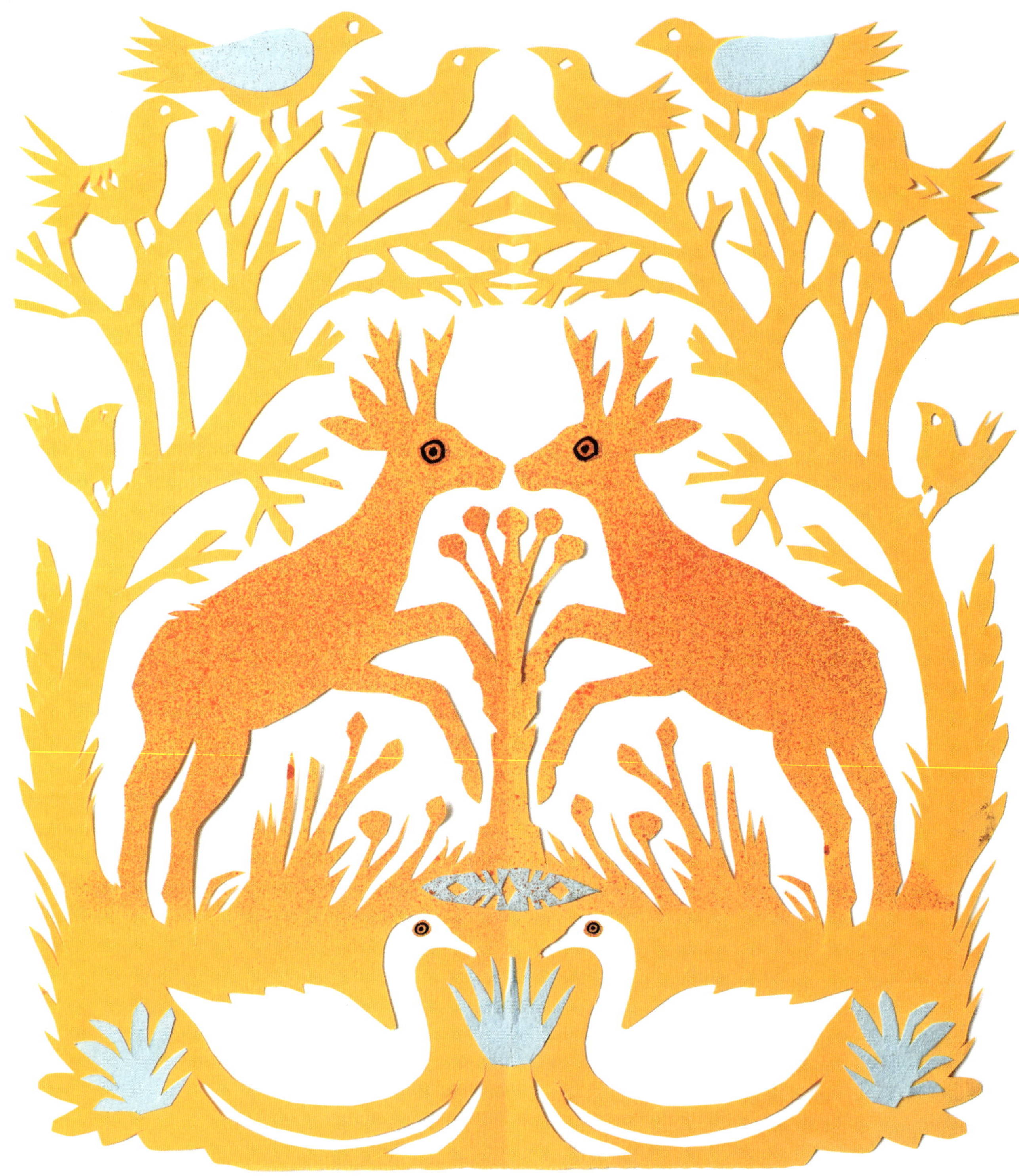

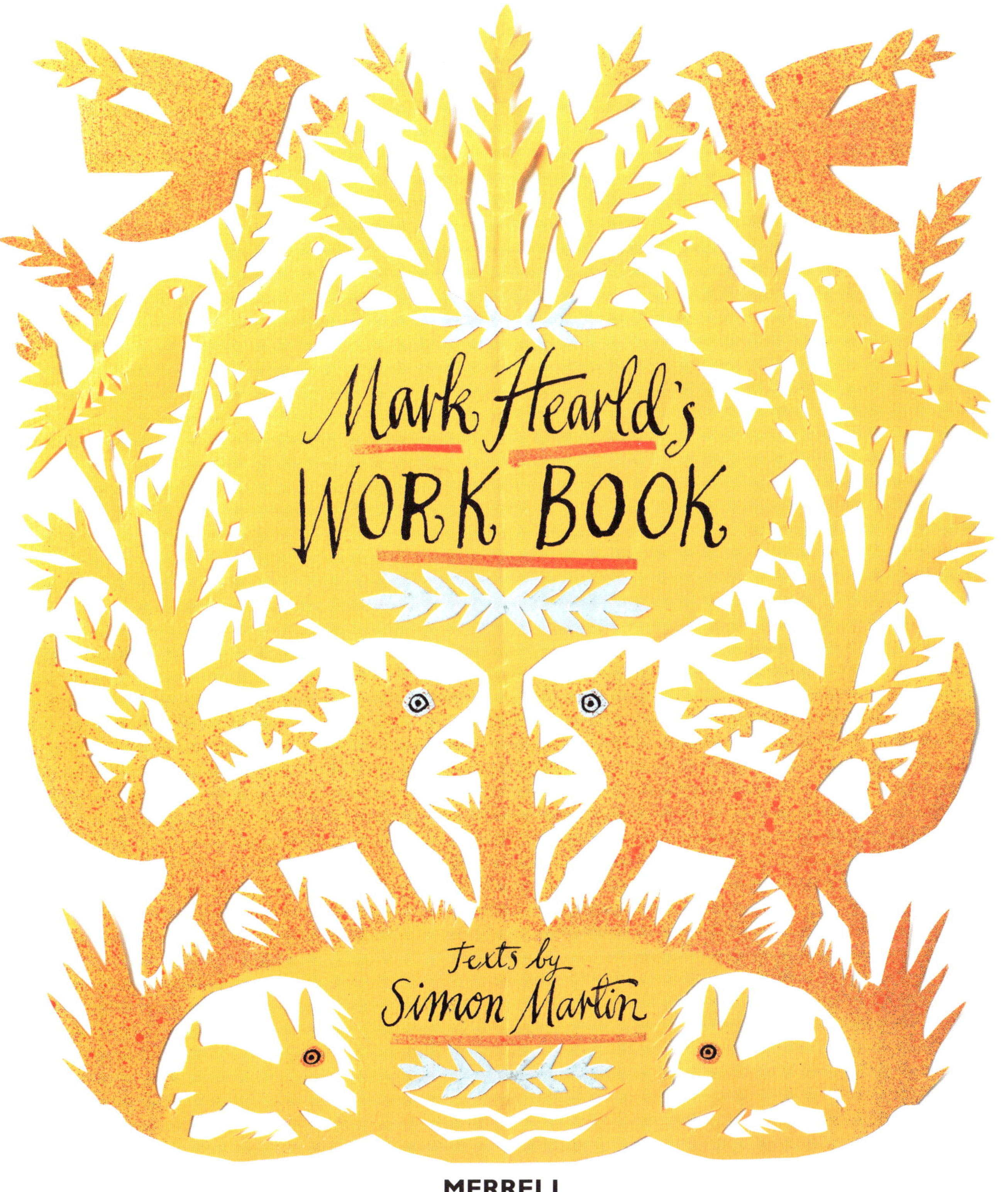

MERRELL

LONDON · NEW YORK

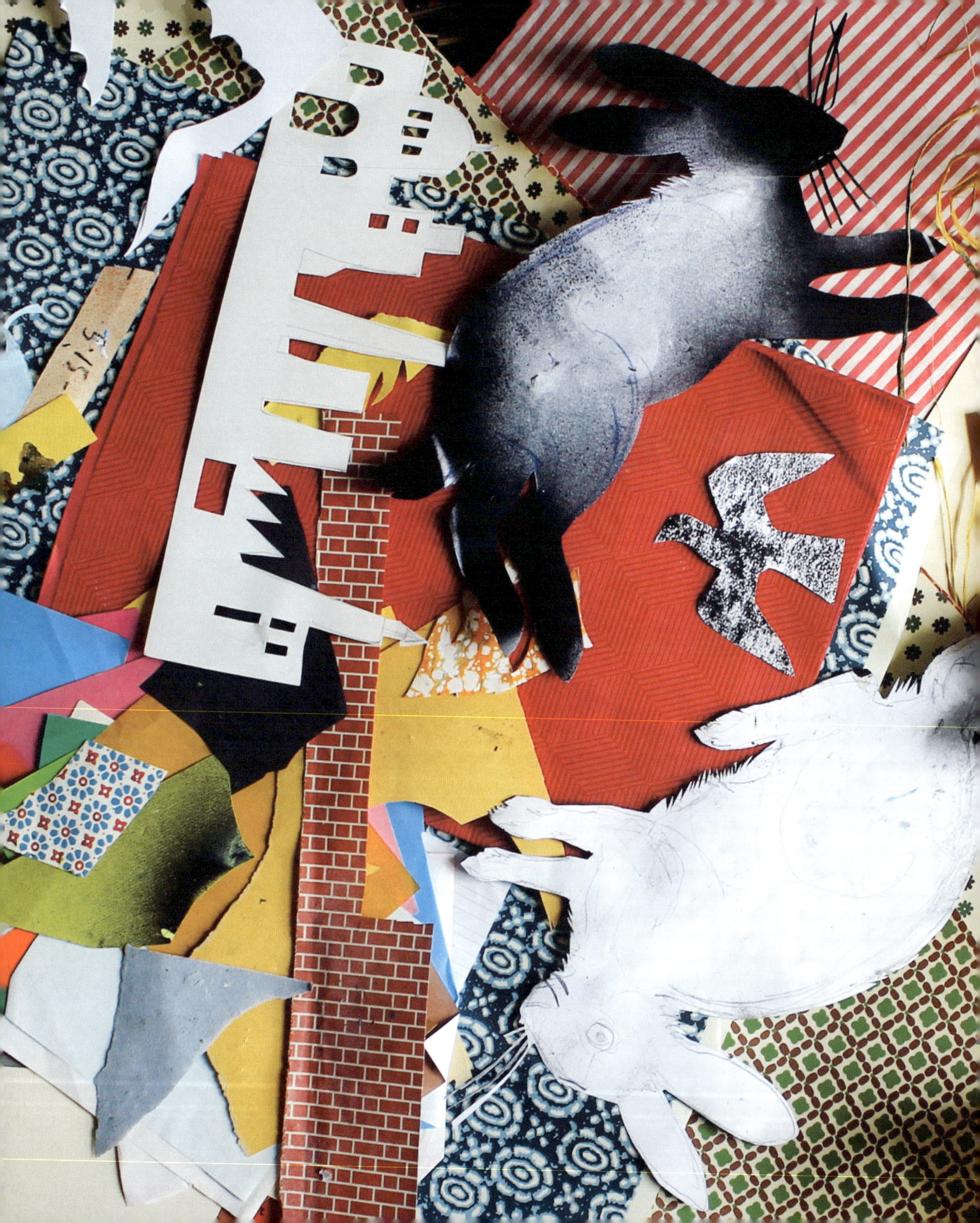

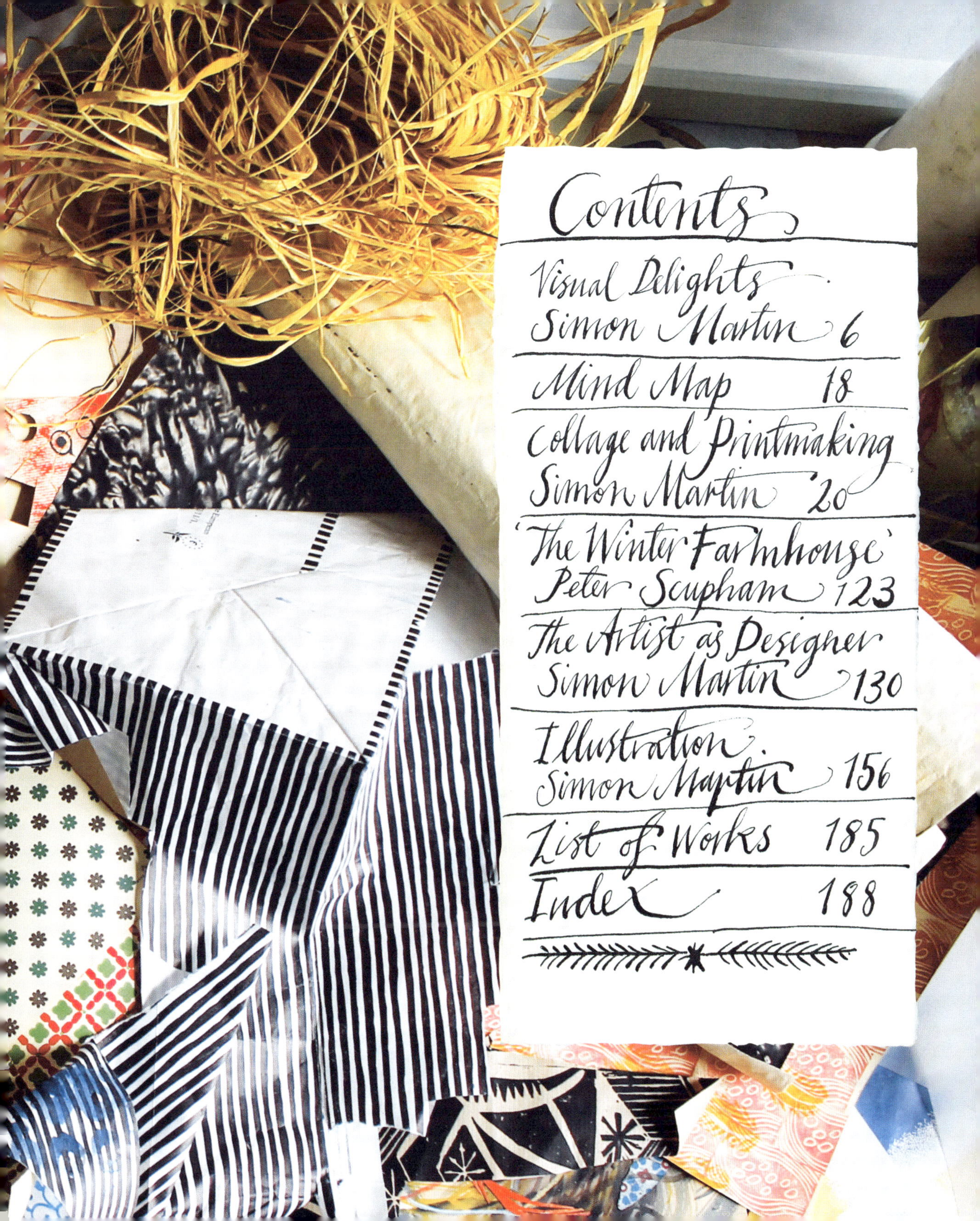

Contents

Mark Hearld's art encourages us to look with fresh eyes at the nature that surrounds us. It celebrates the flora and fauna that we so often take for granted: squirrels in the park, pigeons on the rooftops and gulls on the seashore. His birds and animals are full of vitality and character, whether they be linocuts or lithographs, collaged from scraps of paper, drawn or painted, printed on textiles, or reproduced on a dust jacket. Hearld is a remarkably versatile and creative individual, describing himself not only as an artist but also as a 'collagist, printmaker, designer of this and that, and collector of tat'. He has an unstoppable creativity that can seemingly be applied to any medium with equal skill. Behind this lies a sense of visual delight – a pleasure in creation and an inquisitive mode of looking that reveals the overlooked for all to enjoy.

Hearld's view of nature is inherently English, and is rooted in the seasonal variations of spring, summer, autumn and winter. The birds in his images are those that one might see when looking out of the window: starlings, pigeons, robins and gulls. Finding beauty in the everyday, rather than in picturesque or dramatic landscapes, Hearld focuses on the places where humans and nature come together: farmyards and smallholdings, pigeon lofts, duck ponds, the riverside and ports. Instead of depicting spectacular things, he looks for the extraordinary in the ordinary, presenting a single cockerel or goose in the manner of a prize bull in a folk-art painting. Yet any seeming naivety is actually a reflection of his appreciation for the directness of folk art, and is combined with a sophisticated handling of materials. Hearld's 'child's-eye view' brings a visual immediacy to his subject matter, as if we were seeing these birds and animals for the first time – not as mute specimens, but as creatures imbued with life and individual character.

Hearld relates his art to the notion of 'inscape', a concept used by the nineteenth-century poet Gerard Manley Hopkins to describe the characteristics that give, say, a gnarled tree its uniqueness and make it different from other things. Hearld feels a connection with paintings that focus on the qualities of specific objects in nature, such as *The Magic Apple Tree* (1830; page 8, left), Samuel Palmer's mystical depiction of a tree in Shoreham, Kent, which Hearld appreciates for its 'particularity, its intimate sense of place'. His essentially romantic, pastoral view of the natural world conveys something of the sense of

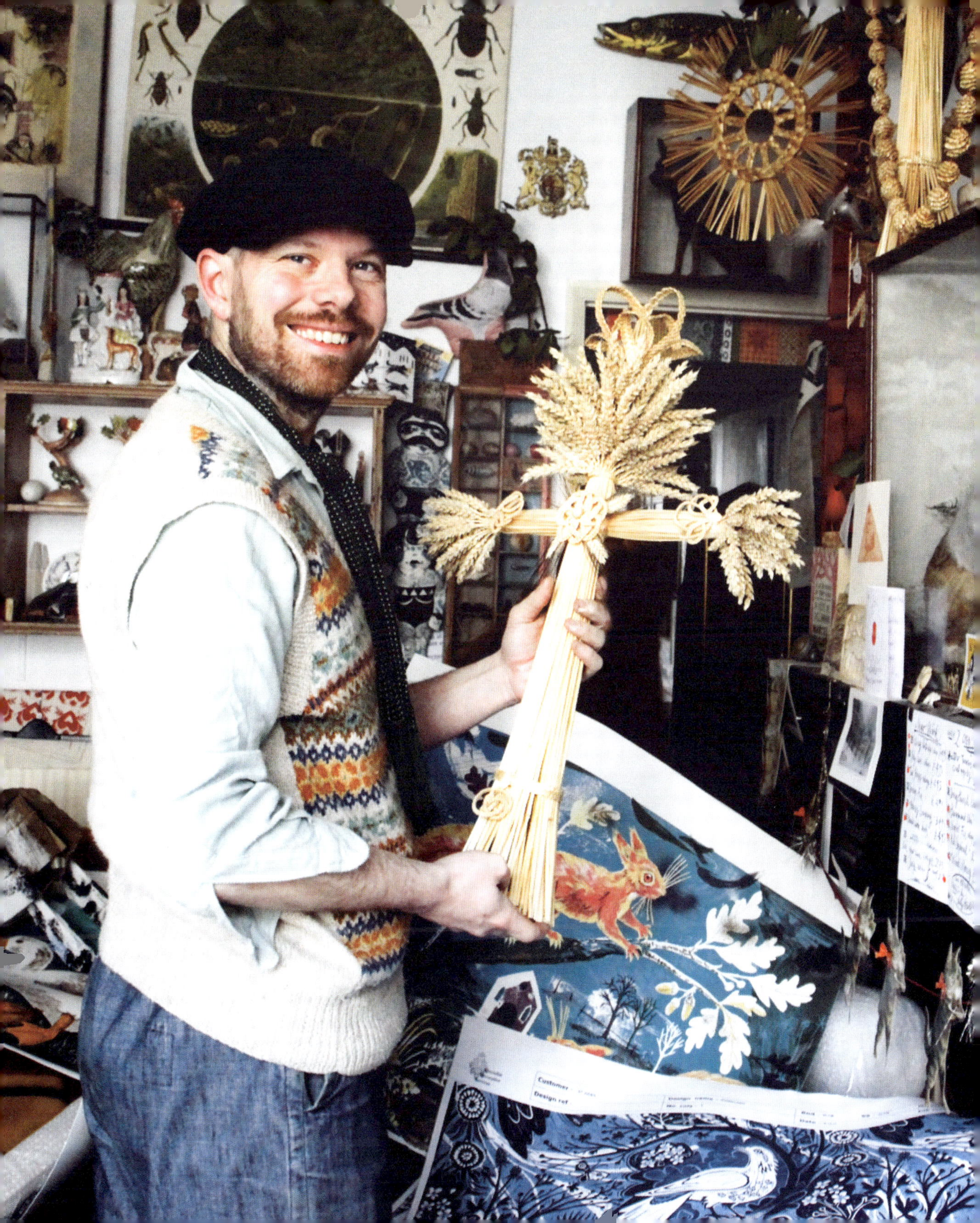

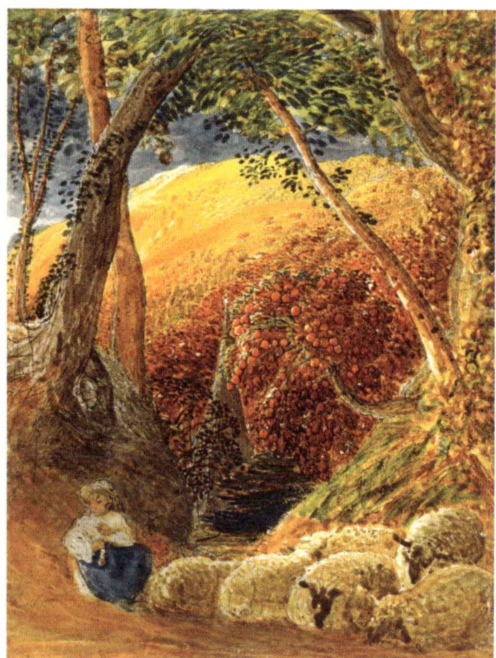

Samuel Palmer (1805–1881)
The Magic Apple Tree, 1830
The Fitzwilliam Museum, Cambridge

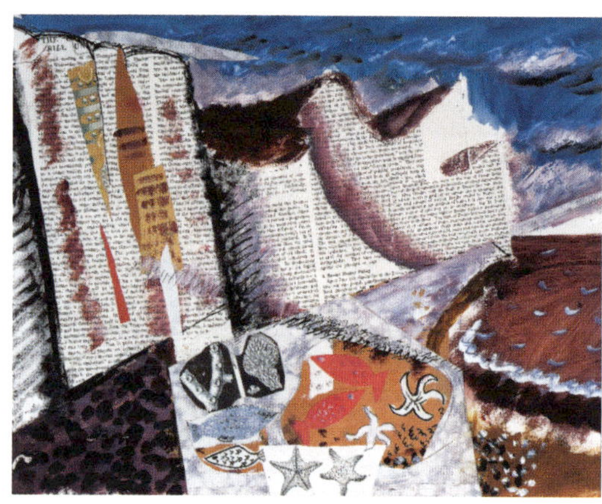

John Piper (1903–1992)
Beach with Starfish, c. 1933–34
Tate Collection, London

yearning that characterized the images of such British Neo-Romantic artists of the mid-twentieth century as Graham Sutherland and John Piper, whose work Hearld admires. 'As a child,' he explains, 'I always wanted to live in the country, but lived in a town. For me, the farmyard was a romantic place full of animals. When I was eleven years old my family moved to Heslington, a village just outside York, and I would hang around our neighbours' farms, Bridge Farm and Botland Farm. There were guineafowl roosting, bantams everywhere, an orchard, decaying farm machinery – they were just the perfect places. It's that coming together of people's ordinary activities and nature; man's intervention in nature. That is the most romantic, or visually rich, set of elements. There is a sense of gritty ordinariness and romance.' His images present not rural idylls but urban scenes and the creatures that many hold in disdain, such as pigeons. 'I love, absolutely love to see nature in the city, animals surviving alongside man', he says. 'I'm drawn to the ordinariness of pigeons, but at the same time to the exquisite beauty of their markings. Even in the most ordinary setting they remind you of beauty.' Hearld believes that his appreciation for nature living side by side with man is wonderfully expressed by a passage from the autobiography of the artist Julian Trevelyan, *Indigo Days* (1957), describing life on the Thames near Trevelyan's studio: 'The broad bend of the river at Chiswick has become so much part of my life that I can conceive of living nowhere else. Besides the river traffic, tugs, barges, sailing dinghies, skiffs and eights, there are the ever-changing states of the tide. It reminds me at times of a Venetian fete; for here the river is at its broadest and most majestic, and beyond the opposite bank there are reservoirs, so that the nearest houses seem very far away. From our garden we look up river to Chiswick Eyot, an island of willows, decorated at either end with a group of swans who are forever cleaning themselves, their long necks turning and twisting ceaselessly.'

At a time when art and life are becoming increasingly digitalized and packaged for mass consumption, Hearld revels in the idiosyncrasies of a scrolling hand-drawn mark or hand-cut paper collage. He celebrates the timeless, often unsung aspects of life that are rapidly being swept away by consumerism. He speaks of 'the importance of throwaway bits and pieces to the collage maker', giving papers that once wrapped some Cox's apples a new lease of life as the jaunty Union Jacks that billow in his cut-out harbours

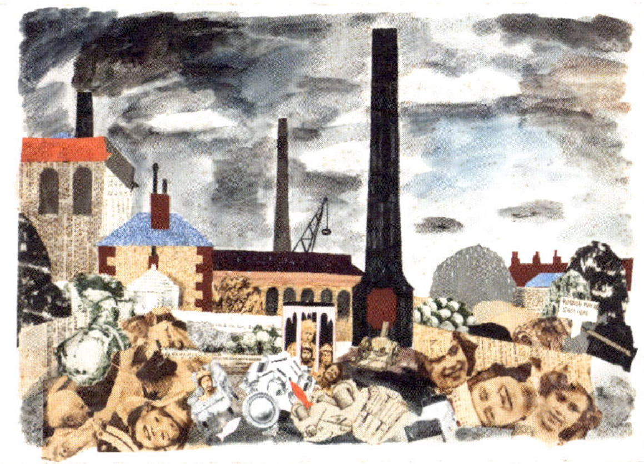

Julian Trevelyan (1910–1988)
Rubbish May Be Shot Here, 1937
Tate Collection, London

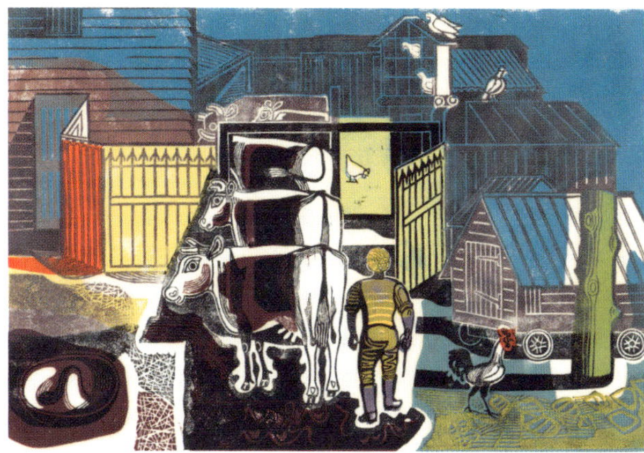

Edward Bawden (1903–1989)
Ives Farm, Great Bardfield, 1956
The Fry Art Gallery, Saffron Walden, Essex

(pages 66–71) and his view of a city's rooftops (page 102). Perhaps his aesthetic reflects the return of a 'make-do-and-mend' mentality, at a time when there is renewed interest in folk art, in growing vegetables in allotments, in limiting the use of pesticides to protect the wildlife in our hedgerows, and in the handmade among young designers and makers. This is not so much nostalgia as a desire to maintain links with the things that give us our identity and individuality and connect us to the place in which we live. Instead of the shiny and anonymous surfaces of 'Cool Britannia', Hearld's work presents the multilayered textures of the 'Englishness of English art'. His work carries forward the spirit of folk art and the modernism of Trevelyan's factory collages of the 1930s (above); the School Prints of the 1940s, a series of original lithographic prints intended to introduce schoolchildren to the work of such contemporary artists as Paul Nash and Henry Moore; and, in the 1950s, the contributions of the writer and artist Olive Cook and the photographer Edwin Smith to *The Saturday Book*, an annual miscellany published between 1941 and 1975. Yet despite these strong influences, and the fact that he sometimes makes knowing visual references to the artists he admires, including Piper and Edward Bawden,

Hearld's imagery is distinctively his own: the vibrant colours, the swirling lines, the idiosyncratic subject matter. It is as if he has picked up the baton of English modernism, presenting it to a twenty-first-century public.

Hearld initially studied illustration at the Glasgow School of Art, where his tutors included the artist Mick Manning, who has illustrated more than sixty children's books. In his teacher, Hearld discovered a kindred spirit who knew a great deal about plants and animals, and who encouraged his students to draw outside – a fundamental lesson for Hearld in the observation of nature. While living in Glasgow, Hearld discovered in the city's museums paintings and drawings of birds and animals by the Edwardian artist Joseph Crawhall. Hearld admired, and was greatly influenced by, the 'energy, life and graphic quality' of Crawhall's depictions of pigeons, magpies, geese and even a domesticated rabbit in a hutch. Hearld also compiled albums of postcards featuring images of natural history by artists as varied as Beatrix Potter, George Stubbs and Eric Ravilious.

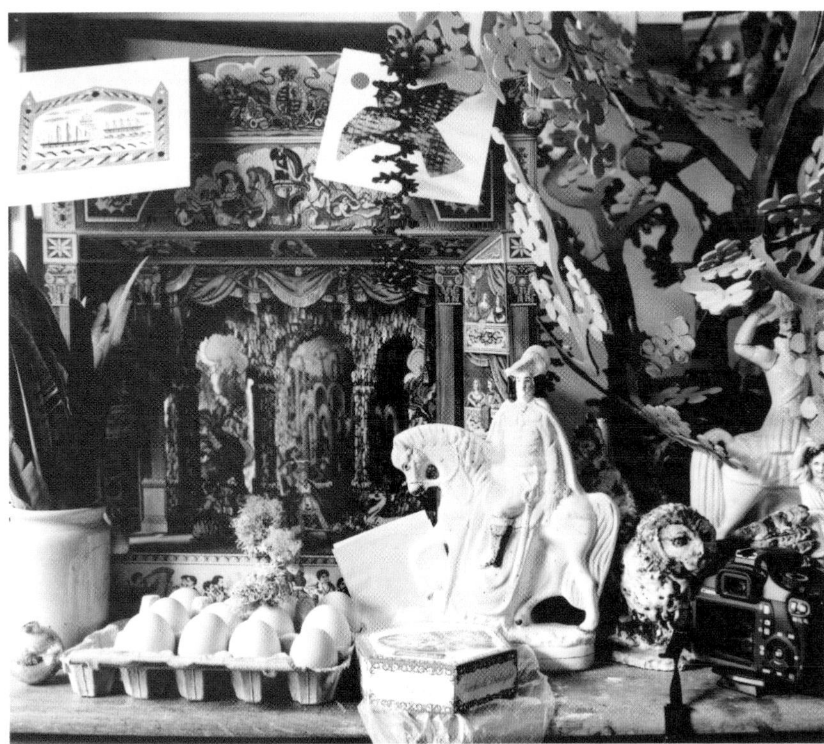

When Hearld subsequently began an MA in natural-history illustration at the Royal College of Art (RCA) in London, he was surrounded by the impetus to be 'contemporary'. As he was depicting timeless subjects from nature, he at first felt out on a limb; fortunately, however, he found himself among people who had a strong connection to the world of mid-twentieth-century British art and design. His tutor, the zoological illustrator John Norris Wood, had attended the East Anglian School of Painting and Drawing, co-founded by the artist Cedric Morris in 1937, and was later taught by the Neo-Romantic illustrator John Minton and by Edward Bawden, about whose own fascination with nature Wood told Hearld 'the most colourful anecdotes'. After graduating from the RCA, Hearld lived in York, where he met the architect and architectural historian John Hutchinson, who had contributed to Nikolaus Pevsner's guide to York and the East Riding, and who owned several lithographs by John Piper. This gave Hearld an opportunity to look closely at such prints by Piper as *Beach in Brittany* (1961–62) – an experience that had a big influence on his way of seeing. He describes Hutchinson as a 'visual mentor' who 'lived out a creative approach to life. His ordinary terraced house was a treasure trove of studio pottery, architectural fragments, Piranesi prints and hand-blocked William Morris wallpaper.' Hearld was inspired by the way in which aesthetics determined his friend's every decision, right down to his choice of cutlery, and this informed Hearld's own approach to collecting objects and living in a visual way. Hearld has never been drawn to the grandest art treasures, and states that in a country house he would most probably be found in the kitchen, as that is where one might see 'real life'. This mindset has perhaps influenced his 'democratic' approach to creating beautifully designed objects that can be used and displayed in the home: printed fabrics for curtains and furnishings, ceramic kitchenware, and wallpaper, among many other things.

Hearld cites the homes of artists and collectors as being great influences on his own approach to living. 'Seeing art objects in a domestic context is always fantastic, as you interact with them in a different way', he explains. He particularly admires Kettle's Yard in Cambridge, the former home of Harold 'Jim' Ede, curator, art collector and friend of such artists as Ben Nicholson, David Jones, Alfred Wallis and Christopher Wood. For Hearld, Kettle's Yard is 'a triumphant marriage of images and objects, natural and

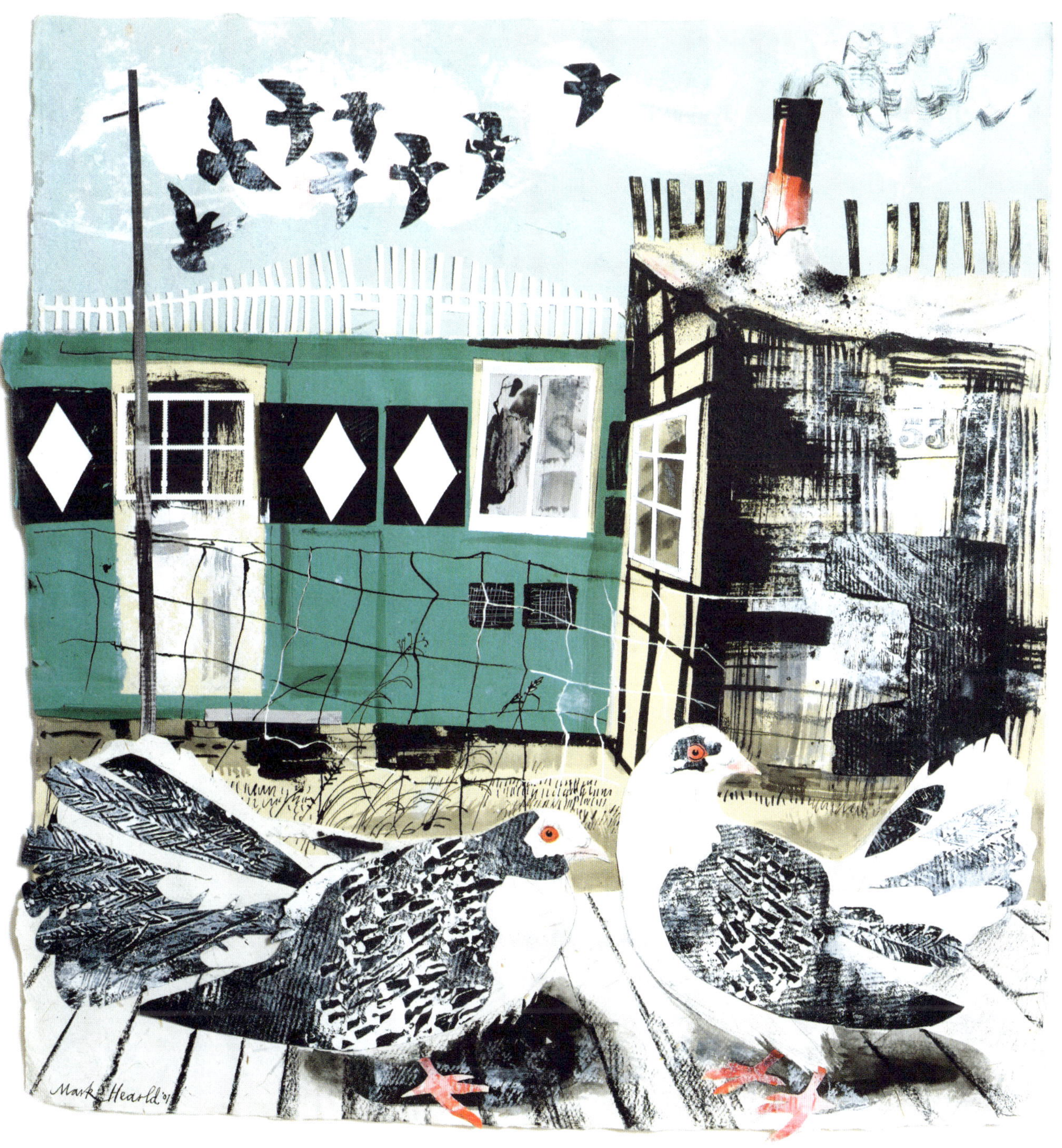

Whitby Pigeon Loft, 2001, collage,
56 × 56 cm (22 × 22 in.)

The mantelpiece at Portland
Street, spring 2012.

man-made. It is so incredibly subtle, and, like any great
collection or space, it creates an atmosphere that is more
than the sum of its parts – as in the case of Dennis Severs's
eighteenth-century house in Spitalfields in London, or
other artists' houses. They have an atmosphere that is to
do with the space *between* things.' Hearld also admires
Charleston in East Sussex, the country home of the
Bloomsbury group, in which every chair, headboard and
door is covered by the vibrant decorations and textiles of
the artists Vanessa Bell and Duncan Grant. 'At Charleston',
Hearld enthuses, 'you had artists working as designers,
and that always interests me. They were creating, and
living in one of their own creations. The Bloomsbury
artwork is playful and about colour; it's most successful
on a door or a dust jacket. Bell and Grant were at their
best as designers. What comes across at Charleston is art
as a way of life, and that is one of my key driving forces.'

Hearld has created his own extraordinary home in York.
A museum of his mind, it reflects his varied interests and
passion for folk art and design. Everywhere one looks there
are visually arresting and fascinating objects and pieces
of furniture, as if Hearld had heeded William Morris's call
to 'have nothing in your house that you do not know to be

useful, or believe to be beautiful' (indeed, one can see a
Morris-designed Sussex armchair that Hearld bought from
a junk shop for £50, while Pre-Raphaelite stained-glass
panels hang in the windows). The walls are lined with
artworks by Hearld and the artists he knows and admires,
while shelves are packed with books on all aspects of art
and design. There are eclectic children's toys, hand-coloured
Victorian toy theatres, rag rugs, corn dollies, a folding
screen covered in Victorian scraps, printed cards and
ephemera, Staffordshire china dogs on the mantelpiece
and flatback figure groups on the sideboard. 'Staffordshire
pottery appeals', says Hearld, 'in that it is joyful, direct and
slightly crude, and in the way it is painted with the right
balance of spontaneity and precision. The figures I have are
often rural – the harvest, man and dog – but I could equally
have chosen them because of the mark-making or the
patterns on a skirt. It's a vigour that the best ones have,
an abstract quality in the decoration. I suppose it's also
a simplification and formalization, of a kind I explore in my
own collage in two dimensions. The figures are sculptural,
but invariably have a pleasing profile, too. There is also
something good about them being a poor-man's art, and
they are affordable and findable. I remember enjoying other

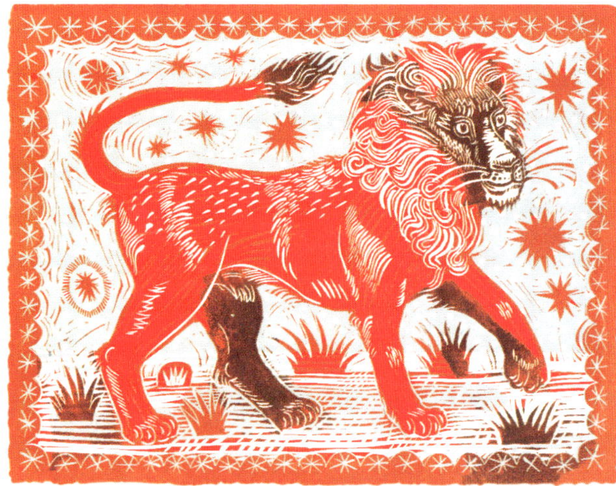

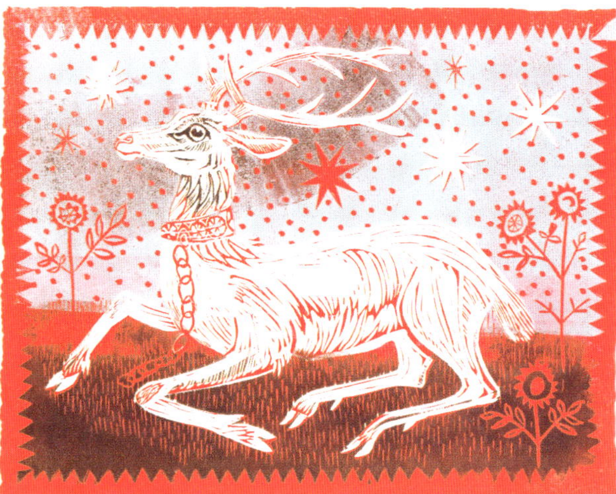

artists' images of them – for example, Dora Carrington's *Beeny Dogs* [1917] and a great line drawing by Bawden from *Life in an English Village* [1949].'

Hanging from a series of wooden pegs in the bedroom is an array of scarves: polka dots, paisley swirls, stripes and other patterns. Perhaps it should not be surprising to learn that Hearld's dress sense is as quirky as his eye for collecting pattern papers and eclectic objects. Rarely does he leave the house without wearing a distinctive scarf, a flat cap, high-waisted trousers or a patterned sweater. 'I see wearing clothes as being similar to making a collage', he explains. 'It's putting different elements together. I've always liked clothes that look strong and functional. I like clothes that look like an artist's clothes. I love hats of all types.' Hearld has become something of a poster boy for Old Town, the Norfolk-based clothing manufacturer that specializes in classic British work wear; he has even appeared in one of its advertising campaigns and an issue of its newsletter, *Evening Star*. Will Brown and Marie Willey of Old Town made Hearld a Pearly King hat, which is proudly displayed. 'I love the folk splendour and theatricality of how Pearly Kings and Queens dress up', says Hearld. 'The materials, black on white, the heraldic

quality – clothes made joyfully by ordinary people.' Also on show in the bedroom are three hand-painted signs bearing the names of Hearld's artistic heroes, including Piper, Bawden, Ravilious, Wood, Carrington, Keith Vaughan, Edward Burra, Peter Blake and Mary Newcomb. Hearld commissioned the signs from a sign-painter in Hull. 'I saw the quality of his lettering and wanted to use him, and it came to me to make a list of the people I admire. I limited my list to British artists, and many of them are Neo-Romantic landscape painters. Although I am more interested in animals, these artists looked at nature with a poetic eye, which is why their work appeals to me.'

Hearld's love of birds and animals is expressed through many of the objects in his home: rag cushions decorated with pictures of cats, deer antlers mounted on the walls and glass cases containing such stuffed creatures as a barn owl, a Manchester terrier, a shelduck and a hare. 'When I was a child,' Hearld explains, 'a family friend had a stuffed barn owl on their mantelpiece. Because of my interest in animals I enjoyed seeing it close up, and never found it morbid. It's to do with wanting to know the *way* something looks, with having it myself, collecting it. The museum-like quality of stuffed animals in cases also appeals. I'm not interested in

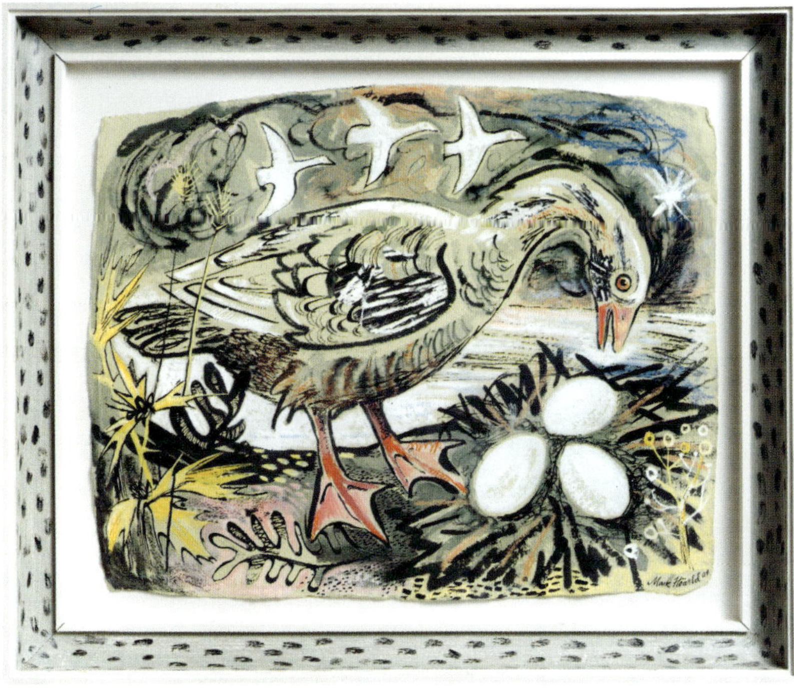

the morbid, fetishistic or macabre element; rather, it's a response to a given animal. I'm generally interested in any depiction of nature. It runs very deep. It's also why I like old Steiff animals.' When discussing his home, Hearld makes reference to an evocative short story by Saki (H.H. Munro) called 'The Lumber Room' (1914), in which the young protagonist discovers a 'storehouse of unimagined treasures' – full of 'wonderful things for the eye to feast on' – hidden away in an Edwardian country house. It is not surprising to learn that many of the items in Hearld's home have influenced his artwork and designs; equally, however, he sees the act of collecting such items, at flea markets and junk shops, as creative, an activity akin to making a collage: 'I was inspired by artists' interiors from the mid-twentieth century – those of Peggy Angus, Olive Cook and Edwin Smith – and also by the Enid Marx Collection at Compton Verney in Warwickshire, by the book Marx wrote with Margaret Lambert [*English Popular Art*, 1951] and by Barbara Jones's *Unsophisticated Arts* [1951]. I have a real interest in the objects that turn up in these books, so I go to car boot sales and collect things. I think finding or buying an object is almost like creating one yourself: both acts satisfy a similar aesthetic impulse. If you make it, it's

a bit more virtuous, but if you find something cheap and bring it home and think, "Aha!" – that's an act of creativity. And then placing it next to other things is like making a three-dimensional collage.'

Sometimes, Hearld is inspired by a specific piece of folk art, as in the case of his drawing of a Staffordshire flatback figure group for *Spitalfields Life* (2012; see page 164), or his collages and prints of squirrels and foxes (pages 34–35 and 93) suggested by the lively cut-outs by Hans Christian Andersen, the nineteenth-century Danish author best known for his children's stories. More generally, however, Hearld is drawn to the graphic quality of folk and popular art, and to their unaffected purity of vision. In common with much of his own work, folk art usually relates to the natural world, and often has a playful immediacy. In 2009 Hearld was invited to curate an exhibition at Scarborough Art Gallery. The result, *The Magpie Eye: A Mark Hearld Miscellany*, brought together all kinds of wonderful objects, intuitively arranged by Hearld to create a sense of visual delight in the everyday and to encourage visitors to make their own poetic associations and connections. He described it as 'a curious hotchpotch of artefacts from my own collection, from the gallery's collection and from creative

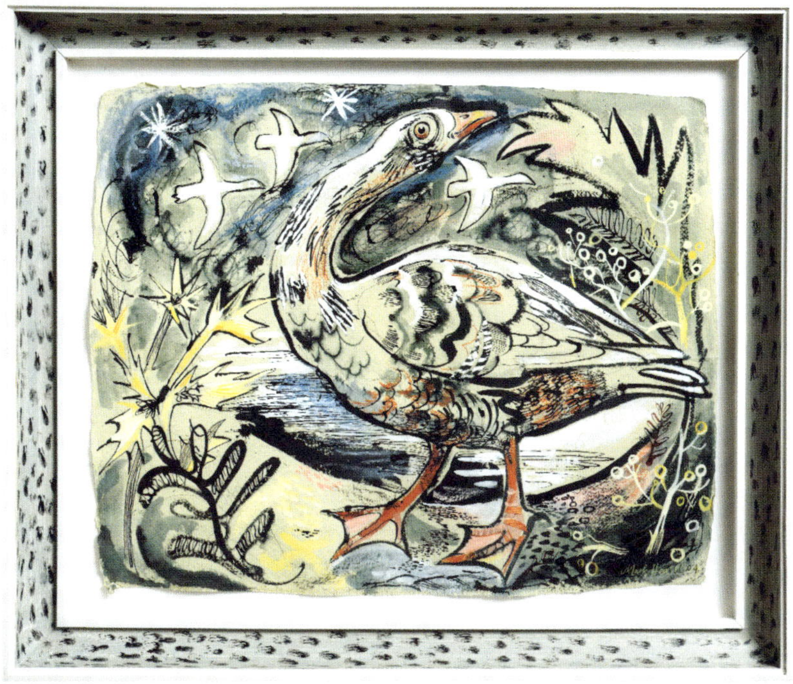

Wild Goose 2, 2004, ink and gouache, 56 × 75 cm (22 × 29½ in.) unframed

In this drawing, the goose is contemplating the journey ahead of it while migrating swans fly past in the starlight. A made-from-memory sketch of the third image in the series is shown below.

friends who have made things specially'. The show reflected Hearld's ability to bring like-minded artists and creative types together, making connections and introductions. He has organized other exhibitions, including *Mark Hearld and Friends* at the Scottish Gallery in Edinburgh in 2009, featuring the potters Anna Lambert, Terry Shone, Ann Stokes and Paul Young, and the illustrators and printmakers Christopher Brown, Jonny Hannah, Michael Kirkman, Ed Kluz, Angie Lewin and Emily Sutton, Hearld's partner. The latter group has been described as the 'New Bardfield' – a reference to the village in Essex where Edward Bawden and Eric Ravilious lived in the 1930s. Yet, while there are common bonds of friendship, shared studio spaces and an admiration for the work of such mid-twentieth-century British artists as Bawden and Ravilious, Hearld feels uneasy with the suggestion of 'revivalism'. Essentially, these artists are interested in exploring man's sense of place in the natural world, and in finding new ways of approaching this subject that speak to contemporary audiences. After several decades in which fine art and craftsmanship have been seen as distinct practices, Hearld and his contemporaries are working across the fields of illustration, printmaking, textile design and ceramics,

frequently in collaboration. The result is often a timeless modernity, which creates new forms from old voices. It is perhaps a conscious reaction to the anti-aesthetic of 'Britart', to digital and conceptual art, instead getting back to a direct connection with materials and an understanding of process.

Anyone fortunate enough to have one of Hearld's collages or prints on their wall, his decorated plates and mugs in the kitchen, or his cushions on their armchair will appreciate his belief in the importance of 'visual delight', which these days is so increasingly rare. Hearld reconnects us with the nature outside our window, and links us back to an English folk tradition that can sometimes seem lost in the fast pace of modern life. He creates joyful images and encourages us all to live visually, seeing the world as if through the eyes of a child.

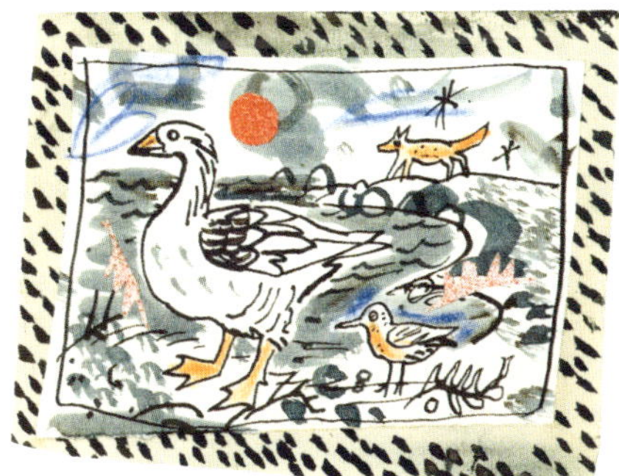

SIMON MARTIN

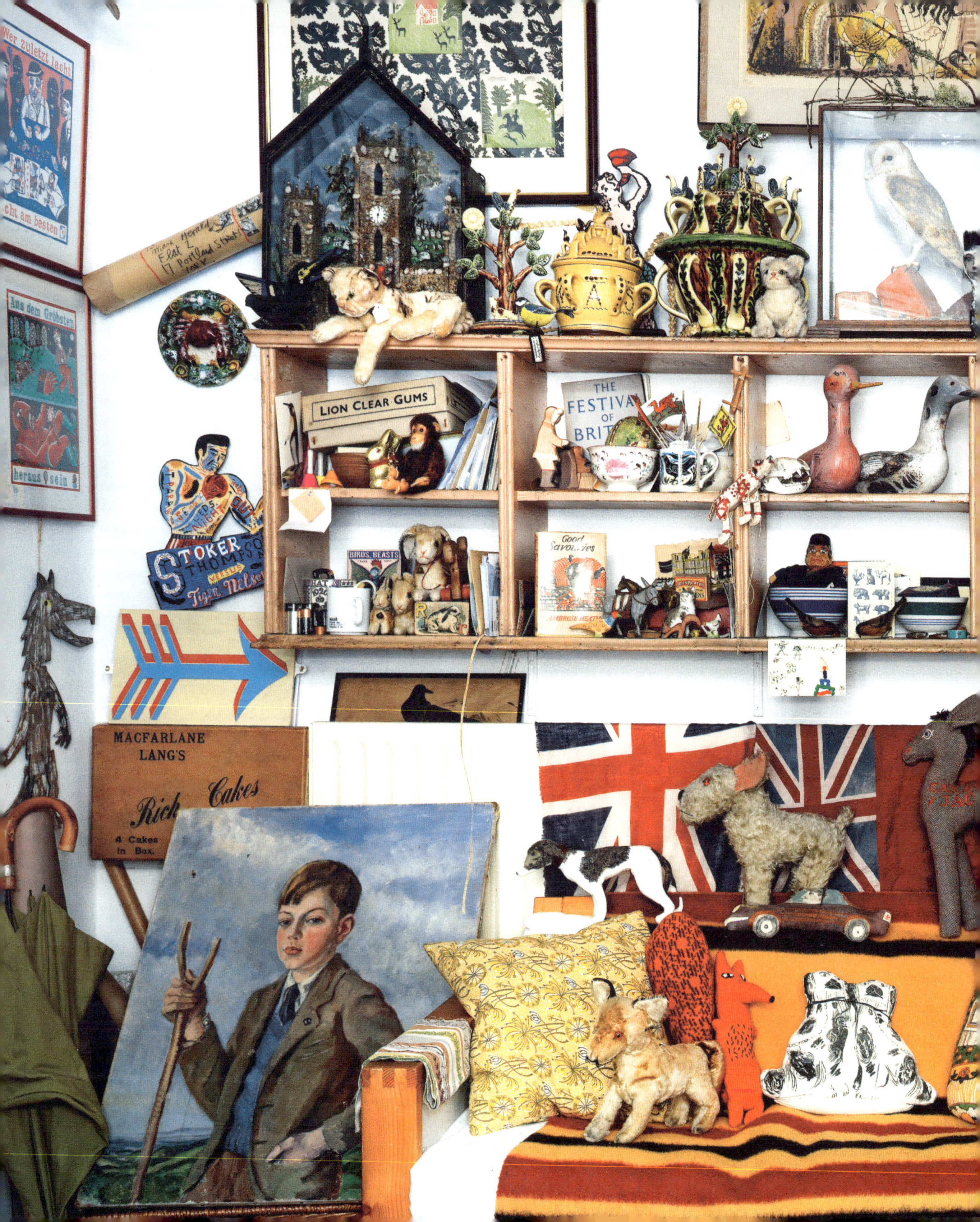

Wer zuletzt lacht
cht am besten
Aus dem Gröbsten
heraus sein
LION CLEAR GUMS
THE FESTIVAL OF BRIT
STOKER
THOMPSON
VERSUS
Tiger Nelson
BIRDS, BEASTS
Good
Savou...es
MACFARLANE
LANG'S
Rich Cakes
4 Cakes
in Box.

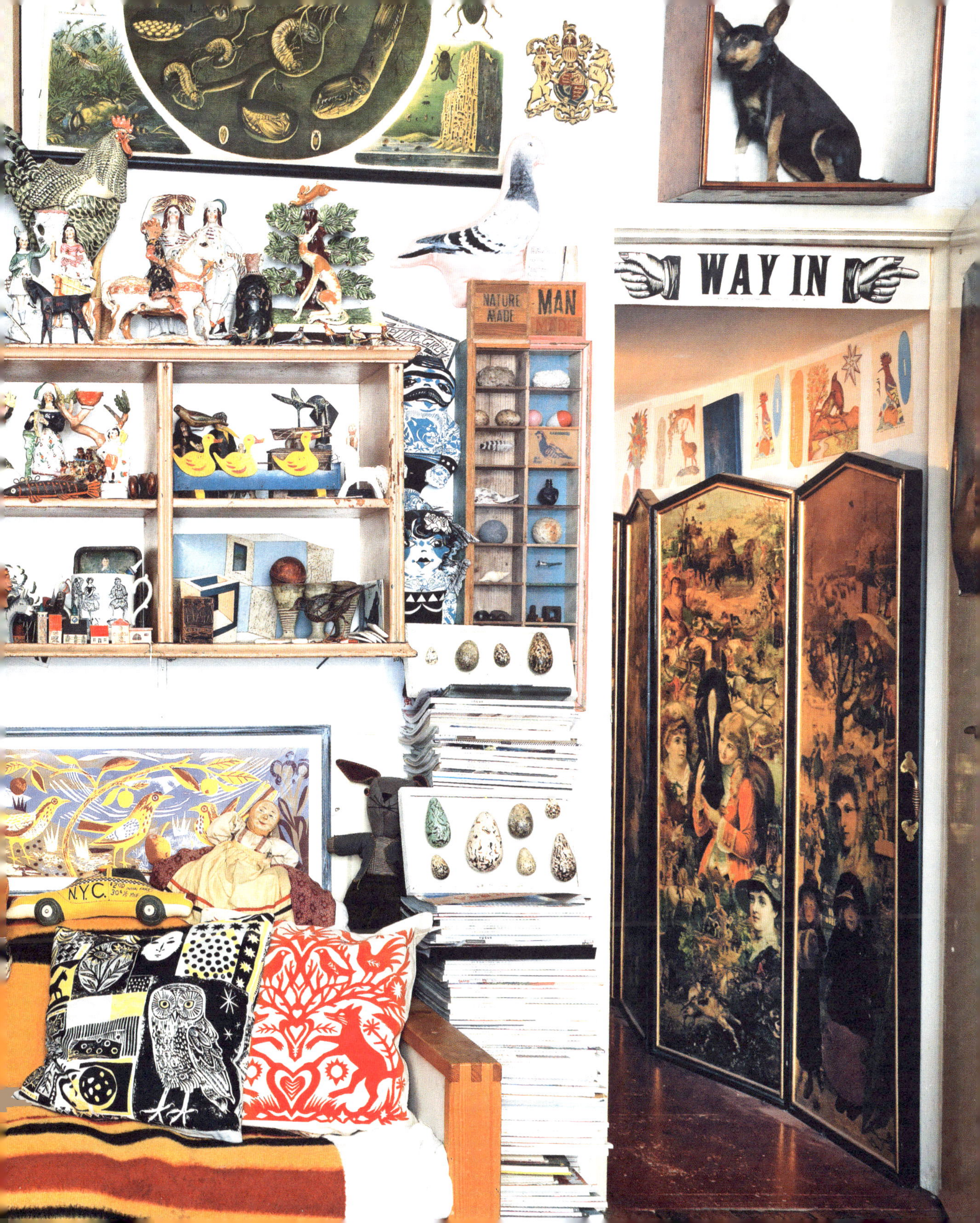

NATURE MADE
MAN MADE
WAY IN
N.Y.C.

RAMP
Geoffry Fuller · Paul Young · Terry Shone

Slipware
Thomas Toft
c17th century

North Devon
HARVEST JUGS

OMEGA
Workshop

CHARLESTON
FARMHOUSE
VANESSA BELL
DUNCAN GRANT

Picasso
SUPREME
CREATIVE

Fitzwilliam Museum

English Pottery

English Delft
(from LONDON
& LIVERPOOL)

decorative painting
painted furniture
Compton Verney

FOLK
ART

SUPERLATIVE
DRAUGHTSMAN

PETER BLAKE
DORA CARRINGTON

H. Matisse

Sign Lettering
Decoy Carving
paper cutting

Eg. Nicholson
Nancy Nicholson

Champions
of POPULAR
ART

Collage

Julian Trevelyan drawing

John Piper

Illustration

Edward Lear
Edward Ardizzone

BLOCK PRINTERS
of Textiles and Wallpaper

William Morris

Martha
Armitage

Josef Frank

John Burningham
Brian Wildsmith
Kathleen Hale — Sendak
Wolf Erlbruch Charlotte Voake

the *DRAWN*LINE*

Johnny Hannah
Emily Sutton Michael Kirkman
Ed K

JN & PN TAUGHT
John Nash
Paul Nash
Edward Bawden
Eric Ravilious
Kenneth Rountree
Michael Rothenstein
Master of the LINOCUT
A CHART
of INSPIRATION'S
Themes and connections
in
Mark Hearld's HEAD
Wallis
KETTLE'S YARD
Christopher Wood
Ben Nicholson
Winifred Nicholson
Alfred
Peggy Angus
John Piper
John Minton
Julian Trevelyan
Graham Sutherland
John Craxton
Lucian Freud
David Jones
Keith Vaughan
Neoromantic
Artists
influenced
by William Blake
& Samuel Palmer
ROMANTIC
English Linear
Tradition
Enid Marx
Barbara Jones
Barron & Larcher
Mary Fedden
Mary Newcomb
BLACK EYES &
LEMONADE
POPULAR ART
EXHIBITION
Amy Husband
Chris Brown
Colin Wilkin
Levin
Discovered in David Mellor's
A Paradise Lost BOOK
Art full of dynamic
Linear ENERGY

Collage is central to Mark Hearld's artistic output. Early in his career he mostly worked in ink or watercolour, but when he began to experiment with collage, he discovered an artistic approach that suited his needs. 'It gave me the capacity to compose in a really strong way', he recalls. 'Suddenly I felt as though I'd found my medium.' Collage held an important place in twentieth-century art, from Pablo Picasso's cubist collages to surrealist assemblages, Henri Matisse's paper cut-outs and the work of such British artists as Julian Trevelyan and John Piper, who used it to introduce an abstract quality into their images. Paper collage enables an artist to take a playful approach to creating images. The different

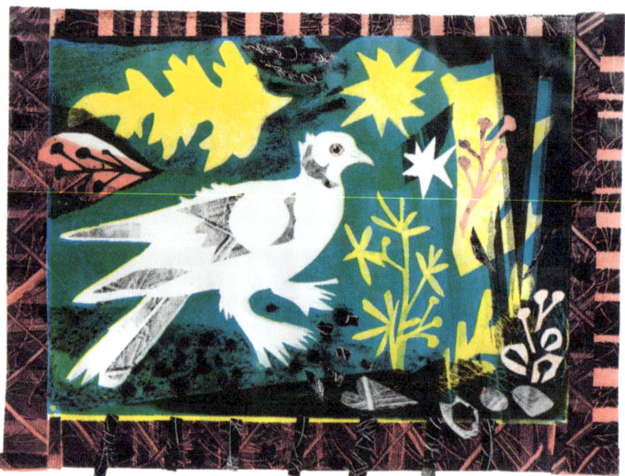

Matisse's Pigeon, 2002, collage and monoprint, 50 × 70 cm (19⅝ × 27½ in.)

layers and textures produce contrasts and tension that the artist can exploit. The act of cutting out abstract shapes that, when brought together, form a recognizable image of a landscape or an animal seemingly full of vitality requires a particularly graphic handling of colour and form. Hearld's approach to collage reflects his 'magpie eye', his collector's instinct for finding visually attractive materials and bringing them together. He particularly admires Victorian découpage screens decorated with cut-out vignettes. 'There's nothing I like better', he explains, 'than trying to find visual equivalents for things just lying around, like a piece of paper that has been used to wrap up some flowers, an old bit of newsprint or a Florentine pattern paper. I enjoy bringing these things together and making them work. I enjoy playing off the tensions of the different materials.'

Often, Hearld uses strips of hand-printed pattern paper to create a decorative frame, as in his *Night Harbour* series of collages (pages 71–73), in which fully rigged boats are seen leaving, or returning to, port by the light of the moon. The simplified collaged shapes of the boats and buildings are a nod to the work of the early twentieth-century artist Alfred Wallis, who, from his home in St Ives, Cornwall, created naive and beautiful boat paintings that are celebrated for their directness and visionary qualities. In the *Night Harbour* series, Hearld is playing with the tension between light and dark forms, as well as emphasizing the close relationship between man and nature, as fish, birds and boats

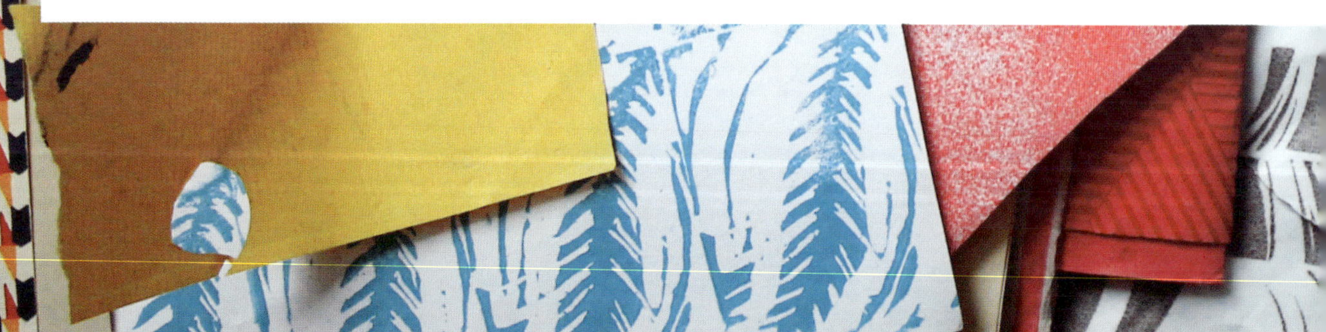

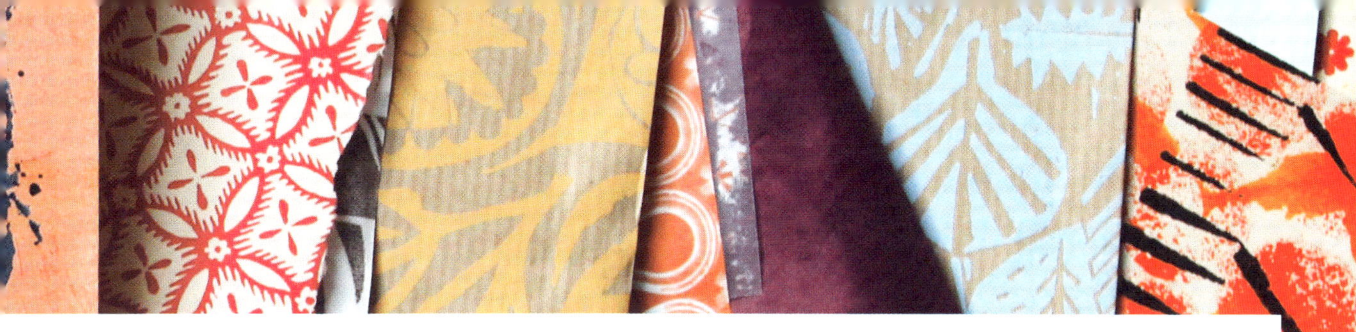

populate the same waters. In a collage and related print called *Salmon Return to the Thames* (pages 74–75), he presents an imaginary scene of freshwater marine life in front of the distinctive outline of the Houses of Parliament. Generally, Hearld is not interested in architecture per se, but in the play of building shapes and in the buildings' relationship with nature, as in his collages *St Paul's Pigeons* (page 103) and *Venetian Fantasy* (pages 112–13). In the latter, found Italian pattern papers are employed to suggest the decorative finials and windows of Venetian Gothic architecture, with a witty use of vintage photographs to add people to the scene.

Hearld's approach to collage has helped him in his understanding of such printmaking processes as lithography and screen printing. In lithography, a technique based on the non-compatability of oil and water, an image is printed from a flat surface (originally stone, but now usually metal) treated so as to repel ink except where it is required for printing. The image can be drawn directly on to the printing surface using grease-based substances, or drawn on to film and then transferred to a printing plate by exposure under UV light. 'Collage really taught me how to print because it's about layering', Hearld explains. 'When I came to make lithographs for the first time, I knew much of what I was doing from having looked at a lot of other lithographic images in old children's books, such as the *Picture Puffins*. I had a good idea of how lithography works –

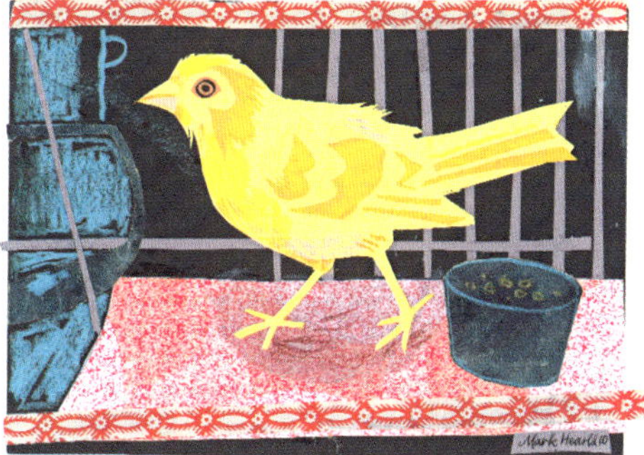

Canary Collage, 2010, collage, 14.5 × 21 cm (5¾ × 8¼ in.)

but I also thought in layers. I could see the potential for bringing different marks into the lithographic process by drawing on to separate pieces of film and layering them up. So in effect I was collaging with the film before making the printing plate, but then obviously the print process flattens everything out. There is something very satisfying about bringing together a range of different marks. The lithographic process is wonderfully unifying because it brings everything together.'

Hearld often works with the Curwen Studio in Cambridgeshire, one of the leading lithographic printmakers in Britain. Established in 1863 (as the Curwen Press; the Curwen Studio, from which the company now takes its name, was set up in 1958), it played an important role in the story of twentieth-century British printmaking. Hearld's first lithograph, *Pigeon Loft* (2005), bears the legend 'Inside they cooed,

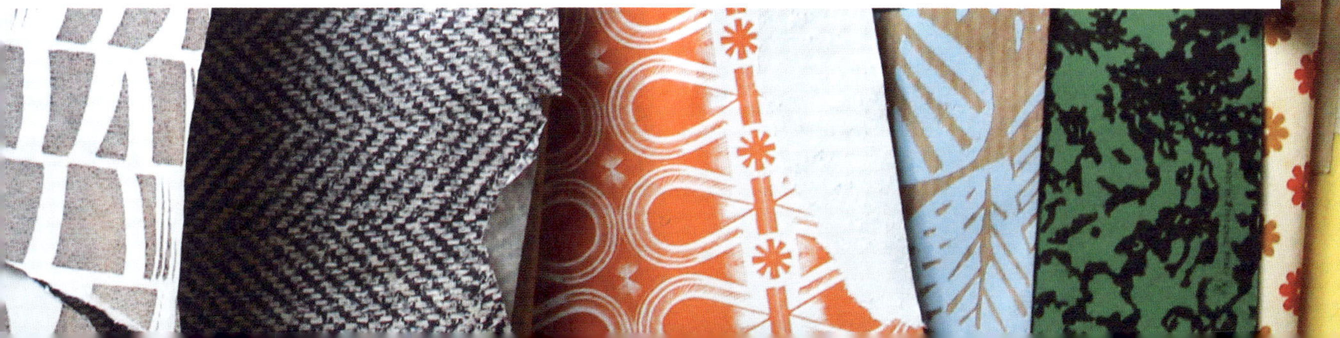

outside they FLEW', as four pigeons watch their fellow birds swooping through the sky to be fed in a farmyard. Initially, Hearld prepared separations of the print on film in his studio. He then responded to these at the Curwen, intuitively building up the image stage by stage and collaborating with the technician who printed it. Also at the Curwen, Hearld has produced a number of frieze-like prints of farmyard imagery in unconventional sizes, such as *Allotment – Goat Husbandry* and *Bramble and Apple Allotment* (pages 84–85), both of which possess a quality akin to that of Piper's *Nursery Frieze* series of the 1930s. The surfaces are animated by different types of activity and animal, while the eye is led across the image by brambles, apple branches, the curve of a basket handle and the boundary fences that enclose the goats. Many of Hearld's prints include witty visual references to artworks of the past: in one lithograph (pages 26–27), a leaping hare takes its cue from a Pisanello painting; a jaunty jay in another print (page 98) seems to be giving both Thomas Bewick's engravings for his *History of British Birds* (1797–1804) and Picasso's aquatints for an edition of Buffon's *Histoire naturelle* a run for their money. Another lithograph, titled *Pick Your Own* (page 99), reveals a quirky sense of humour that not only plays on that quintessentially English activity of picking one's own strawberries, but also makes a knowing nod to British design history through a reference to William Morris's iconic textile design *Strawberry Thief* (1883).

In 2008 Hearld was one of four artists commissioned to produce a lithograph to mark the fiftieth anniversary of the establishment of the Curwen Studio, and his poster-like print, *Printing with Spirit* (page 29), pointed to the studio's origins in the Curwen Press, which produced many commercial posters. His playful image – a cat chasing a bird within a blue border embellished with red stars and squares – captured the mood of the work of many of the artists who had preceded him at the studio. The decorative border in this and other prints, such as *Rooster and Railway Carriage* (page 32), which was commissioned by the Higgins Art Gallery and Museum in Bedford, evokes the printed frames of the School Prints from the 1940s (see page 9). As most schools were unable to frame the prints, each artist included a decorative border within their image so that the prints could be pinned directly to a wall. Another commission, a poster print entitled *British Art at Tate Britain* (pages 30–31), features London pigeons swooping around the iconic portico of the gallery. The horizontal format and the interplay between text and image recall the Shell transport posters of the 1930s, and the classic London Underground posters of the 1920s and 1930s that encouraged their viewers to visit various landmarks.

Printmaking is a democratic process that enables Hearld to produce affordable and original artworks for the enjoyment of a larger audience than that for his one-off works. He also creates linocuts in limited editions. Hearld's fluid line is ideally suited to the depiction of

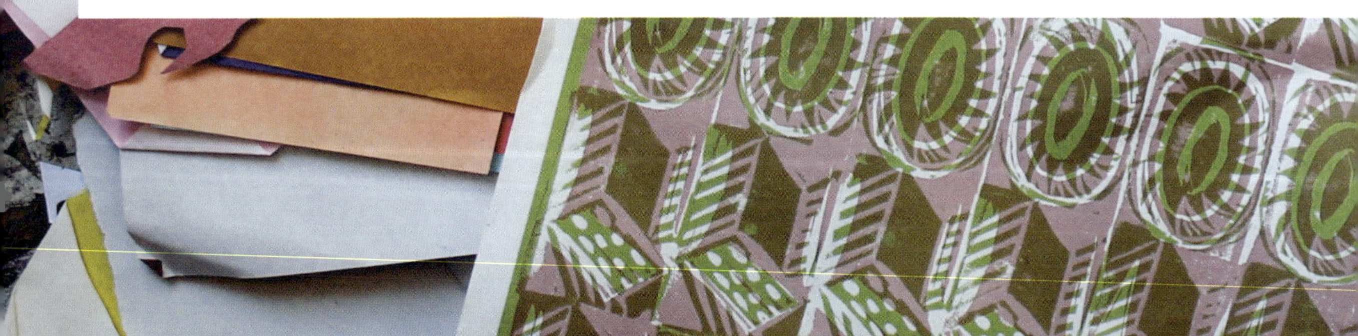

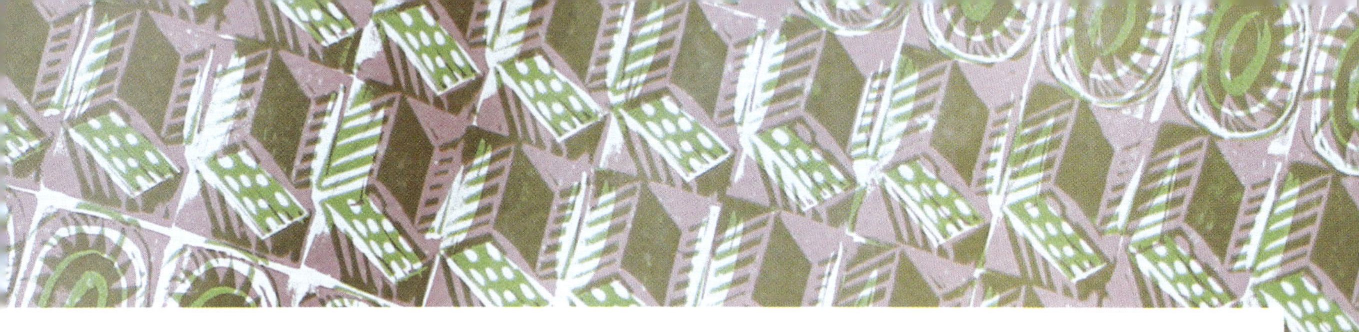

animals and birds in linocut, since it captures a sense of movement. In *Ballindalloch Blackbird* (page 39), the eponymous bird, its beak full of linear grasses, looks poised to take off for its nest. Linocutting requires a different approach from drawing. The weight of the tools and the way in which they cut mean that Hearld has to work with the lino, as it has such a strong character of its own. 'What I enjoy about linocutting', Hearld observes, 'is the directness: it's such a physical, immediate process. You commit to a mark and then it prints. Once you've established the compositional structure, the cutting directs each mark. It has its own life from that point on, and you allow the cutting tool to lead you with the mark-making.' Hearld creates an interplay of positive and negative spaces to animate the decorative surface of the print, with plant forms standing out against the black or white background. The directness of printmaking particularly appeals to Hearld: 'I like the act of inking something up, laying it down and printing it on paper.'

SIMON MARTIN

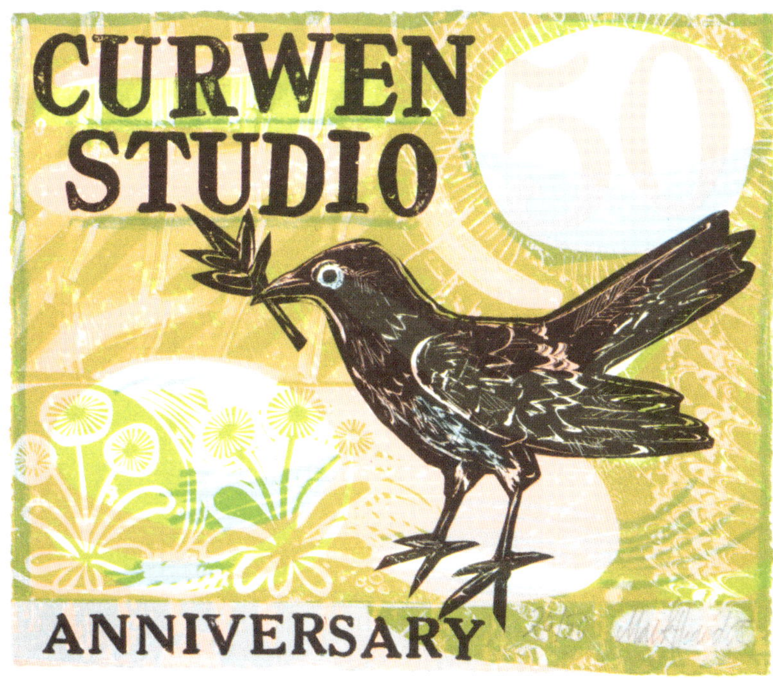

Curwen Studio anniversary print, 2008, lithograph, 25.5 × 30.5 cm (10 × 12 in.)

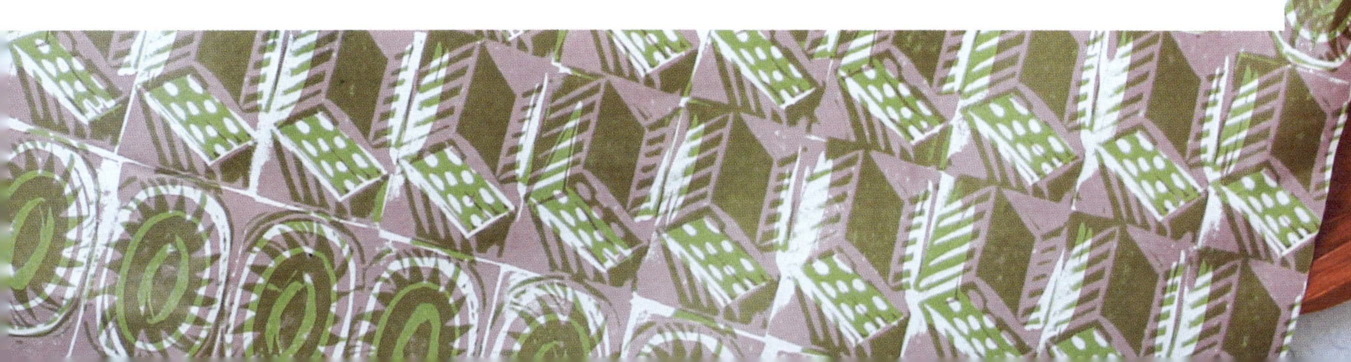

Lithographs

I have long admired the quality of lithography; its capacity for nuanced, tonal washes is unique in printmaking. Before I'd ever made a lithograph, people said to me that my work seemed akin to the School Prints of the 1940s (see page 9). I became a fan of images by John Nash and Julian Trevelyan, and of Barbara Jones's *Fairground* (1946), a copy of which hangs on my stairs; I also own two John Piper lithographs. My interest in mid-twentieth-century artist–designers gave me a familiarity with the autolithographic process used by the Curwen Press and the printer W.S. Cowell. I was invited to try out lithography at the Curwen Studio, and the sight of my image on press for the first time still has a certain magic.

Spangled Cock Bird (opposite, top) and Winter Birds (opposite, bottom)

These lithographs were printed at the Curwen Studio, on the same plate at the same time. Making them was entirely life-affirming. Their creation followed a period of illness, so to be better and making work felt like a gift. *Winter Birds*, in particular, is a joyful celebration of creativity and life. The image below shows the working drawing for the finished print; my collages, by contrast, are entirely improvised, and I rarely make sketches. It's interesting to note that both prints have been made using the same colour palette.

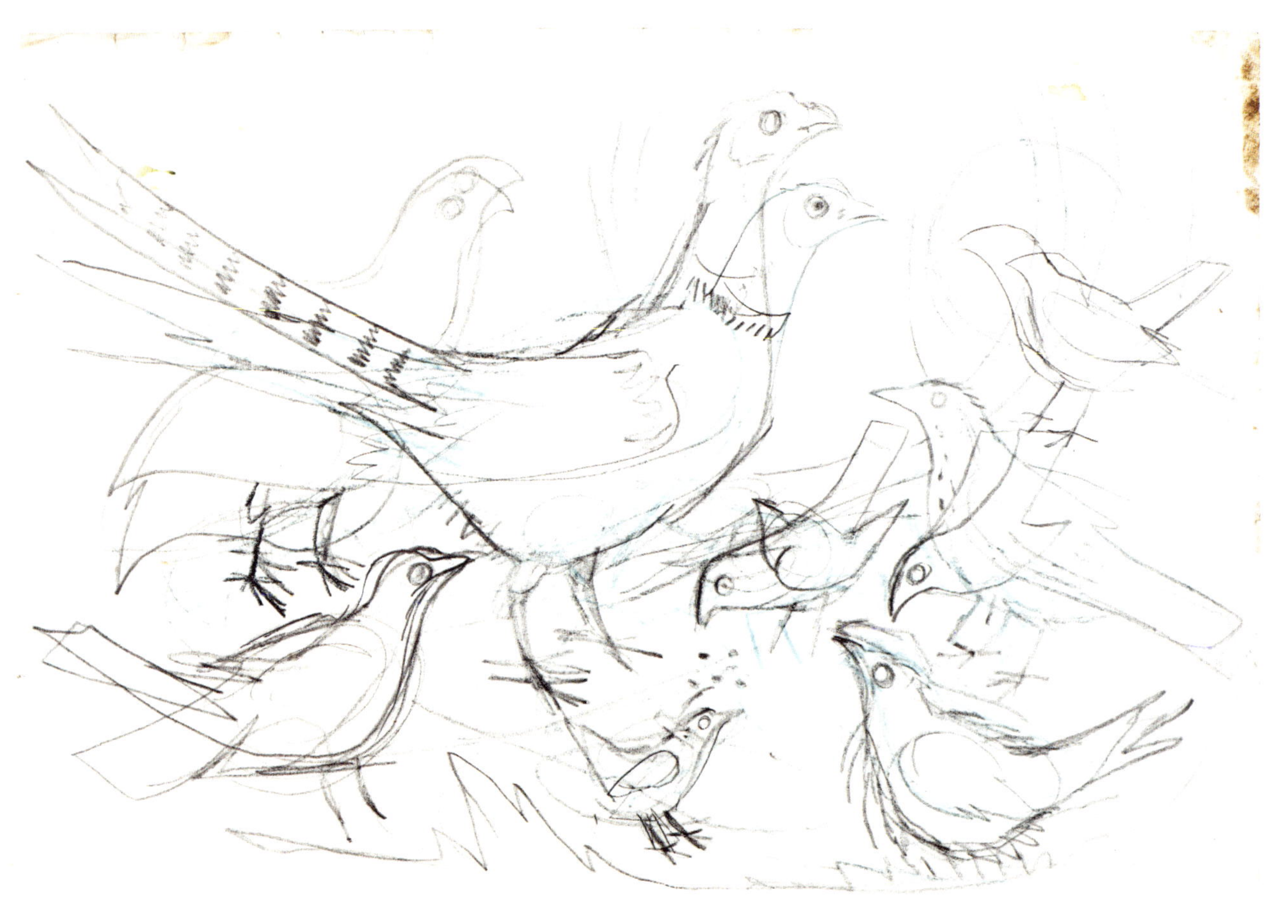

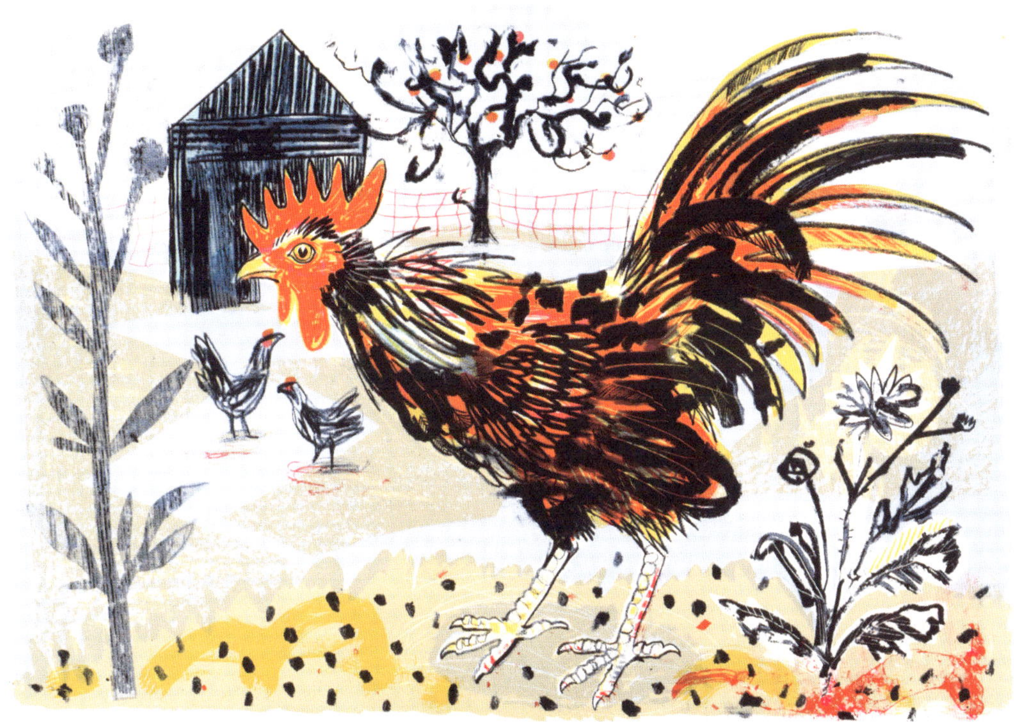

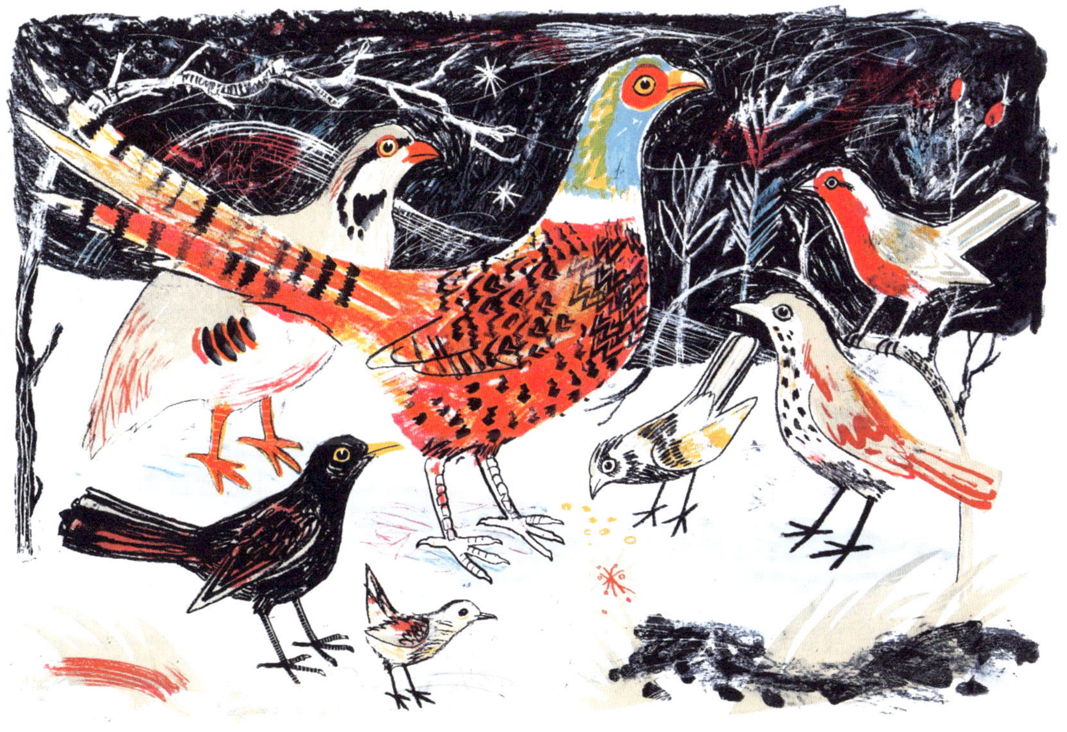

Pisanello's Hare

During a week spent in Umbria, central Italy, I had hoped to see a hoopoe, but alas it remained elusive. At home, thinking about hoopoes, I remembered a favourite painting, Pisanello's *The Vision of Saint Eustace* (c. 1438–42), which features a hoopoe and a hare. This prompted me to make a visual tribute not only to the creatures but also to Pisanello himself. The leaping hare must also take its inspiration from the hare in *Masquerade* (1979), the children's book by Kit Williams, which was a favourite of mine while I was growing up. The small tortoiseshell butterfly is in honour of what turned out to be a Red Admiral in Pisanello's *Portrait of an Este Princess* (c. 1436–38).

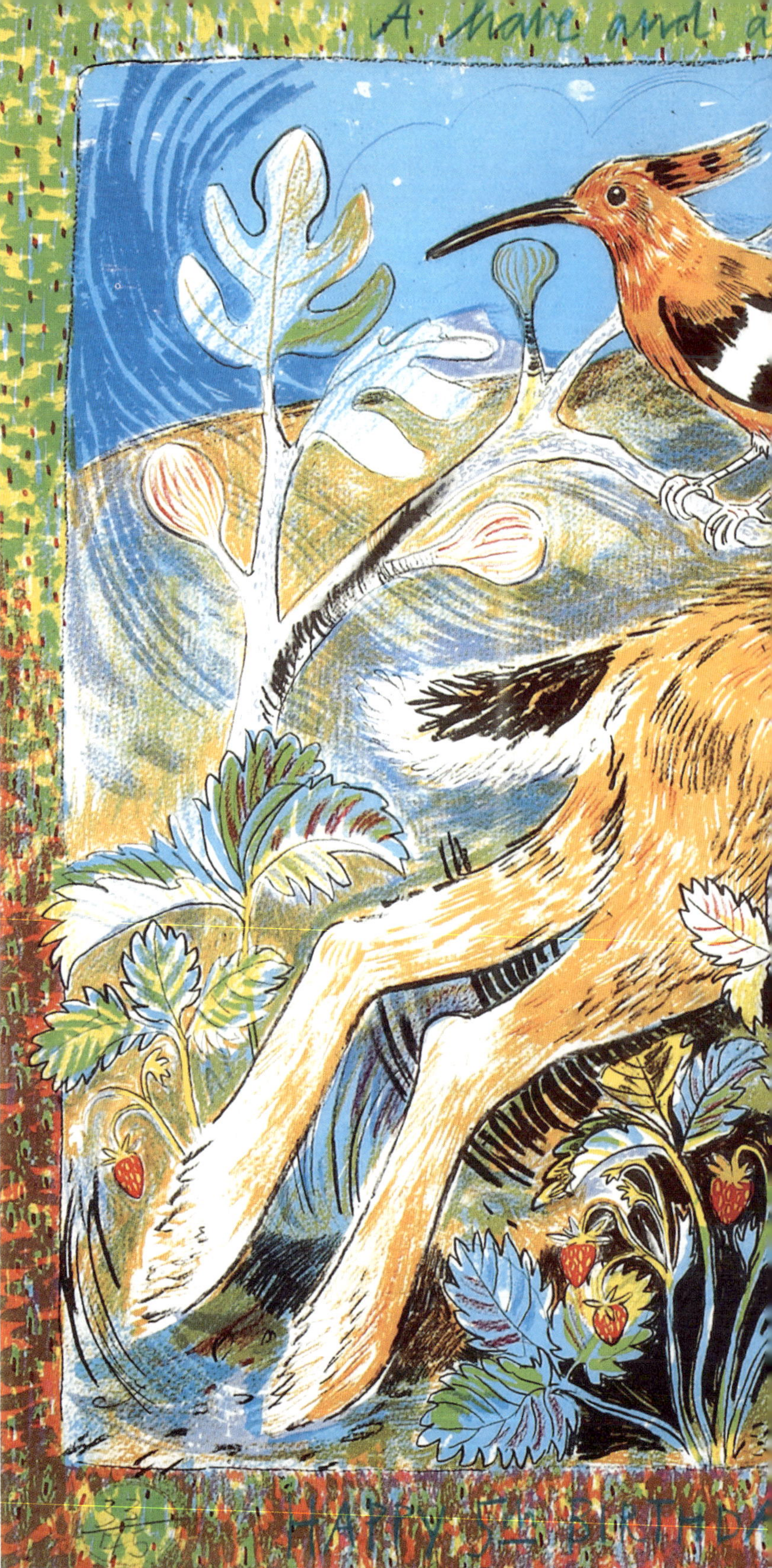

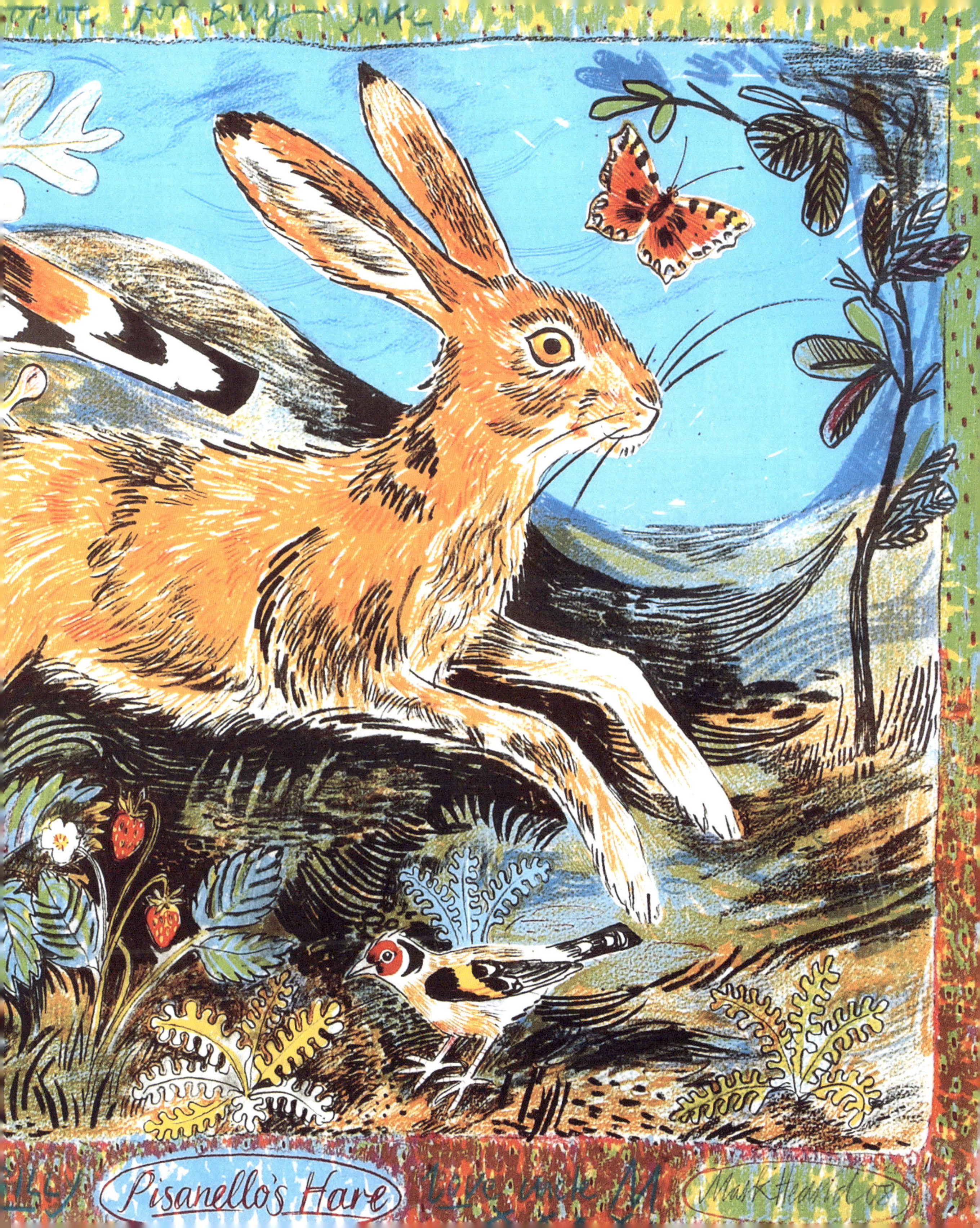
Pisanello's Hare
Mark Hearld

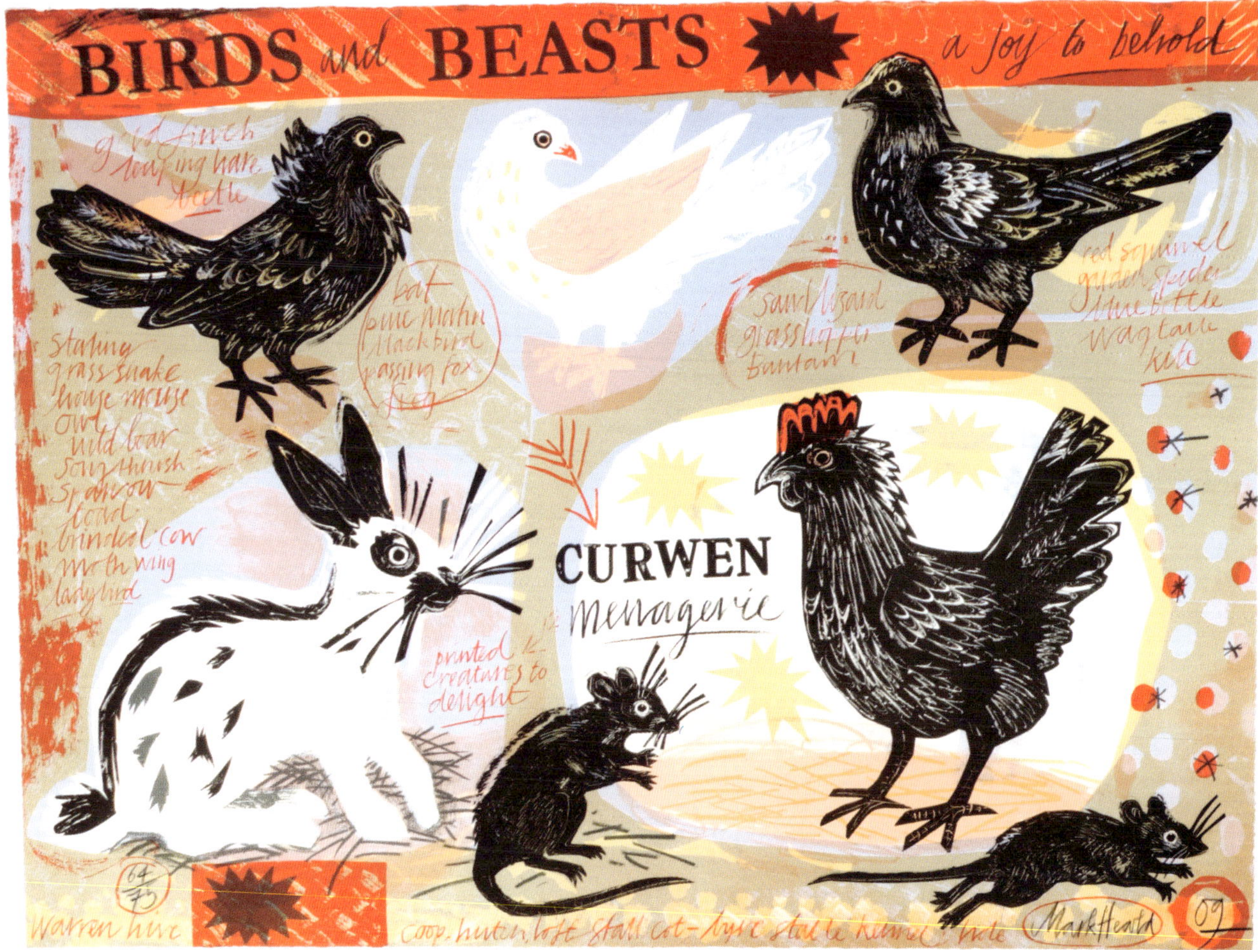

Curwen

I've worked at the Curwen Studio since 2005, and have
made twenty-five editioned prints, which has given me
a wonderful opportunity to experiment with the process.
An admiration for 1940s autolithographic illustrated books
had taught me a lot about working with colour separations
and making the most of a limited palette by overlaying
transparent colours to create chromatic greys. The first print
was daunting, but entirely exciting; I haven't looked back.
The opportunity to collaborate with the printmakers at the
studio still feels like a luxury. Generally, I spend a couple
of days preparing separations at home, then two days in
the studio making plates, mixing colours and proofing.

Curwen Menagerie and Printing with Spirit

In 2008 I was asked to make a print for a display in Tate Britain celebrating fifty years of the Curwen Studio. Set up to enable artists to work on their own plates, the studio was an offshoot of the Curwen Press, so I felt it would be appropriate to make an image that celebrated Curwen's roots in commercial printing. In *Printing with Spirit* I used monoprinted films and Italian rubber stamps to create some of the layers, and kept the colour palette limited but festive. It works with a poster-like directness. *Curwen Menagerie* followed; it's a record of my favourite animals, with a couple of black rats thrown in for mischief.

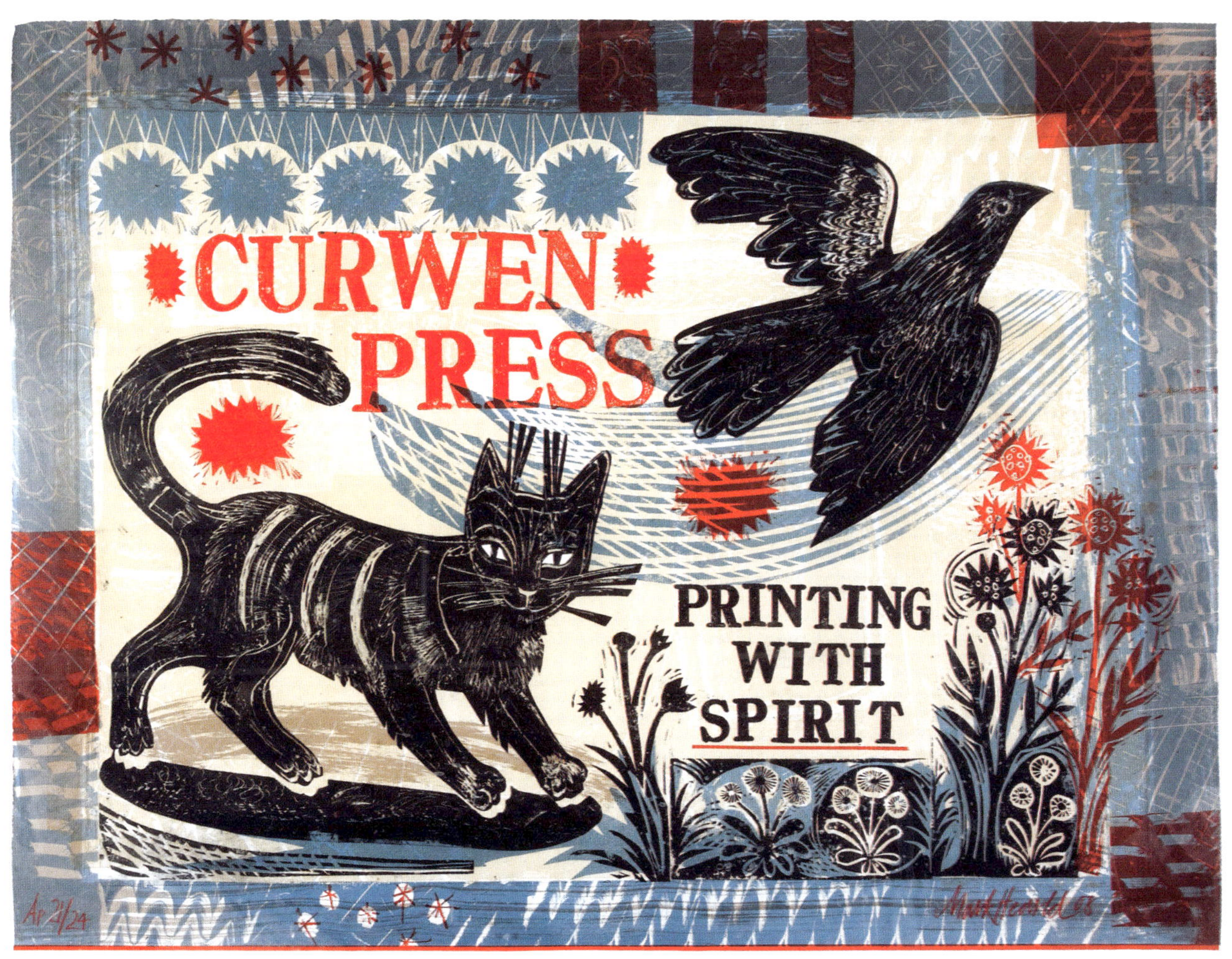

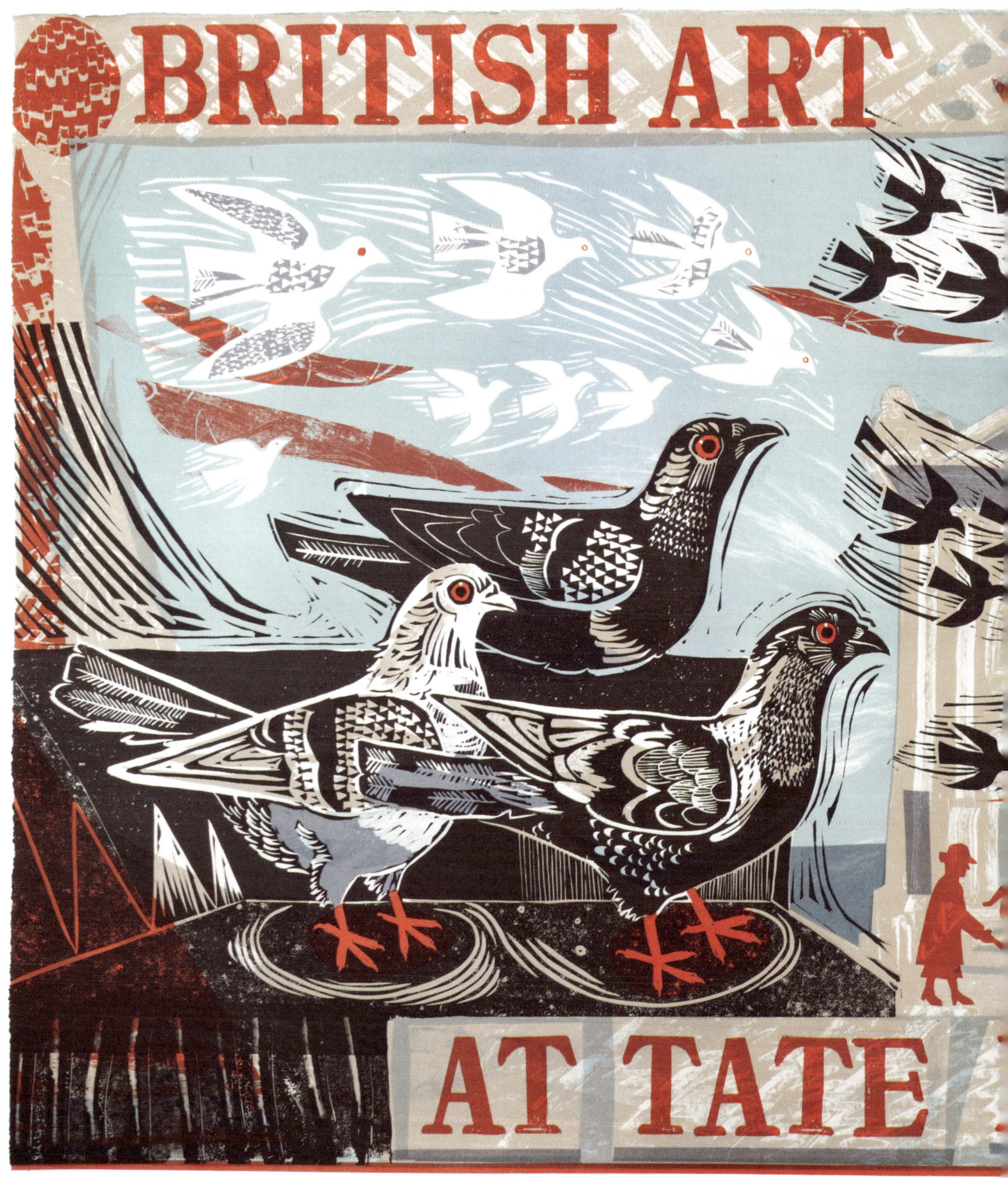

BRITISH ART
AT TATE

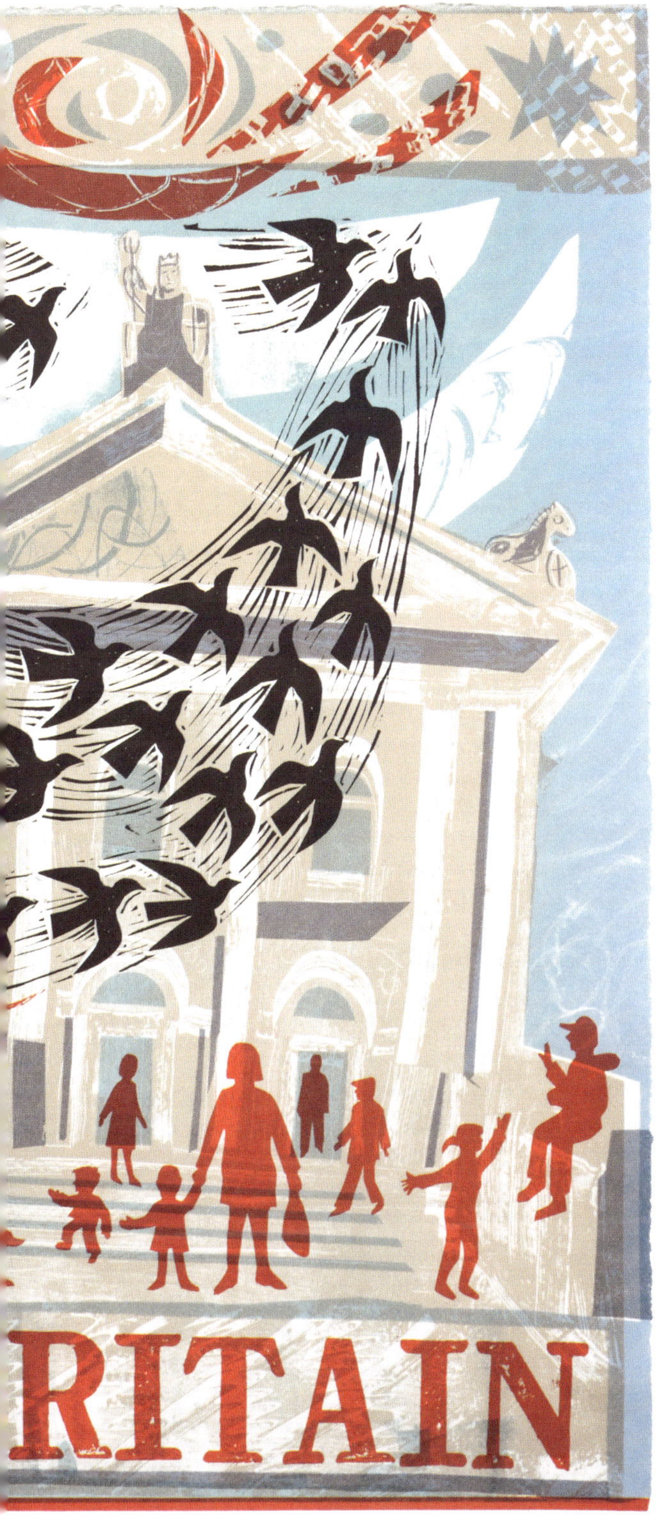

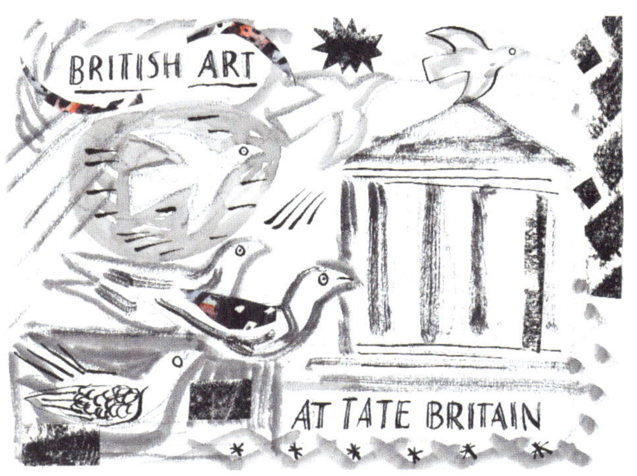

British Art at Tate Britain

When asked by Tate Britain to make a print to sell in its shop, I wanted it to relate to the *Printing with Spirit* lithograph that had been displayed there previously (page 29). It shares a graphic, poster-like aesthetic with that earlier print, with three London pigeons looking on as a flock swoops past the gallery's portico and visitors in the form of paper cut-outs mill about on the steps.

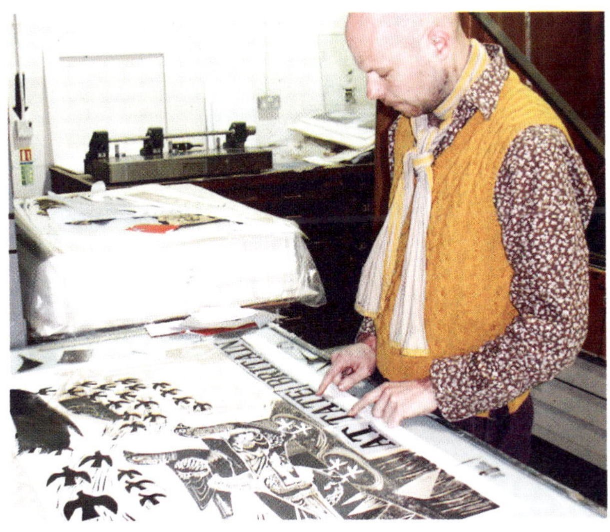

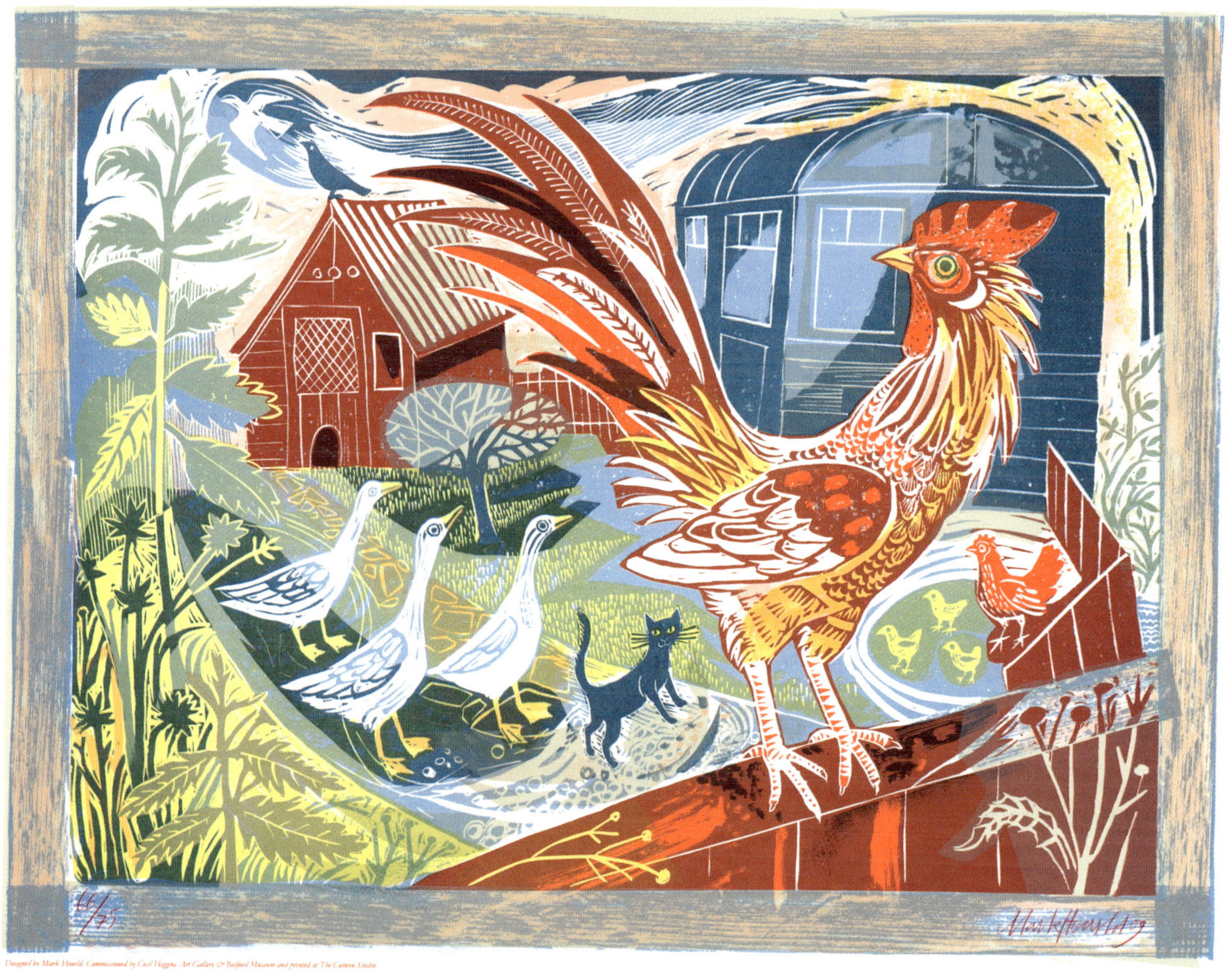

Rooster and Railway Carriage

In 2009 I was commissioned by the Higgins Art Gallery and Museum in Bedford to produce a print to accompany an exhibition of the work of Edward Bawden, who had donated his archive to the gallery in 1986. Printed at the Curwen Studio, where Bawden produced a number of images, the work began as a linocut, but was developed and printed lithographically. It was sold to raise funds for the gallery.

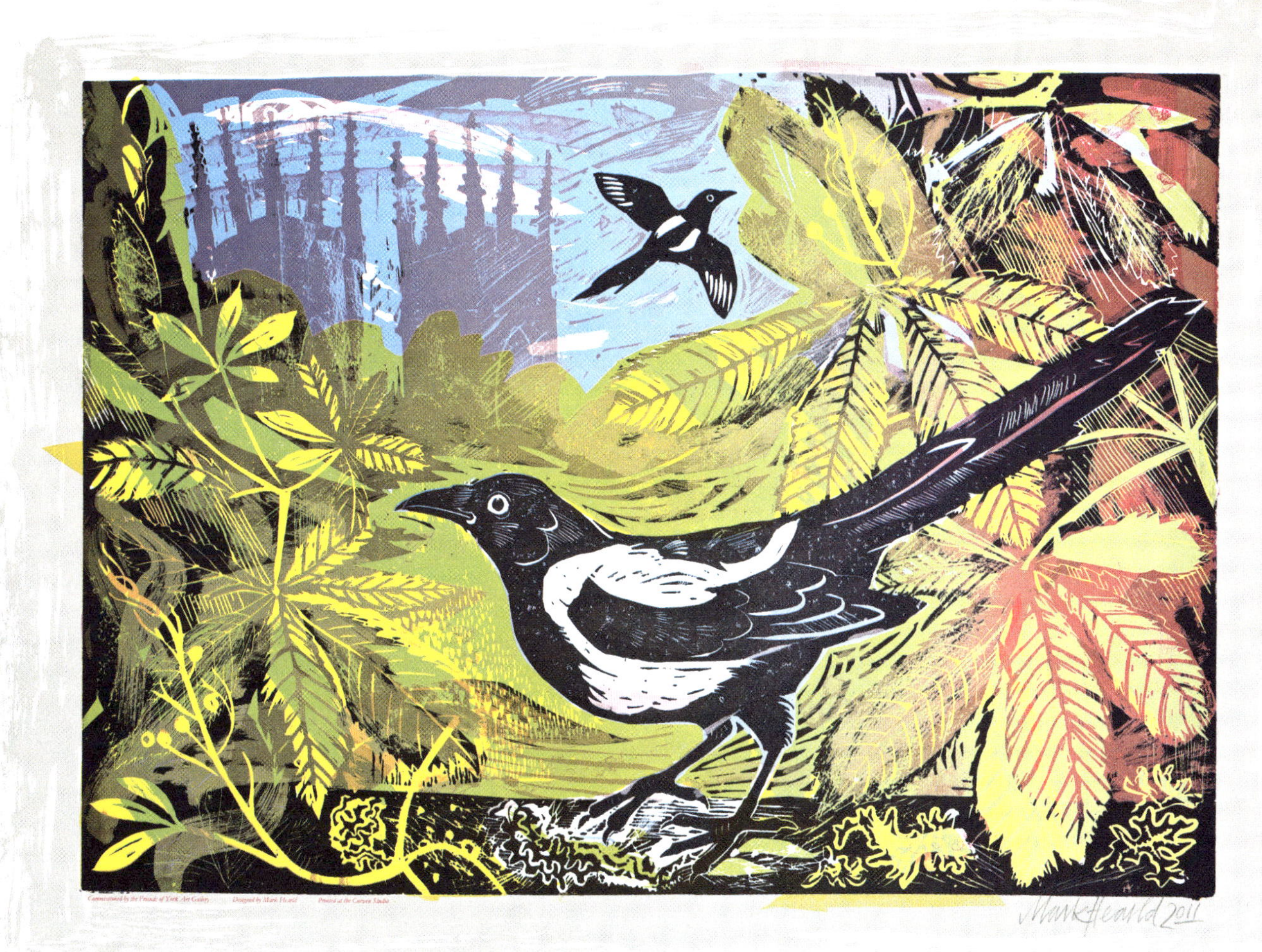

Minster and Magpies

A walk along the city walls in York in late May was the inspiration for this lithograph. I always enjoy taking a bird's-eye view, in this case through a canopy of horse chestnut trees. I decided to feature the magpie with some trepidation. Although it is a handsome and highly intelligent bird, it is also an egg thief and a rogue – one for sorrow, or, in this case, two for joy. It was commissioned by the Friends of York Art Gallery and printed at the Curwen Studio.

Hat Box Squirrels (far right)

The title of this print requires
explanation. It stems from an image
of a fine hat box, block-printed
with scampering squirrels, that
I found in the pages of an old copy
of *World of Interiors* – and then
promptly lost. Initially, I made
a collage, *Squirrels in Parkland*
(below), in response to the
remembered image; this collage
then developed into a lithograph
at a later date. The sketch of the
original hat box (right) does not
do it justice.

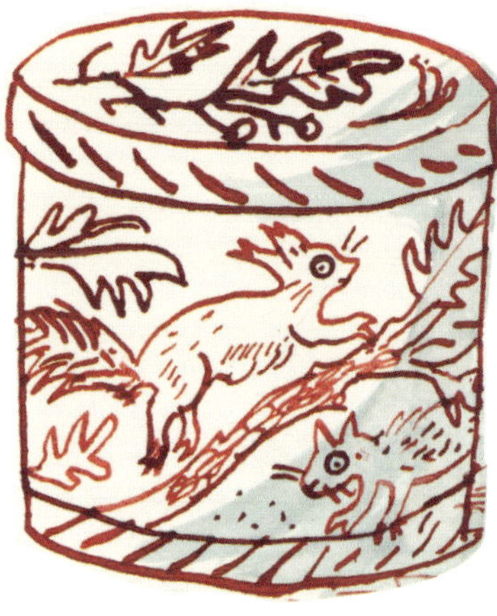

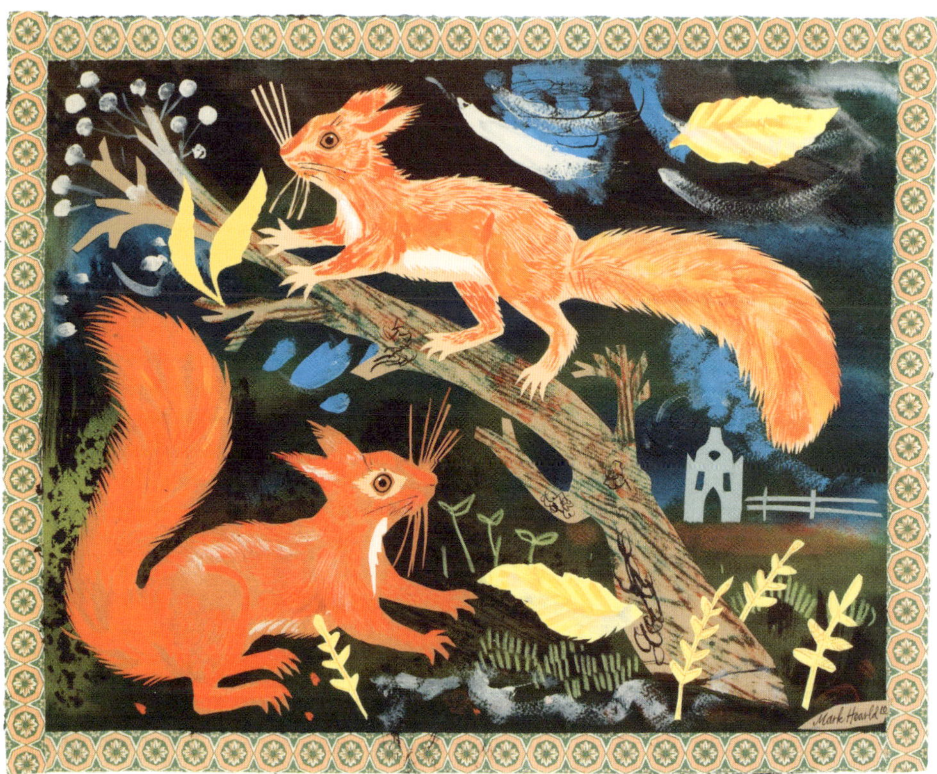

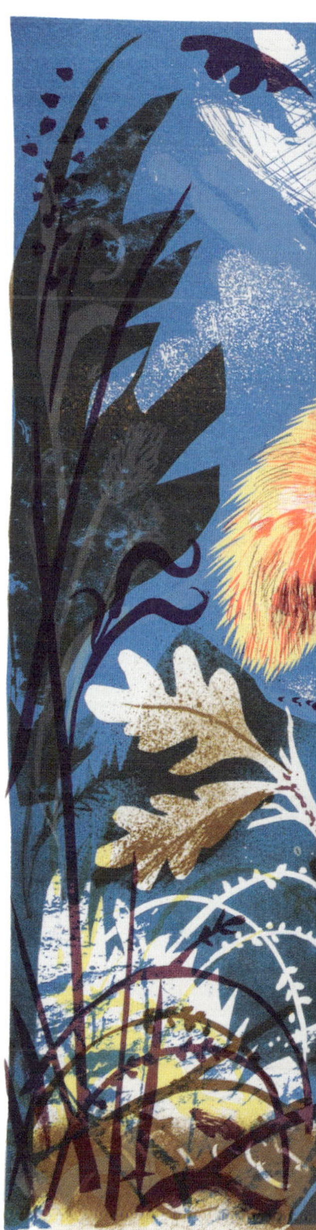

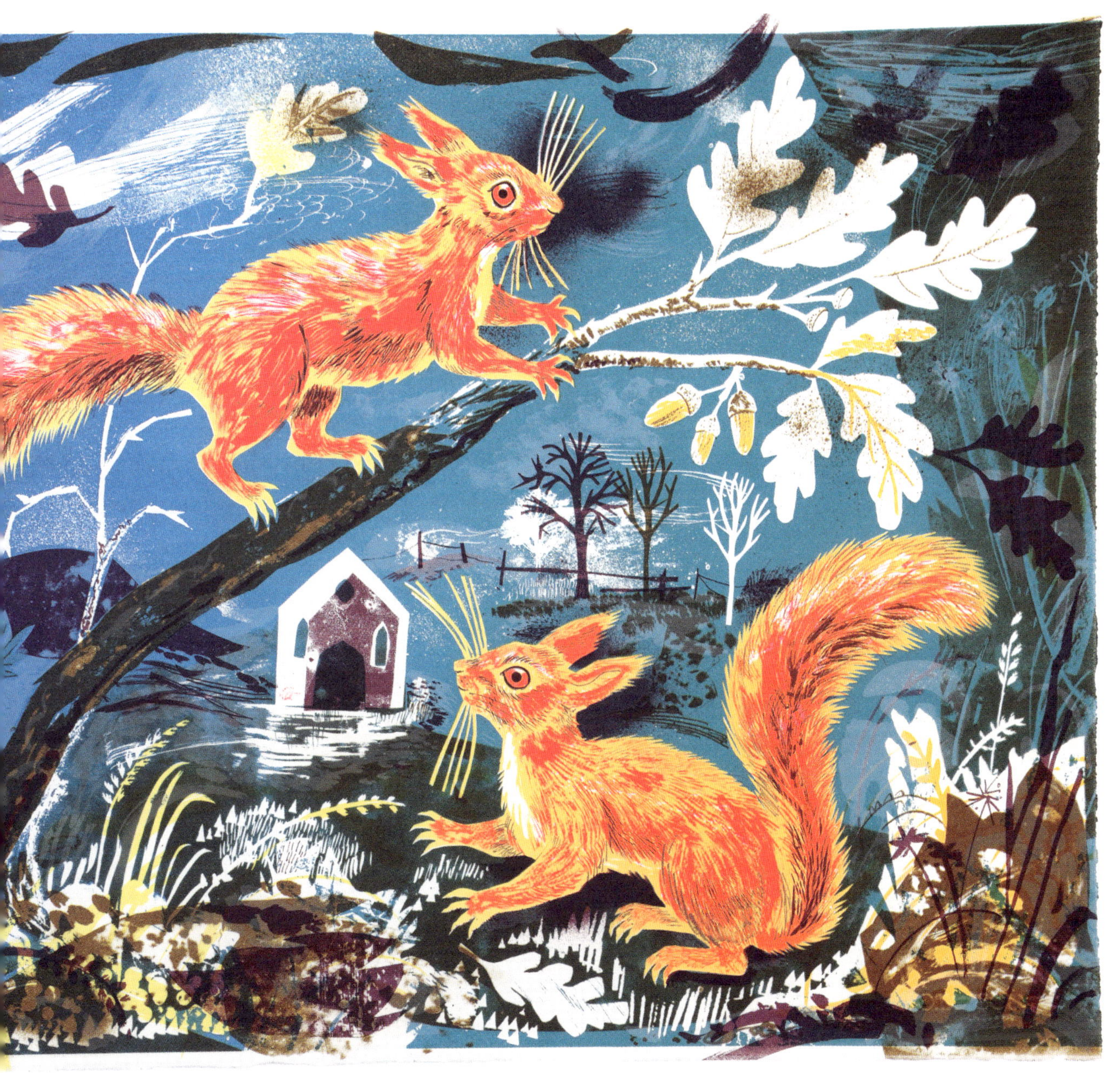

Linocuts

In its simplest form, linocutting is about black and white. The image is created by removing areas of surface that you do not wish to print. The composition is determined by tonal counterpoint, that is, black against white, white against black. Success with the medium is achieved through a subtle application of contrasts; intricate patterned marks provide a foil for bold expanses of ink. White paper comes to life with the residual, inked-up marks left by the cutting tool. Picasso and Bawden demonstrated a masterly grasp of the medium, the former for the animation in each image, the latter with his command of decorative pattern.

The use of two colours creates a strong visual effect, which is often enough to create a rich sense of atmosphere. In *Sea Change* (below), which was the first linocut I made in collaboration with Dan Bugg at his Penfold Press in York, a gull on the shore looks out to sea; the sea holly and sea kale provide textural dynamism and were a joy to cut. A flock of starlings en route to a roost in *Starlings on the Shore* (opposite, top) appears sharply silhouetted against the moonlight. In *Geese and Fish* (opposite, bottom), the bold patterning of the scales of a fish adds a decorative energy to the composition.

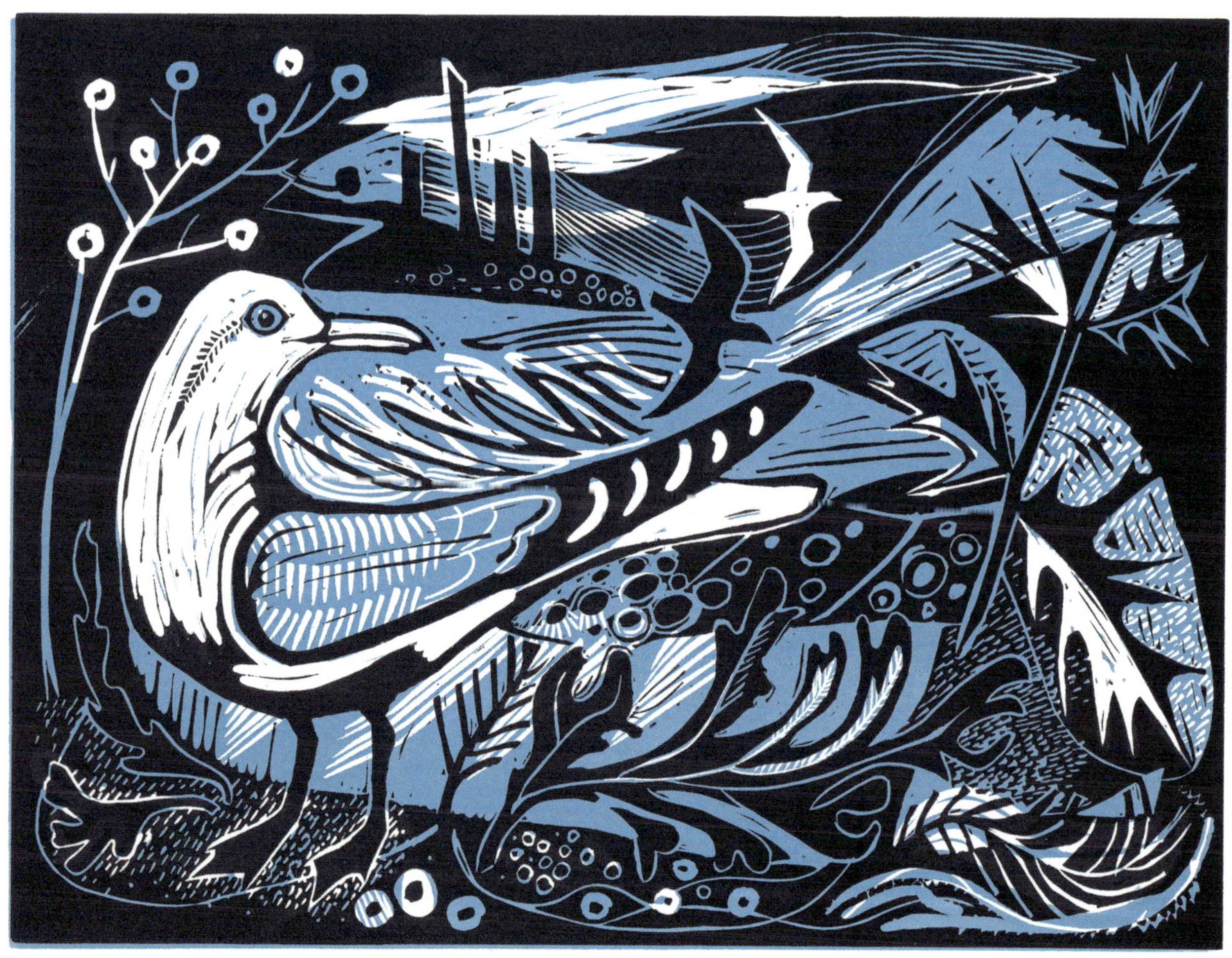

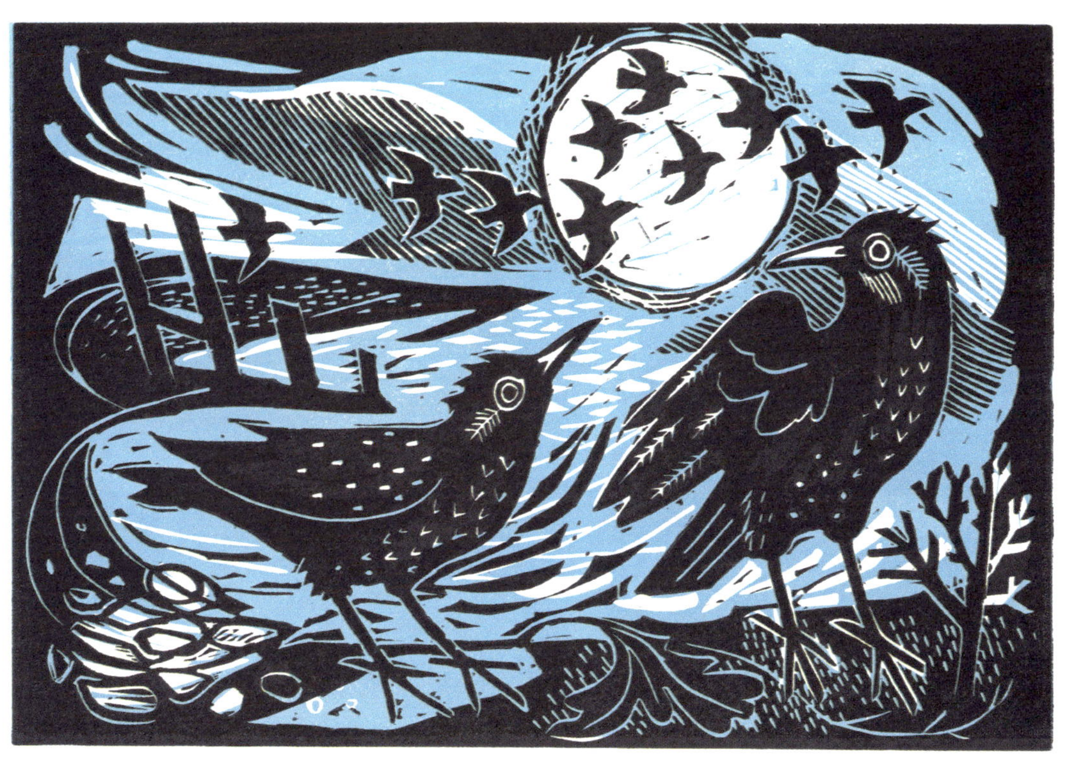

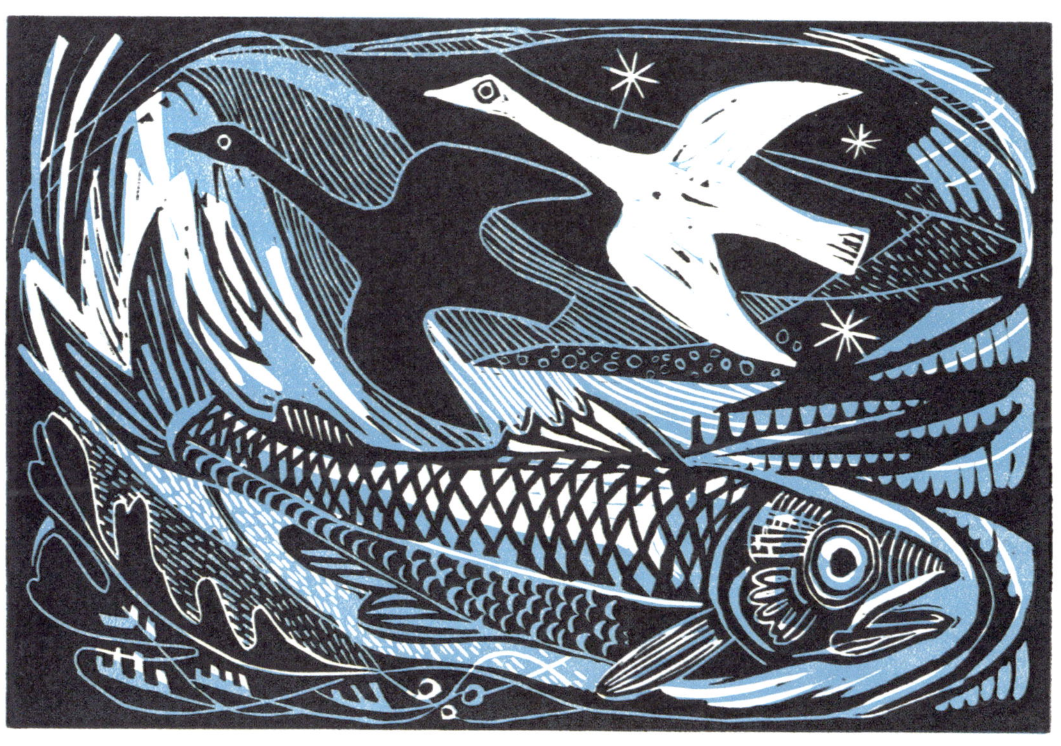

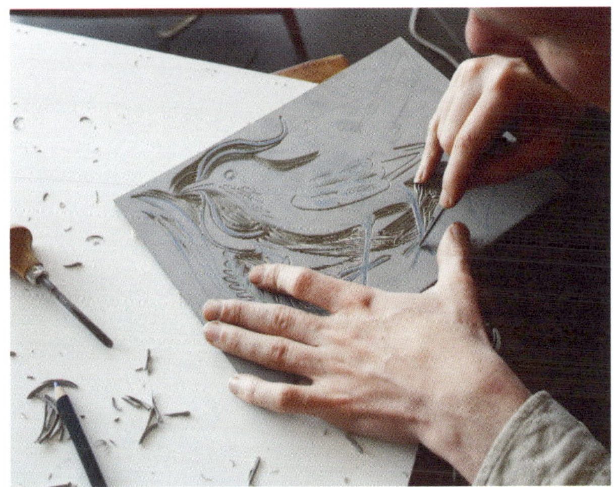

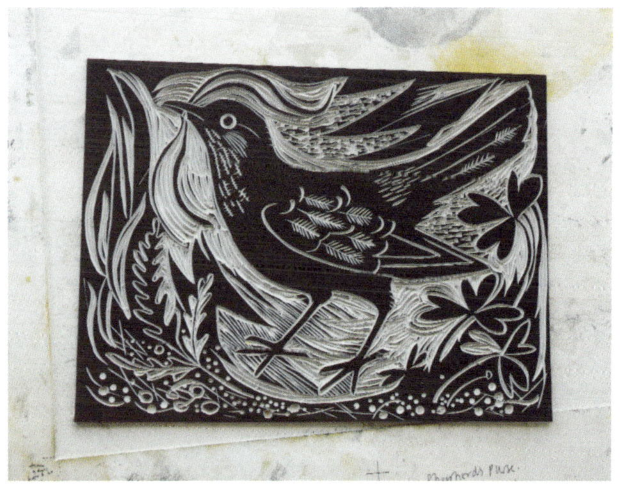

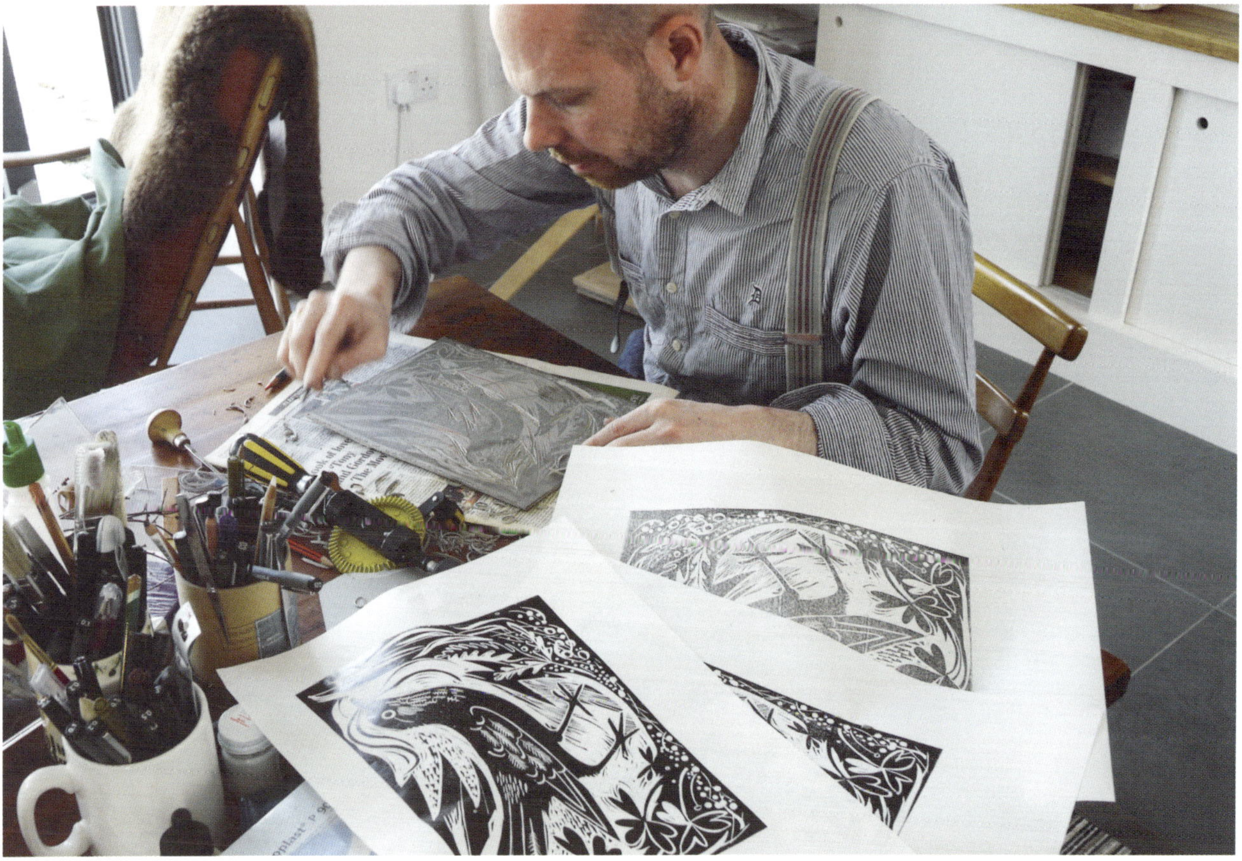

Ballindalloch Blackbird

This image, cut in Scotland, took me by surprise. After a long walk in Speyside with Angie and Simon Lewin of St Jude's (see page 133), I came back tired and uncertain that I had any work in me. However, the satisfying form of a blackbird took shape easily. Perhaps my familiarity with it as a subject and the clarity of its silhouette won out. The edition was printed in Angie's studio and published by St Jude's.

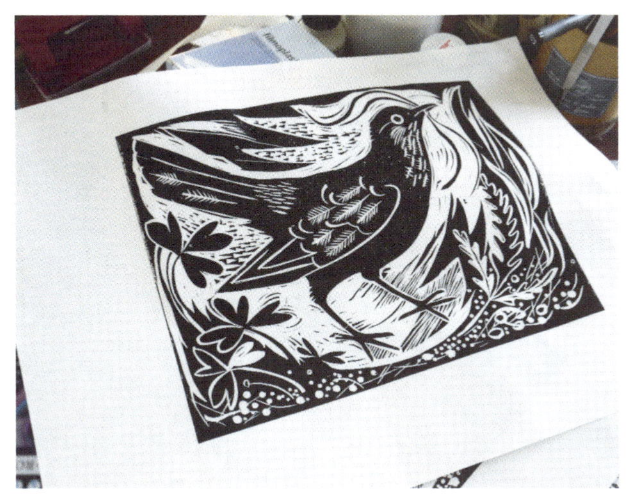 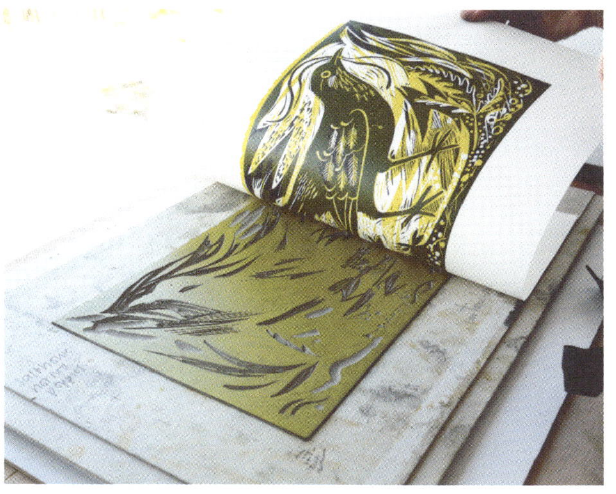

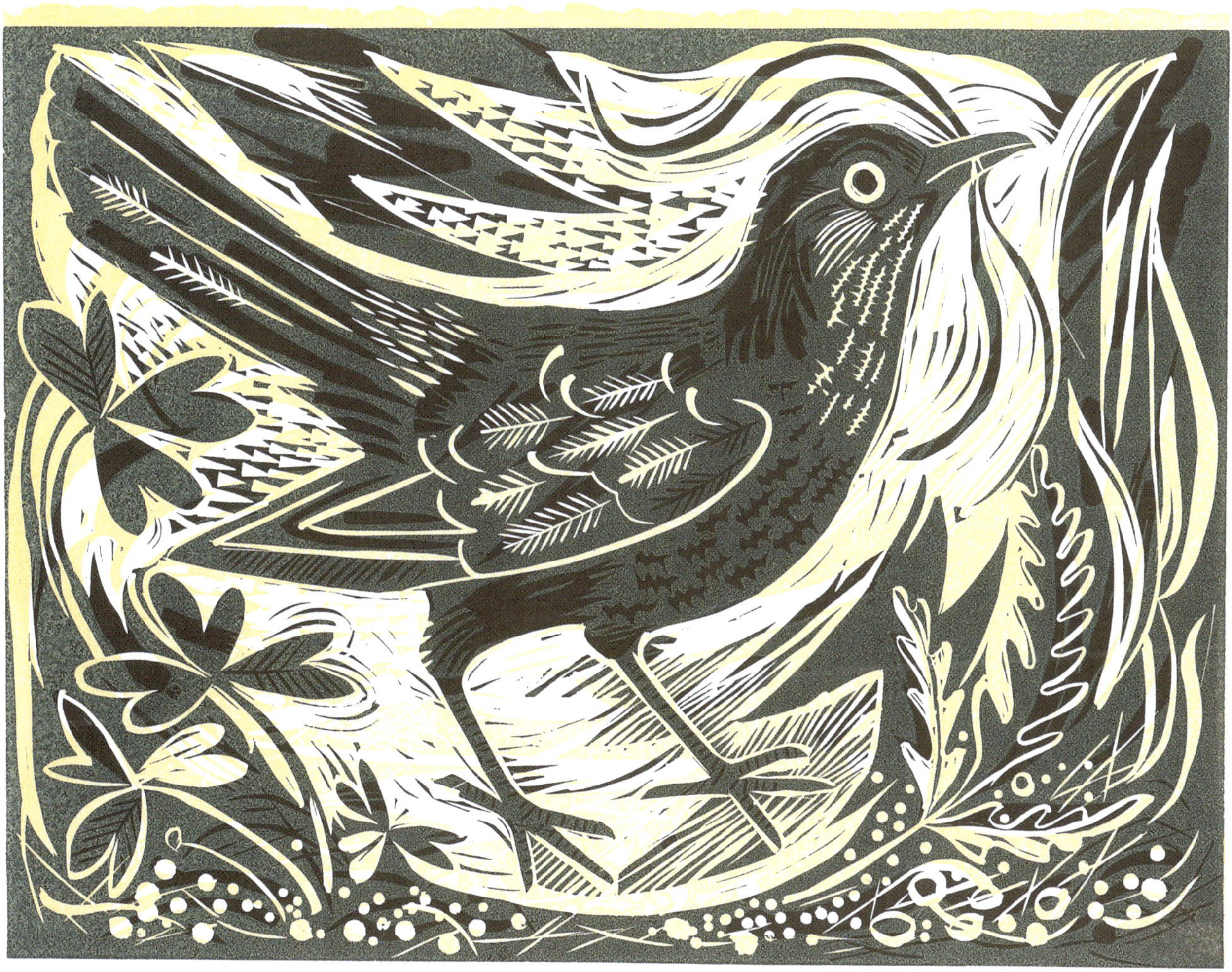

Turkey

Invariably, by the first week in December any Christmas exhibitions are on the wall. I can then begin making a Christmas card or print to send to family and friends, an activity I always look forward to. Perhaps it's over the top to put an A2 print in the post, but it was great fun to edition eighty black-and-white prints in a day.

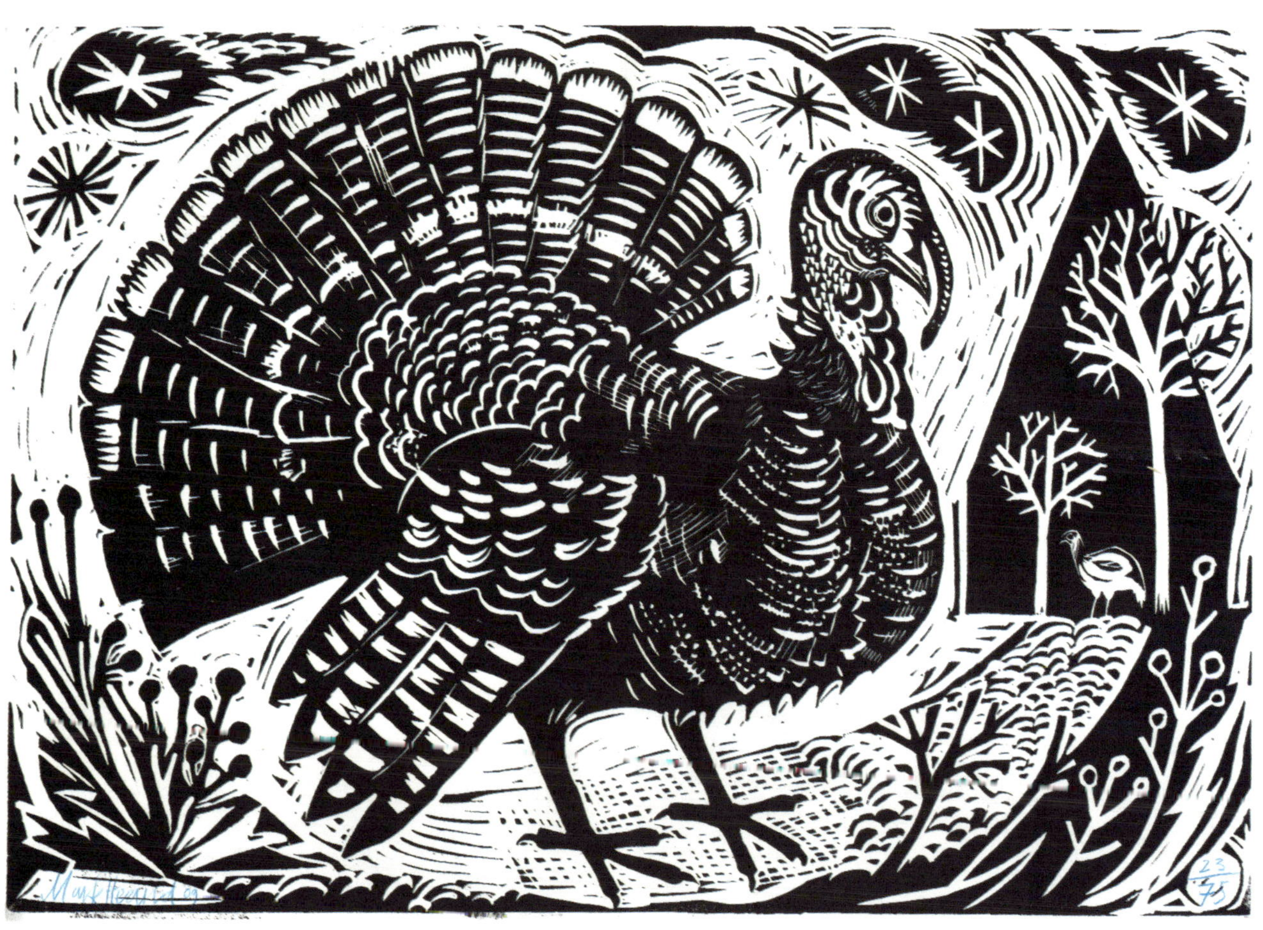

The Boar's Head

'The boar's head in hand bare I, / bedeck'd with bays and rosemary.' So begins 'The Boar's Head Carol', sung in glorious polyphony by the Oxford folk band Magpie Lane, and played in Terry Shone's Whitby pottery (see pages 144–45). It rooted itself firmly in my head, and provided me with a subject for the Christmas print of 2011.

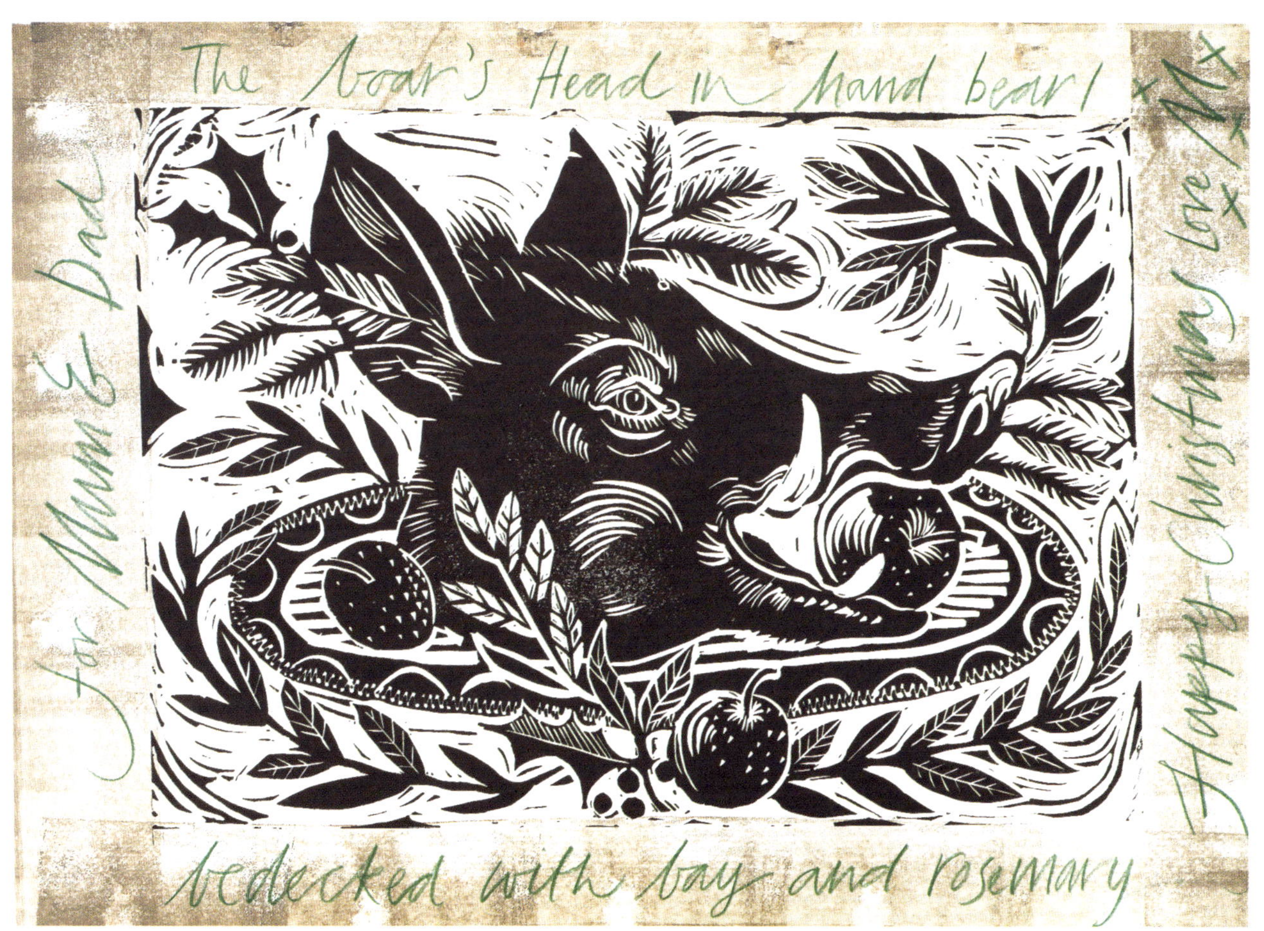

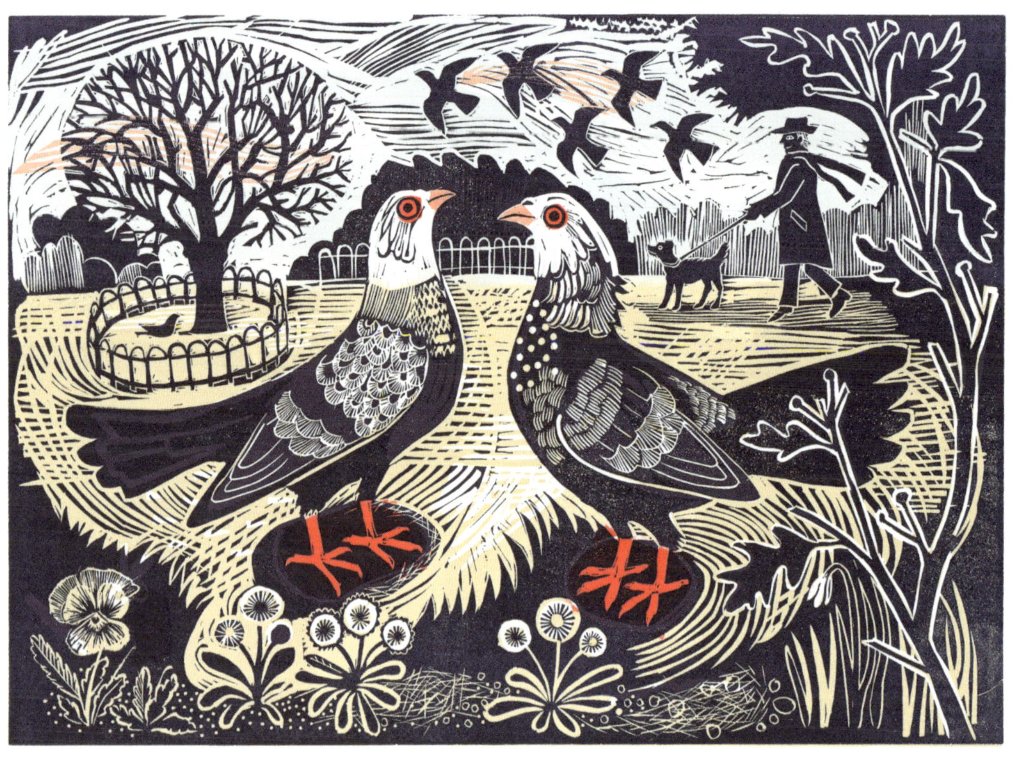

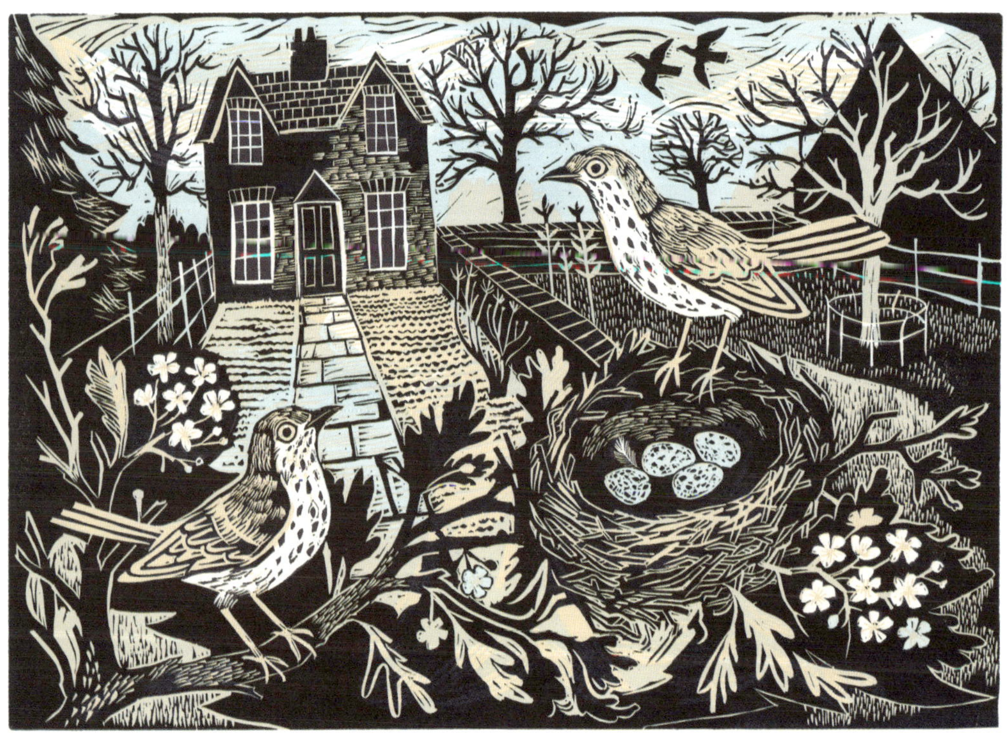

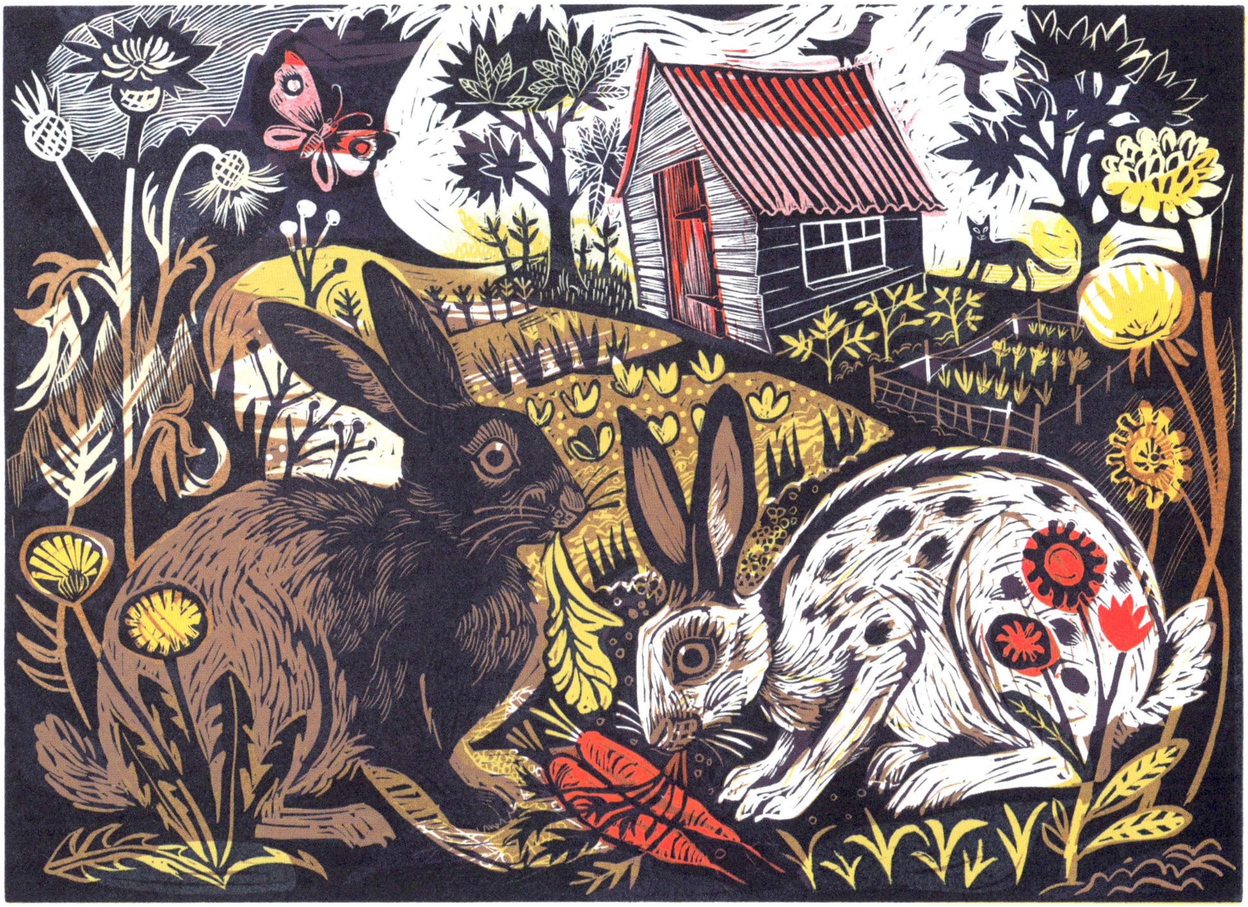

I worked with Dan Bugg to produce these multi-block linocuts, mixing the colour and proofing each print before leaving him to print the edition. I made *Pigeons in the Park* (opposite, top) for inclusion in the exhibition *In the Spirit of Edward Bawden and Eric Ravilious* at the Fry Art Gallery in Essex (2007). I wanted to pay homage to Bawden without being seen as a pallid imitator. The formality of the birds' pairing worked well, and led to a group of involved multi-block linocuts. *Thrushes' Nest* (opposite, bottom) followed, in which the hawthorn flowers are a nod to the treatment of blossom in William Morris's textile *Blackthorn* (1892). It's particularly satisfying when a limited colour palette says it all. The idea for *Salad Days* (above) came from the collage *Carrot Crop* and, by extension, the wonderful rabbit-shaped tureen in the Fitzwilliam Museum in Cambridge (see pages 80–81). The domesticity of a rabbit in a vegetable patch has a resonance that runs deep, maybe as far as Beatrix Potter's Peter Rabbit in Mr McGregor's garden. This is perhaps the most ambitious linocut I've attempted so far, and when I look at it I'm inspired to tackle another.

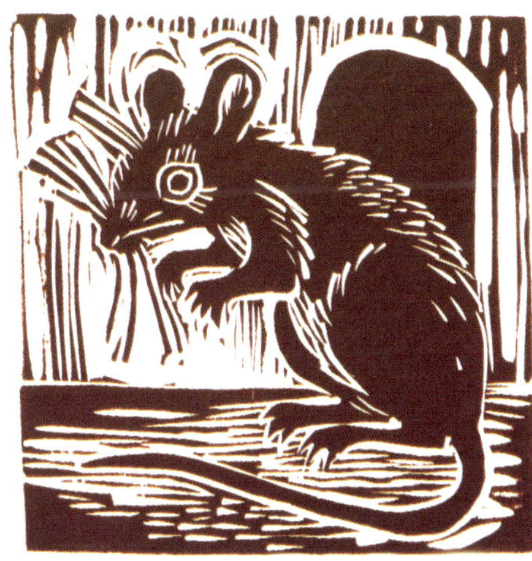

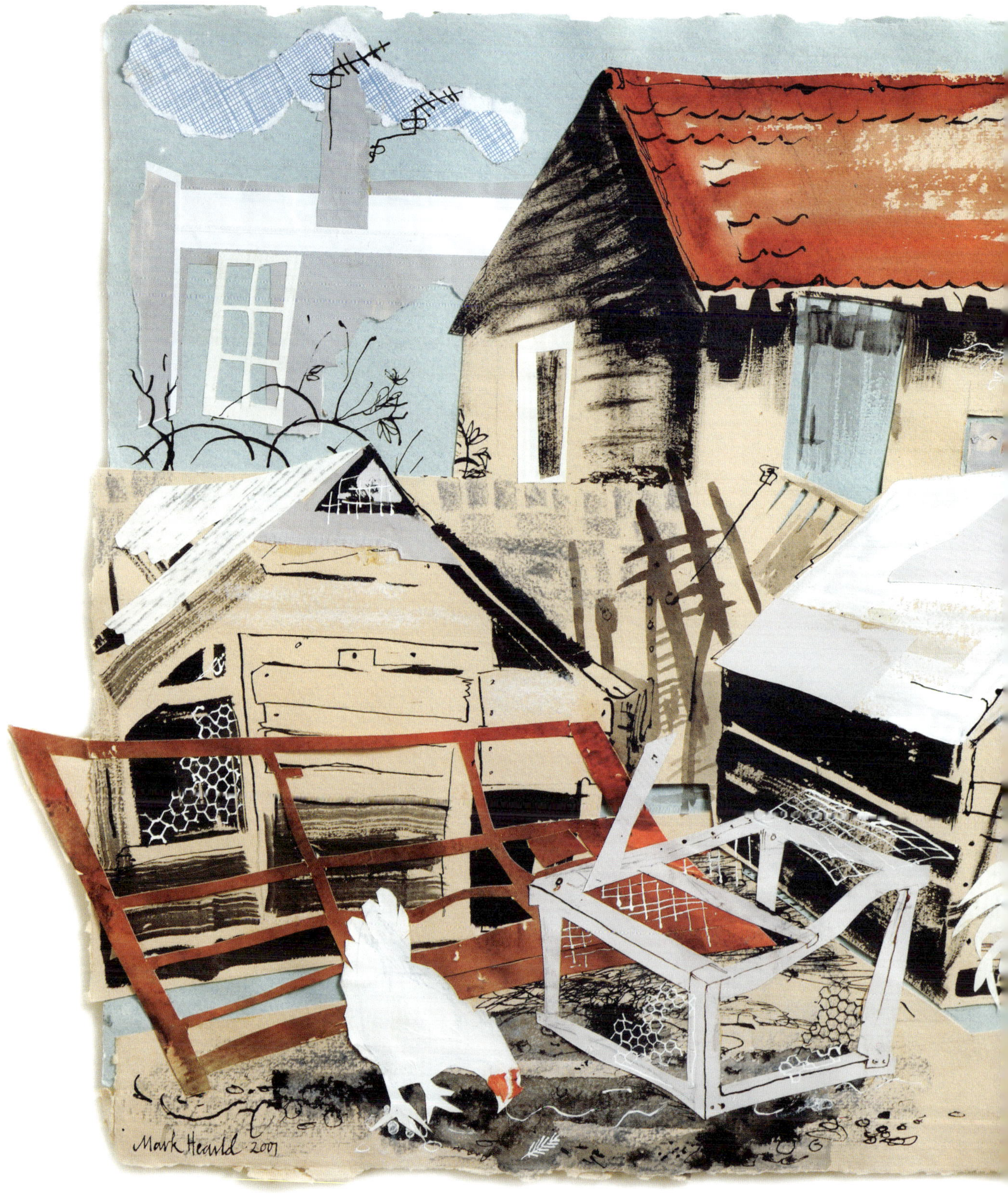
Mark Hearld 2007

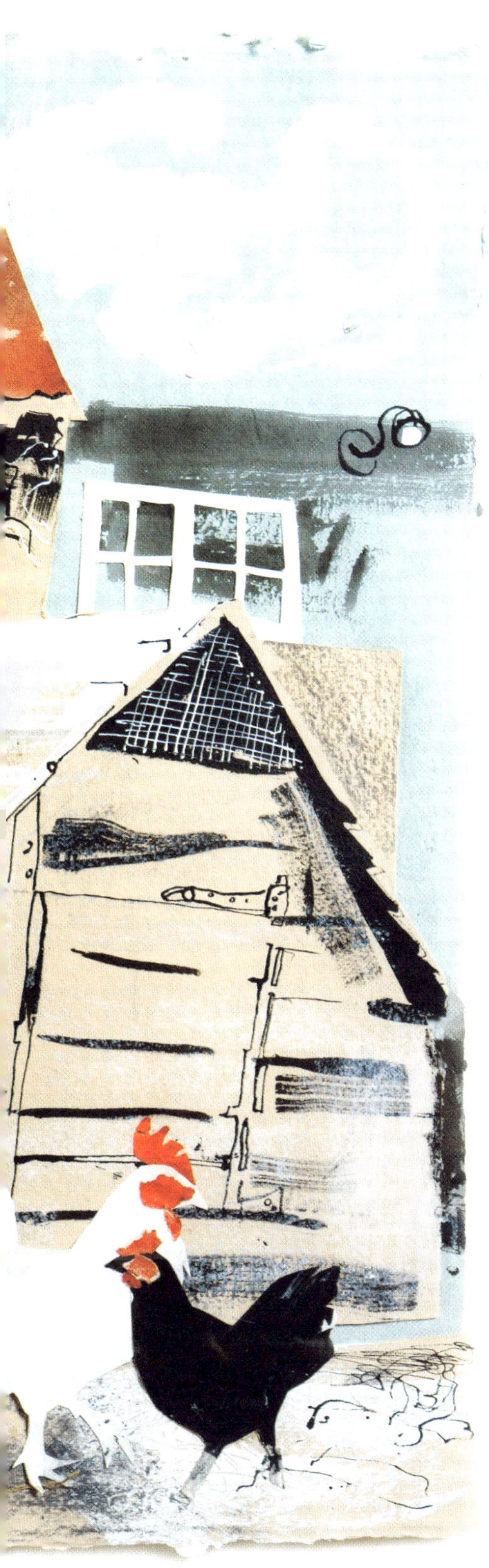

Farmyard

Rusting farm machinery, the vernacular detail of a hen house and chicken coop, an orchard full of apple trees, nettle patches hiding broody hens, swallows nesting above the ponies in the stables – farmyards are full of hidden corners and the layering of history. John Piper talked about 'pleasing decay' in relation to grand ruins, but the phrase also fits the most wonderful aspects of the stackyard or smallholding. As a student, I spent the holidays drawing hens and geese from life. The concentrated period of looking gave me an intimate knowledge of these birds, which I still draw on today. It's important to return to direct observation, to top up the visual memory, but it's also liberating to remember that it's perfectly valid to invent.

Botland Farmyard

This collage has a special significance for me: it is the first collage I ever made, created outside and on the spot, from direct observation, on the farm just around the corner from my family home in Heslington, North Yorkshire (see right). The rusted gates, night arks and coops, arranged in a wonderful clutter, are fantastic graphic elements to snip out of paper – abstract, structural forms that provide a dynamic informality and a terrific sense of 'pleasing decay'. The use of the insides of envelopes for pattern and texture seemed adventurous at the time, informed by the work of Julian Trevelyan and John Piper. All subsequent chickens appear with eyes.

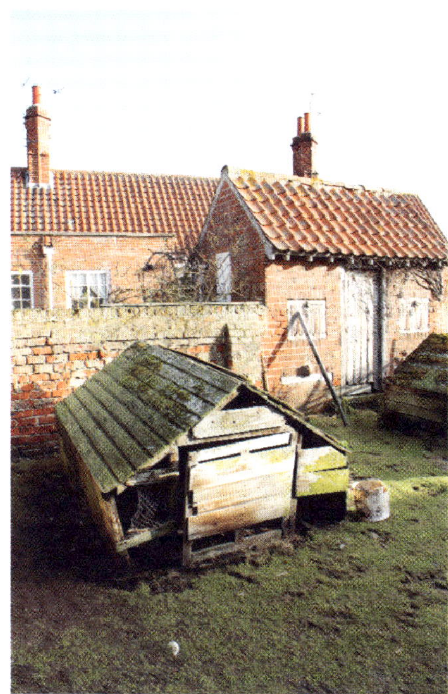

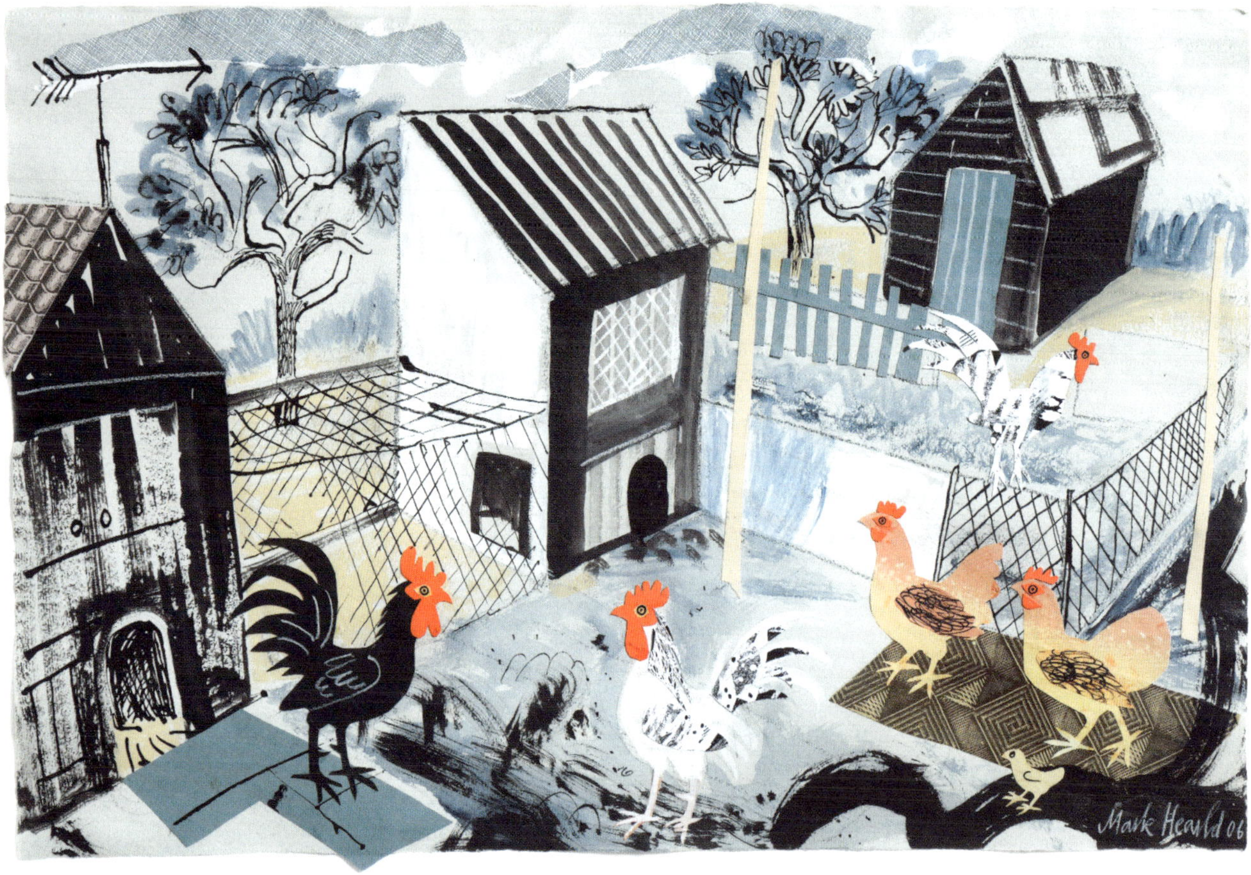

Hens and Coops

The contained space, framed by
a ramshackle collection of wire
netting and picket fences, is a
key feature of this smallholder's
chicken run.

Black Hens and Eggs (right)
and Barred Cockerel
(opposite)

Black Hens and Eggs features
pattern papers from Florence, the
Curwen Press and a stationery
shop in New York. I am particularly
pleased with the crackled eggs.

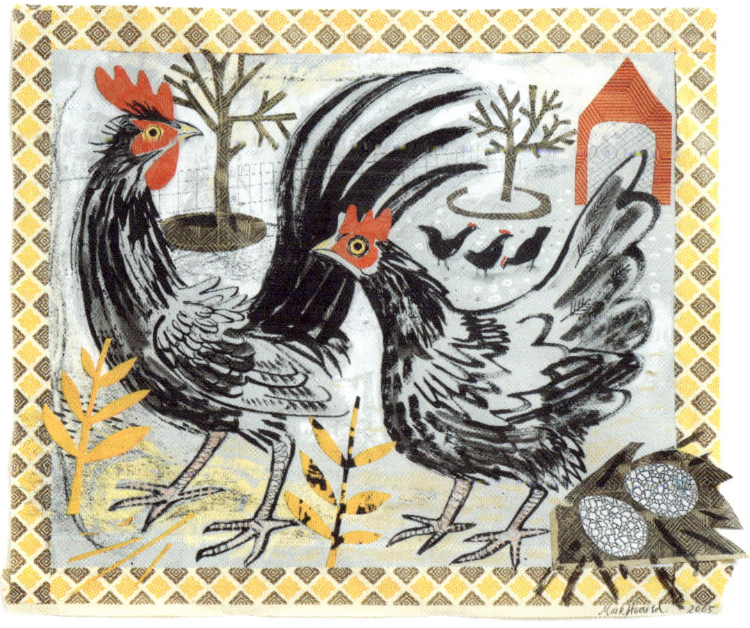

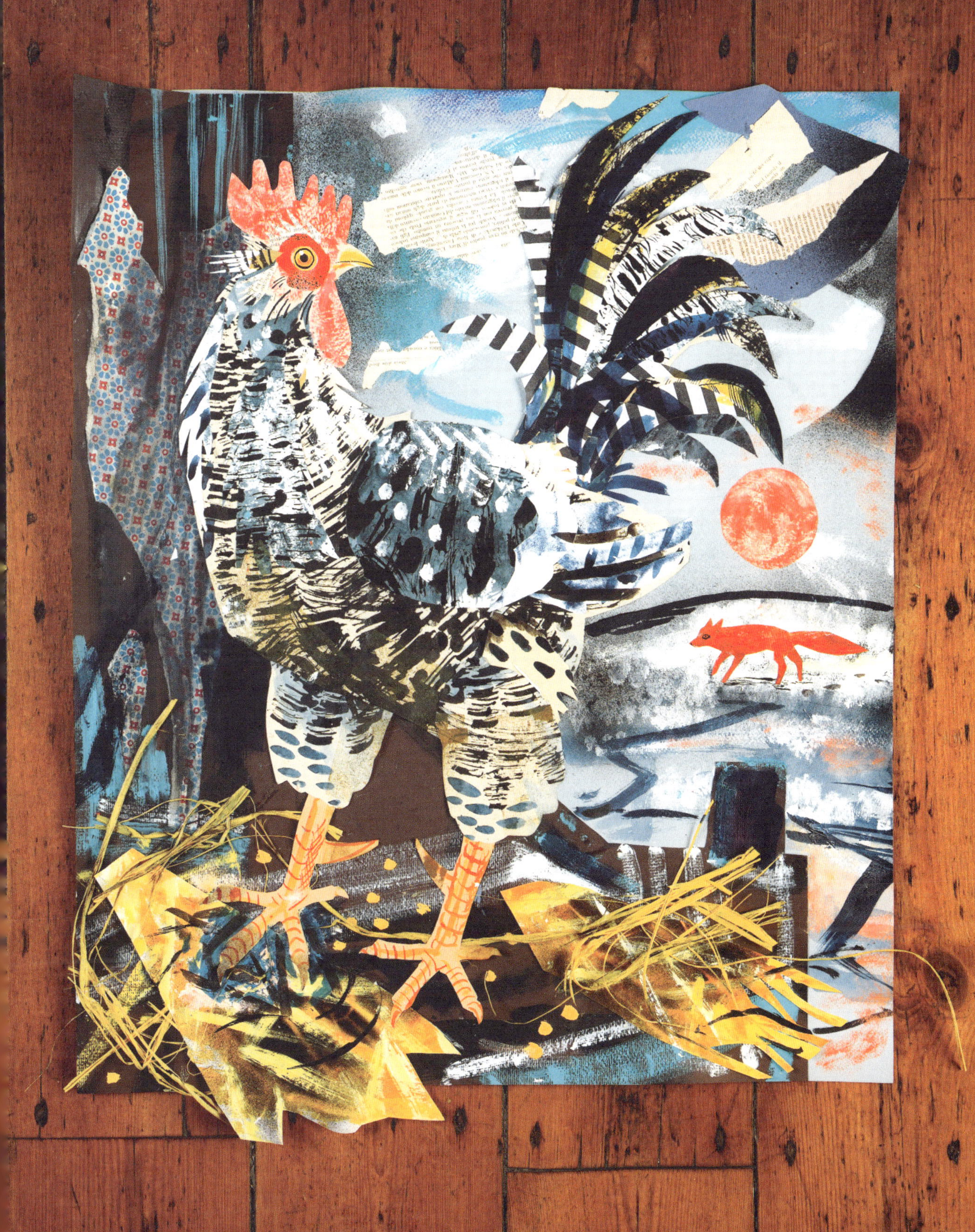

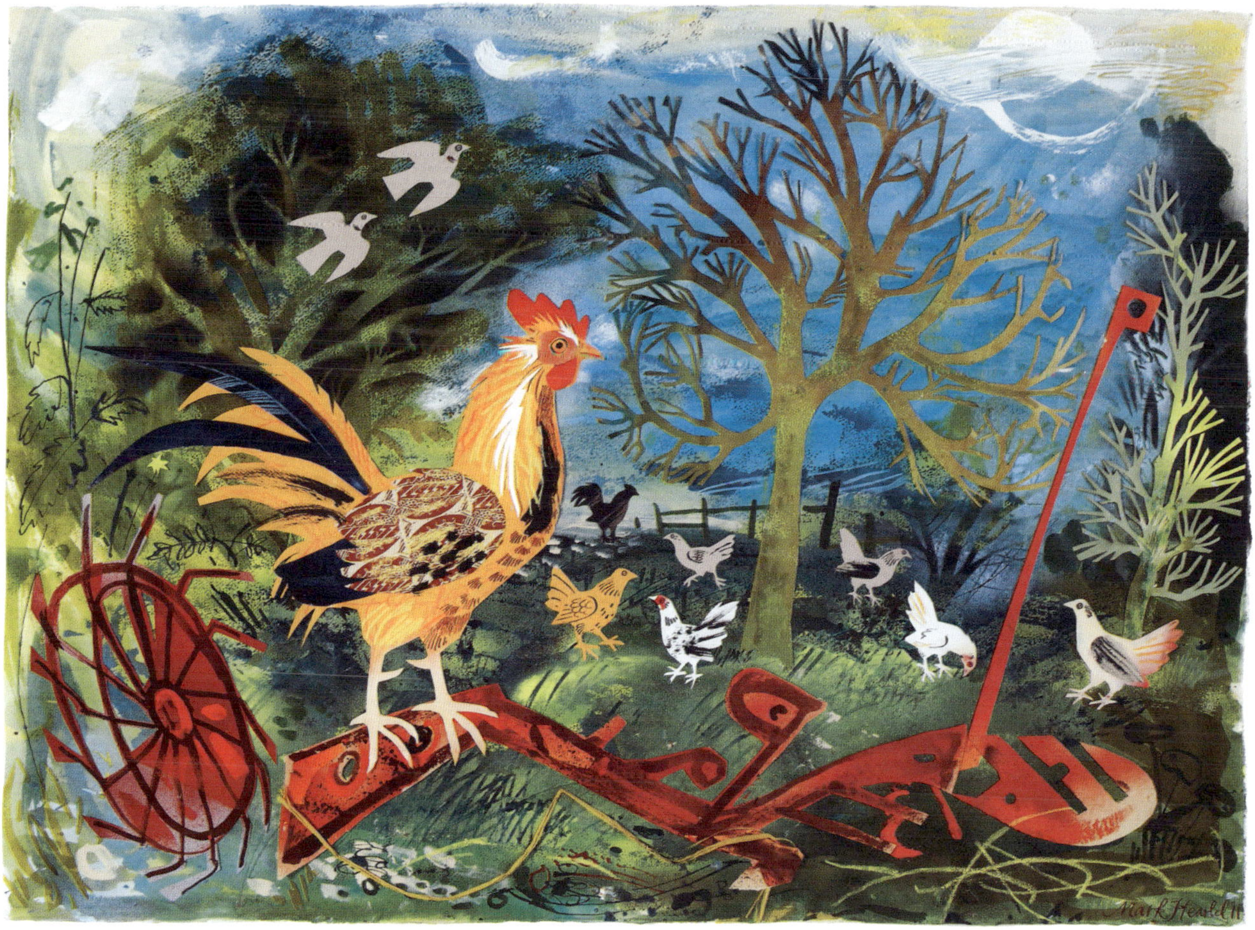

Cockerel and Farm Machinery (above)

The imposing decorative plumage of a cockerel is a gift to the collagist. Its graphic profile and high colour command the attention and offer dynamic possibilities for image-making. In this piece, a Curwen Press-printed endpaper designed by Enid Marx is the perfect visual equivalent for the wing markings. The piece of farm machinery is entirely fabricated, but lends the scene an element of abstraction and a hard edge.

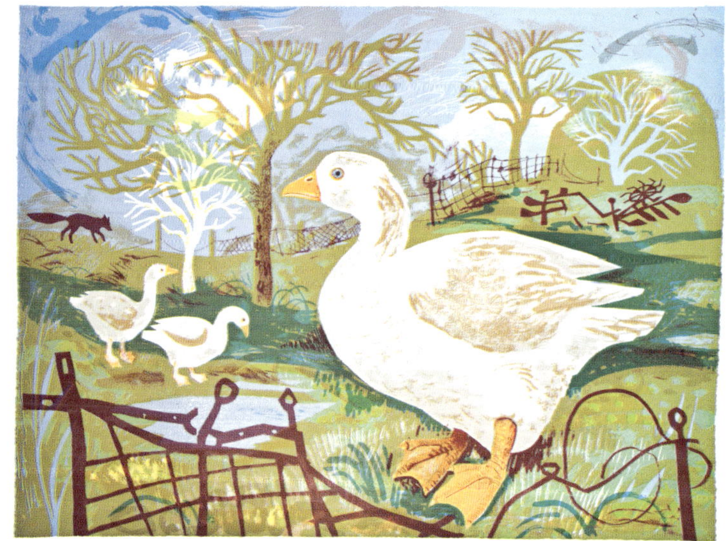

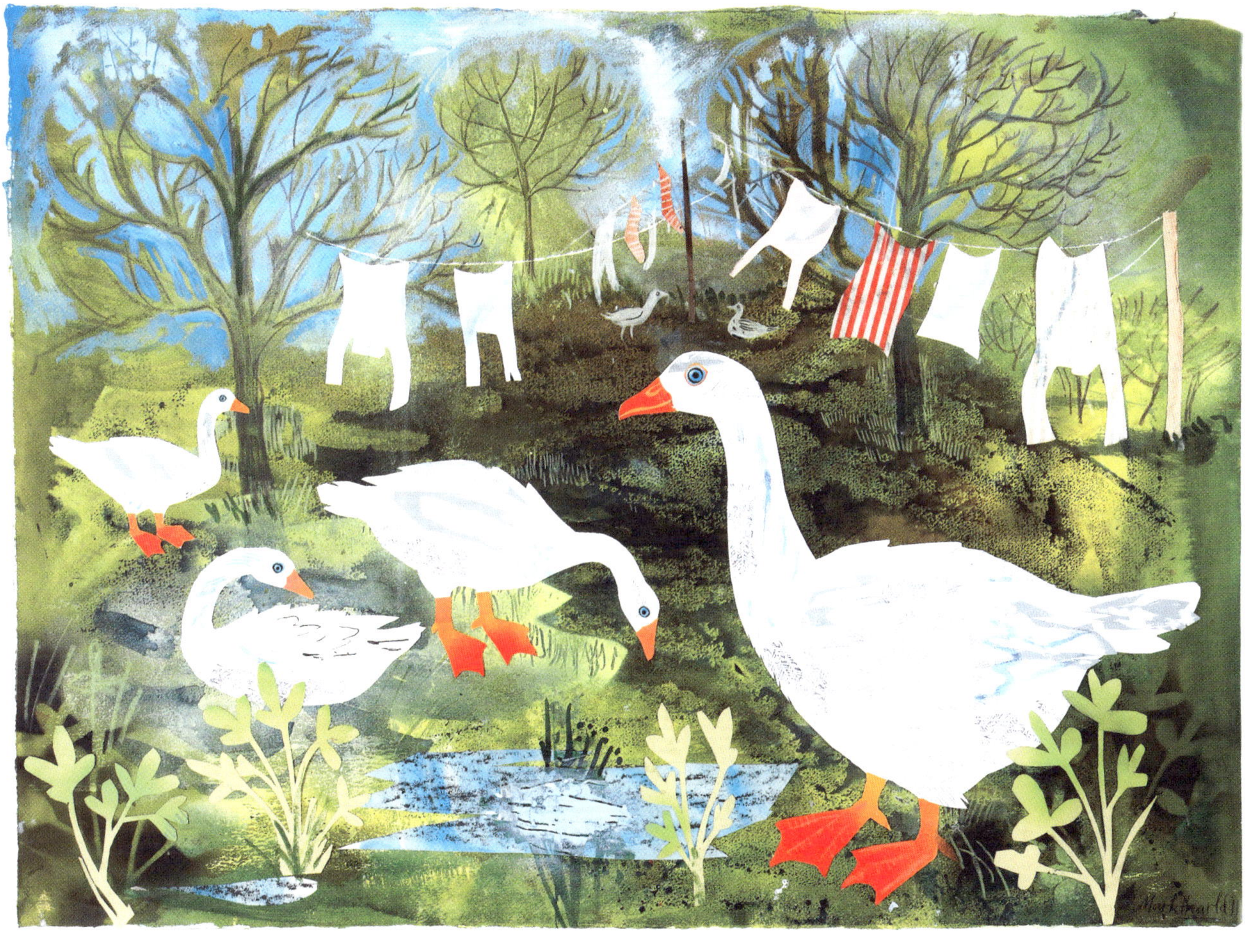

The Orchard

The orchard at Bridge Farm in Heslington is where I saw through an artist's eyes for the first time – in effect, seeing nature anew, with the excitement of all the visual possibilities it provides. The smell of apples in the early autumn led to an image, *September Windfalls* (1997), that caught the spirit of the place, with Red Admiral butterflies feeding on rotting apples. It's the ordinariness of the orchard that is at the same time its special beauty: a green space, with geese drinking from galvanized zinc washtubs, framed by the arcing boughs of the apple trees. I made the collage *Orchard Geese* (above) and, more recently, the lithograph *Orchard Goose* (opposite, bottom) in response to a favourite location.

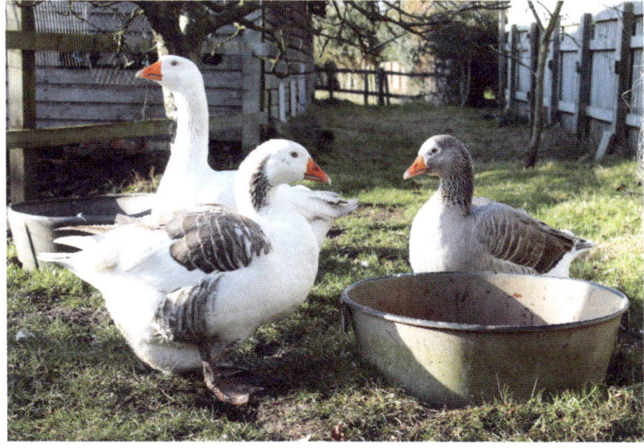

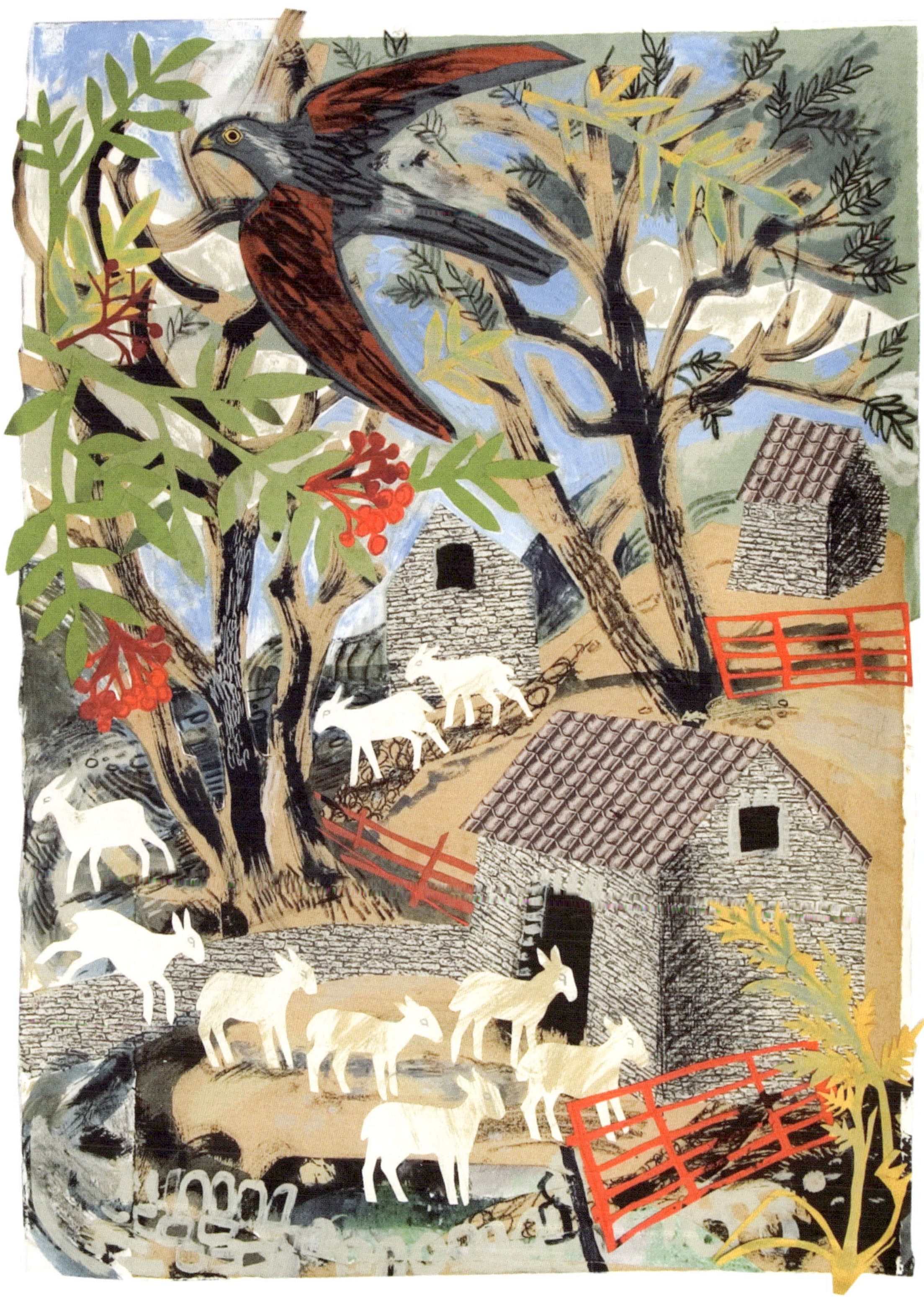

Kestrel Flight (opposite)

Cheviot hill sheep have
appealingly large ears: their
silhouette cuts out well. In
this collage, made in the studio,
I was interested in the stillness
of the stationary sheep and
the animation in the maverick
sheep determined to join them.
A passing bird of prey adds
another point of focus to the
work, another moment in time.
Working from memory allows you
to bring together in one image
a series of different events.

Uttely's Ducks

A stay at Michael Kirkman's
family cottage in Coverdale, North
Yorkshire, proved an inspiring
week away. I made two collages on
the spot, and am pleased with the
vitality and sense of place they
evoke. In *The Tin Hut, West
Scrafton* (page 52, top), the sheep
sheds have a random quality that
would have been hard to invent.
With *Uttely's Ducks*, the visual
editorial decisions made with
the onset of rain worked to the
image's favour; the ducks waddled
obligingly to and fro, ending up
at the bend in front of me. The
importance of working from
nature is knowing what to include
and what to leave out.

Duck and Drake

In certain images, you hit upon
a colour combination that sings.
Here, the cadmium-yellow beak
and the warm blue sky hold
the whole composition together,
offset by the sharp green of the
waterside plants.

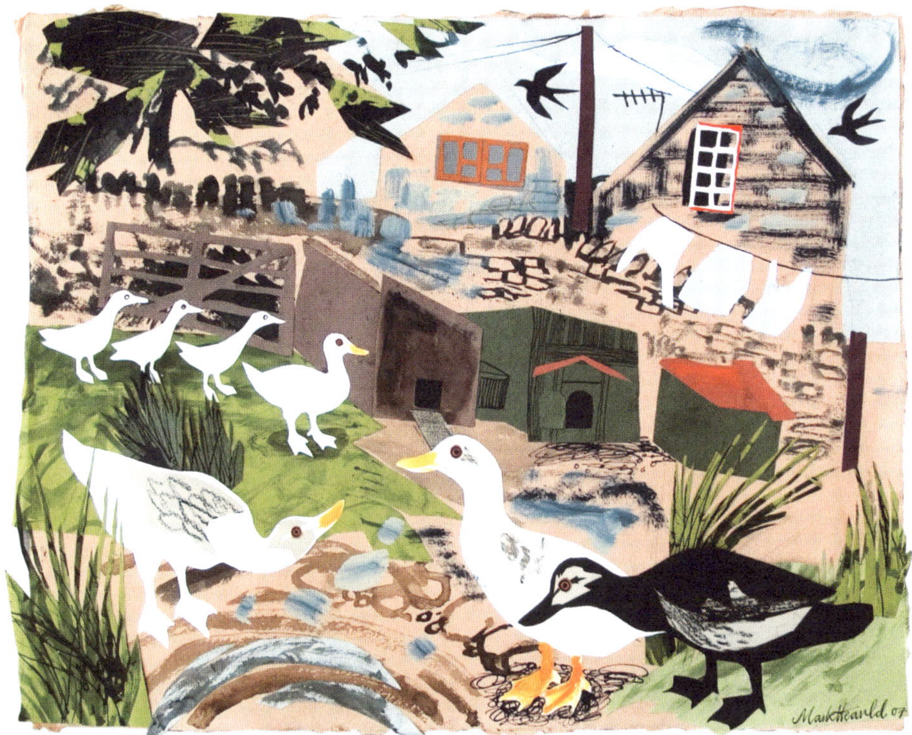

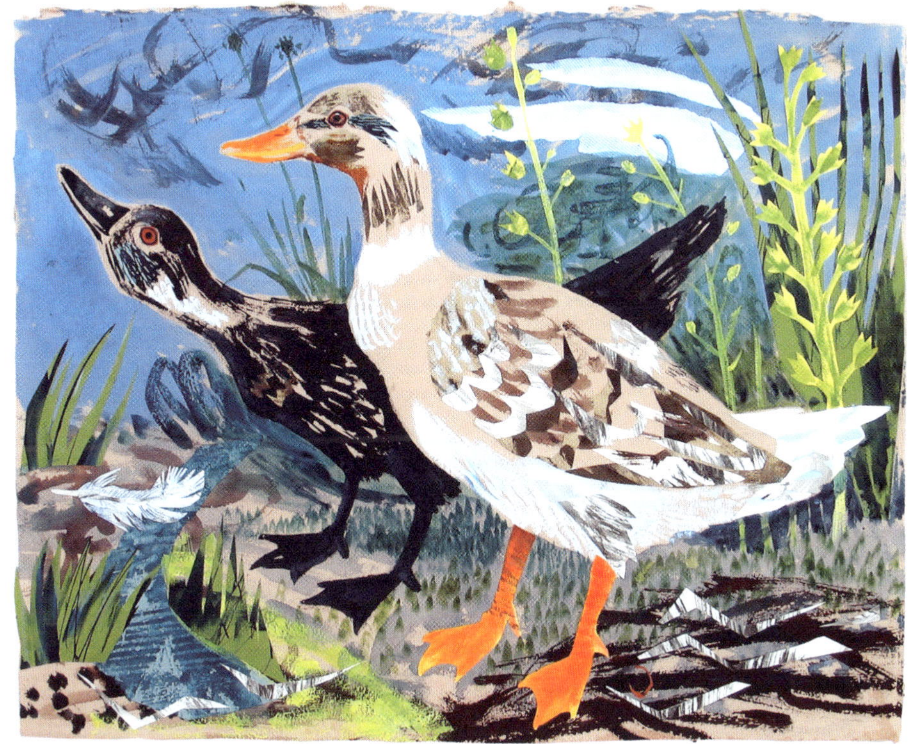

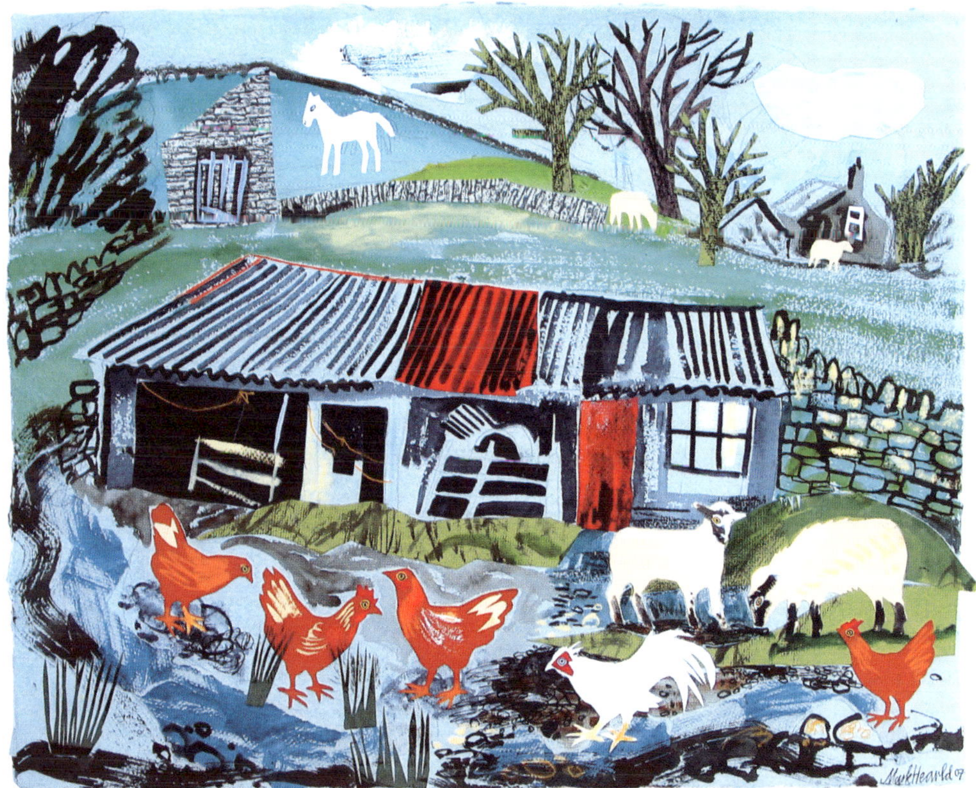

The Tin Hut, West Scrafton

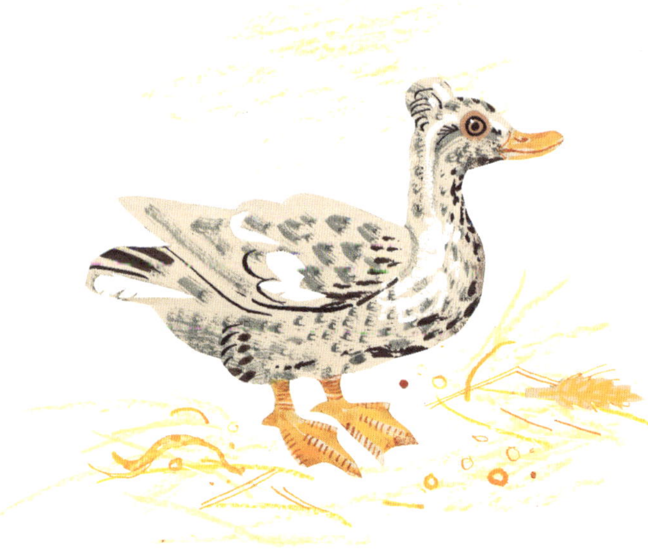

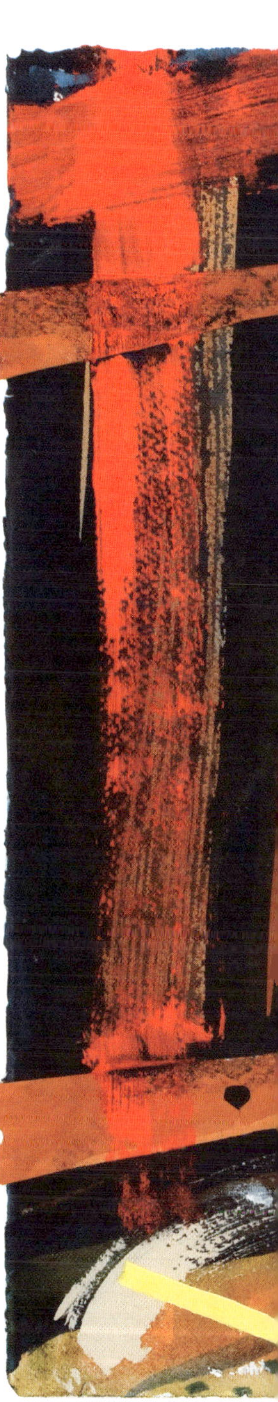

Duck (right)

The simplicity of this collage –
a benign-looking duck in a
formalized farmyard – responds
to the directness of folk art.
I particularly enjoyed creating
the surface of the rusty door
that frames the space.

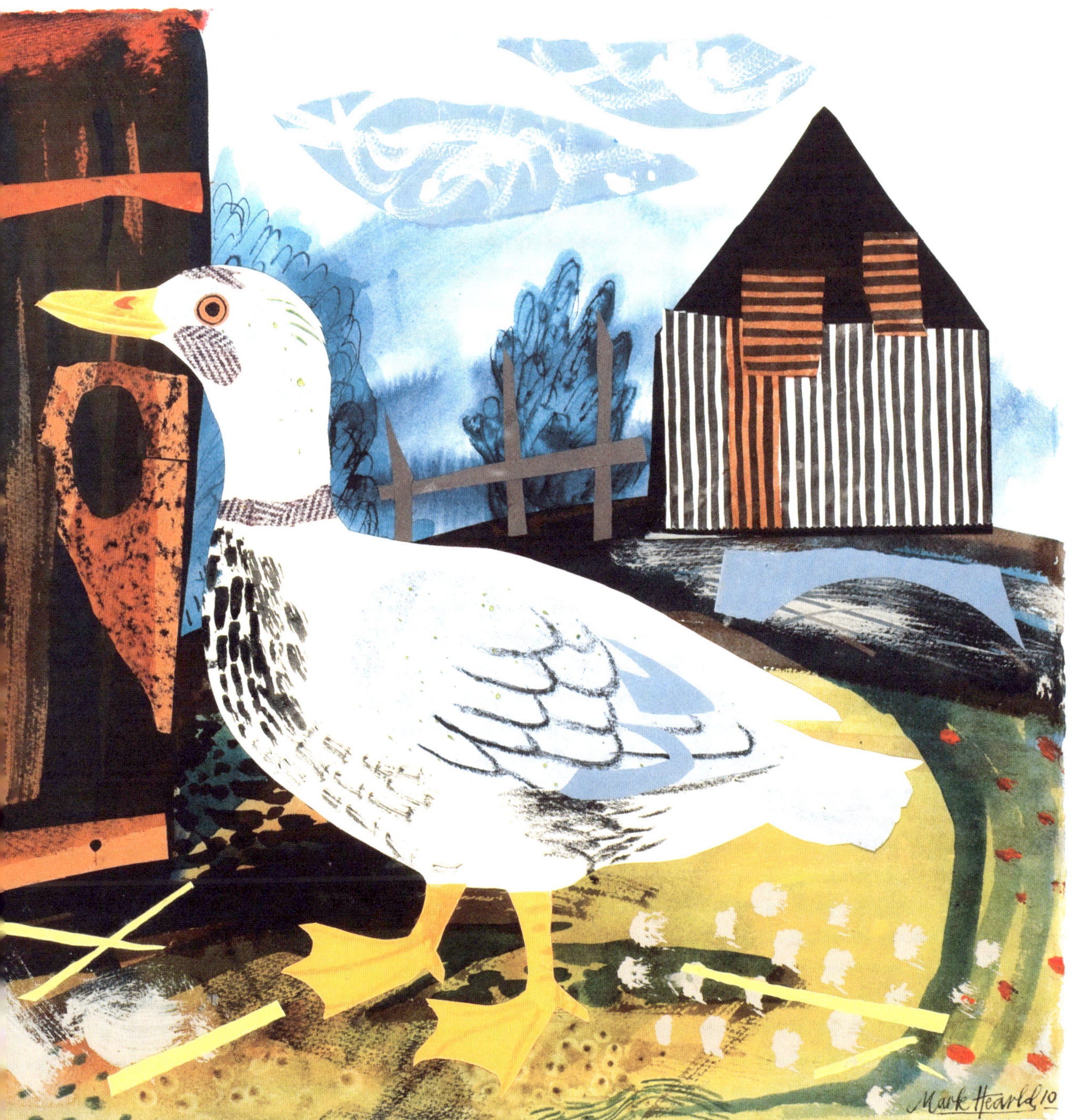

Mark Hearld 10

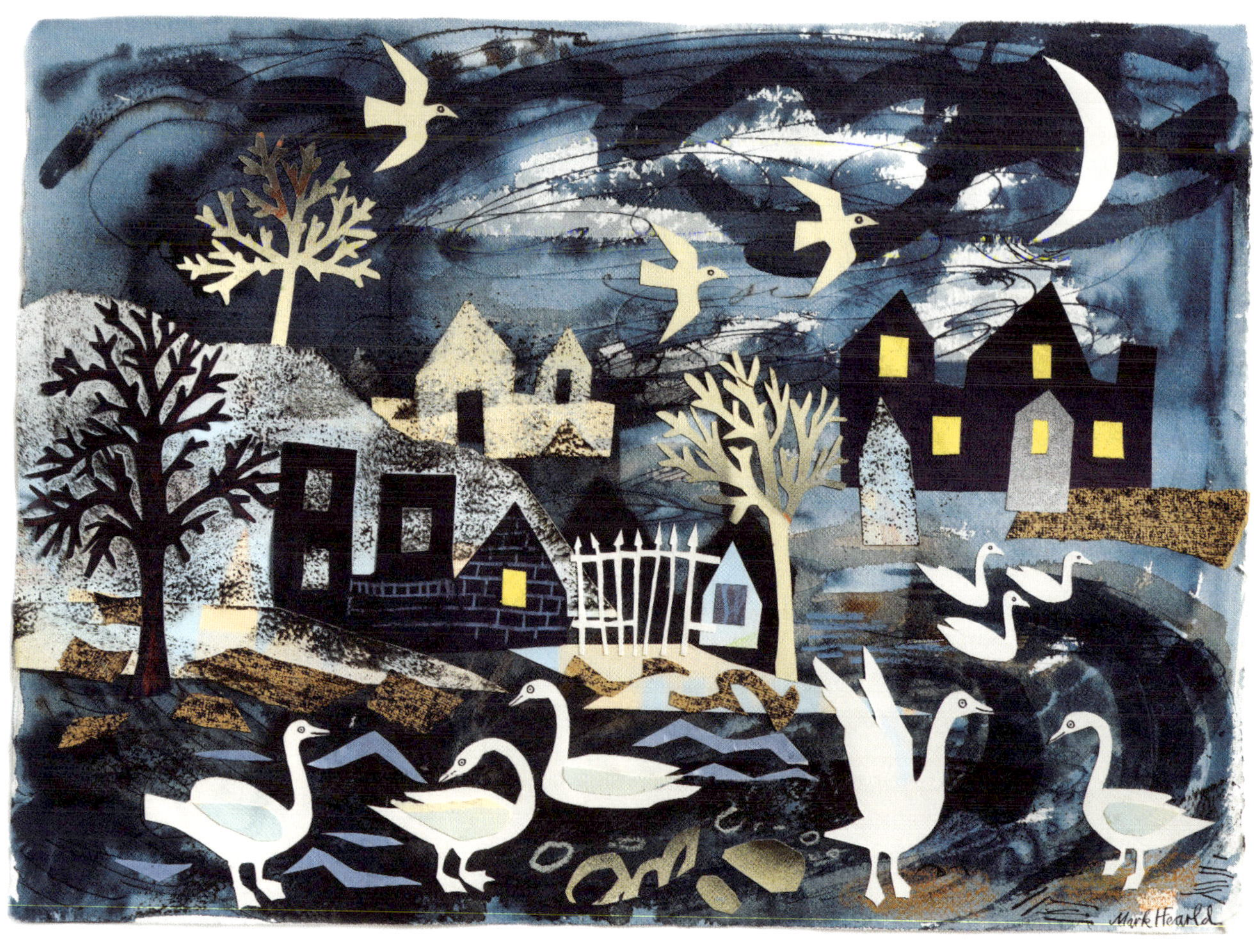

A Romantic Eye

As a student, I was greatly inspired by *Paradise Lost: The New Romantic Imagination in Britain* (1987), an exhibition of Neo-Romantic British art from the 1940s and 1950s at the Barbican Art Gallery in London. The sense of atmosphere redolent in the drawn landscapes, featuring night skies and crescent moons, caught my attention. At the Royal College of Art, reading Elizabeth Bowen's novels and Alain-Fournier's *Le Grand Meaulnes* (1913), I felt a longing for the farmland and scrubby lanes near my parents' house, and for summer walks through the stubble fields in the early evening. The landscape at dusk is visually inspiring.

Night Swans

The beauty and form of the swan never escape my attention; the bird's whiteness creates a pleasing contrast with its environment. The description of the Thames seen from Durham Wharf in Julian Trevelyan's autobiography *Indigo Days* (1957; see page 8) comes to mind whenever I revisit riverside swans and birds as a subject.

Harvest Moon

A large, outscaled moon hanging
low in the sky – a well-established
source of inspiration for landscape
painters – is richly evocative of
early evenings in September. This
work was used for the cover of
Peter Scupham's collection of poems
Borrowed Landscapes (2011).

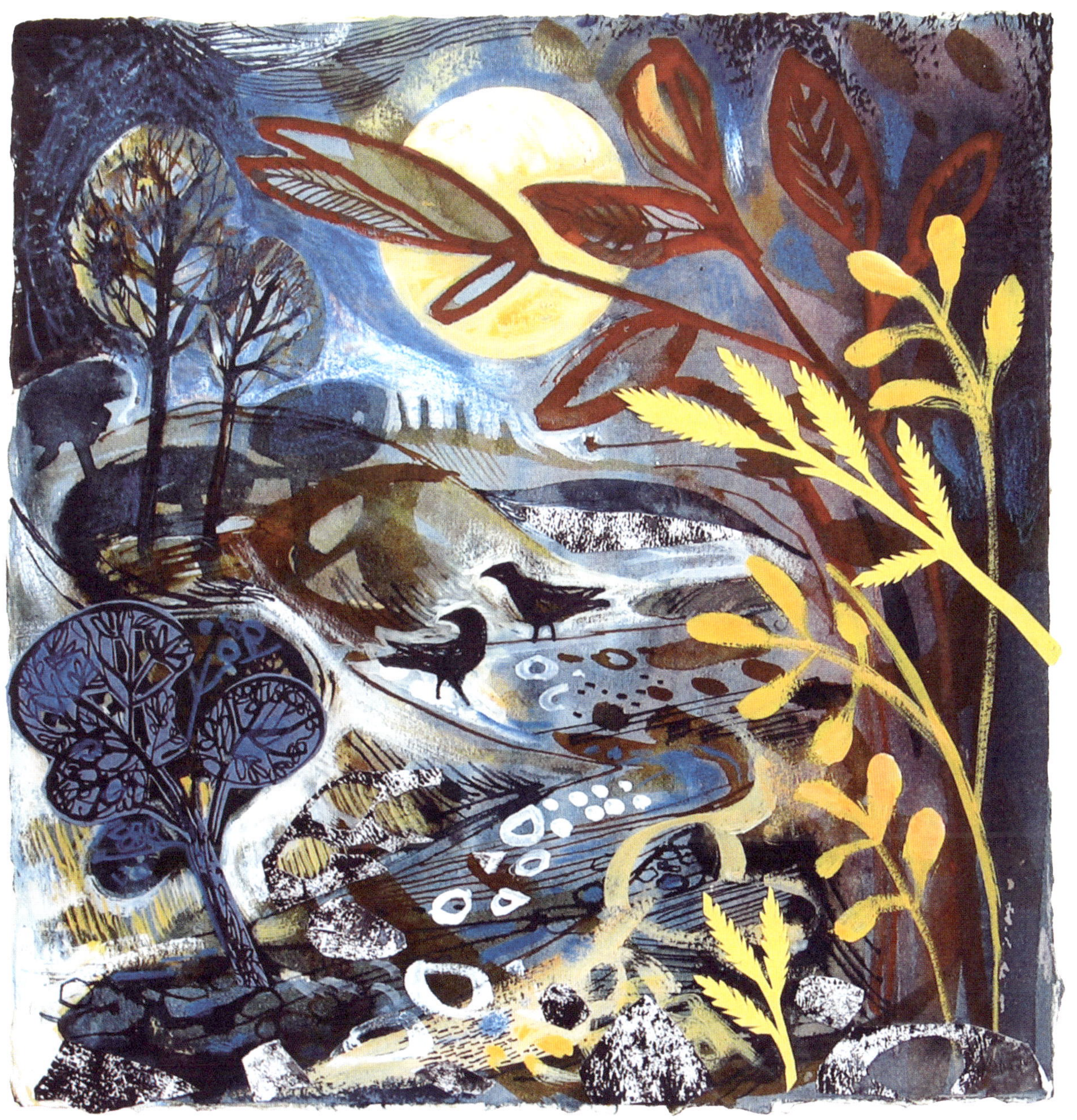

Owl Flight

The sight of a barn owl quartering
a field and fluttering, moth-like,
at dusk resulted in the collage
Owl Flight (below). The image
was so satisfying that I decided to
take it further and develop it into
the lithograph *Owl Flight* (right).
The foliage in the print relates to
the collage *Harvest Moon* (page 55),
which was made at the same time,
and in a similar spirit.

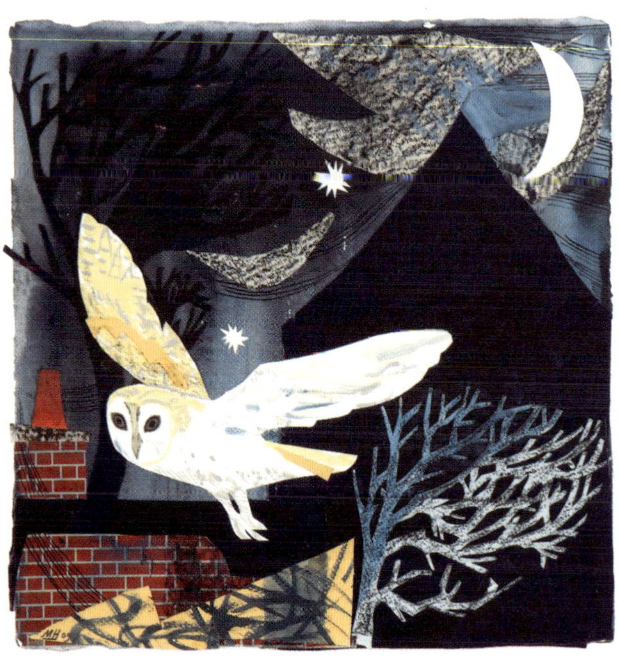

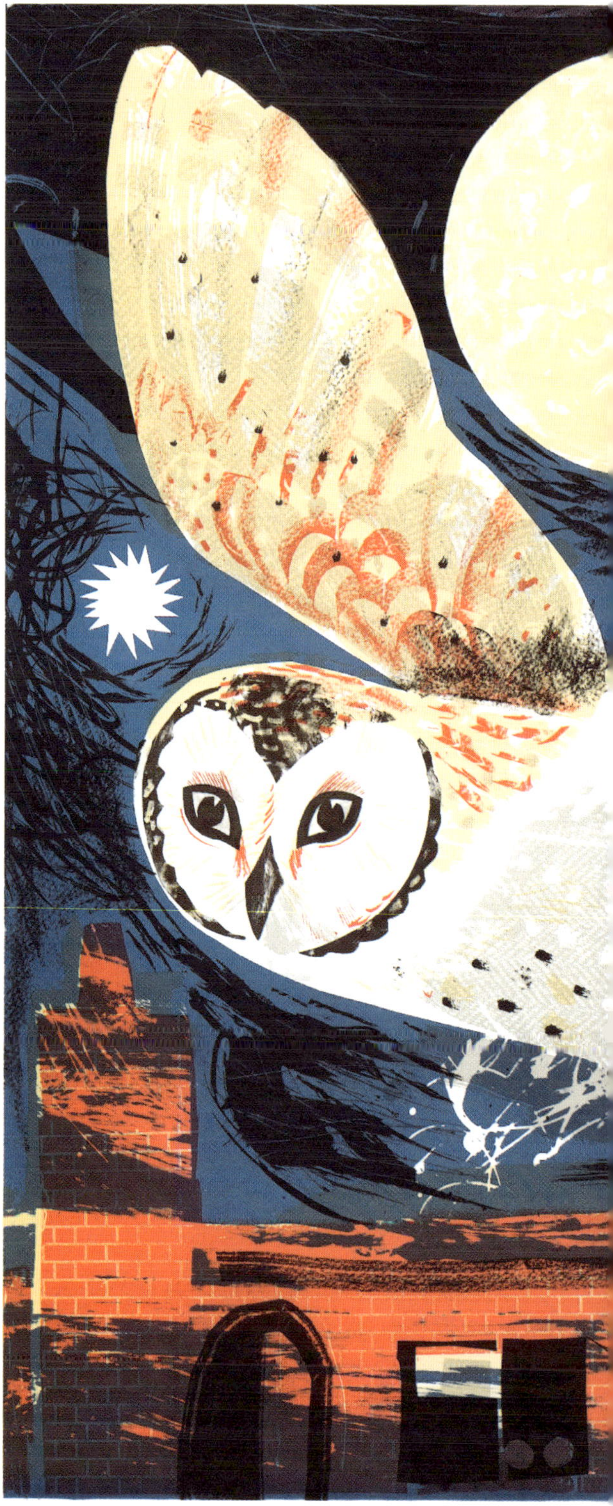

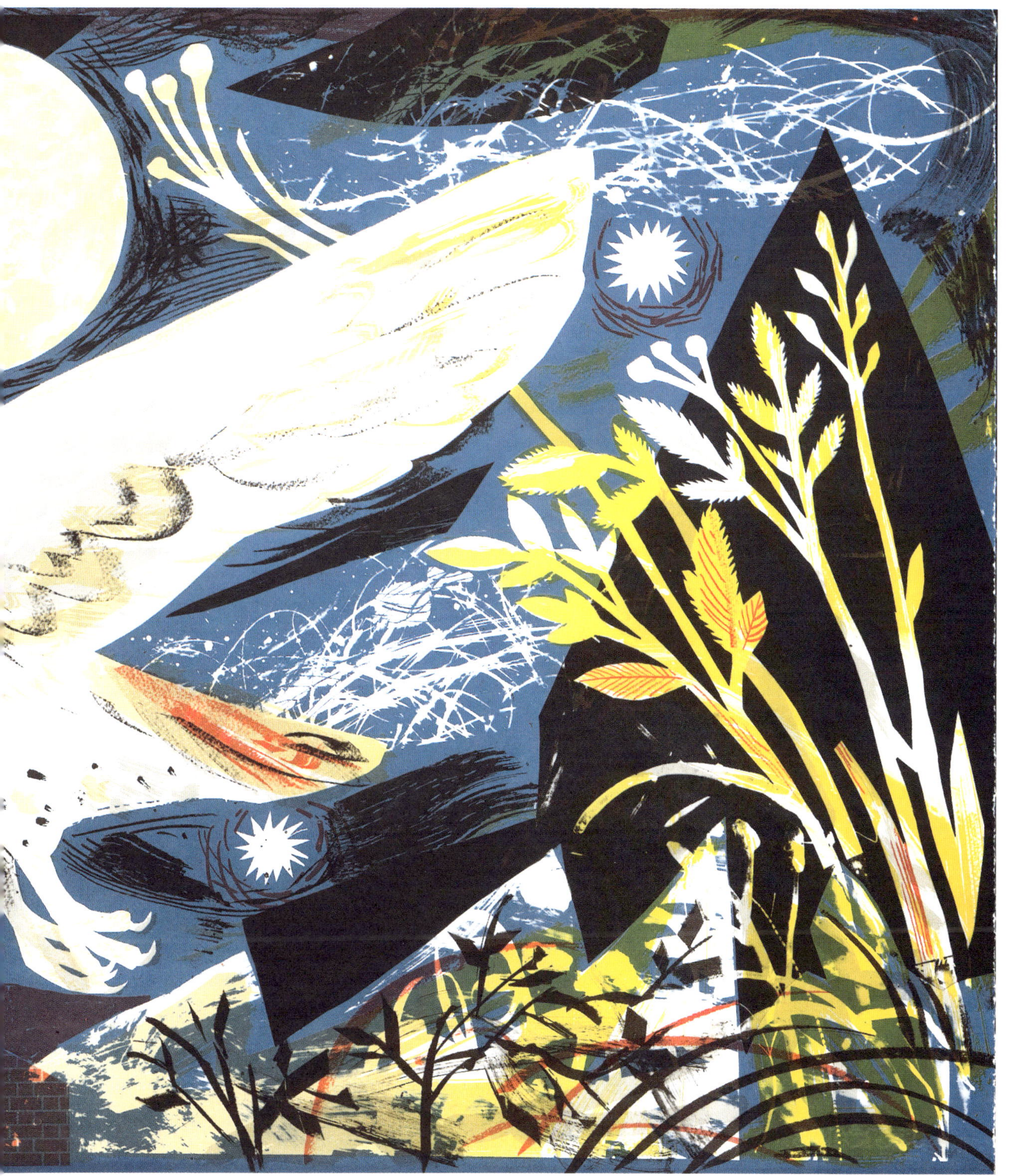

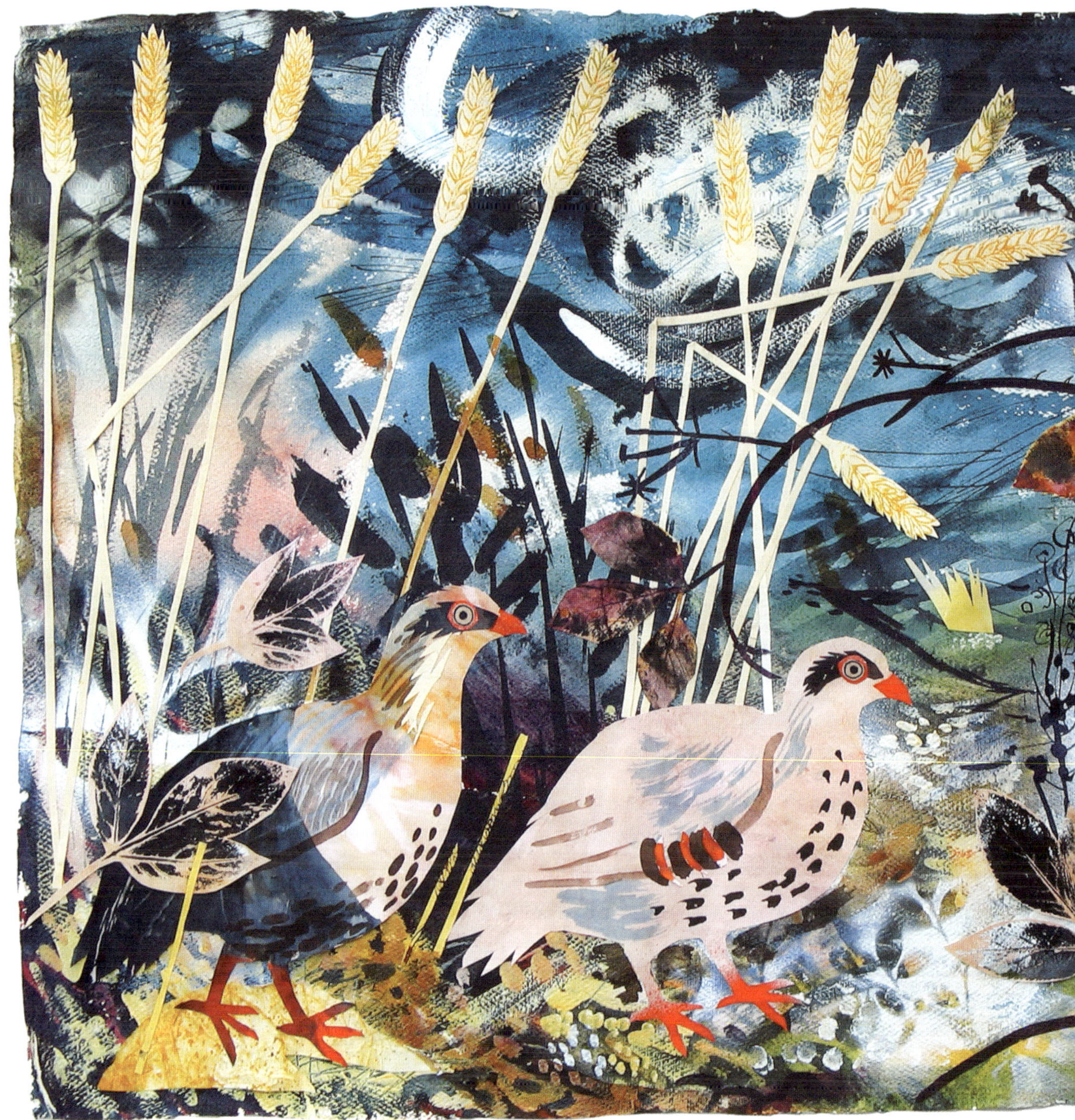

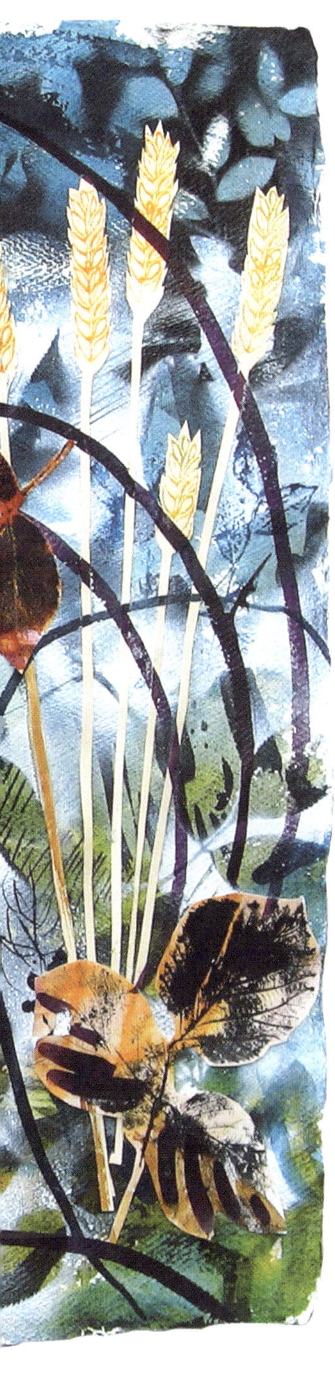

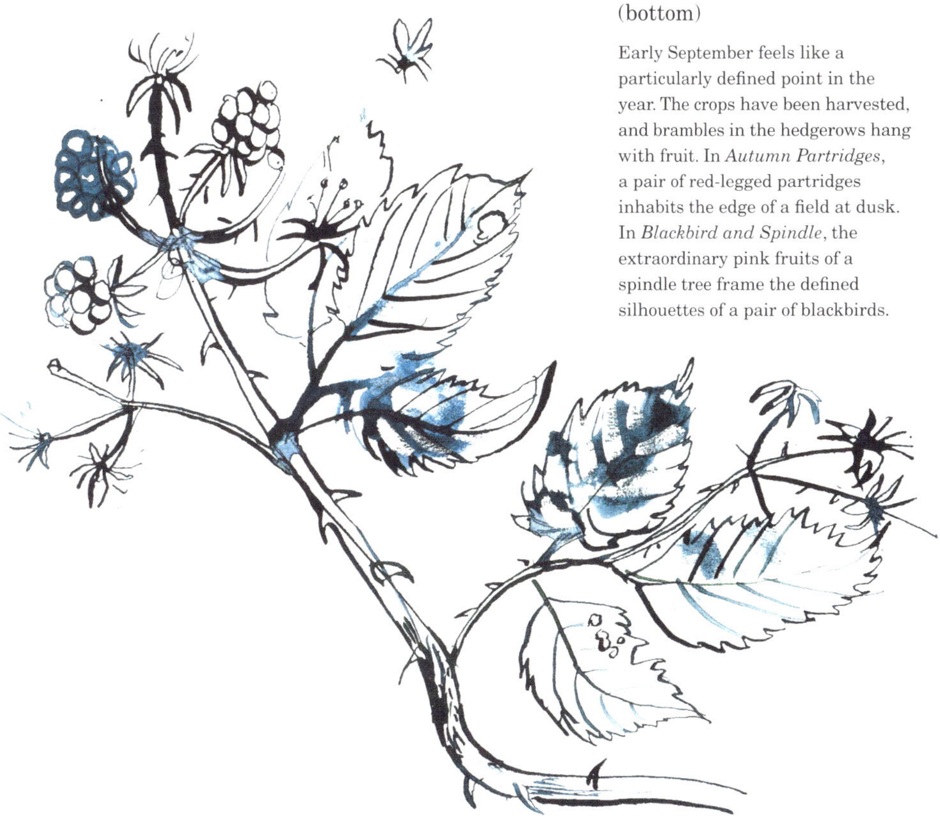

Autumn Partridges (left)
and Blackbird and Spindle
(bottom)

Early September feels like a
particularly defined point in the
year. The crops have been harvested,
and brambles in the hedgerows hang
with fruit. In *Autumn Partridges*,
a pair of red-legged partridges
inhabits the edge of a field at dusk.
In *Blackbird and Spindle*, the
extraordinary pink fruits of a
spindle tree frame the defined
silhouettes of a pair of blackbirds.

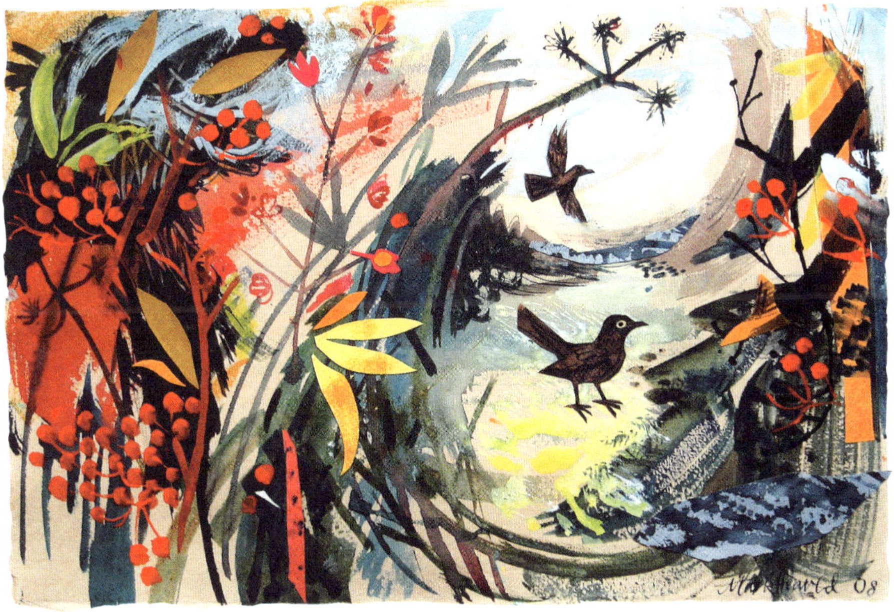

Jackdaws

Some people find members of
the crow family sinister. To me,
however, they are fascinating birds
to watch, their antics mischievous
and entertaining. They are sociable
birds, too, and the jackdaws here
are eyeing up a flock of rooks flying
to roost. My collage marks the
moment before night comes and
all will be quiet.

Allotment Fox (overleaf)

Evening dog walks through the local
allotments bring you into contact
with nature at the edge of the city.
I'm still waiting for a fox to cross
my path.

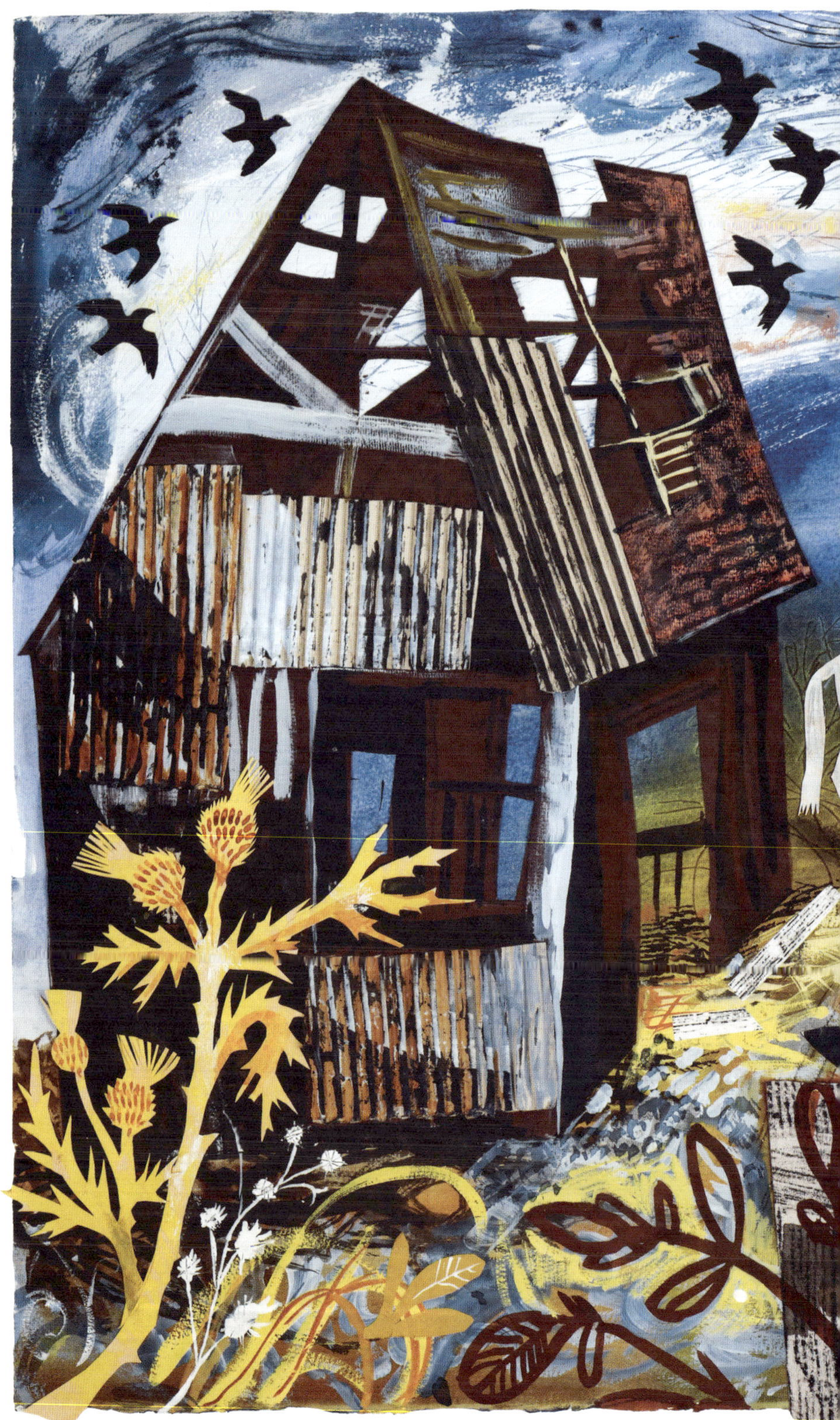

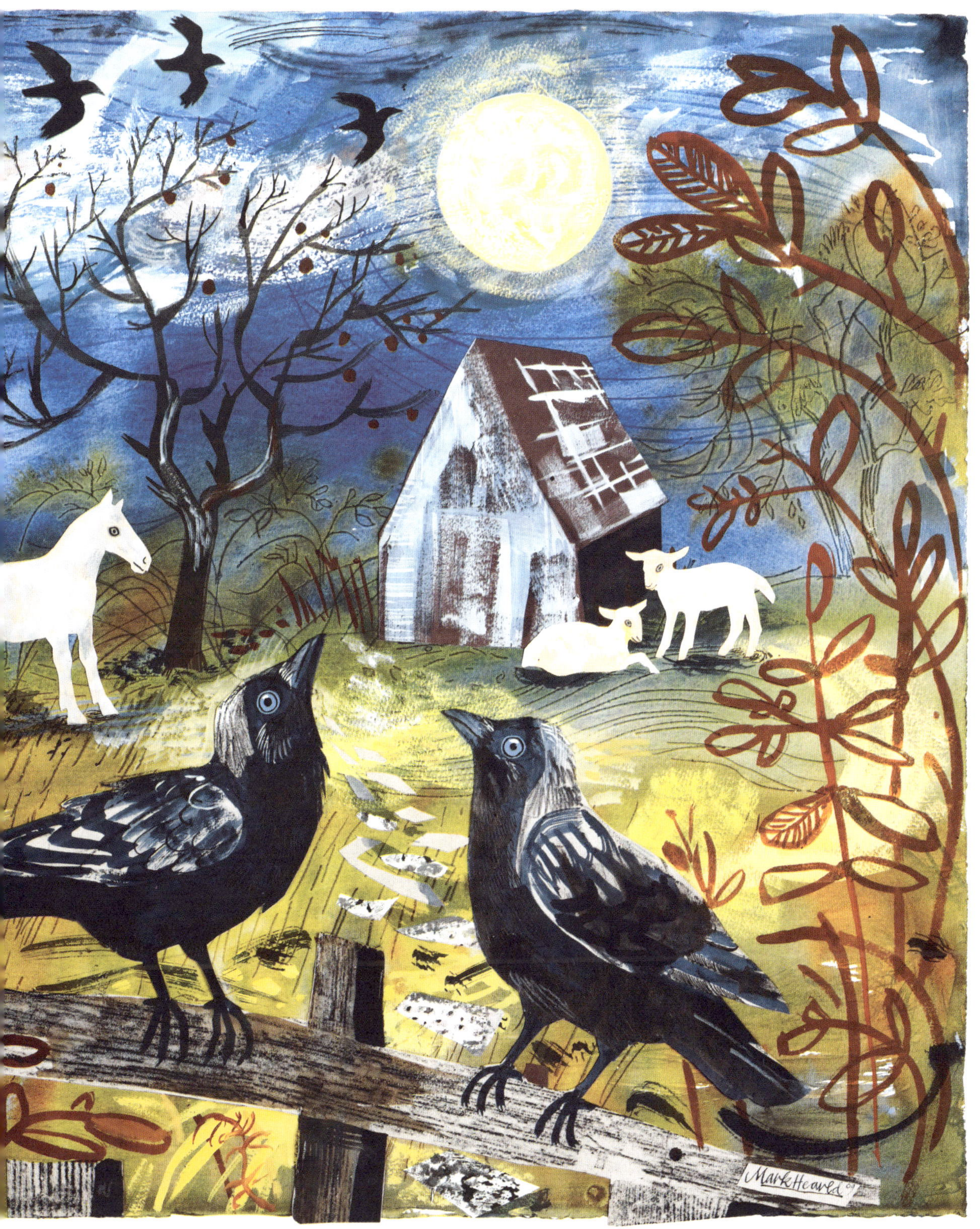

Mark Hearld 09

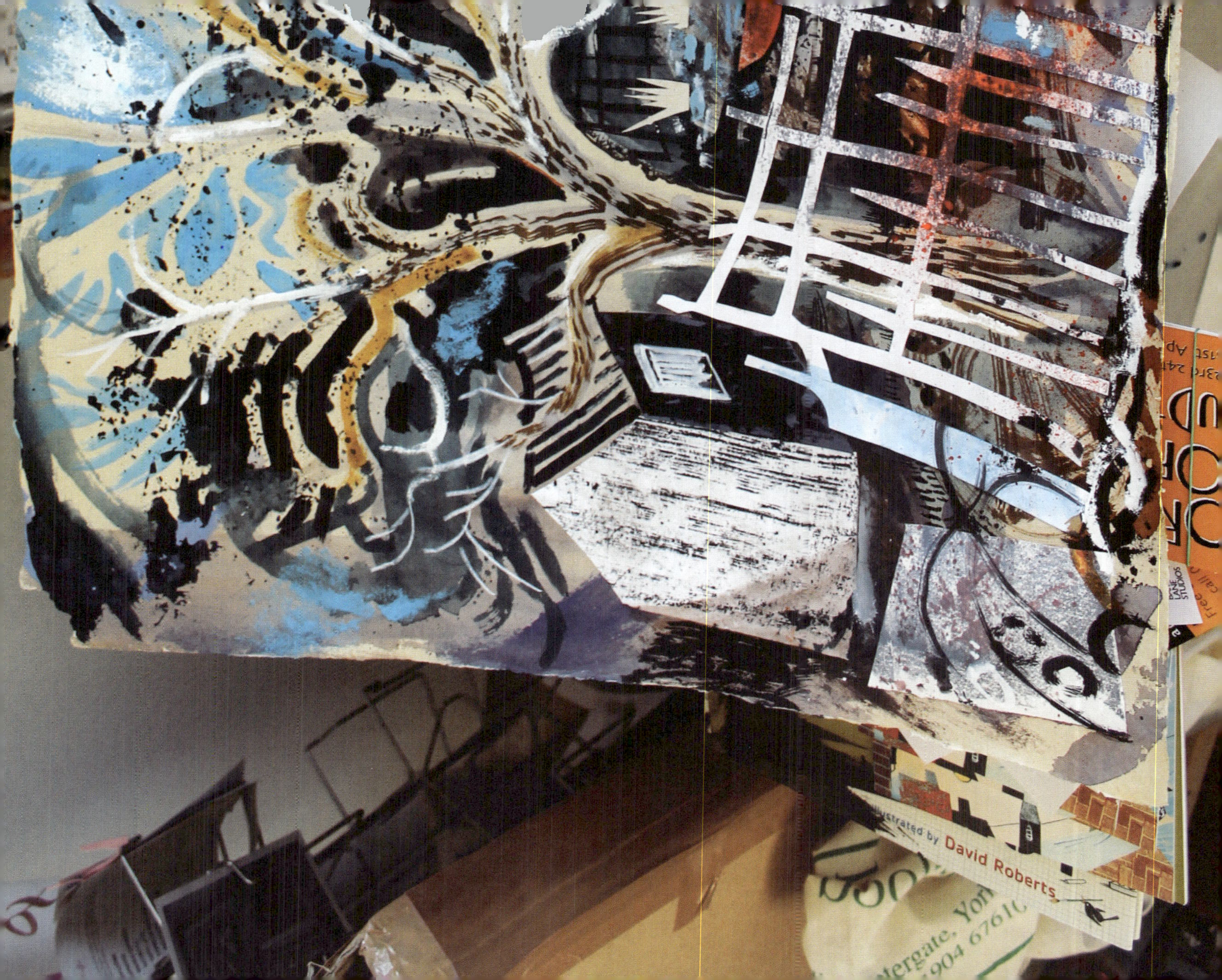
Illustrated by David Roberts
ergate, Yor
904 6761
Free call
LANE
STUDIOS
23rd 24th
1st Ap

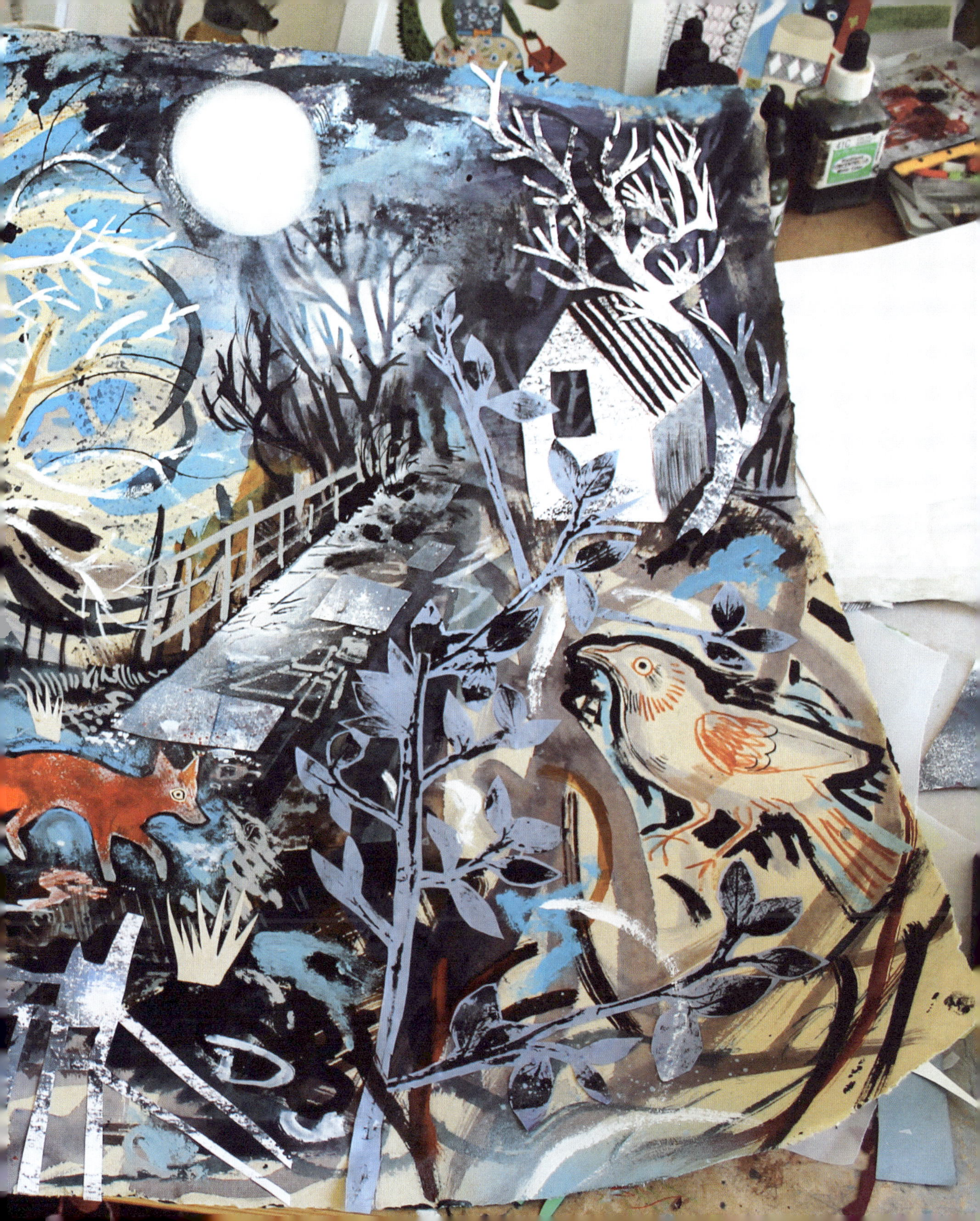

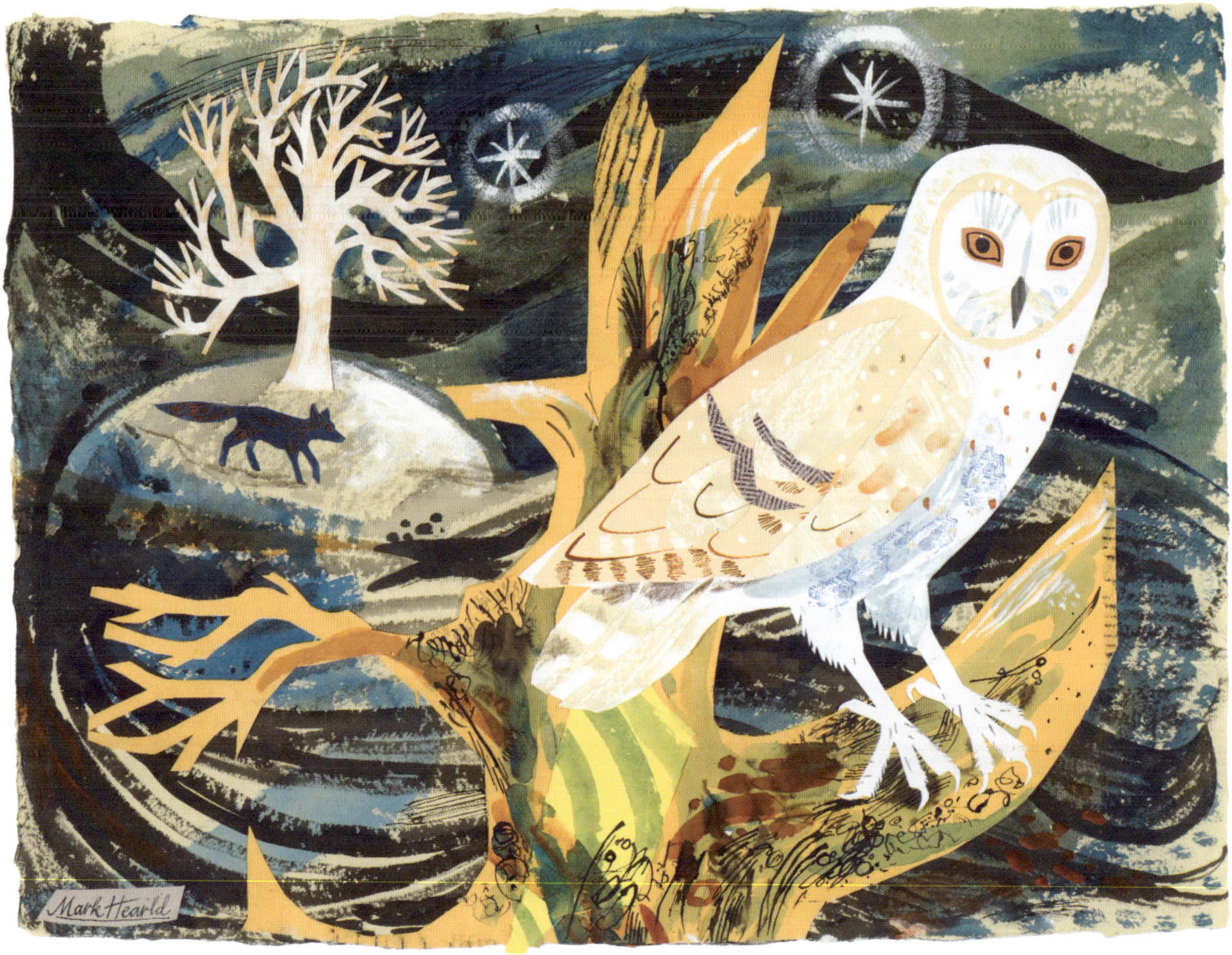

The Owl and the Fox (above)

Thomas Bewick, one of the greatest bird artists of all time, renowned for his *History of British Birds* (1797–1804), had a particular talent for making a perching bird or sitting duck seem animated and alive. In this collage of a barn owl, inspired by Bewick's compositions, I was interested in the strong form of the gnarled branches of a dead tree, and in capturing the poised liveliness and ghost-like otherness of this wonderful bird. The die-cut barn owls shown right will eventually become one of three concertina cards for the Norwich-based publisher Art Angels.

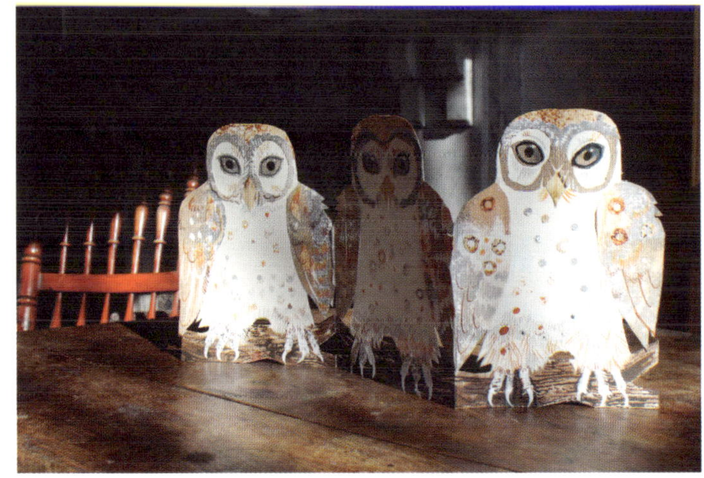

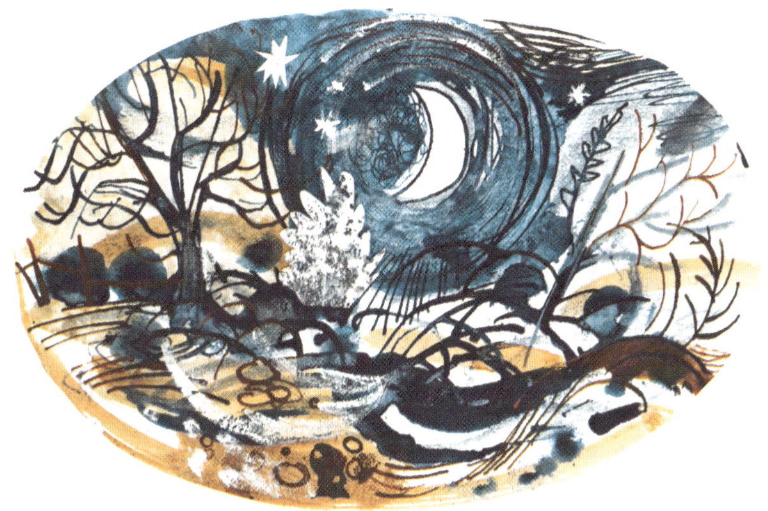

Twilight (below)

Why is it that dusk feels so visually atmospheric? Samuel Palmer and William Blake explored the half-light sublimely. Here, I felt the urge to try to capture it with cut paper and ink, the two birds in the image flying towards the encroaching nightfall.

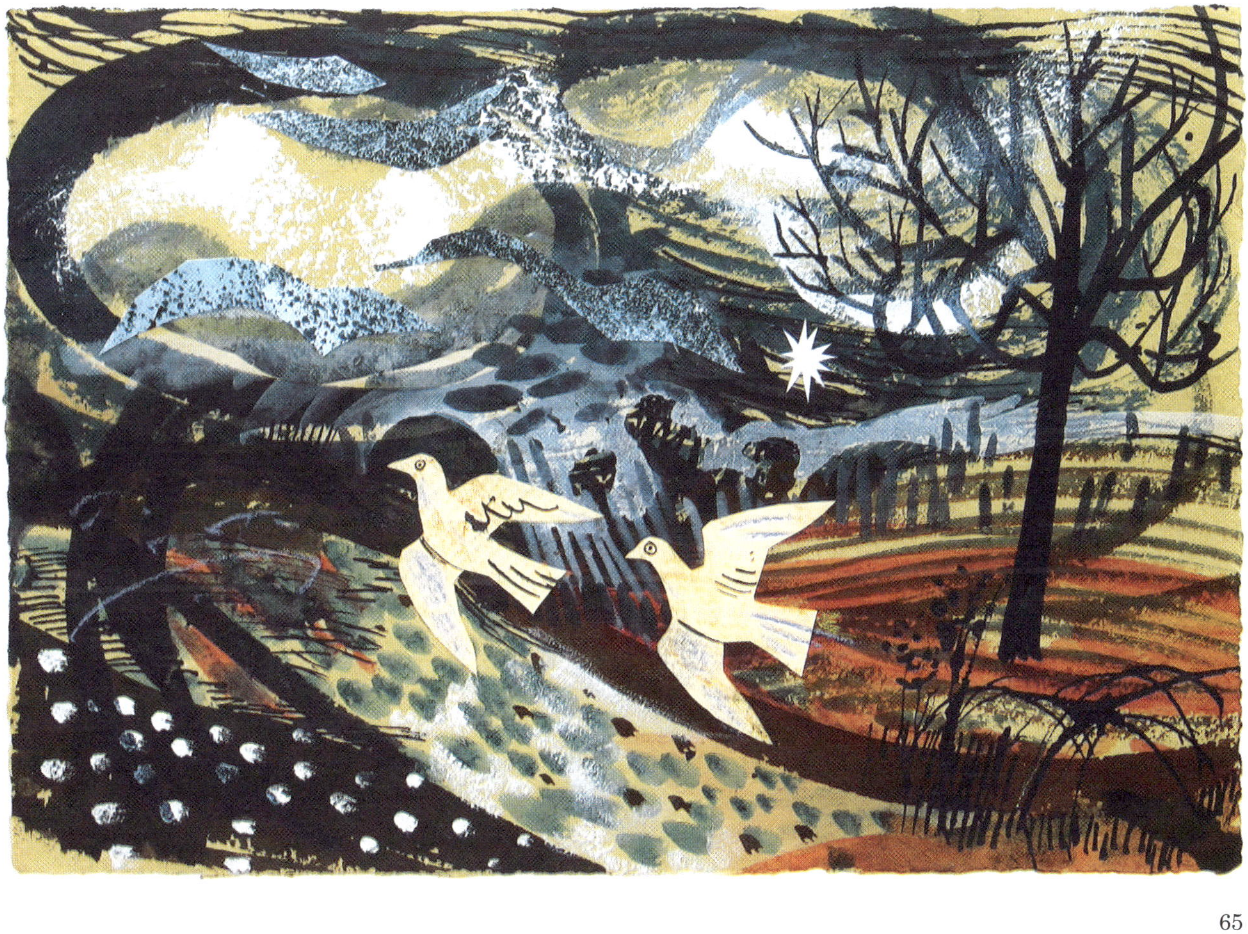

Seashore

The seaside brings back memories of childhood holidays: beady-eyed herring gulls up close or taking chips from your hand in flight; the saltiness of Edward Ardizzone's *Little Tim* books; found treasures picked up on the beach, a feather, a broken shell, a piece of glass dulled by the tide. The otherness of the seashore is rich in inspiration. The natural palette of sand and sea contrasts beautifully with the high colour of the plastic flotsam and jetsam washed up on the shore. Fishermen's huts and grounded boats, shingle and rock pools all offer endless creative opportunities to explore.

Agnus Rose (below)

A northerner at heart, I feel a deep connection to the Yorkshire coast, but the East Anglian coast has its own beauty. This image is not drawn directly from anywhere in particular, but recalls the shingly creeks and accumulation of fishermen's huts at Southwold in Suffolk.

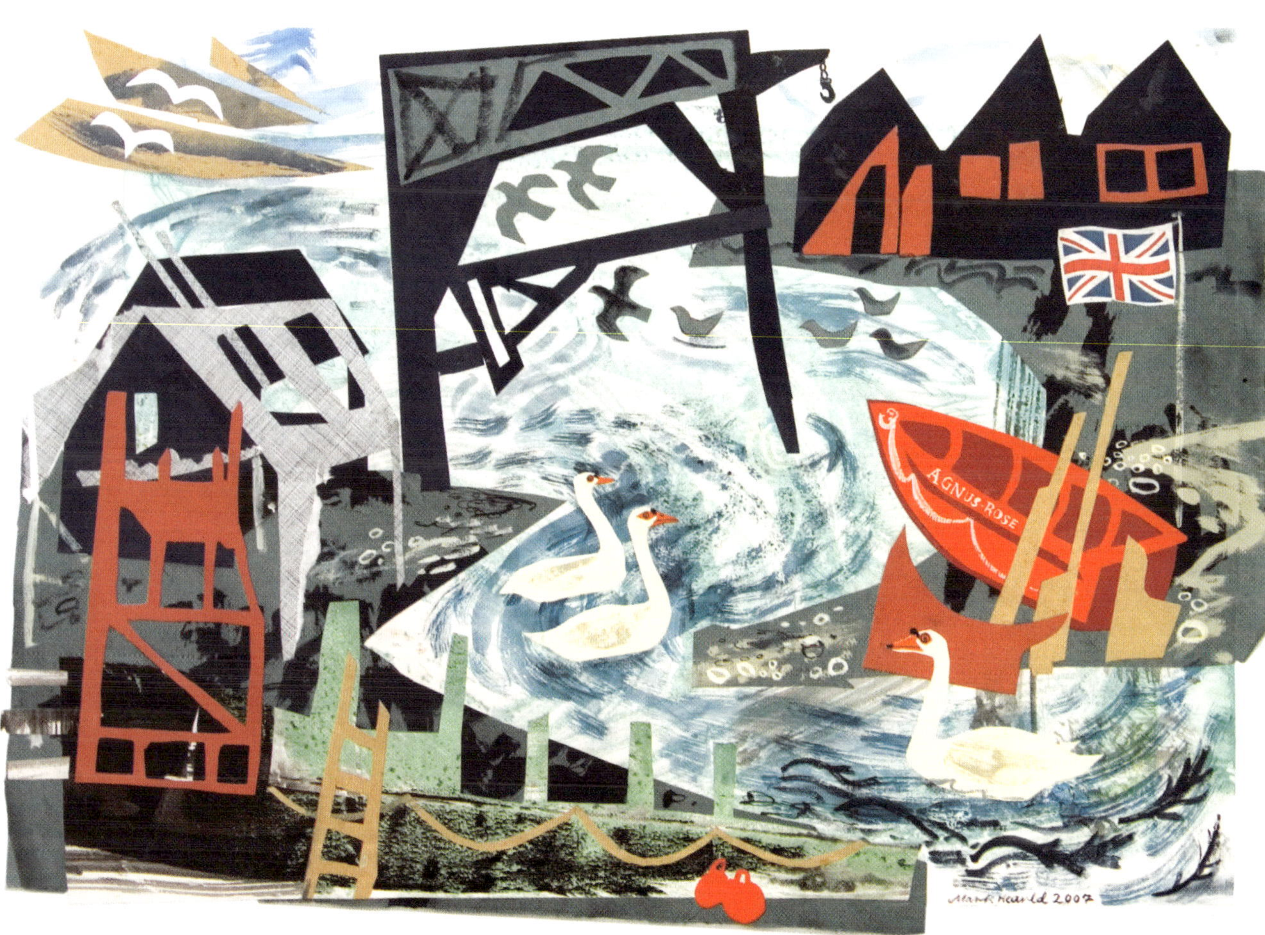

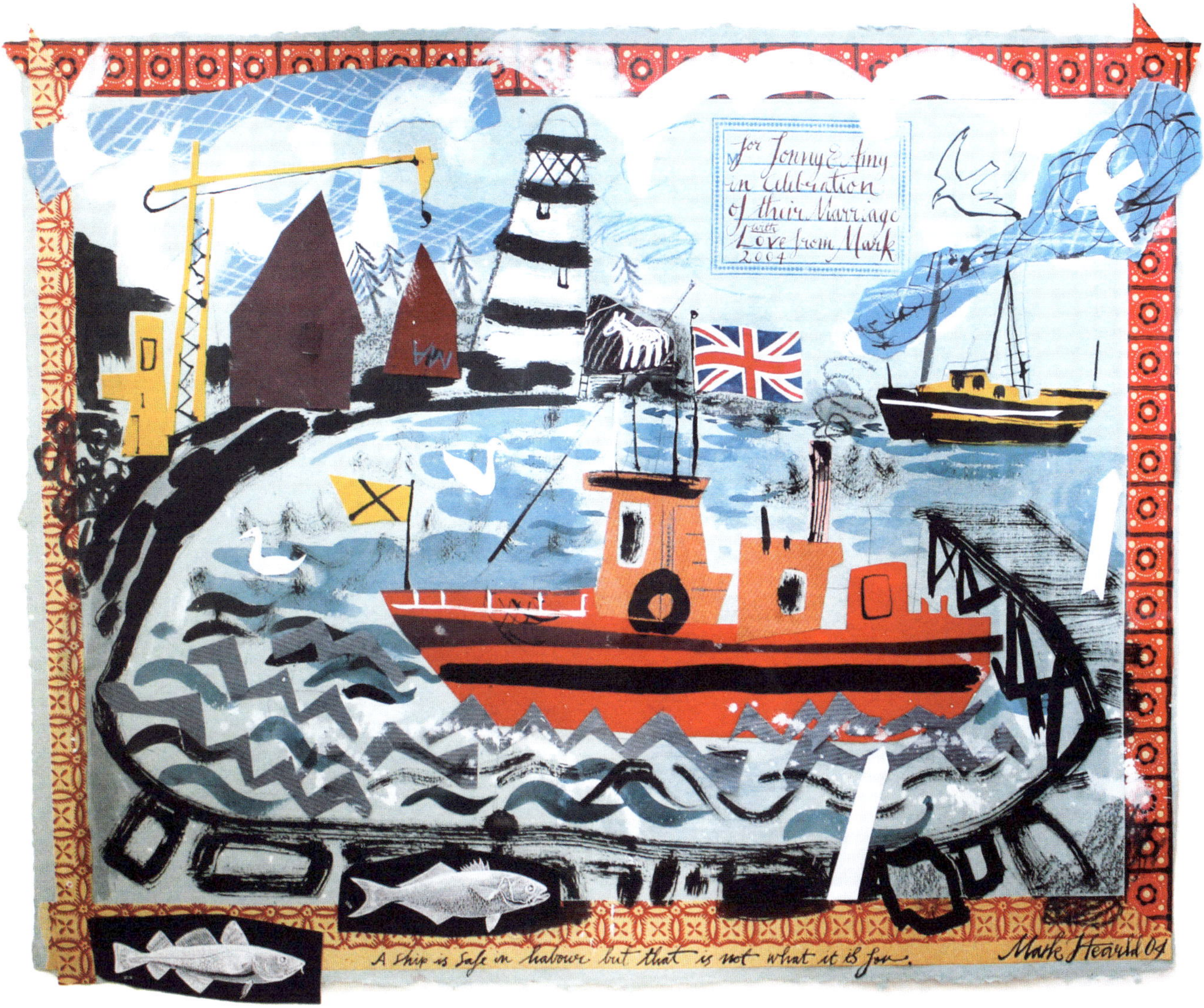

Harbour (above)

A ship is safe in harbour, but that's not what ships are for. This collage was made to celebrate the marriage of my best friend, Jonny, to Amy in 2004. I imagined them setting out on a voyage together.

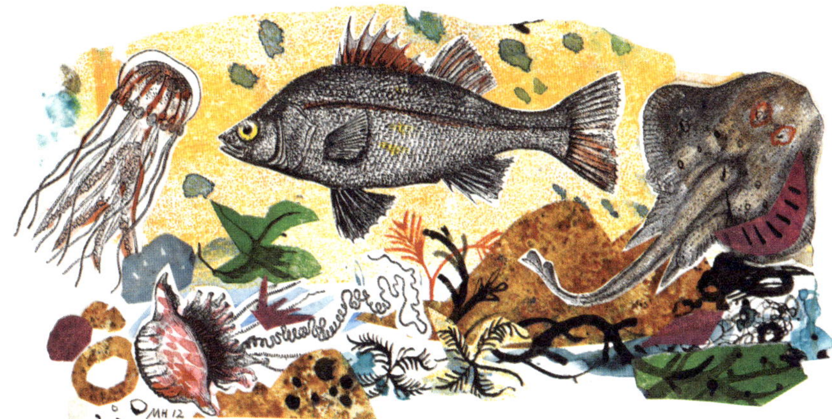

Seaside Fantasy

A fish-and-chip shop from
Scarborough, seashells and
watching gulls, such as the
one featured on the decorated
Gull platter (opposite, bottom),
come together in an image that
celebrates the popular appeal
of the British seaside. This
collage was made to accompany
The Magpie Eye, my exhibition
at Scarborough Art Gallery
(see page 14).

On the Harbour Pottery Roof

The Chinese Chippendale-style
roof lantern on top of the
harbourside pottery in Whitby,
where I make pots with Terry
Shone (see pages 144–45), is a
perfect example of John Piper's
'nautical style', with views up the
Esk Valley and out to sea. A flag
billows and raucous gulls cavort.

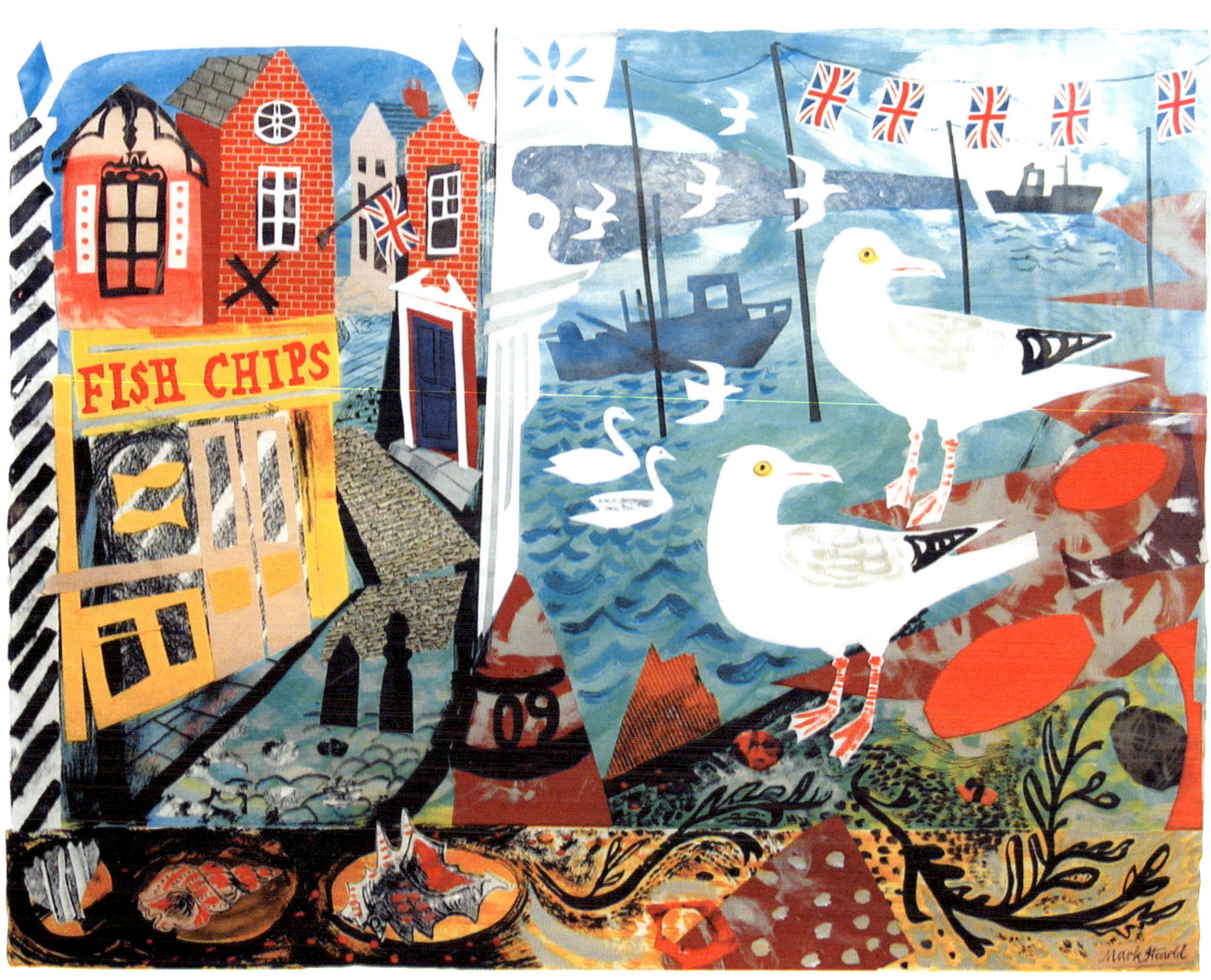

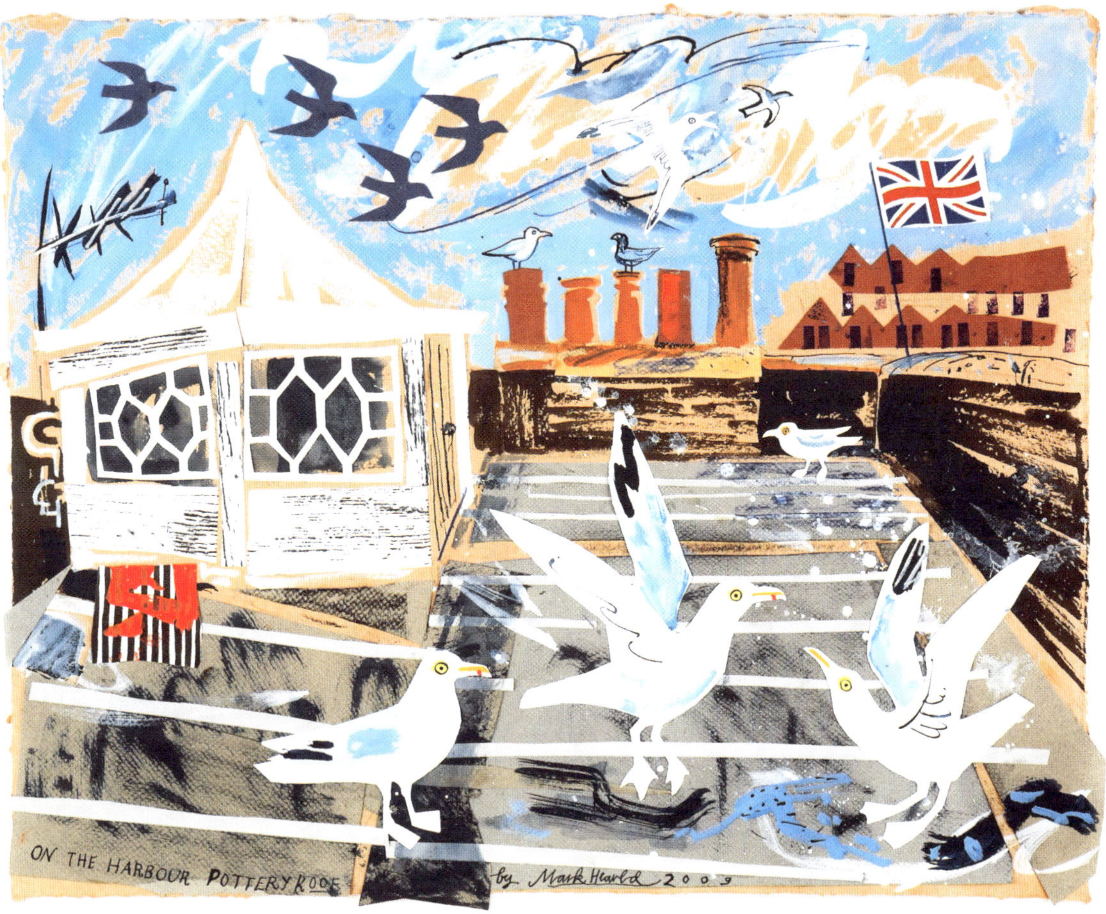

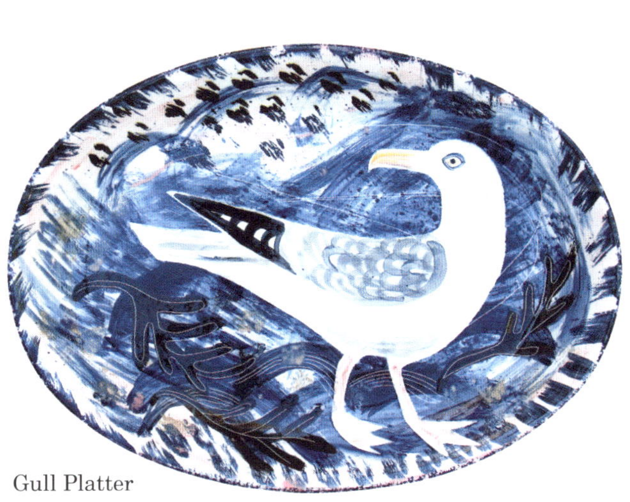

Gull Platter

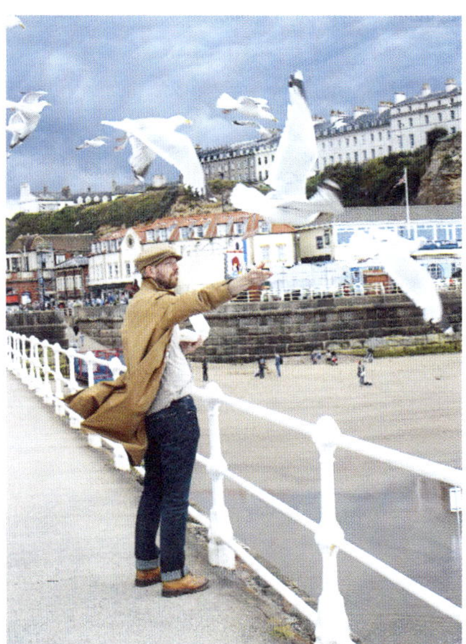

Em. S.

A birthday collage for Emily.

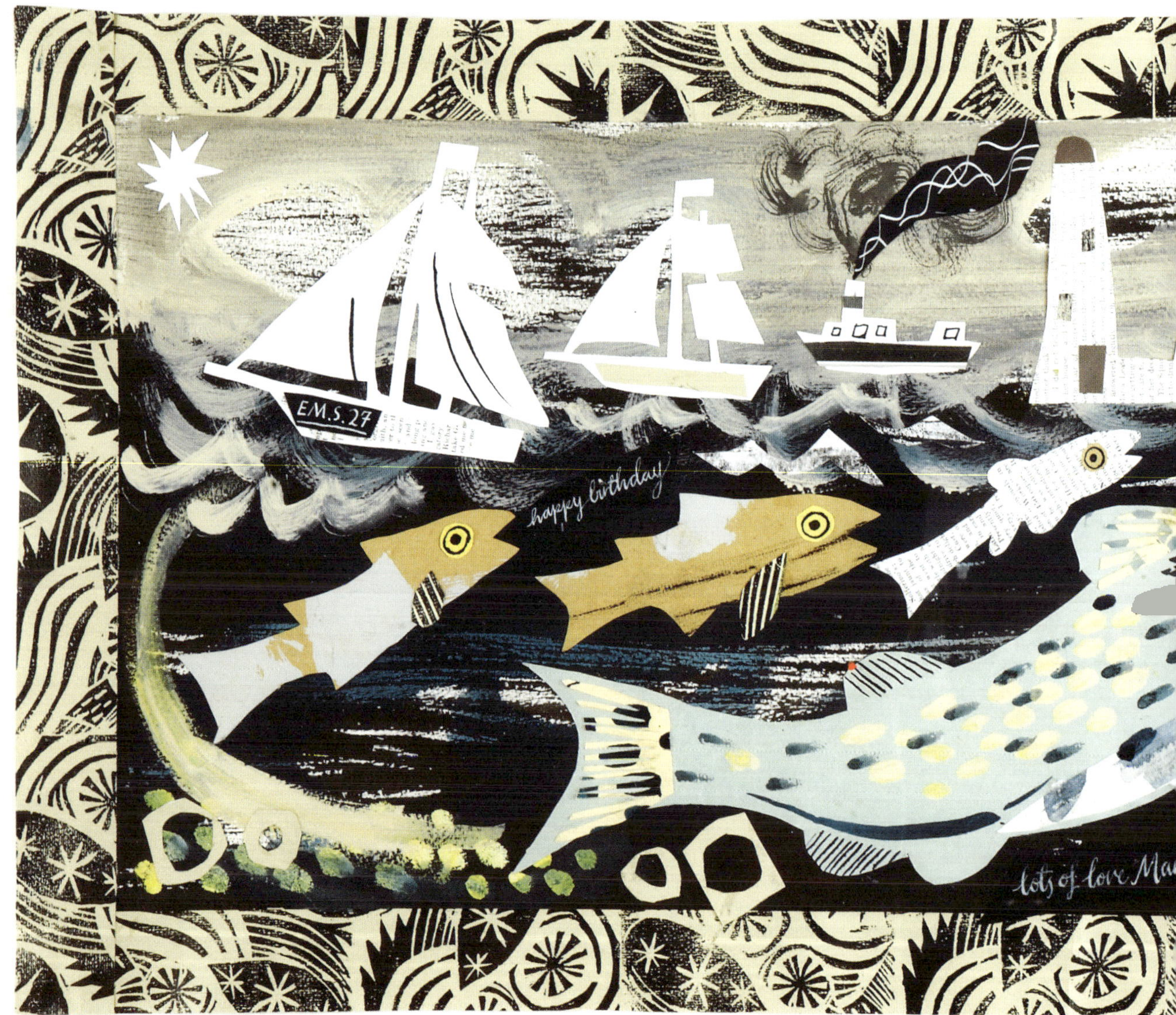

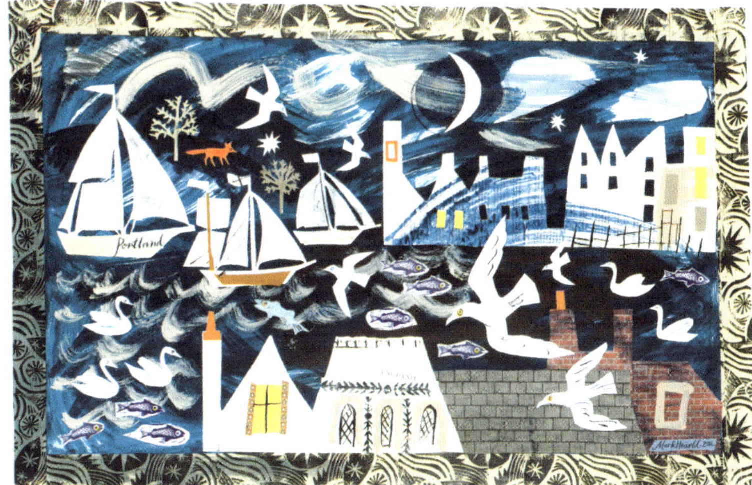

Night Harbour

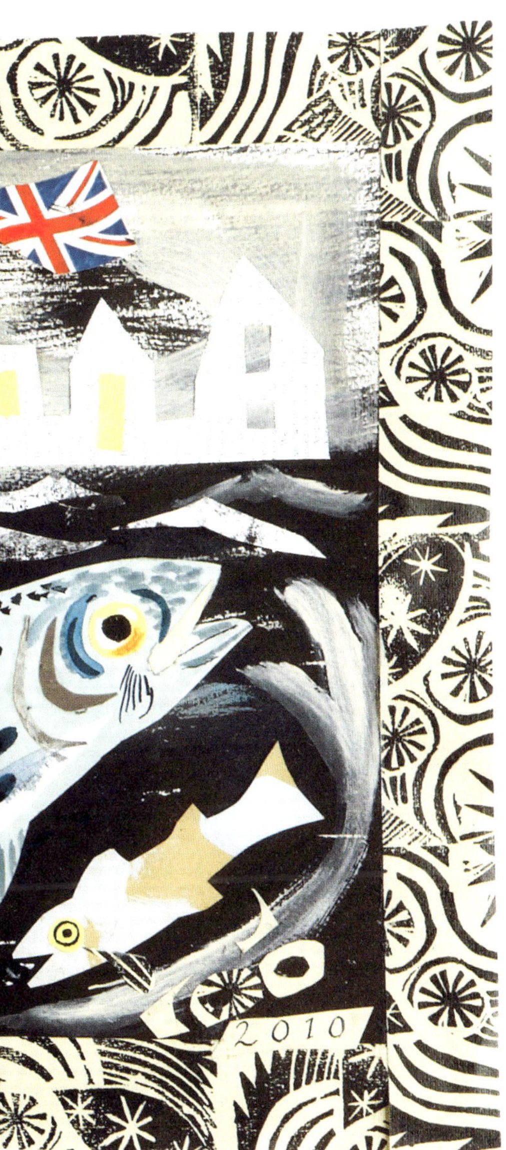

Moon, River

I began a series of images about the sea with the intention of it being black and white, but, inevitably, as the work developed other colours crept in to suggest the harbour at night. Beginning this way gave the body of work a visual structure and logic that made it particularly satisfying to work on. I intentionally took liberties with scale in the way that Alfred Wallis might have, such that a large, indeterminate fish may dwarf some quayside buildings. The important thing was to create a sense of pictorial truth, rather than naturalistic proportion. The eye can accept a large fish and a tiny harbour if the elements are positioned with conviction and certainty; each element works on one level as itself but also as an abstract visual component within the overall composition.

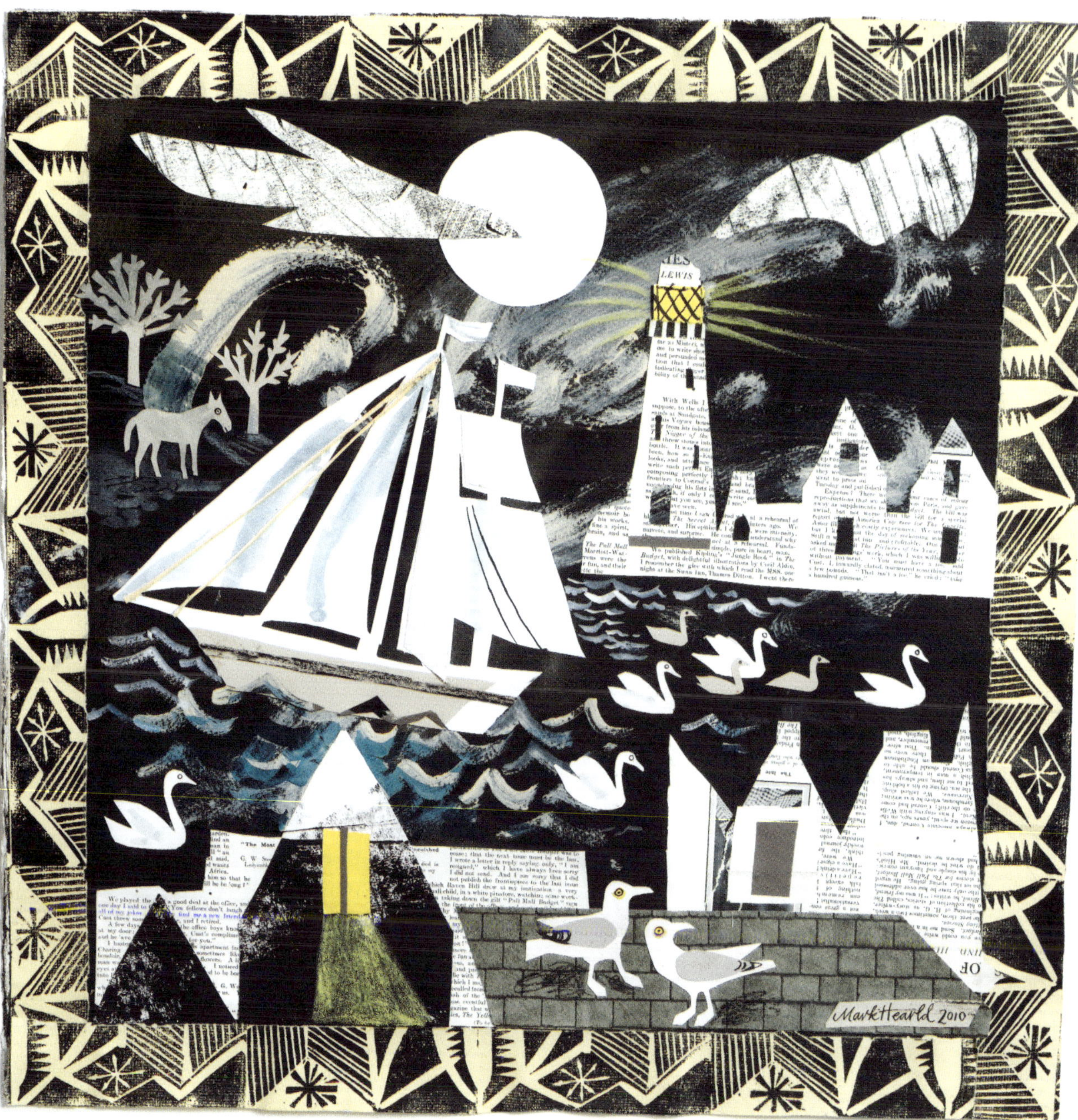

LEWIS
Mark Hearld 2010

Lewis Lighthouse (opposite)

Looking at Picasso's cubist collages, I always enjoy the games he plays with different materials. His experiments encouraged me to use the recycled printed word as texture; here, the text is from a 1920s art journal. The word 'Lewis' was a particularly appropriate find, and gave the collage both its title and its location in the Outer Hebrides. A grey horse looks on in the moonlight.

The Yellow Boat (right)

The Yellow Boat was one of a series of images made for an exhibition curated by Iris Weaver, co-founder of the Fry Art Gallery in Essex, to coincide with the Aldeburgh Festival of 2010. With Alfred Wallis at the helm of the ship, I felt liberated in my use of scale: fish as big as boats shoal through the night sea. It was great fun giving each fish an individual character.

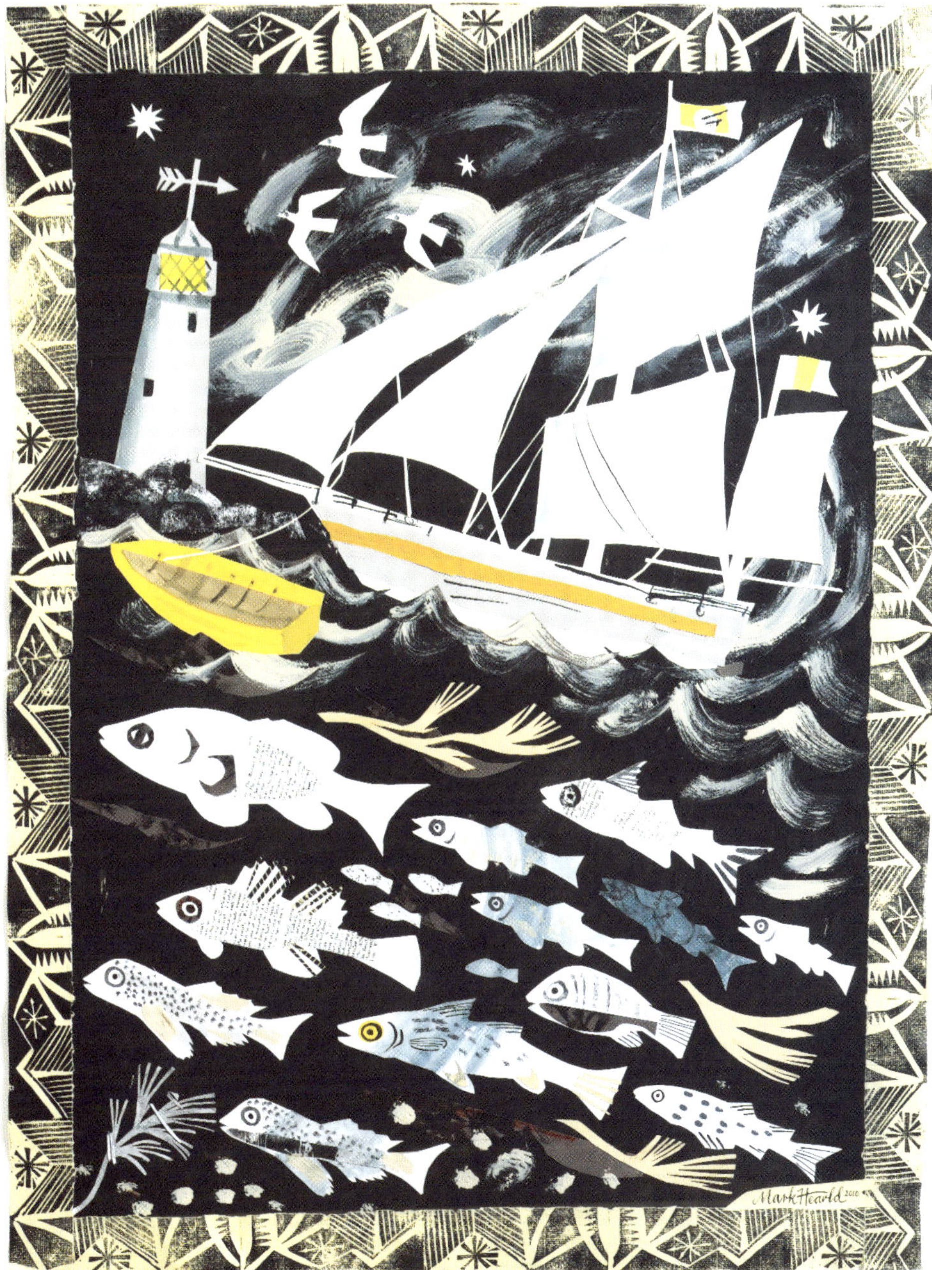

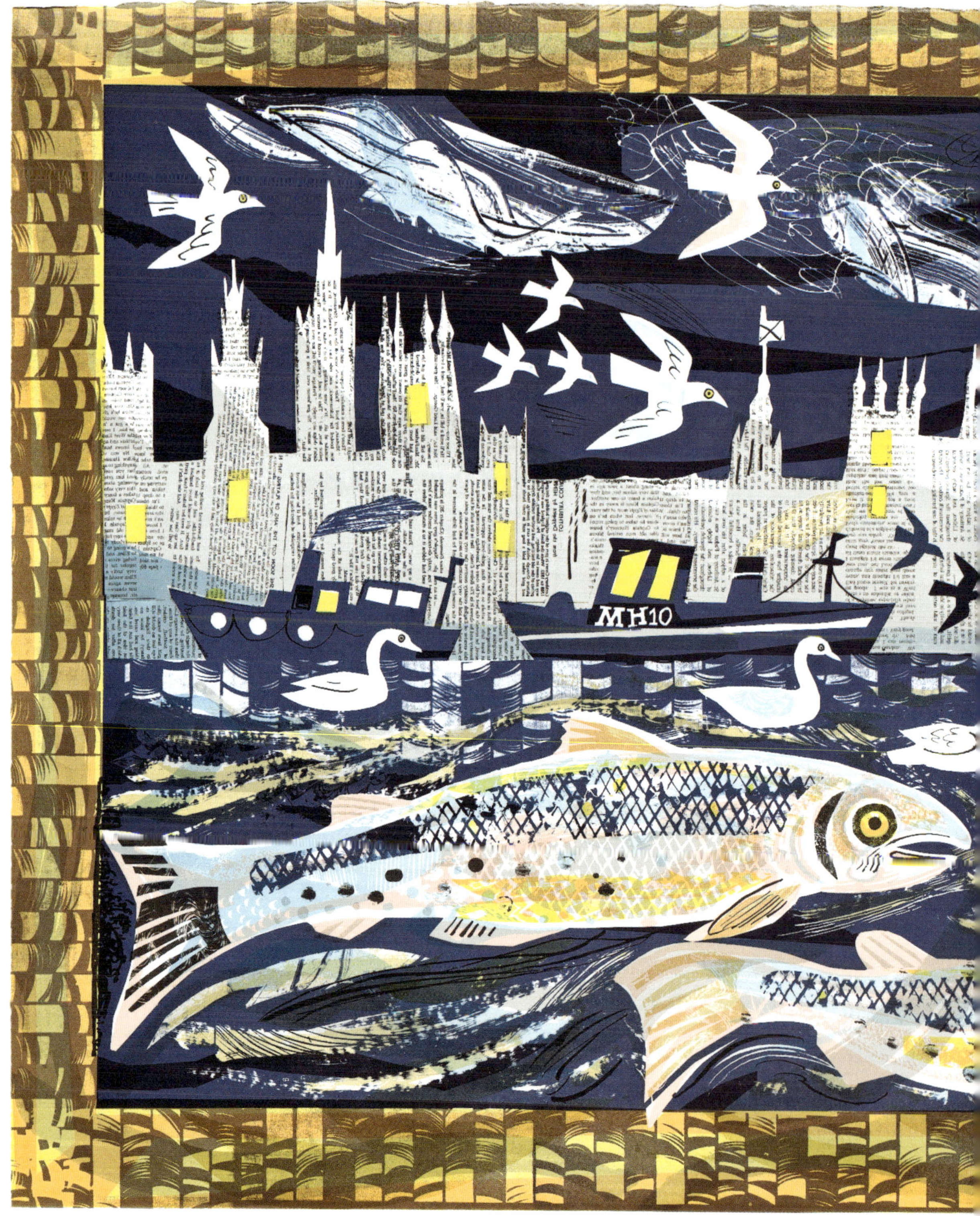

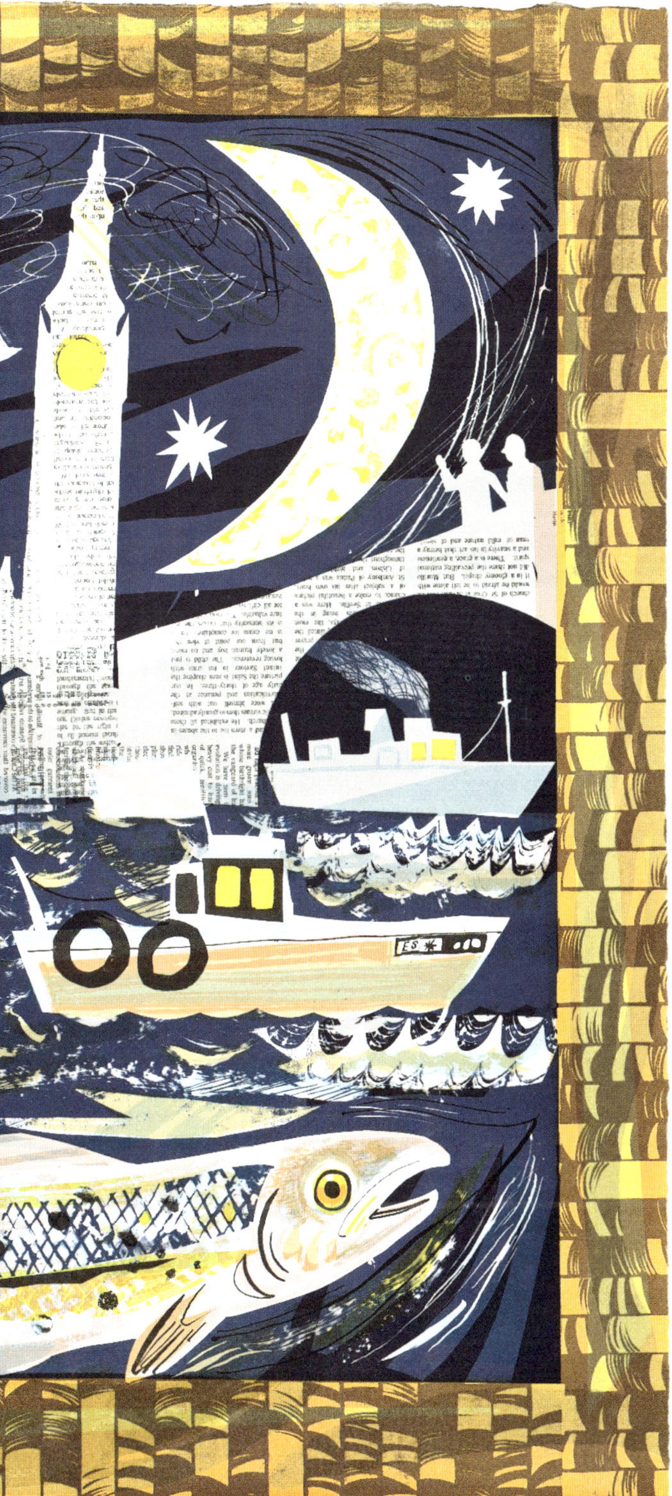

Salmon Return to the Thames

This print, made to coincide with the *St Jude's in the City* exhibition of 2010 at London's Bankside Gallery, was inspired by an item on the radio about the improved water quality in the Thames and the possibility of salmon once again spawning in the river's upper reaches. The romantic notion of such a majestic fish swimming past the Houses of Parliament suggested a fantastic combination of images. I got so carried away by the compositional possibilities that my fish are actually swimming out to sea, rather than upstream. However, a sense of dynamic movement was of paramount importance, and elements moving from left to right always appear more animated. The pages from a 1920s art journal were used to suggest the texture of the buildings.

Thames Cormorant (overleaf)

People often ask me, 'What will you do next?' Each new work tends to be related in some way to the one that preceded it. *Thames Cormorant* draws on the experience of creating *Salmon Return to the Thames* (left), and features the same riverside roofline. It was commissioned in response to the print, to celebrate the life of a person whose office looked out over the Thames, and who loved boats, sailing and birdlife.

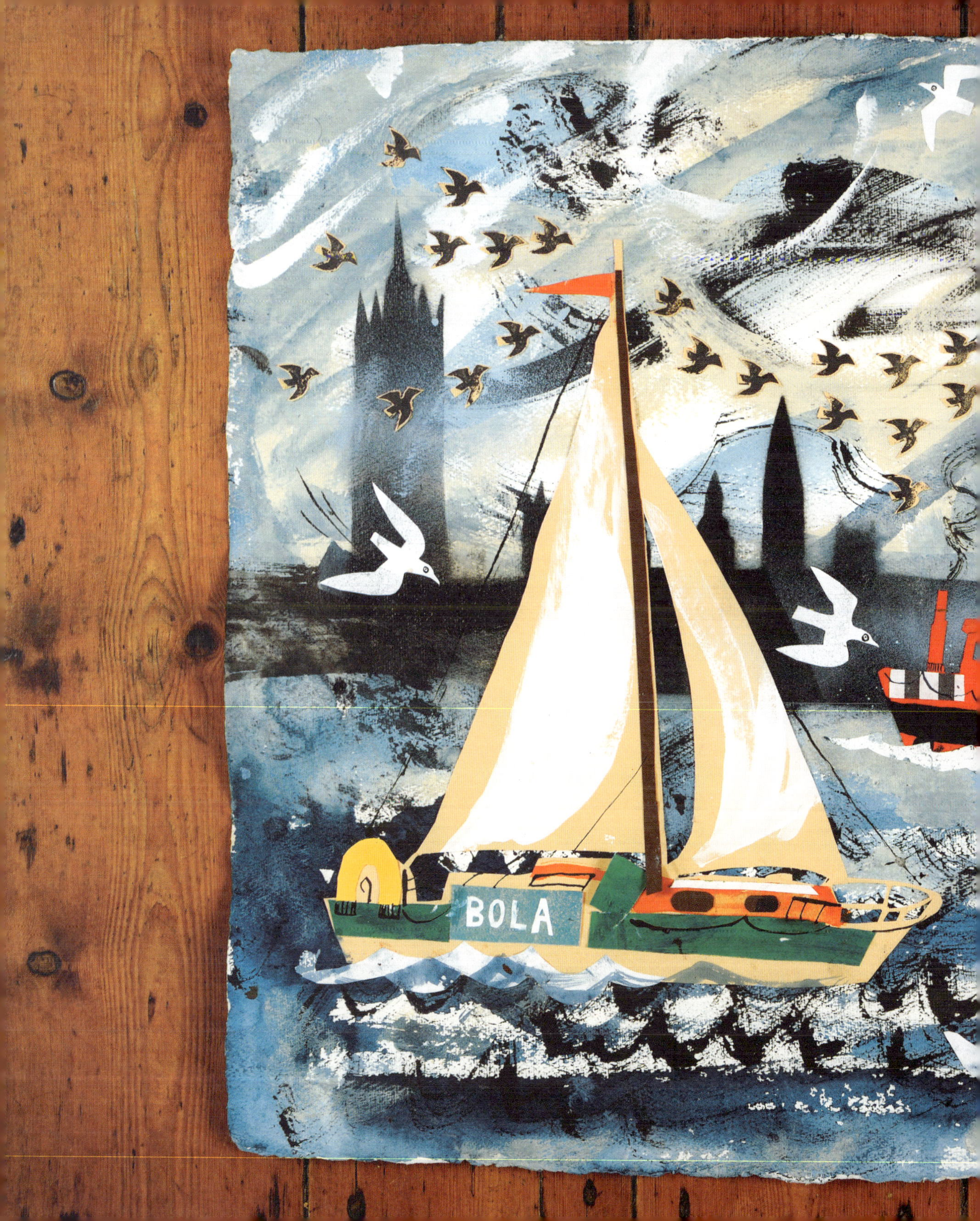
BOLA

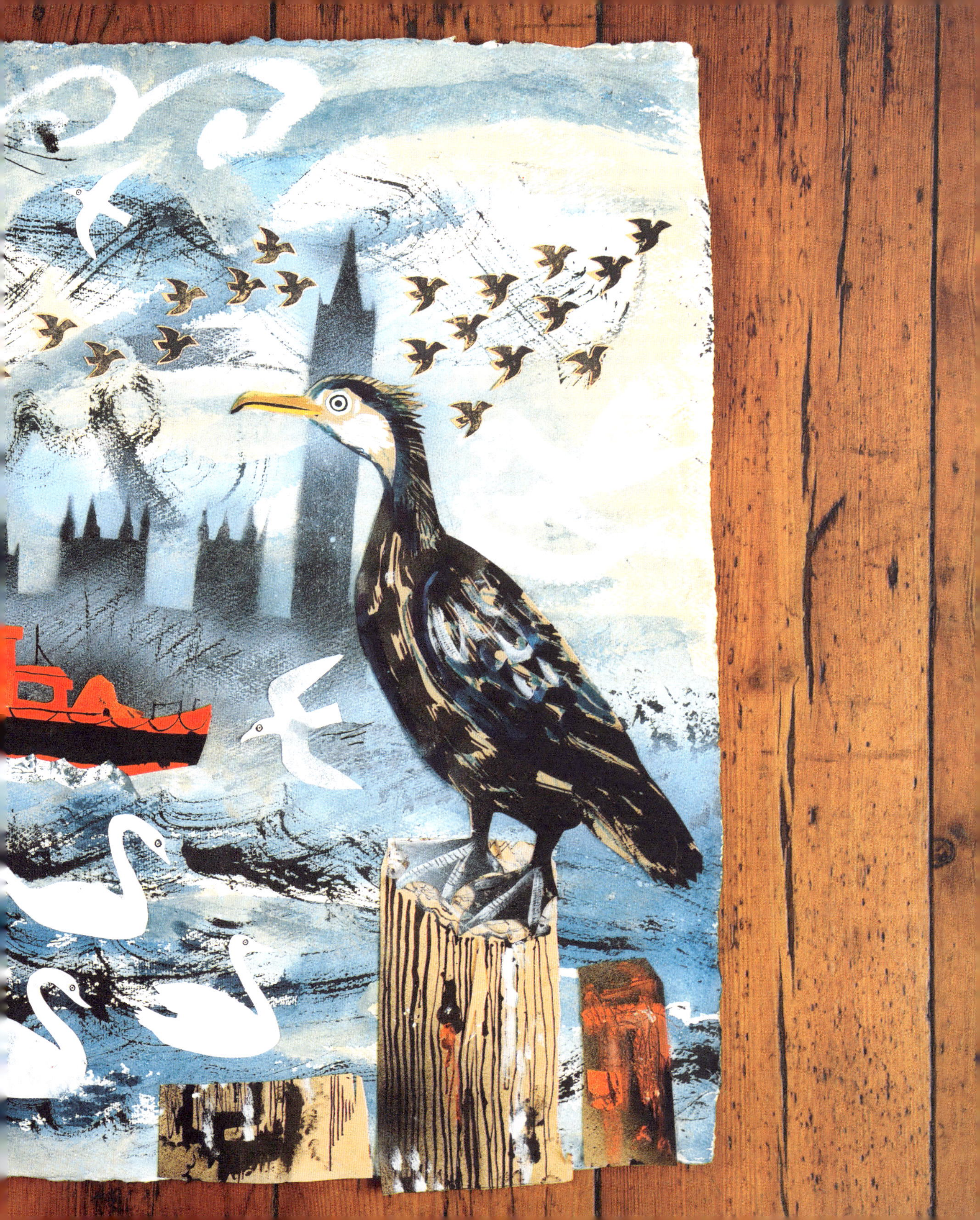

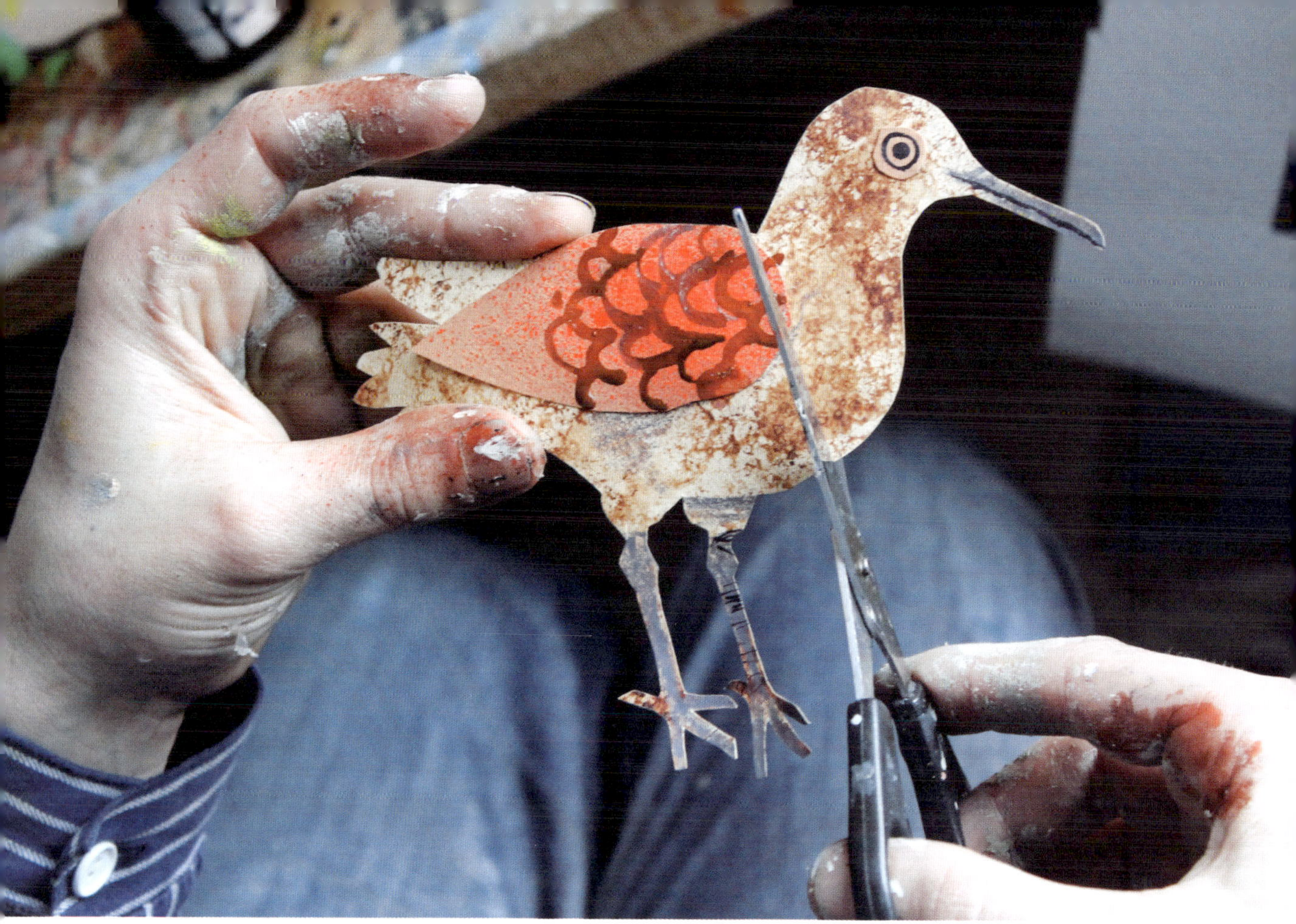

Shore Bird (right)

A beach at high tide, full of waders busy at the water's edge, is a subject I've explored many times. The shape of these birds, their long legs and bills fit for purpose, is a gift for the collagist's scissors (above).

Postal Fish and Box Work (opposite)

Alex Godfrey – friend, artist (as Alex Malcolmson) and gallery owner – celebrates his birthday a couple of days before mine, and whenever possible I try to make him a present. Our shared interest in flotsam and jetsam provided raw material for the small box construction and inspiration for the postal fish.

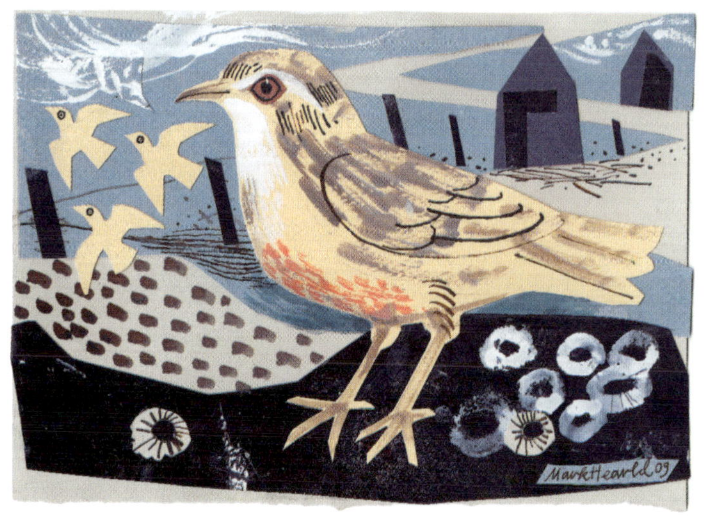

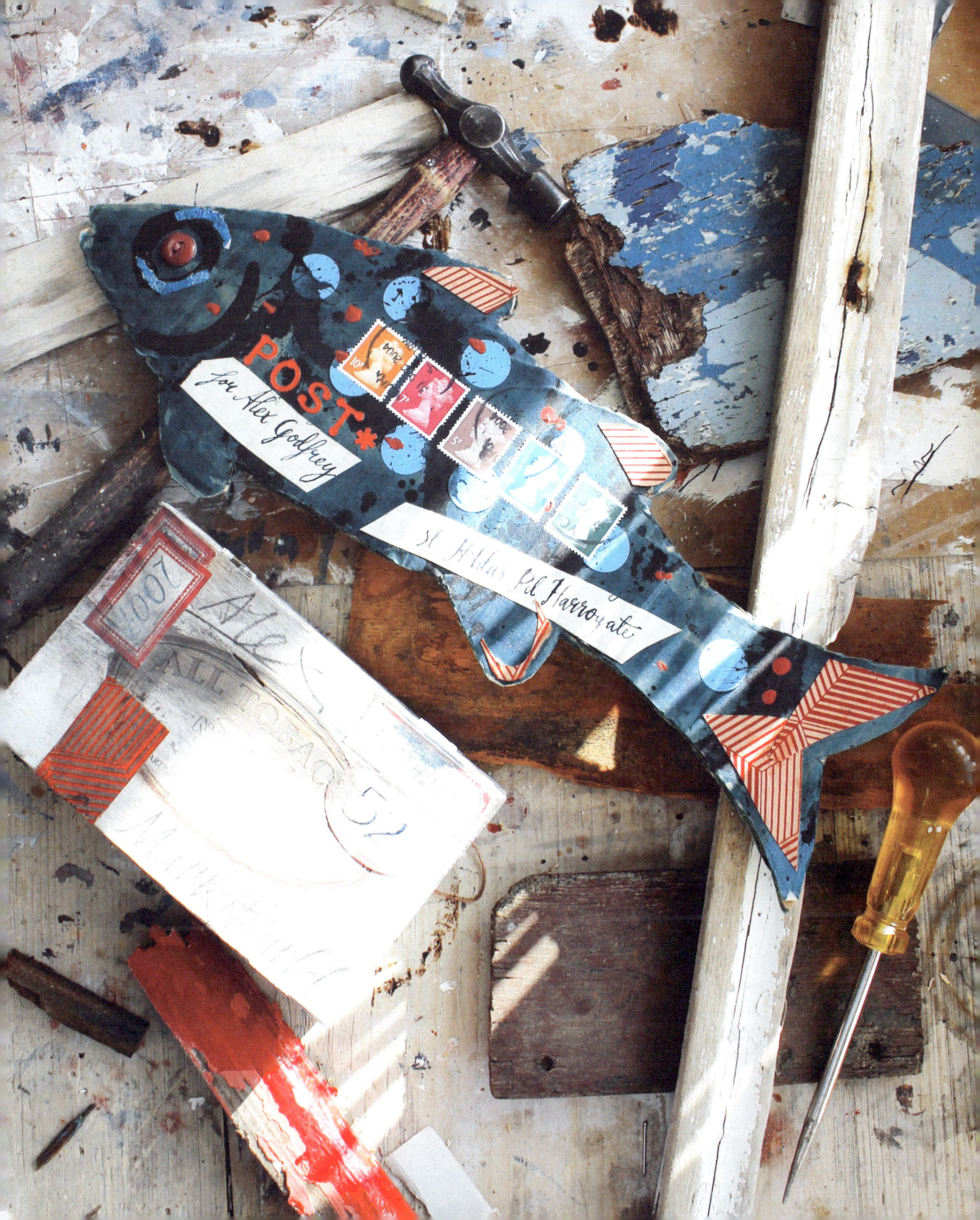

POST *
for Alex Godfrey
St Hilda's Rd Harrogate
2007

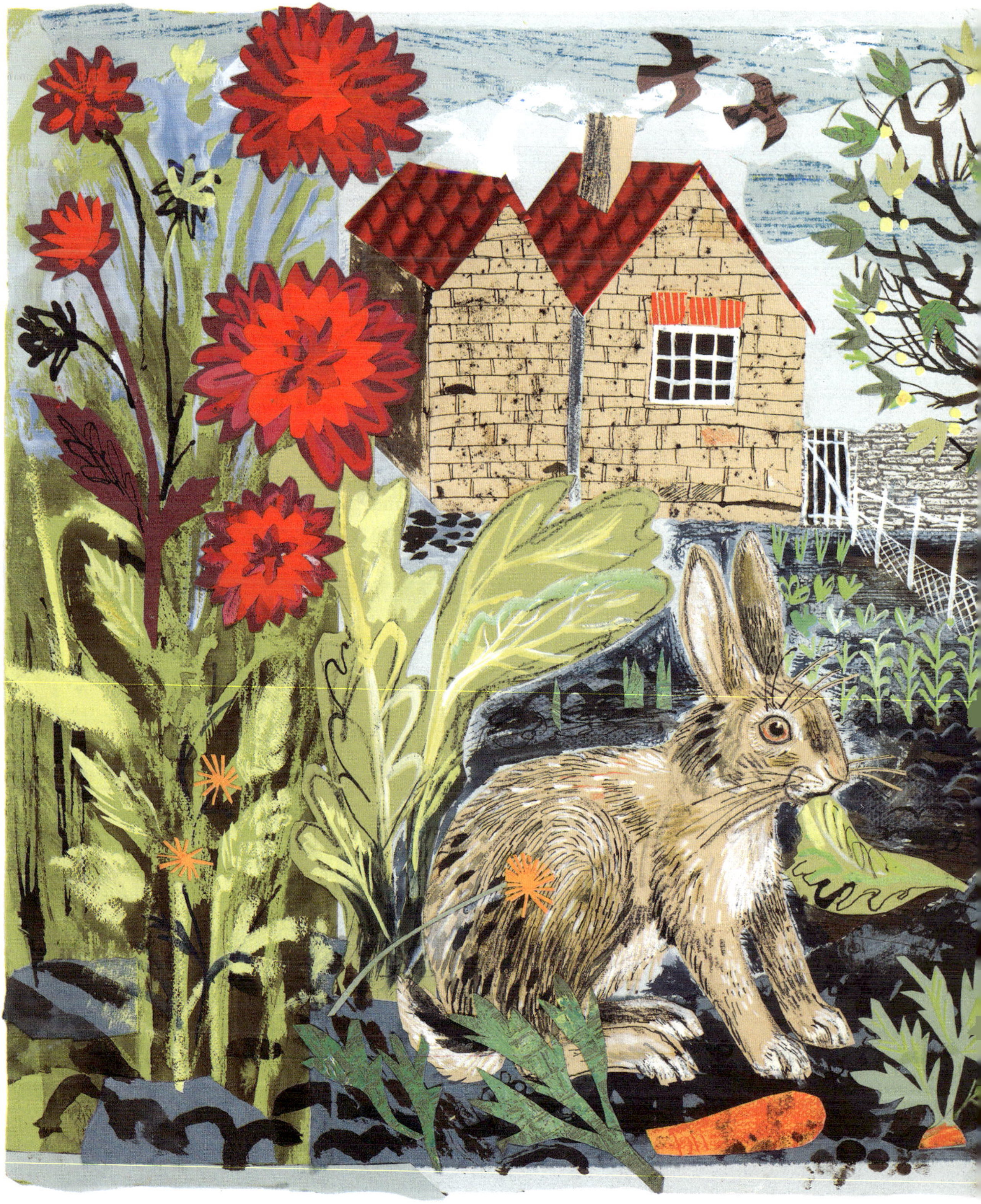

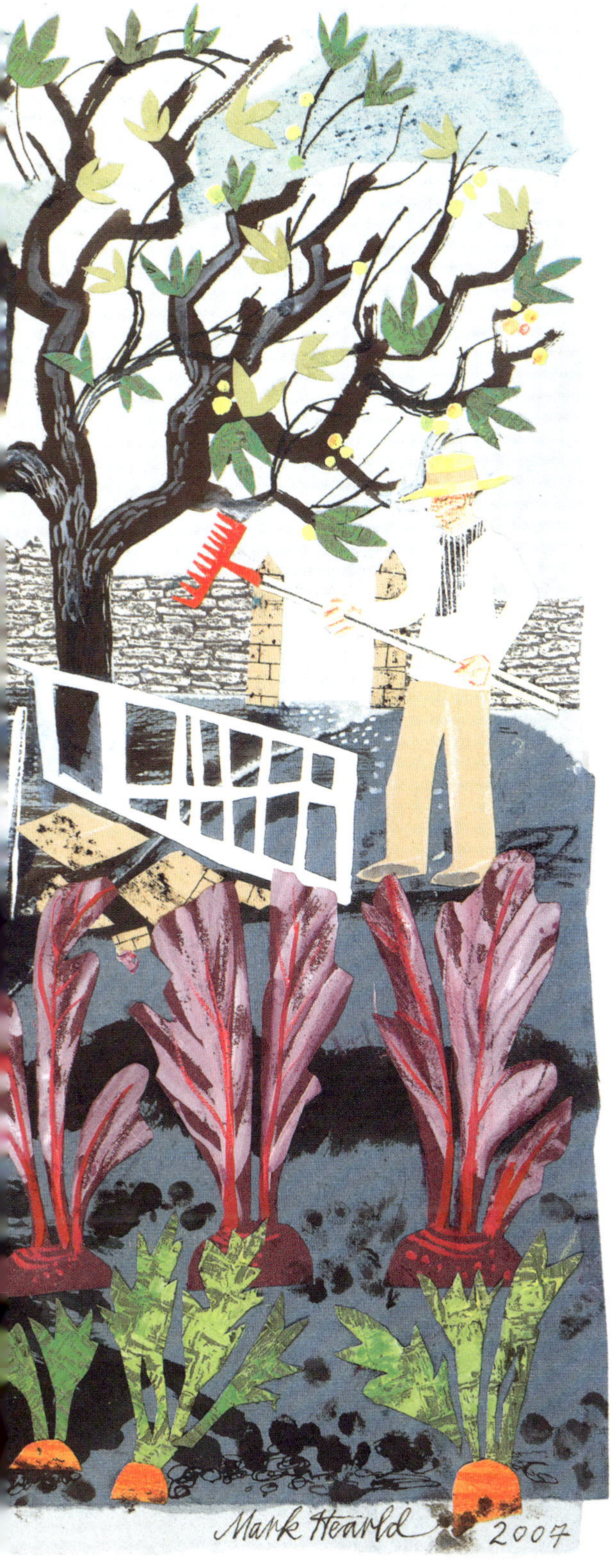

Allotments

Allotments, often located at the edge of town, are a haven for wildlife. There's something about the improvised order of each individual plot that is visually rich. Apple trees and rank brambles frame neat rows of carrots, beetroot or lettuce. I am drawn to the informality and intricacy of the spaces, which lend themselves to the qualities of a collaged image. In late summer, raucous dahlias vie for attention; fruit hangs from the branches of trees, ripe for the plucking; the allotment-holders' hens scratch; and the pigeon-fancier's flock circles overhead. Patched-up sheds and chicken-wire divisions define cherished spaces in which man and nature come together.

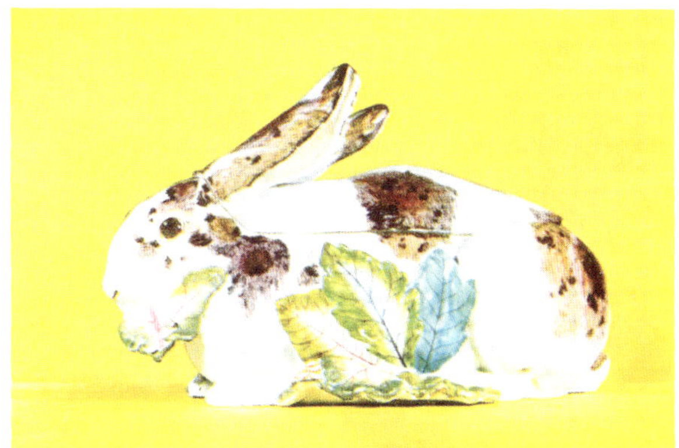

Carrot Crop (left)

Sometimes, a title provides the starting point for an image; such was the case with *Carrot Crop*. I enjoy the tension between the impertinent rabbit and the gardener, who is still unaware of the animal's presence. No trip to Cambridge is complete without a visit to the Fitzwilliam Museum to see the Chelsea soft-paste porcelain rabbit tureen (above), which munches on its own salad leaf.

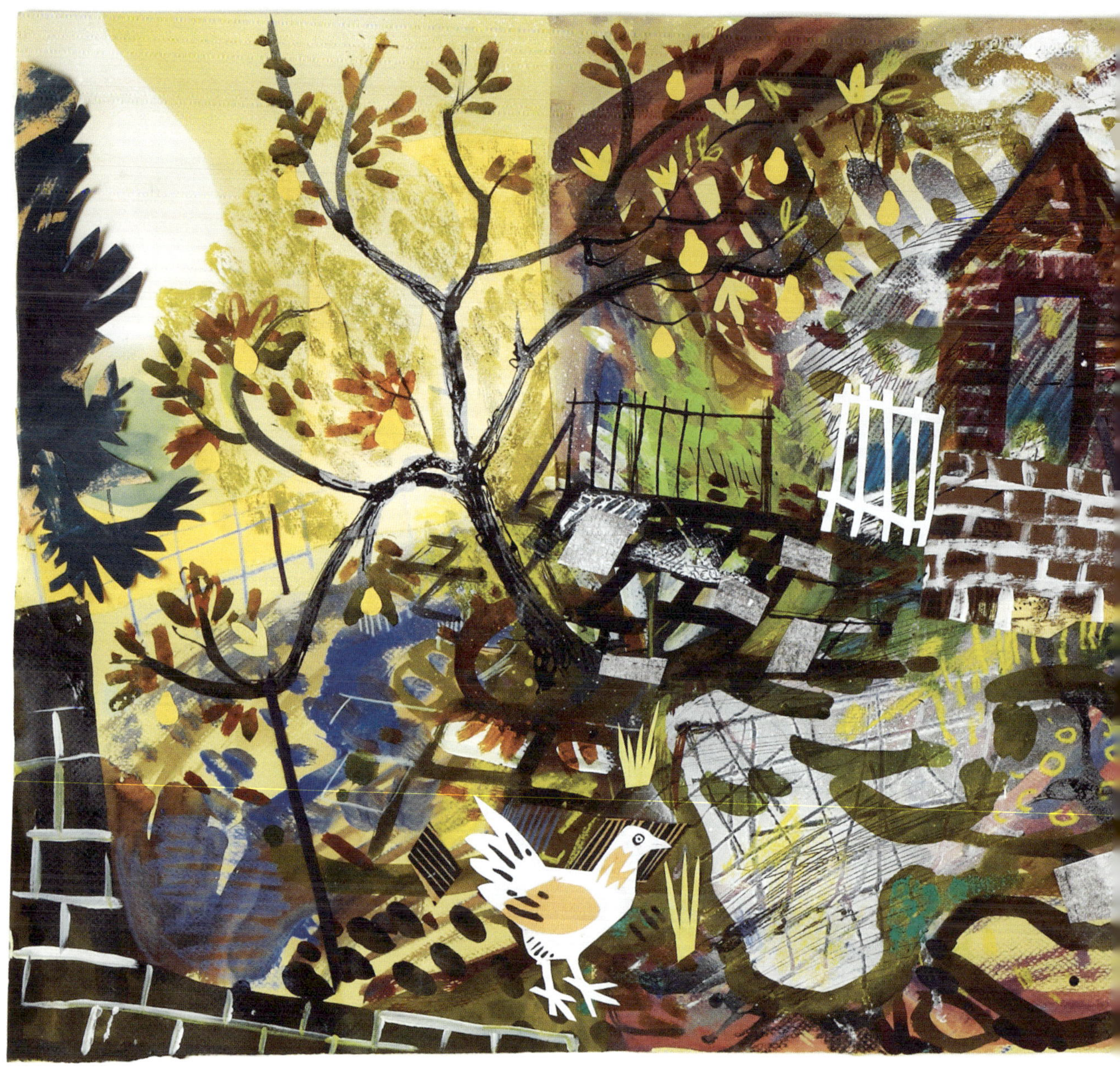

The Quince Tree

A September lunch of pecorino cheese and membrillo made from the quinces growing in my friend's garden gave rise to this image. We sat outside, and I took several quinces back to the studio for inspiration. In this work, the allotment has run wild, but the quince tree, drawn from memory, hangs with fruit.

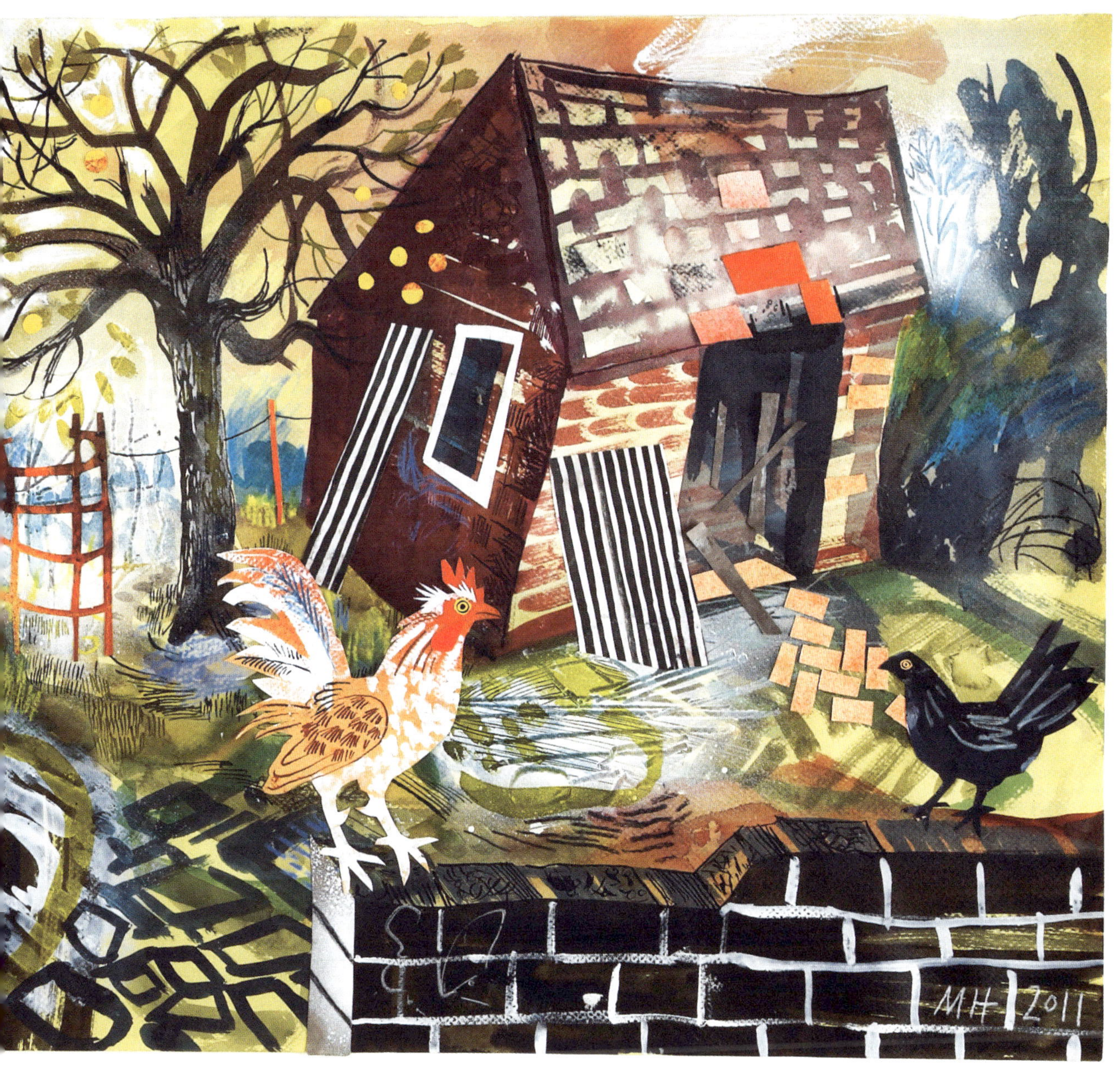
MH 2011

Allotment – Goat Husbandry (right) and Bramble and Apple Allotment

The *Nursery Frieze* prints of the
1930s, which appeal to adults
and children alike, are among my
favourite lithographs by John Piper.
I felt the frieze format was ideally
suited to the creation of a pair of
images rich in life and rife with
incident: a goat tries to escape,
dahlias bloom and apples ripen as
a gardener carefully tends his plot.
My treatment of the allotment
relates to the School Prints of
the 1940s (see page 9), French
lithographs and the Père Castor
lithographic children's books first
published in 1936 (opposite).

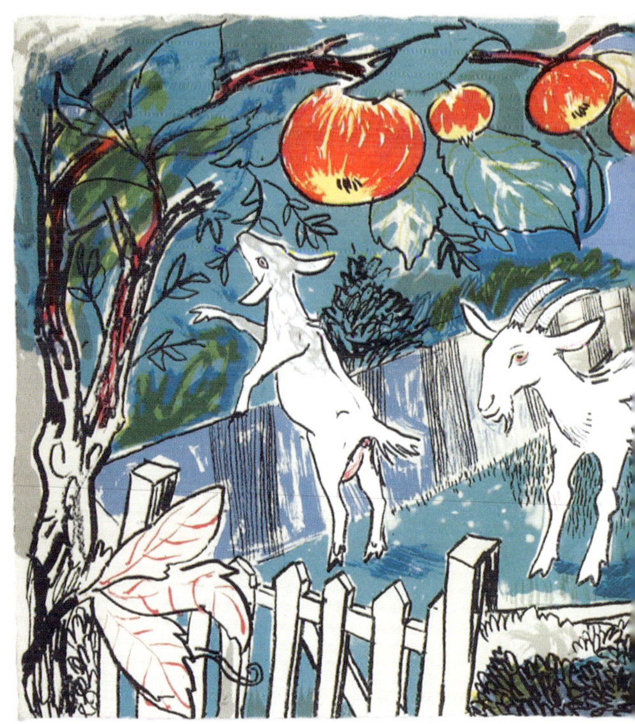

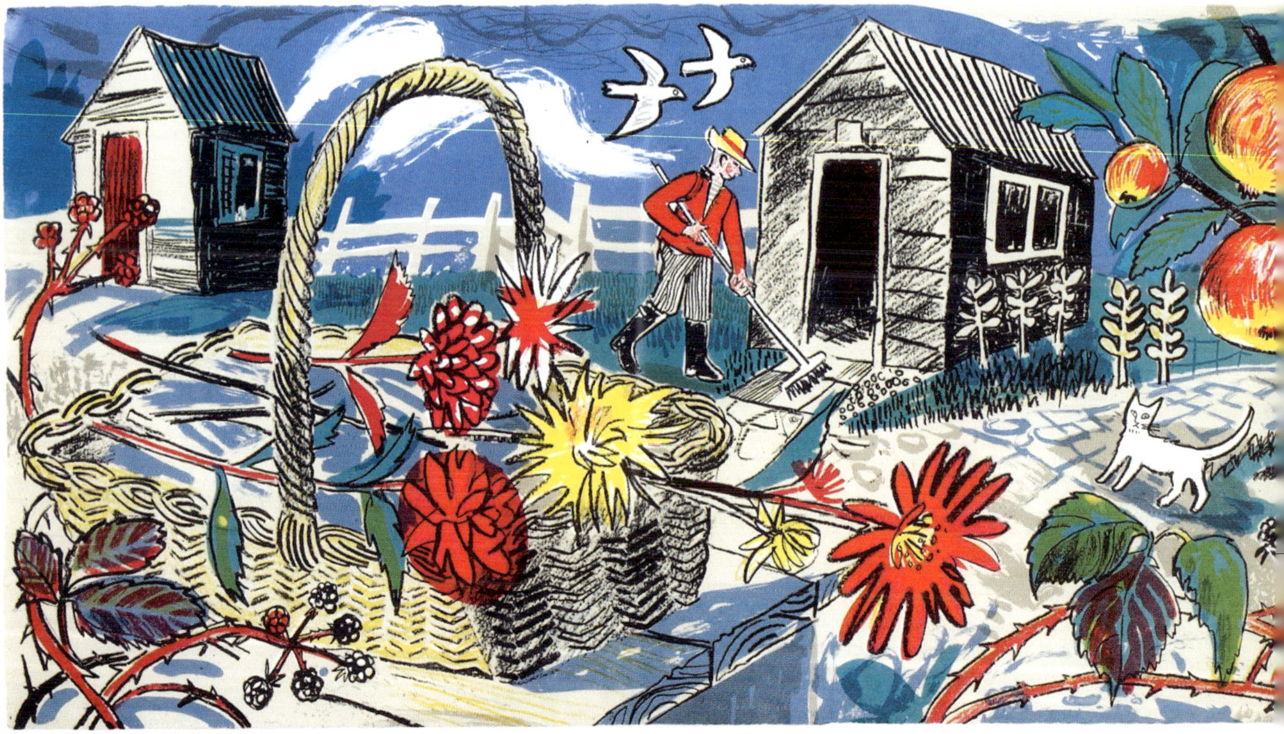

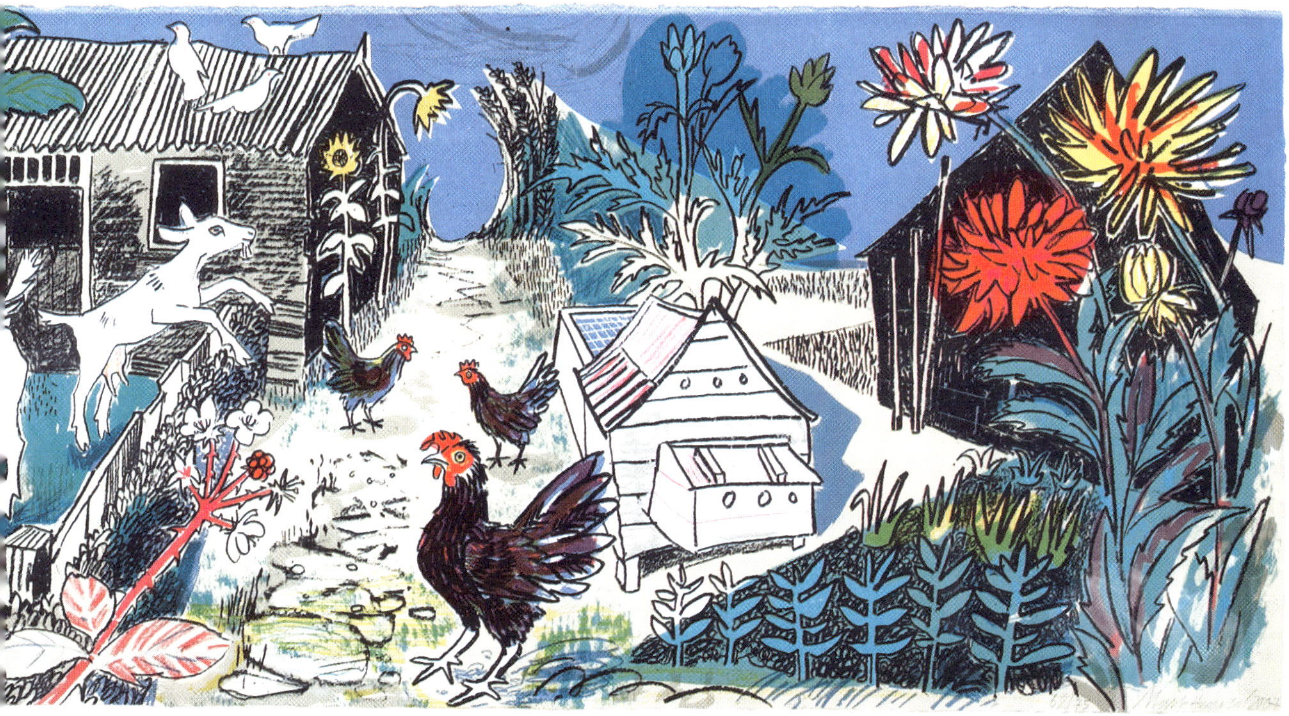

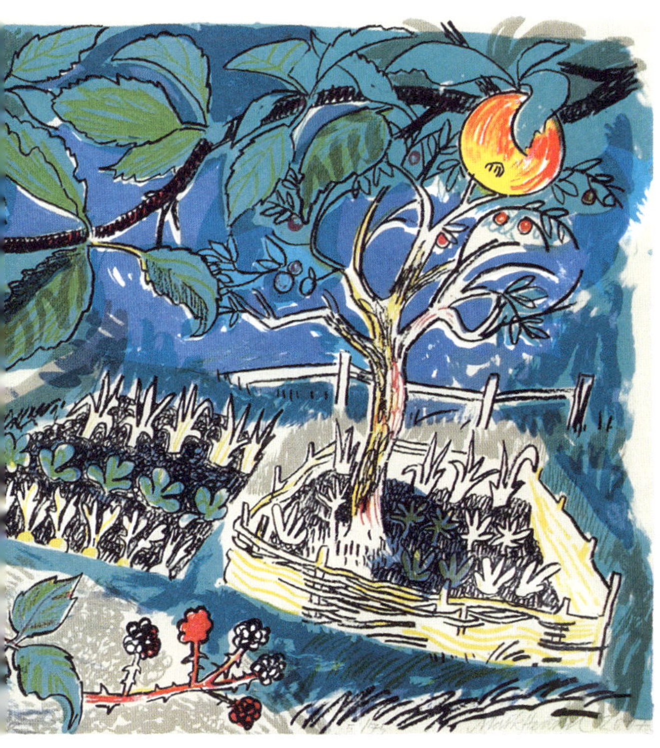

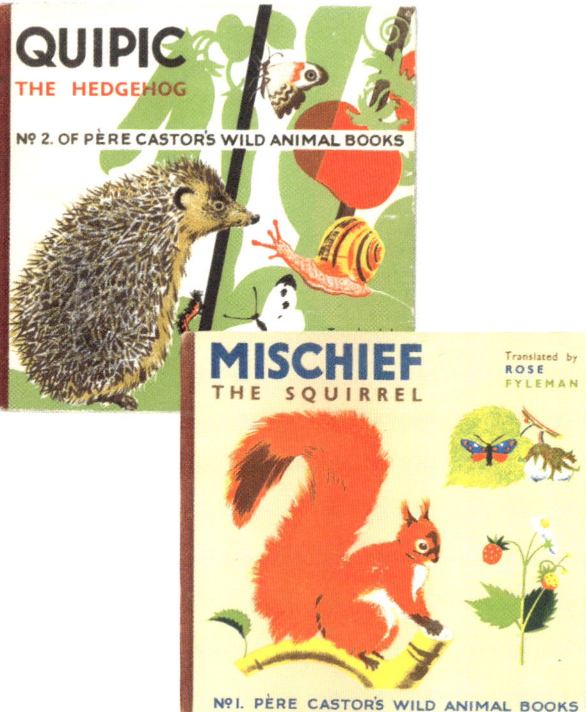

QUIPIC
THE HEDGEHOG
No. 2. OF PÈRE CASTOR'S WILD ANIMAL BOOKS
MISCHIEF
THE SQUIRREL
Translated by
ROSE
FYLEMAN
No. 1. PÈRE CASTOR'S WILD ANIMAL BOOKS

It is rare for me to make an image
without a creature in it. Here, in
Blue Shed (right), the bold shape
of the allotment shed holds the eye,
and weeds flourish at the edge of
the plot. The gaudy splendour
of dahlias, depicted in *Autumn
Splendour* (below), has a seasonal
draw for me; the high colour of the
flowers, at times brash, continues
until the first frosts.

I used spray paint and real
leaves for the foliage in the collage
Autumn Thrush (opposite and
overleaf). The sappy green paper
was a monoprinted leftover. The
thrush brings life, energy and an
important sense of scale to the
image, and sets the prowling cat
firmly in the background.

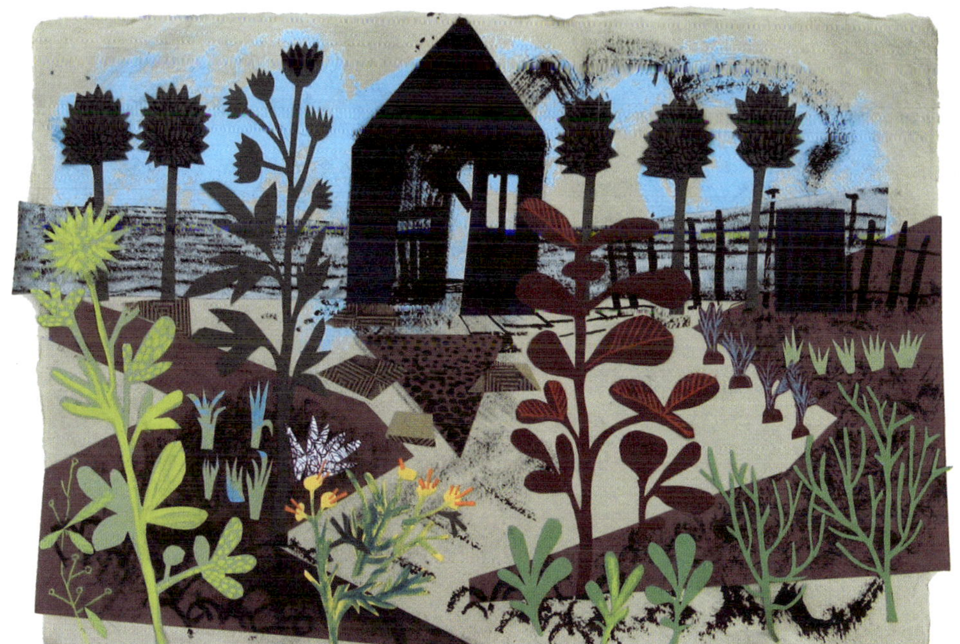

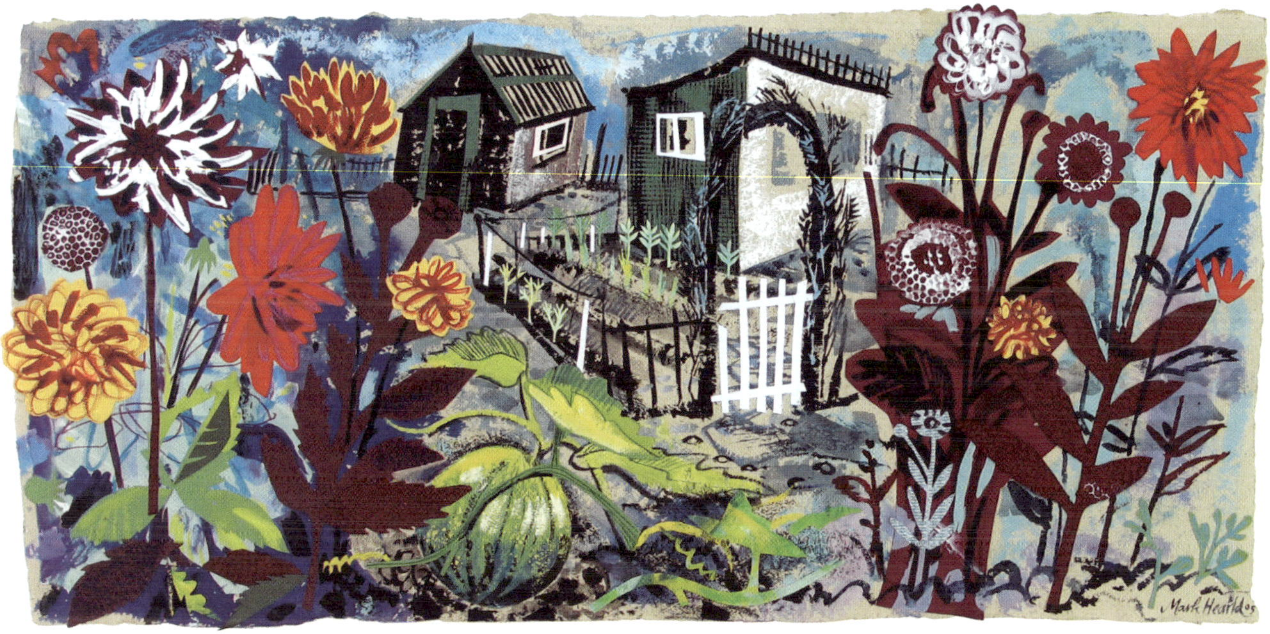

86

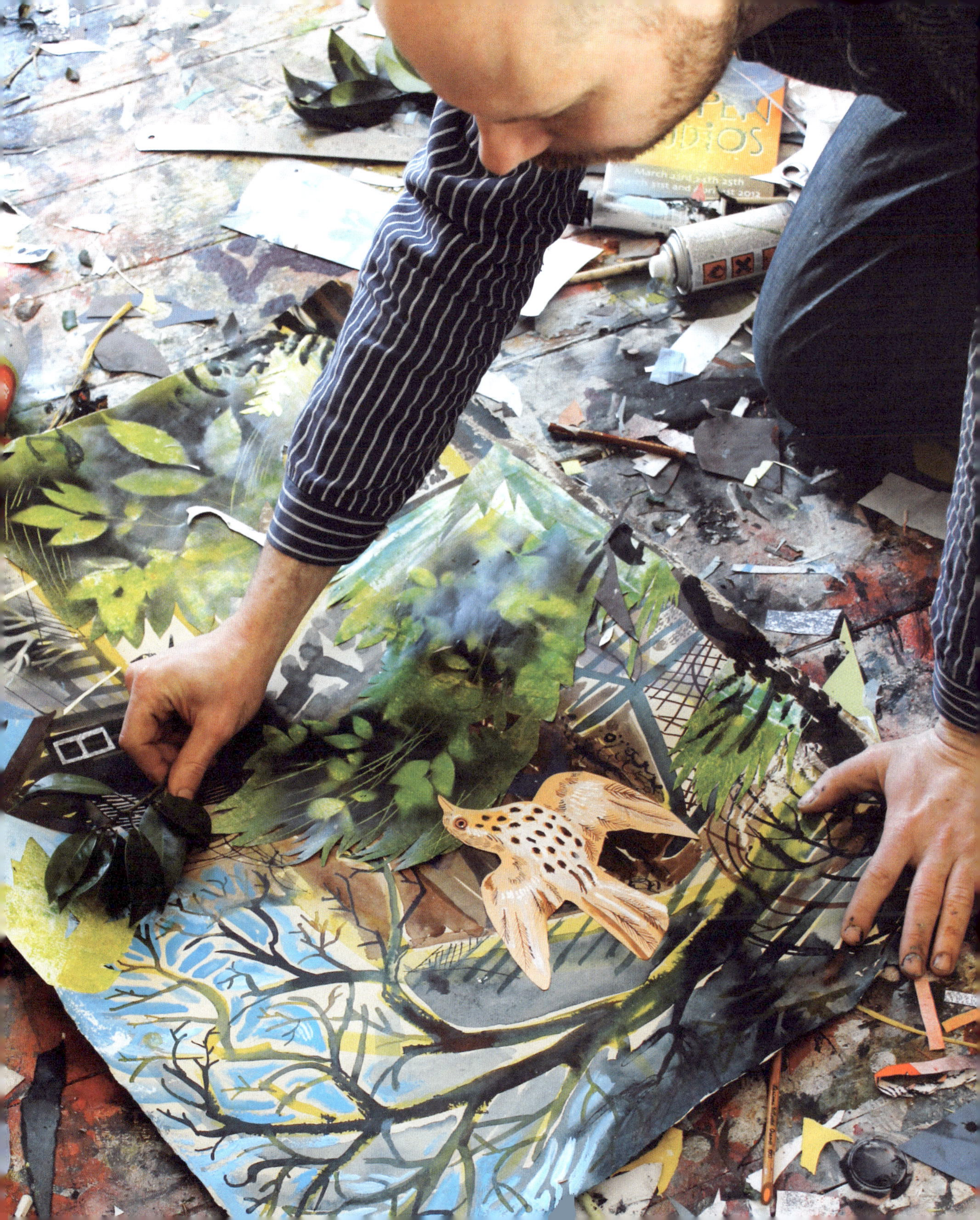

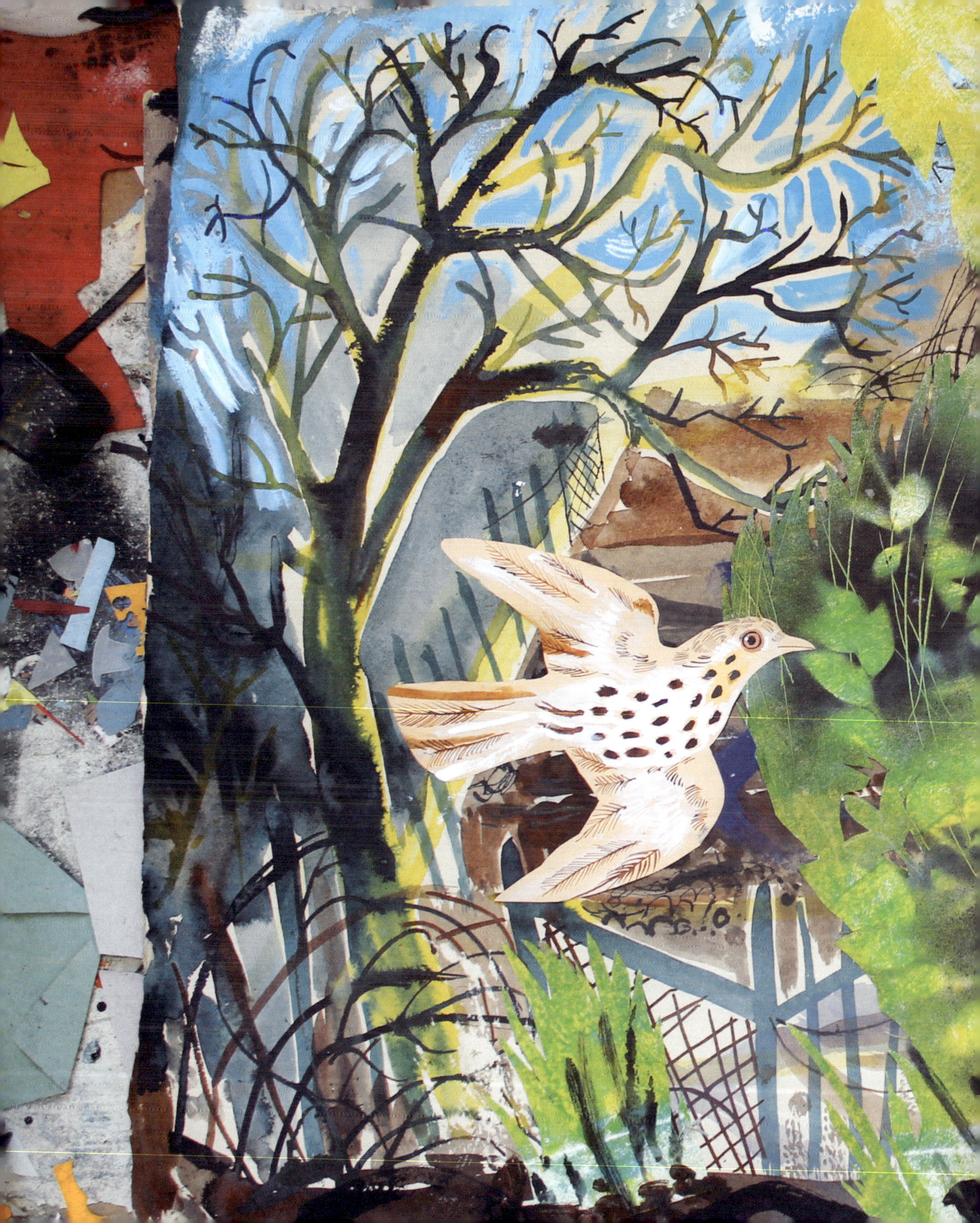

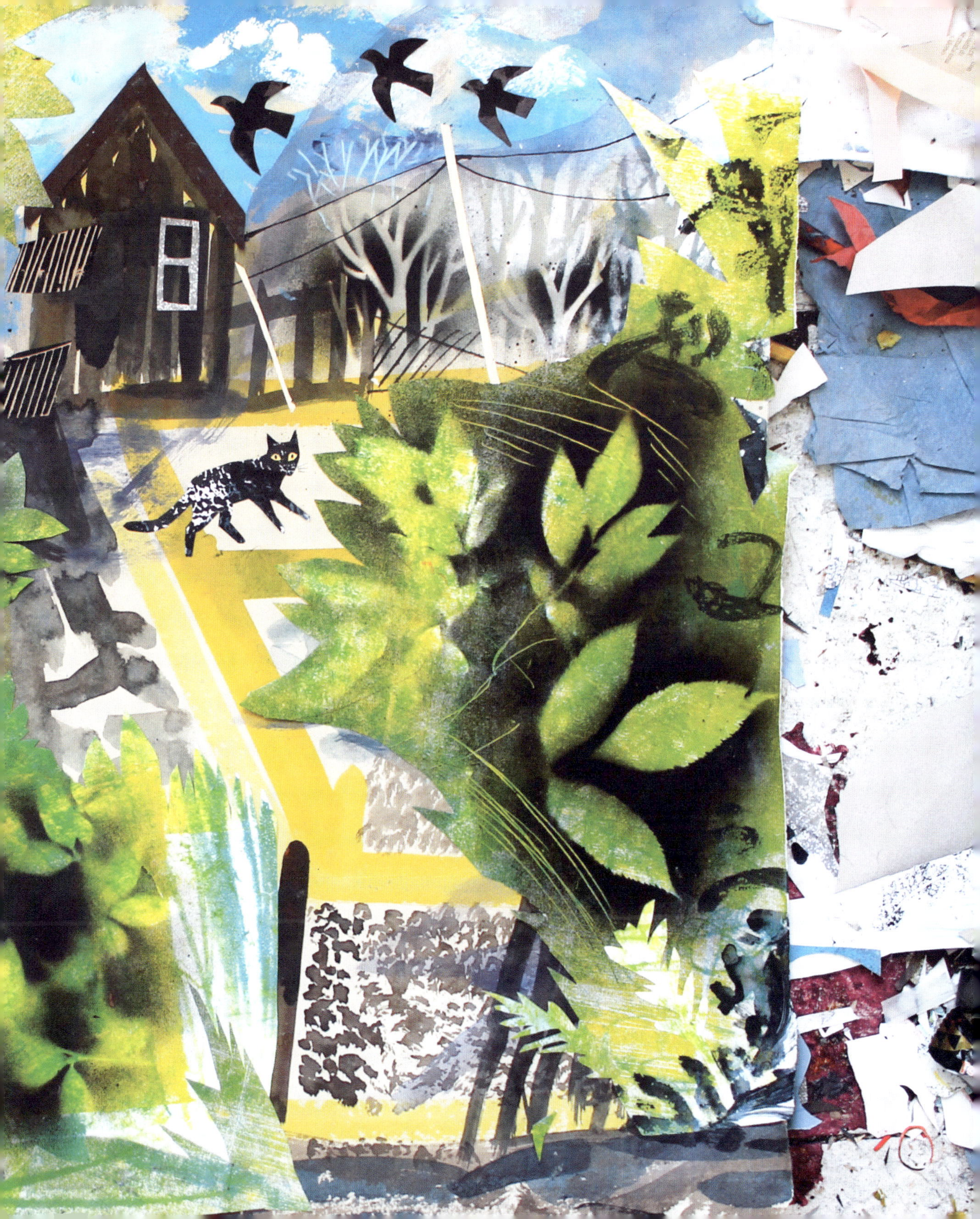

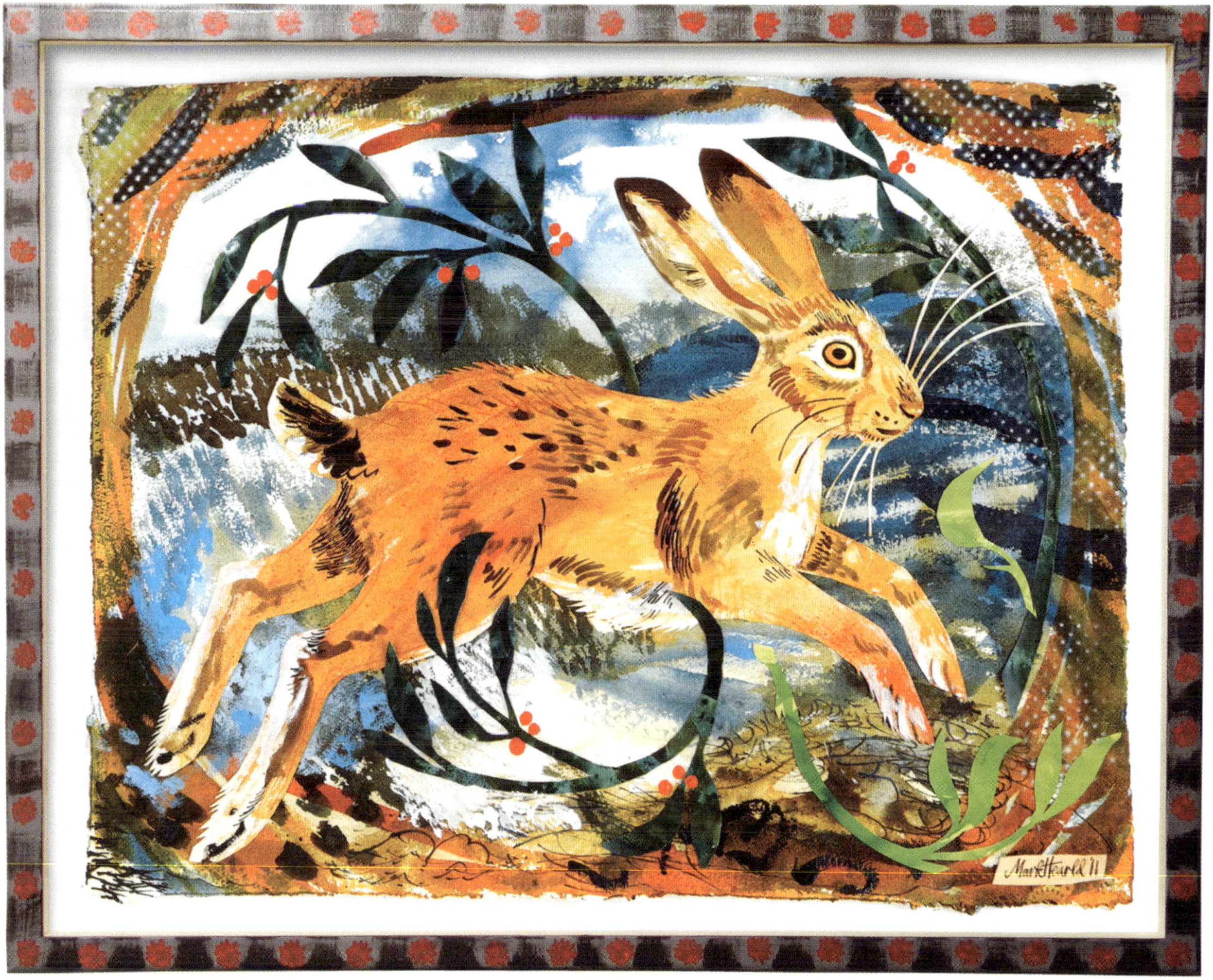

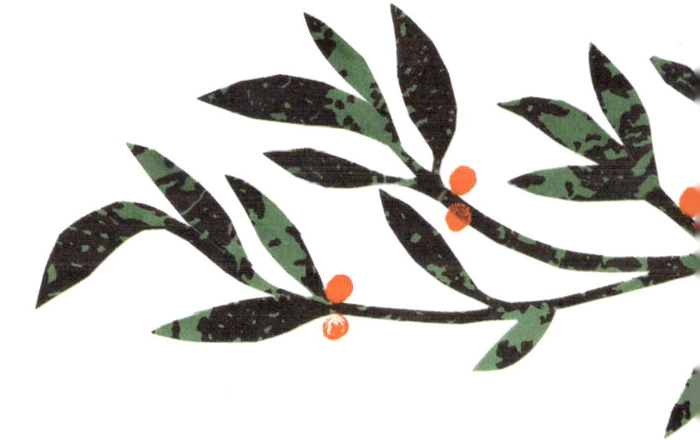

Birds and Beasts

I have been fascinated by the natural world for as long as I can remember, and creatures have been the focus of my drawings since I was at primary school. My subject matter has come instinctively, and I'm particularly interested in images of the natural world in the work of other artists. Most of the birds and animals to which I feel drawn are those that I might encounter on a walk up the lane with the dog, in the local allotments or in my own garden. The ordinary beauty of a blackbird in the snow is entirely compelling.

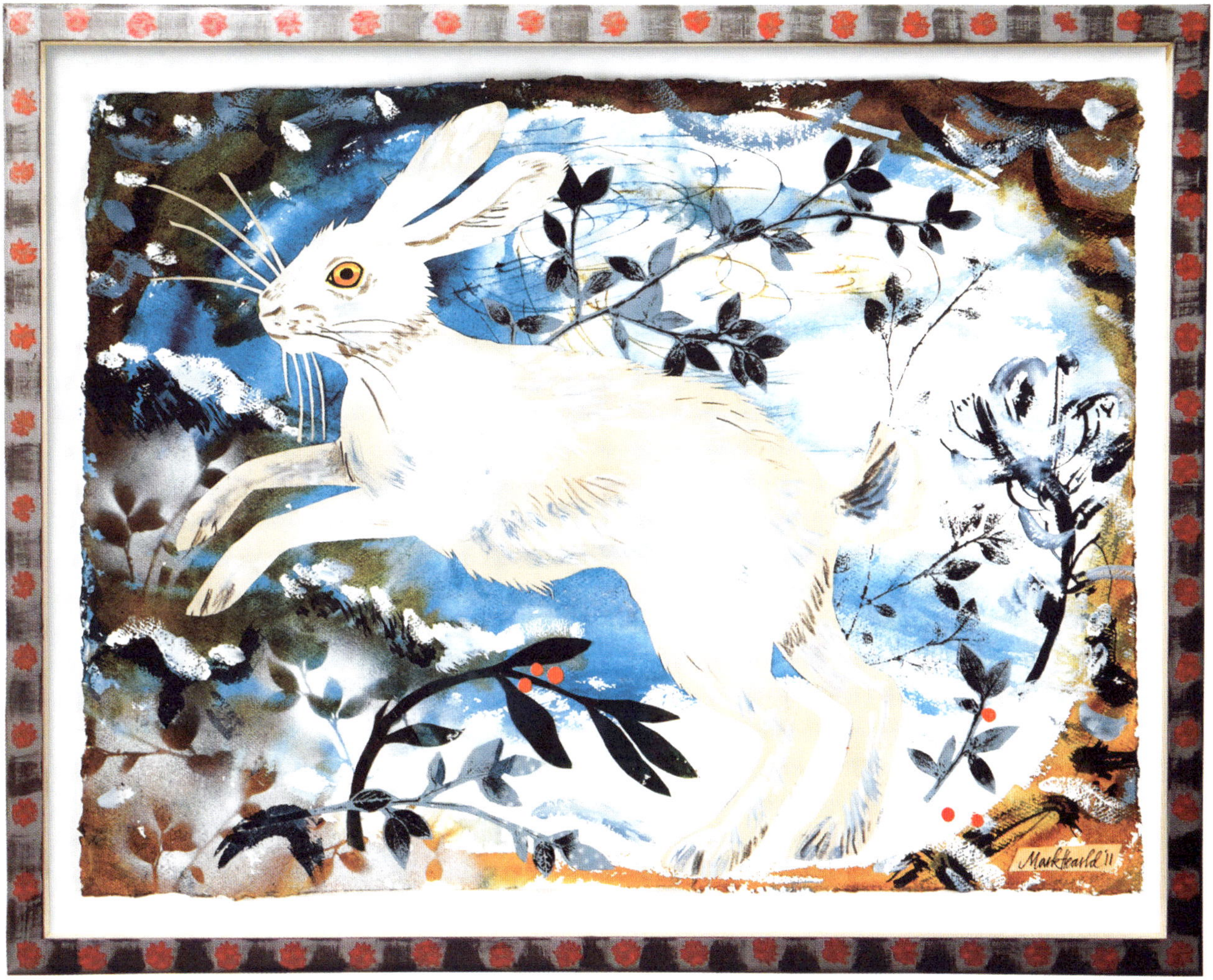

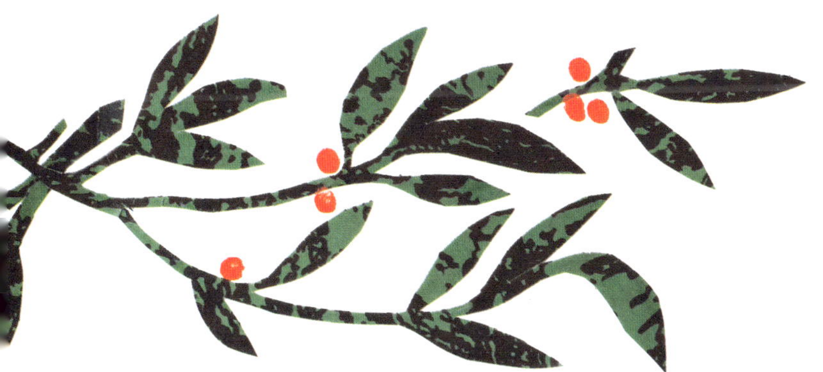

Brown Hare (opposite) and
Mountain Hare

These collages were made as
a pair for the Museum of British
Folklore's Christmas exhibition
of 2011, *The Paper Hare*. The
exhibition's title gave me a good
excuse to make more hares. Each
has a festive garland of evergreen
and a hand-decorated frame in the
folk-art tradition. *Brown Hare* is
now in a private collection in
Pittsburgh, Pennsylvania.

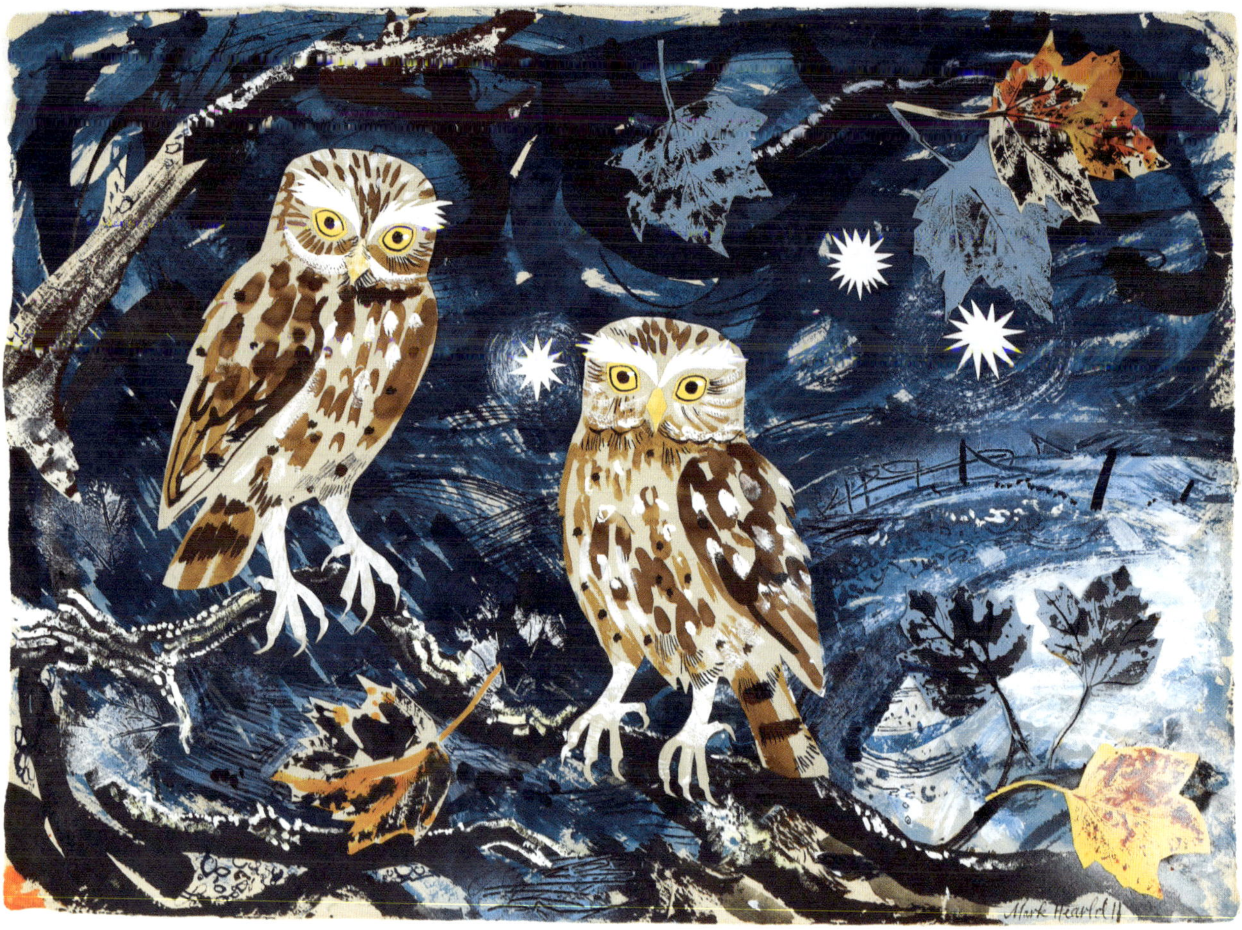

Little Owls

At Emily's family home, a nest box put out to attract barn owls became a home for a family of little owls. On dog walks, I would have frequent encounters with the birds, whose strange, piercing gaze is very beguiling.

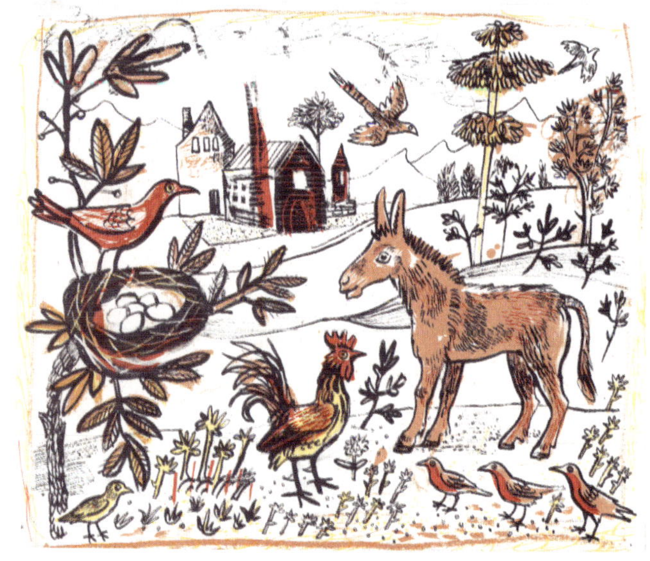

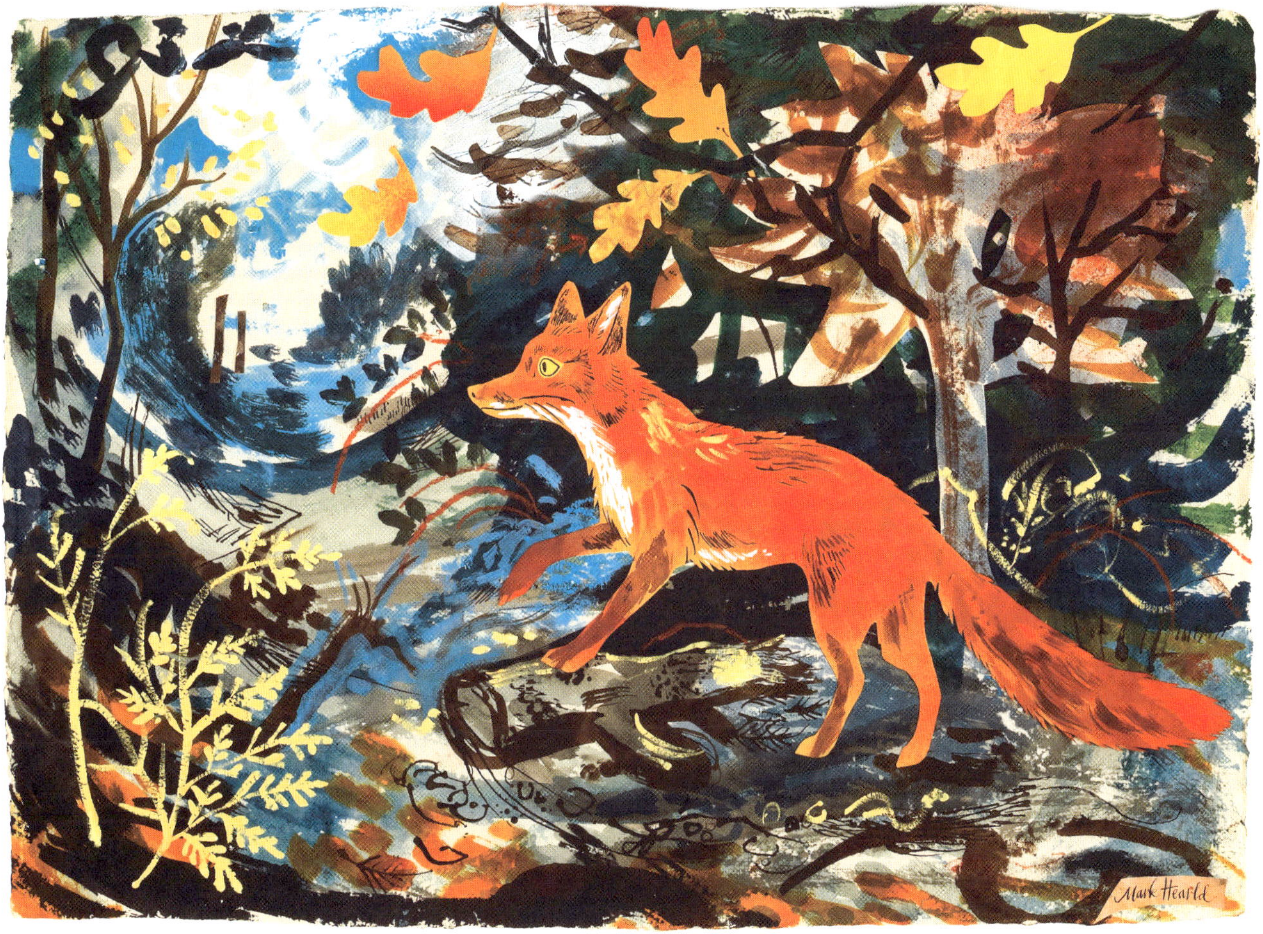

Curwen Mail-Outs (opposite,
bottom, and right) and
Fox (above)

While working at the Curwen
Studio, I had great fun contributing
to some lithographic mail-outs by
the artist Andrew Curtis; both the
donkey and the fox (right) were
made very quickly for this purpose.

My collages rely on the graphic
profile of individual animals. The
unmistakable silhouette of the fox
occurs in many of my works, and it's
interesting to compare the stances
of the foxes in pieces made five years
apart: the Curwen mail-out and the
collage (above), which was inspired
by a close encounter with a dog fox
in a country lane. In both images,
I was concerned with capturing the
essence of such a beautiful creature.

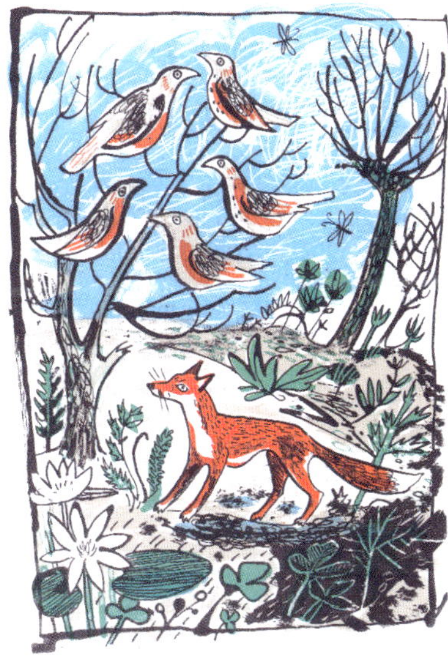

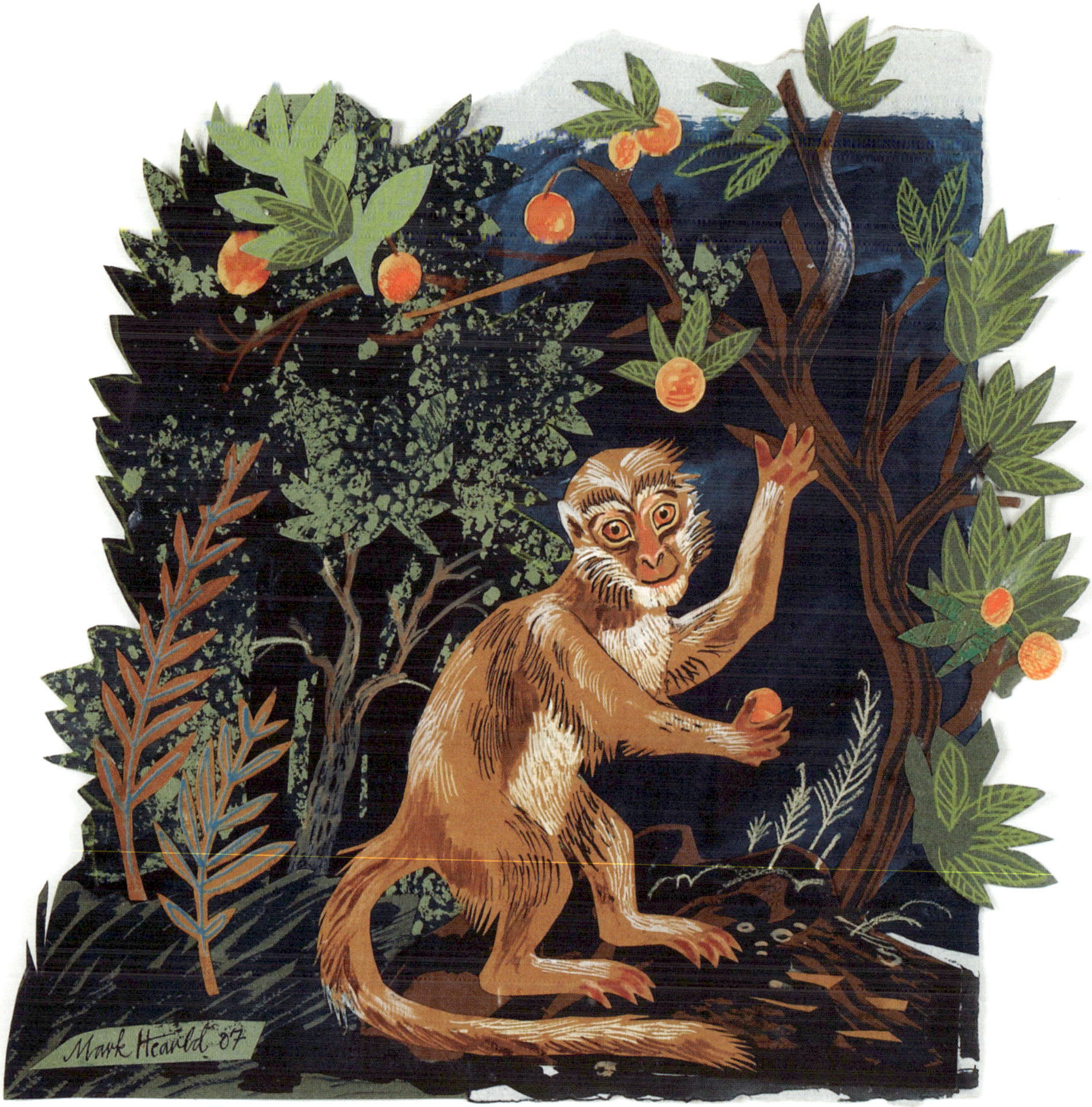

Macaque

George Stubbs, eighteenth-century
horse-painter extraordinaire,
also painted a very fine macaque
(*Portrait of a Monkey*, 1774). This
collage is a small homage to the
great man.

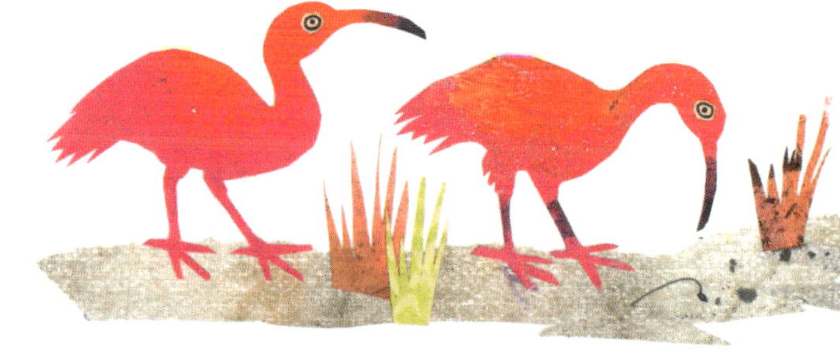

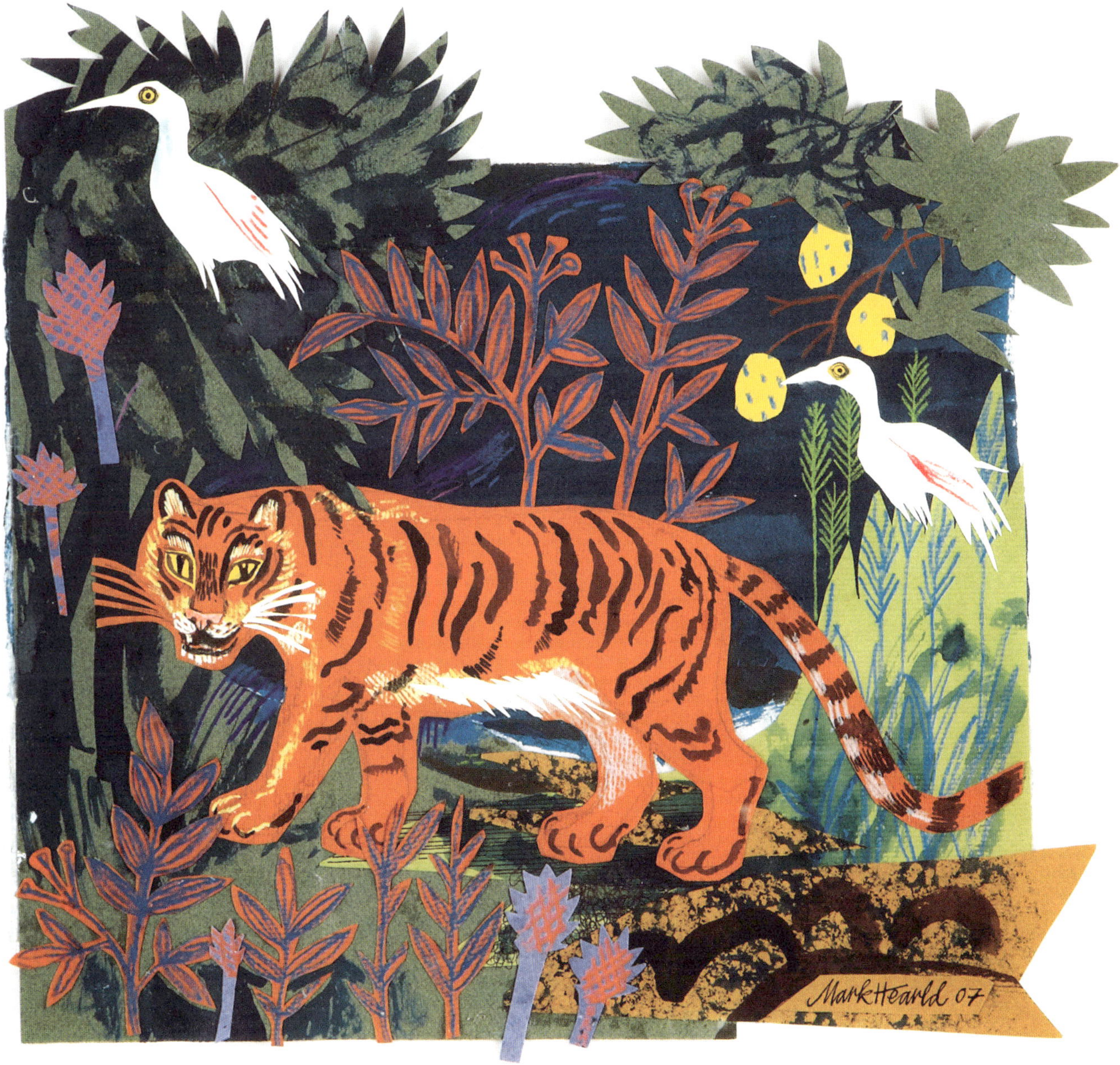

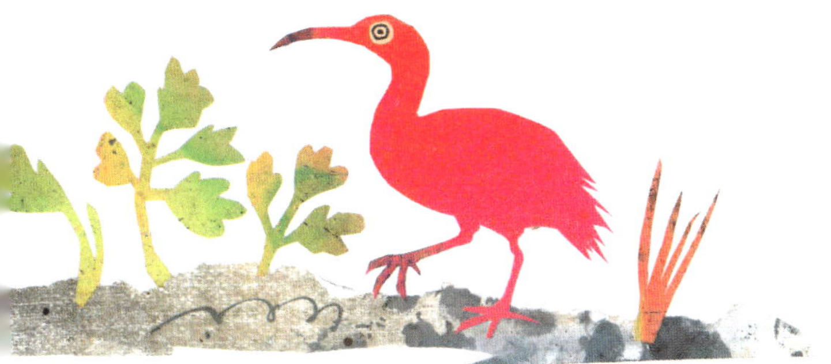

Tiger

I am usually inspired by common-or-garden birds and animals, but once in a while you need to go for the exotic. The triggers for this image were a 'Tyger! Tyger!' needlepoint (possibly by Mrs William Blake) seen in a photo of the potter Ursula Mommens's house, and a woodcut by the artist Dora Carrington.

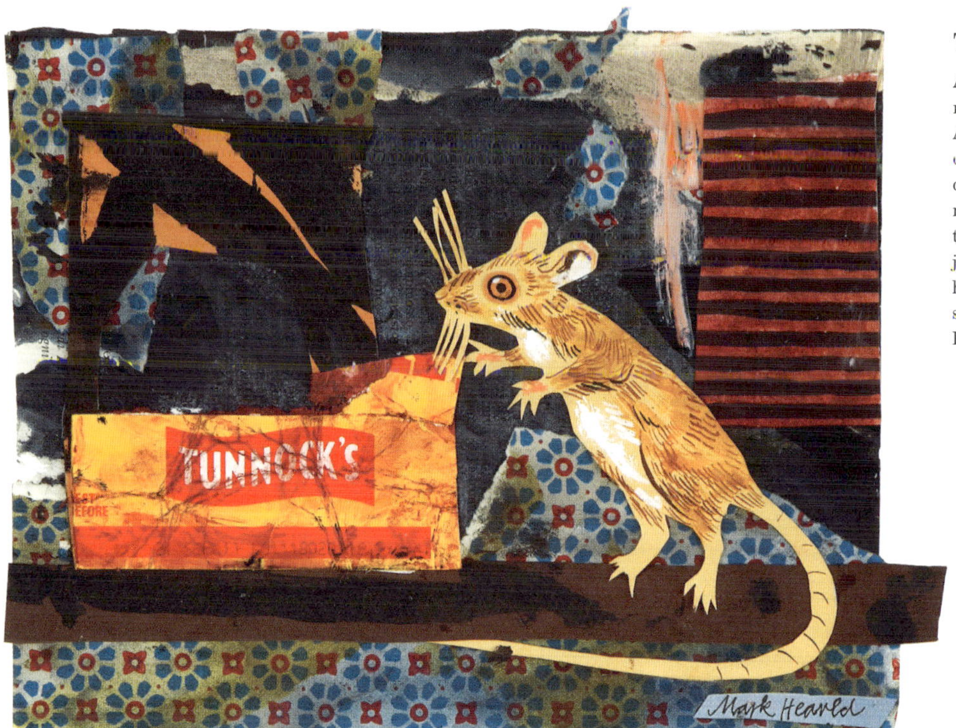

The Portland Street Mice

A single wood mouse in my kitchen rapidly became an extended family. Action had to be taken when I put on a shoe and found it full of grains of corn stashed there by one of the mice; another had chewed through the collar of a Vivienne Westwood jacket. I caught all the mice humanely, eventually, and have since made many images of the Portland Street mice.

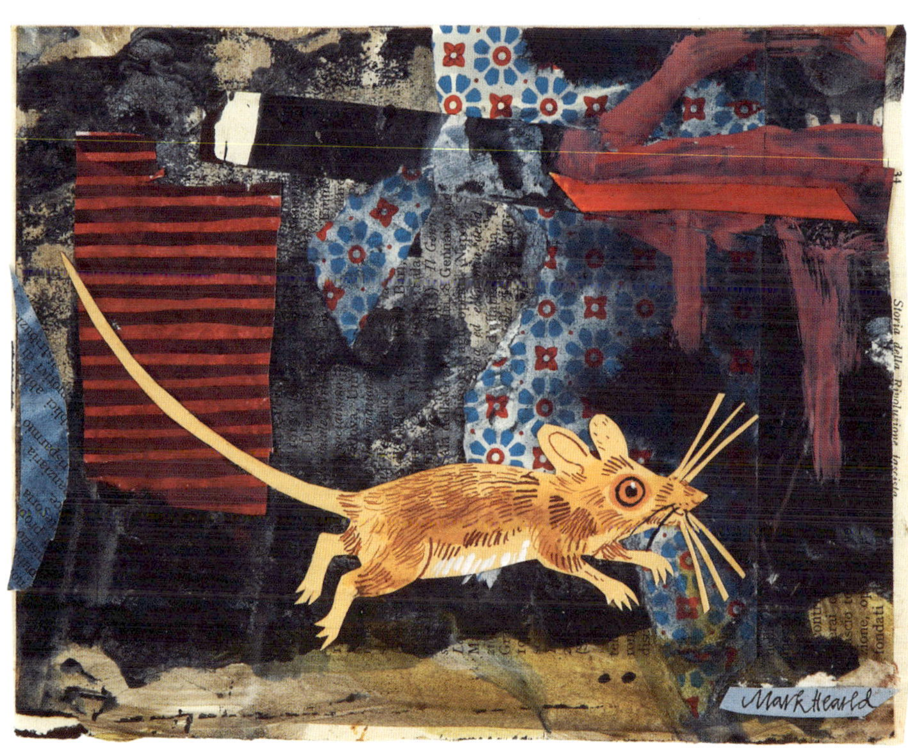

On the Pantry Shelf

… is the polite title for this work. It could have been called *There's a Rat in the Kitchen*, but I feared the word 'rat' might deter potential buyers. With collage, I'm usually concerned with the arrangement of elements on the picture plane, rather than the illusionary recessional space that's so compelling in Dutch still-life painting, but here the lump of cheese is firmly described in three dimensions. The rat, meanwhile, brings a note of narrative mischief.

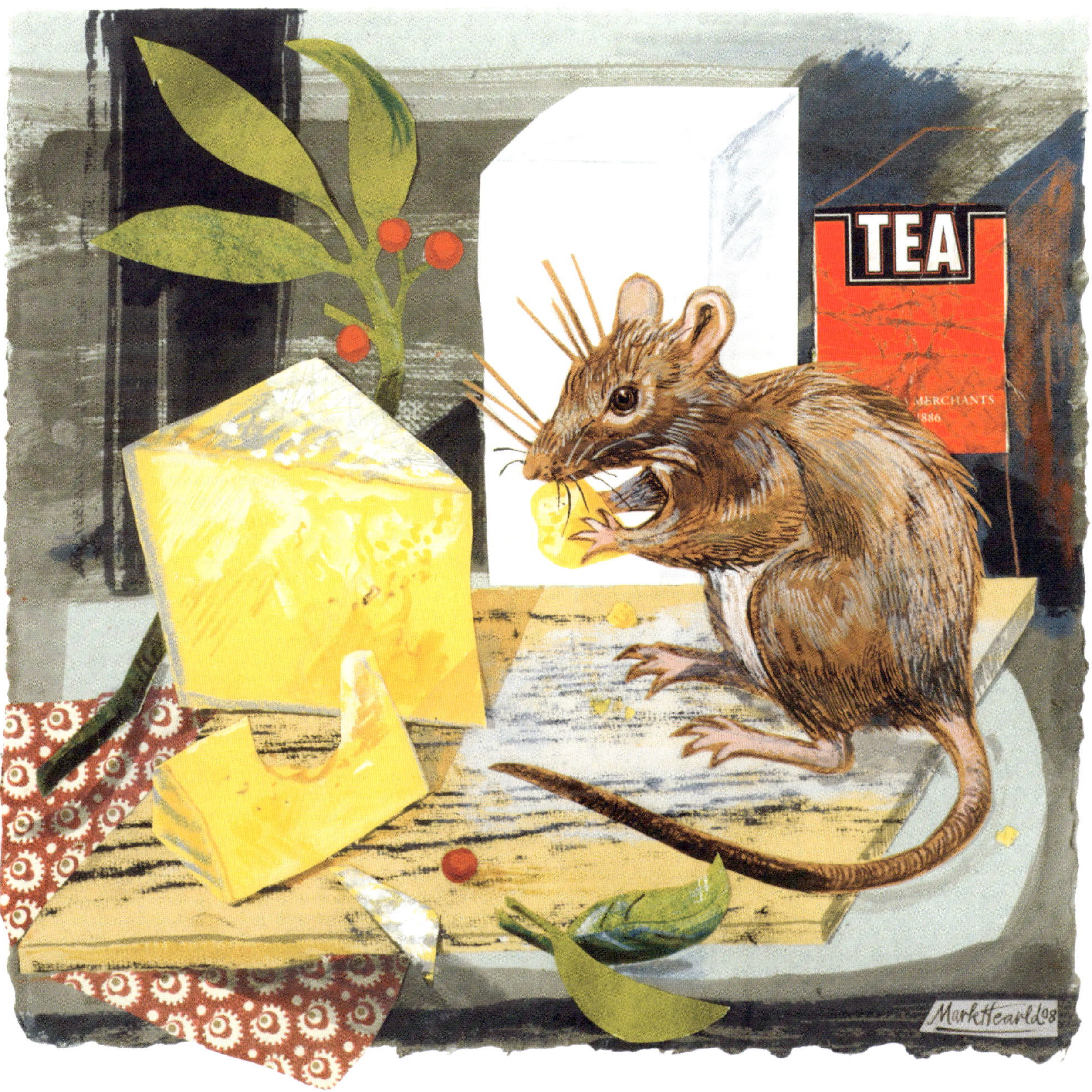

Jay and Pick Your Own

These prints were made on one
plate using the same range of
colours. They demonstrate how the
same, limited palette can be used
to create contrasting images.

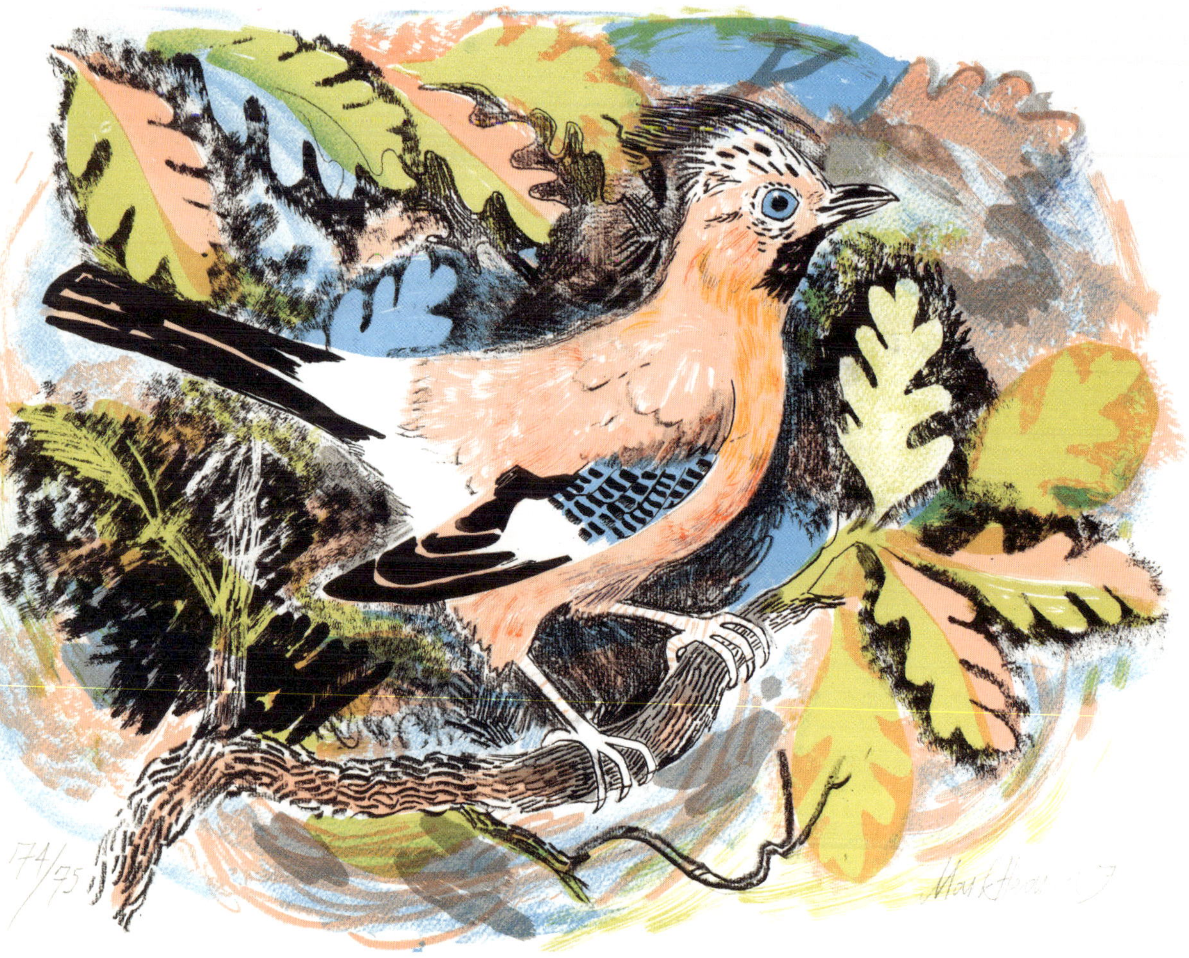

Bullfinch, Cock Sparrow, Wren, Chaffinch and Goldfinch

Birds are a constant source of
fascination. A blackbird hopping
across your path on a morning
walk or a singing chaffinch perched
overhead are small but incredibly
life-enhancing experiences in the
everyday, feeding the soul and
inspiring creativity.

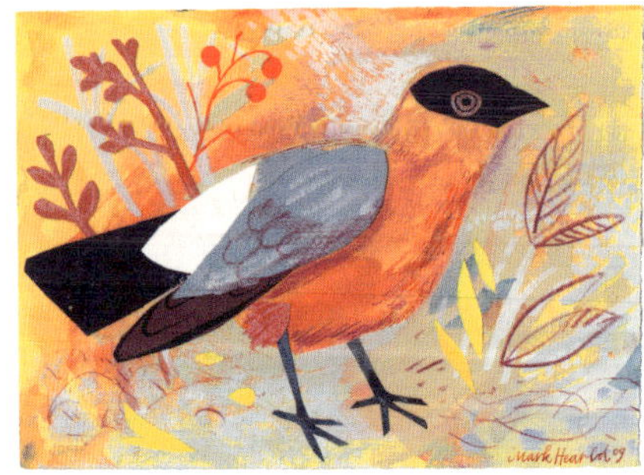

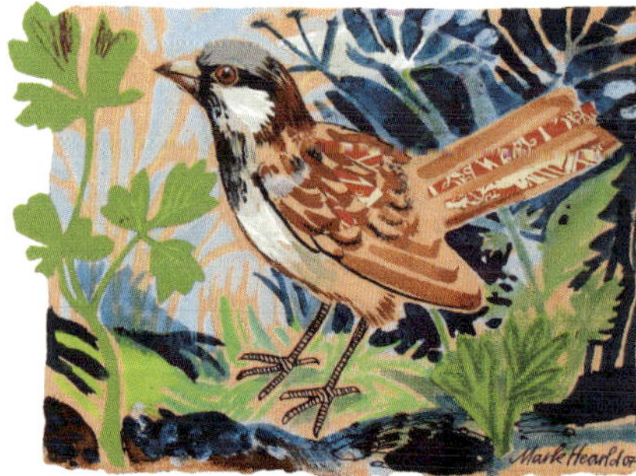

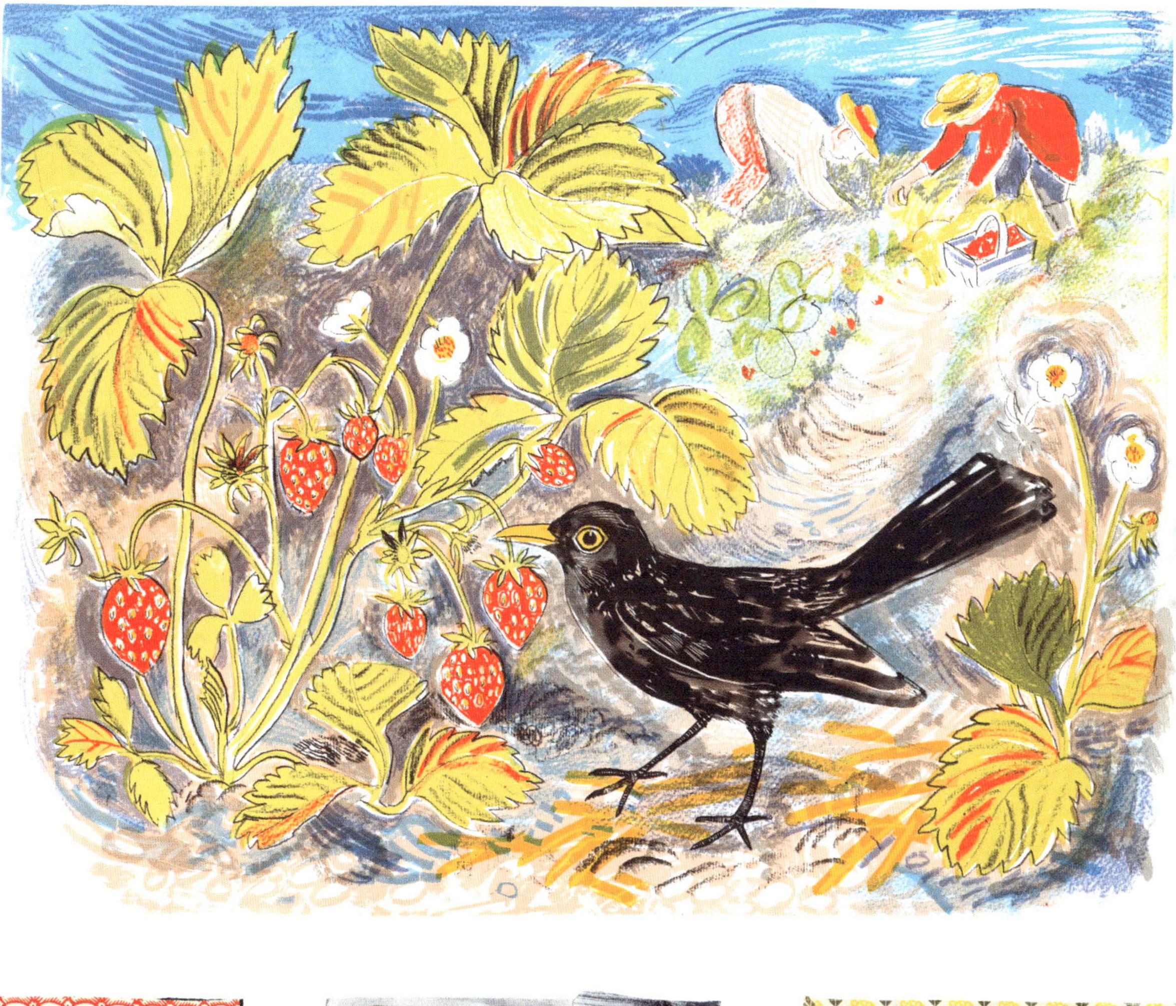

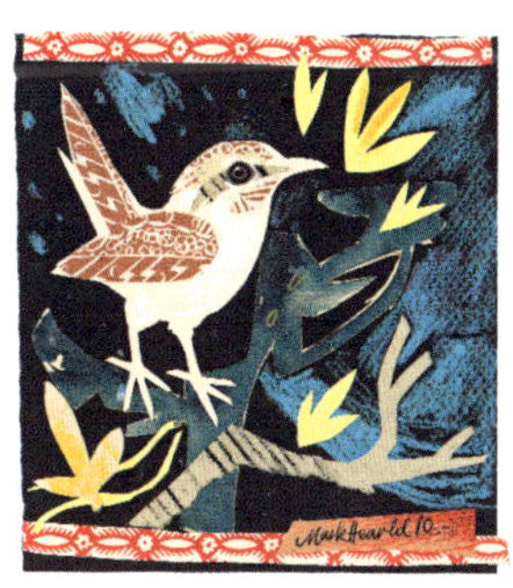

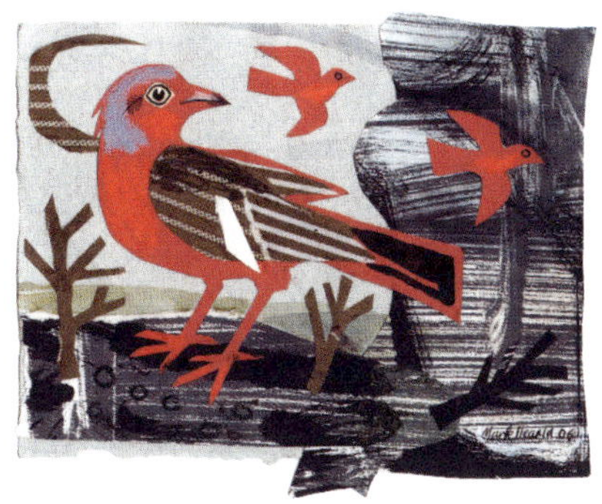

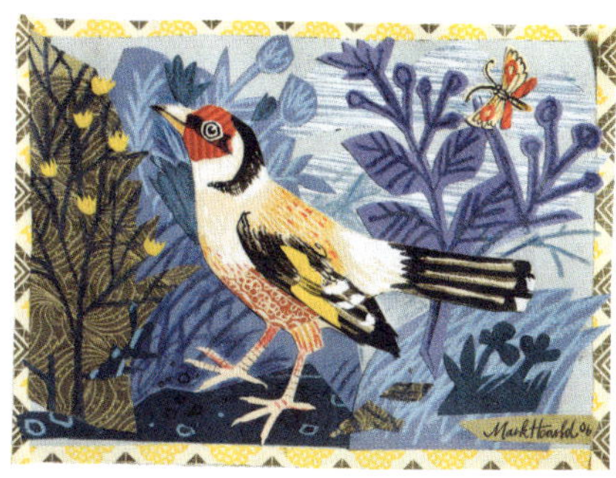

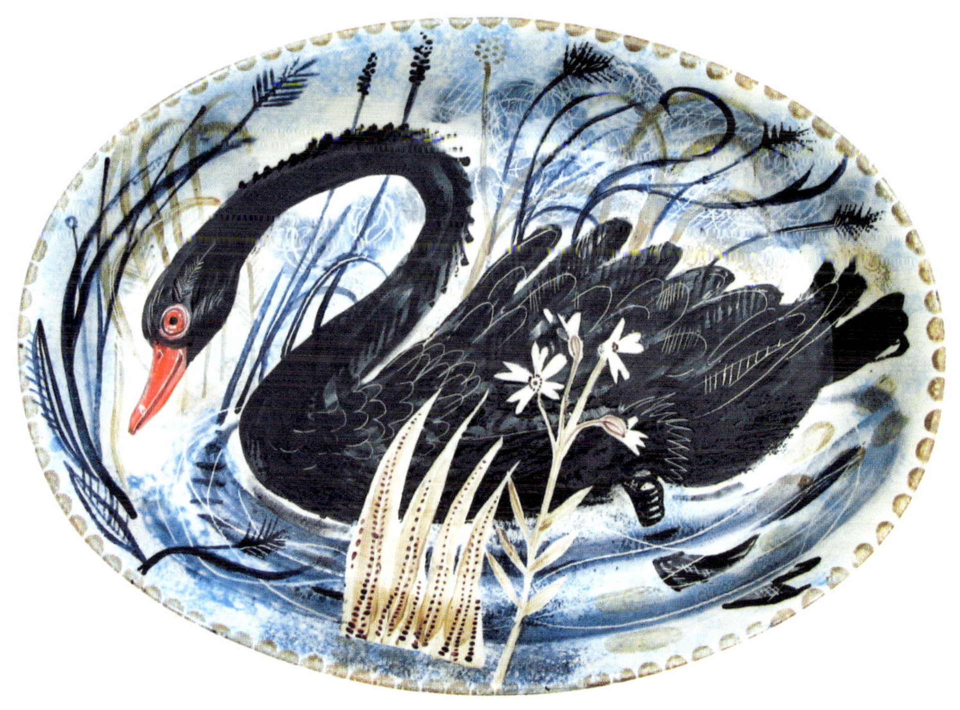

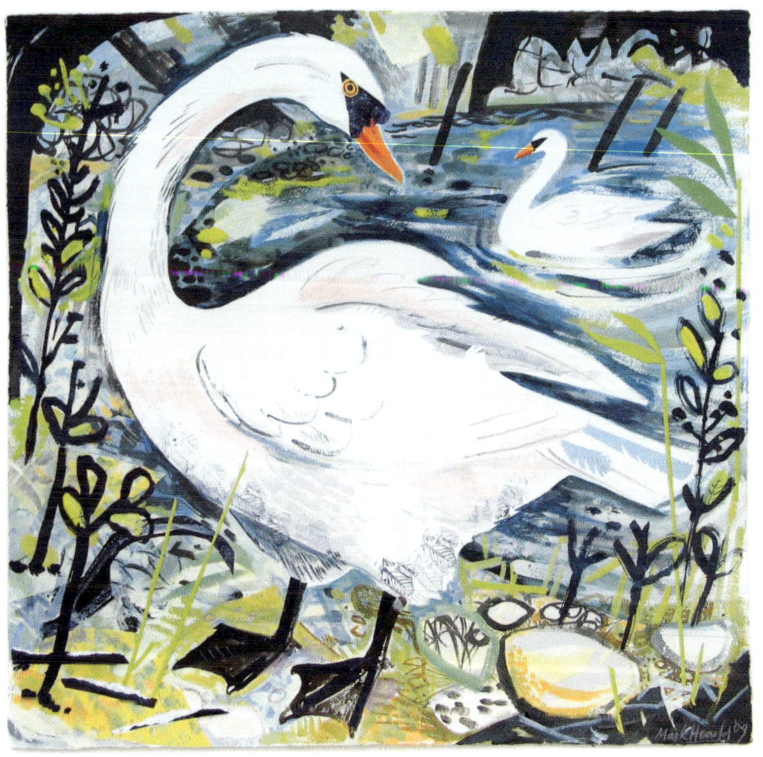

Black Swan Charger

The swan on this charger has a quality that reminds me of Arts and Crafts design. I admire very much the formalization that the potter William De Morgan gave to animals and birds. Each of his ceramics is a piece of design, but his creatures always keep a lively character.

Mute Swan

Mute swans are incredibly beautiful birds, graceful on the water but rather grandly ungainly on the riverbank.

Black Swan

For this collage, made outside
on the banks of the mill race at
Buttercrambe, North Yorkshire,
I used a piece of Curwen Press
endpaper designed by Sarah
Nechamkin in the 1940s. I don't
think I'd be quite so cavalier today.

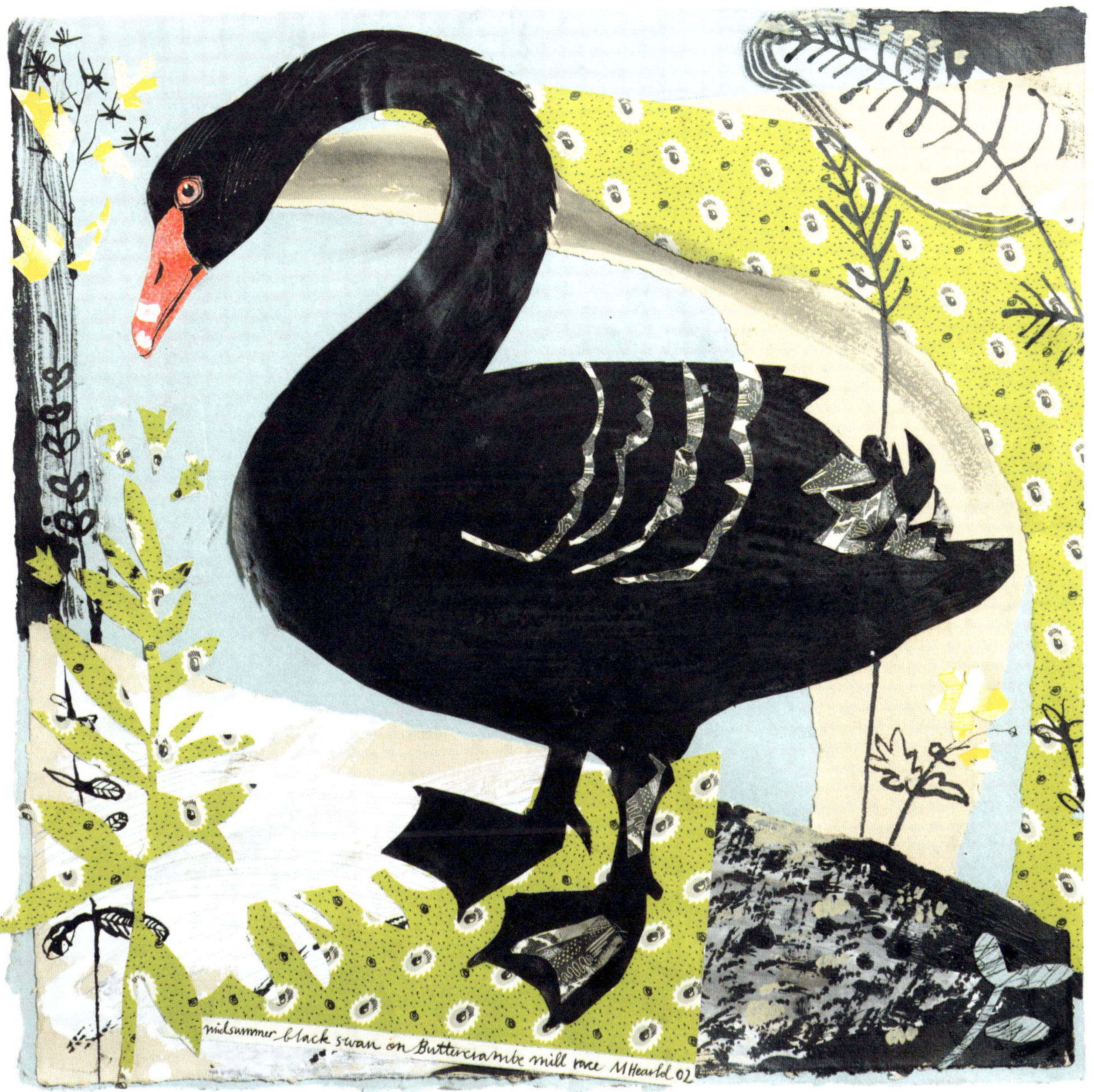

Over the Rooftops

It is well known that I have a soft
spot for the pigeon – a maligned,
beautiful bird that survives in
the heart of man's world. To see a
flock of variegated pigeons catching
the light as it shifts direction in
the sky lifts the soul. The very
ordinariness of pigeons on a rooftop
is easily overlooked, but I find their
presence a welcome reminder of
nature outside the window.

St Paul's Pigeons

This small collage, only A5 in
size, was used as the invitation for
the *St Jude's in the City* exhibition
of 2009 at the Bankside Gallery,
which is just across the Thames
from St Paul's. What could be more
appropriate than London pigeons
wheeling past the cathedral's dome?

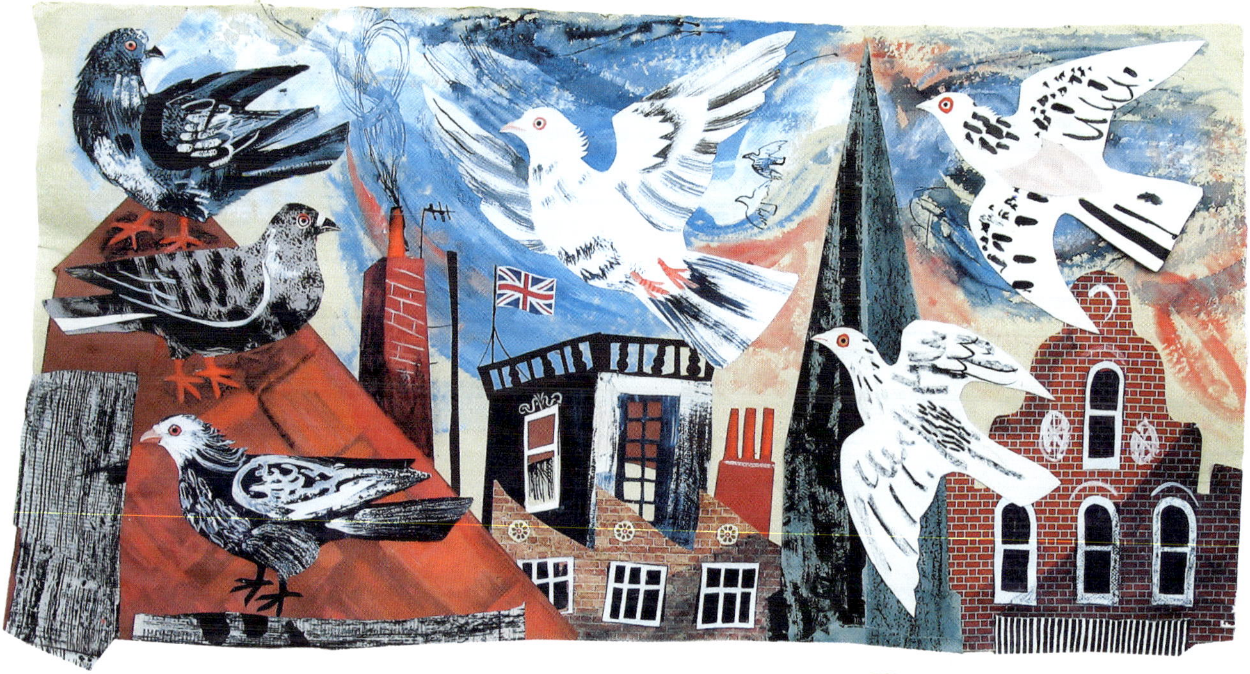

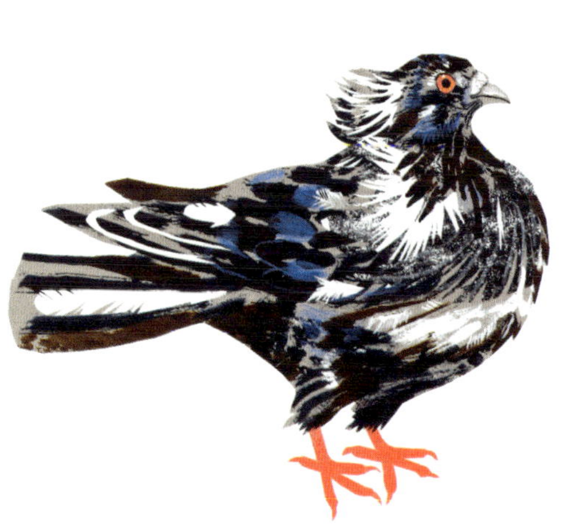

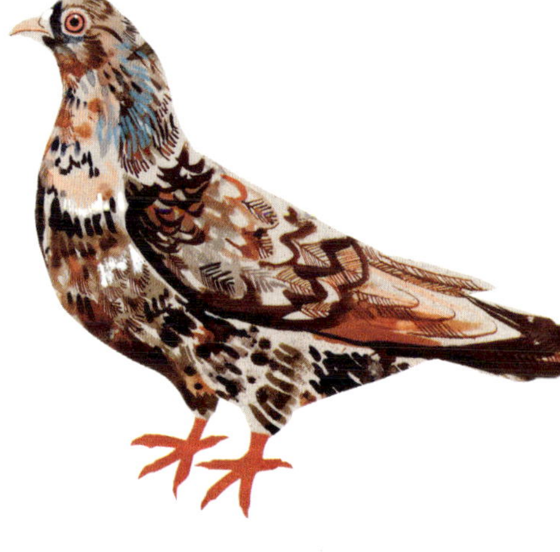

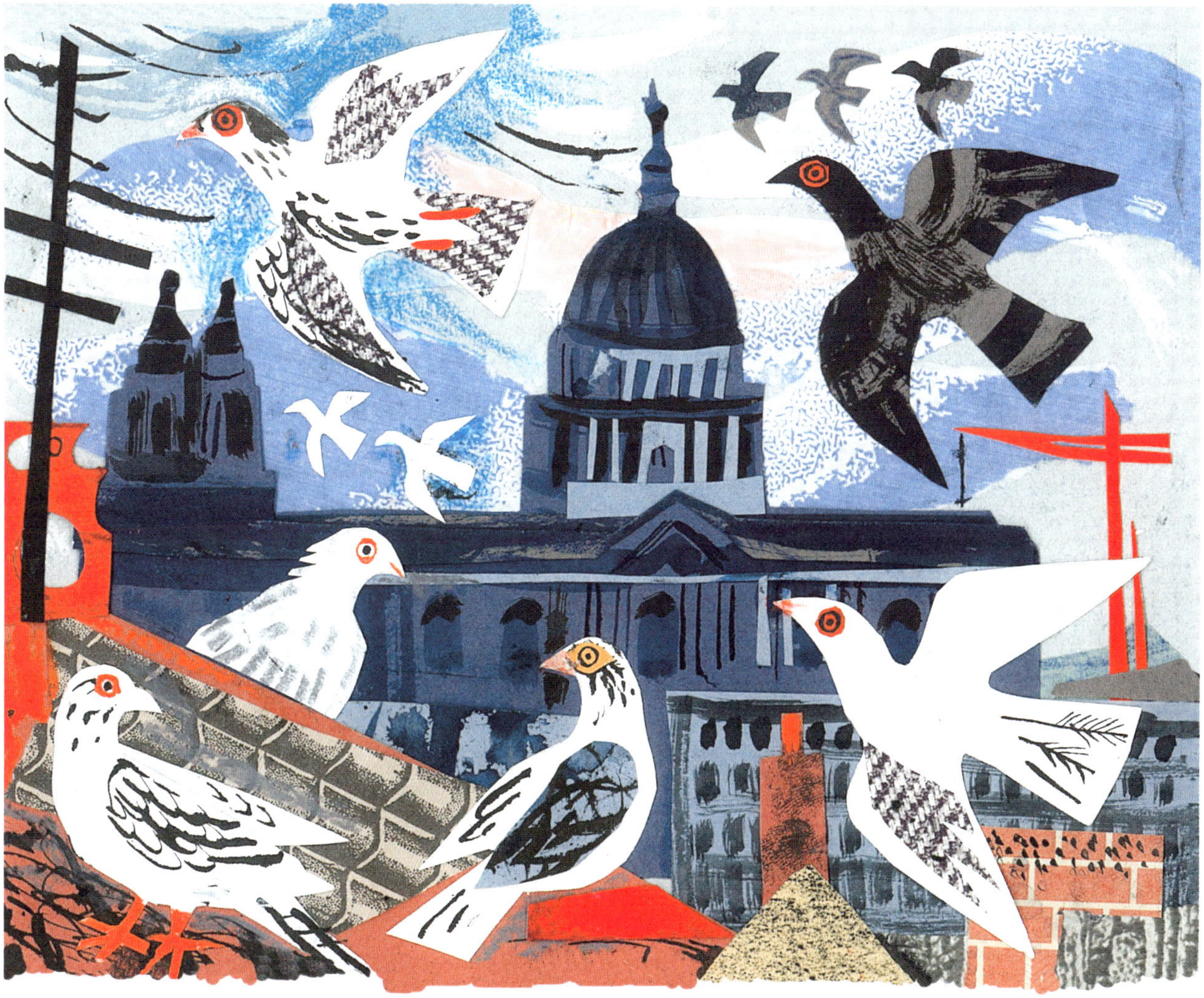

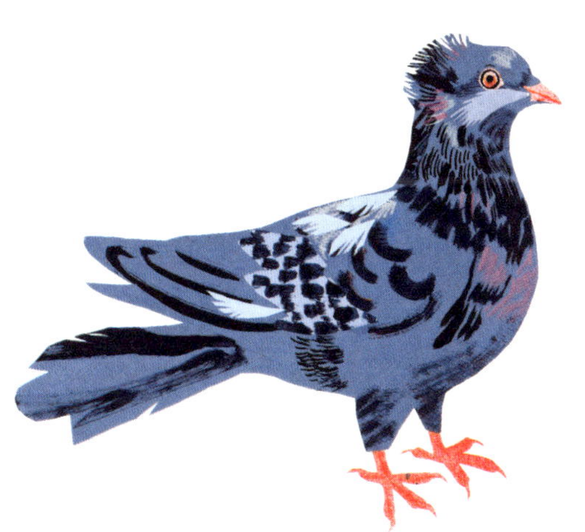
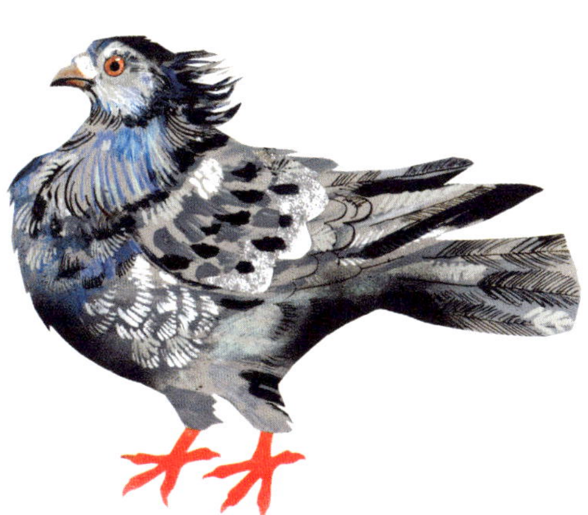

Starlings

A 'murmuration of starlings' is
a wonderful collective noun; the
bird itself, maligned by some, is
one of my favourites. Its spotted,
iridescent plumage and cheeky
antics are a delight to observe
in the heart of the city. An
ubiquitous creature, its numbers
are sadly diminishing.

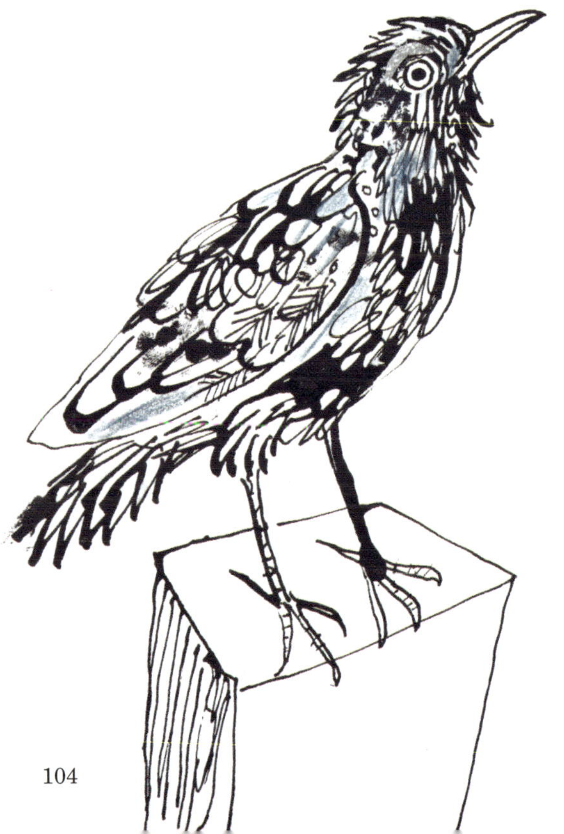

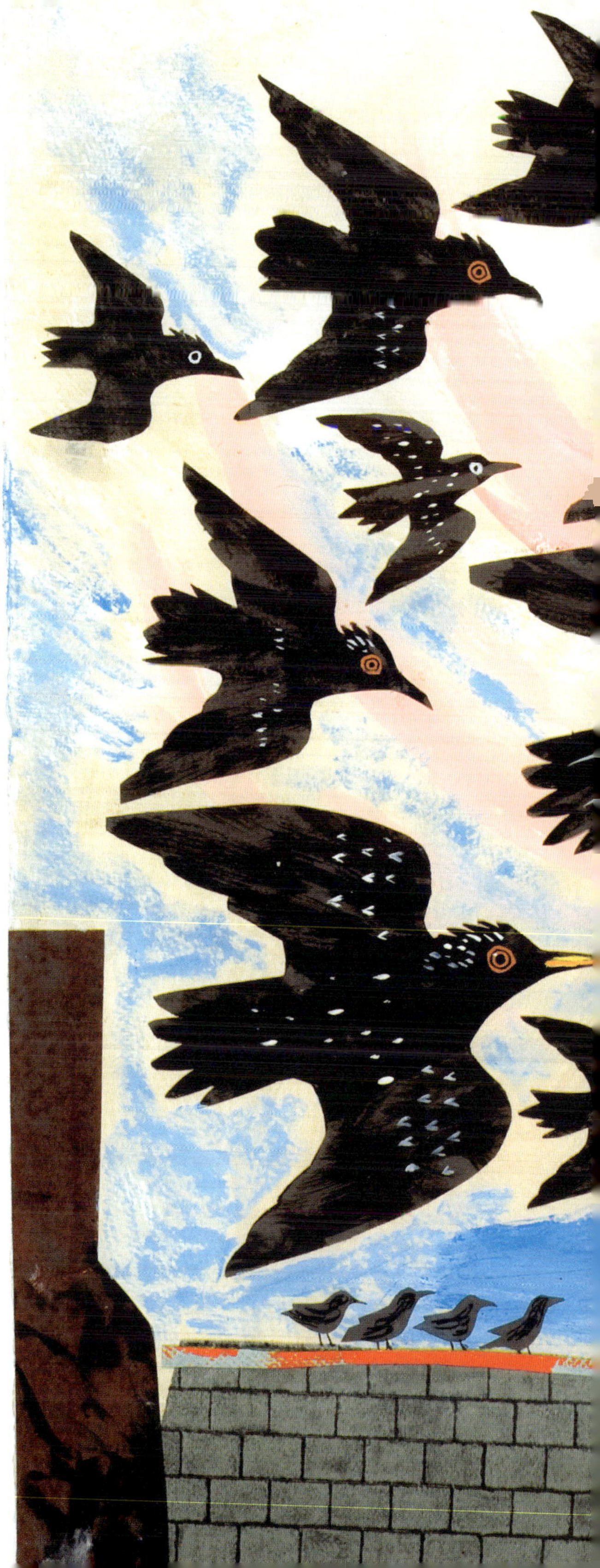

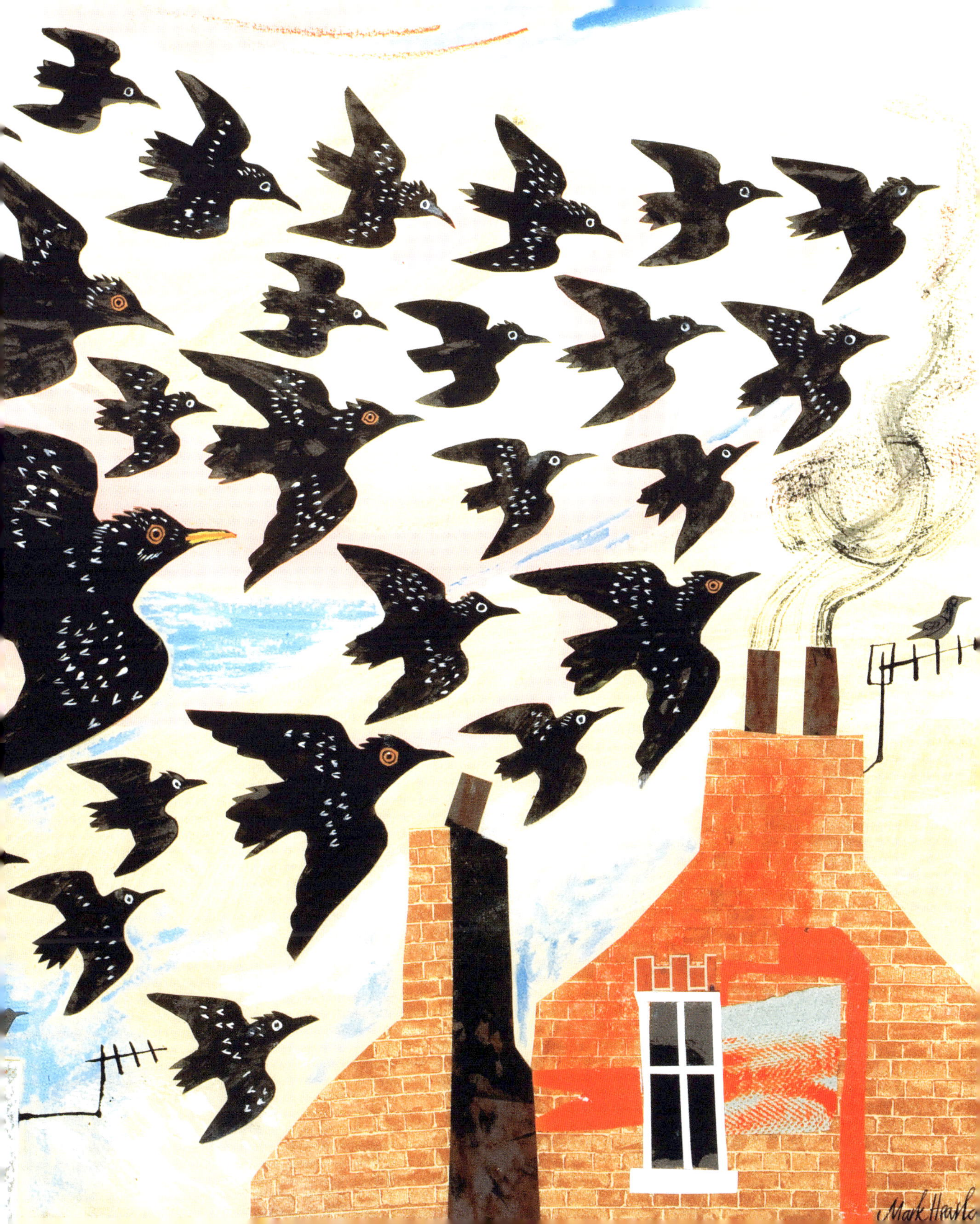

Mark Hearld

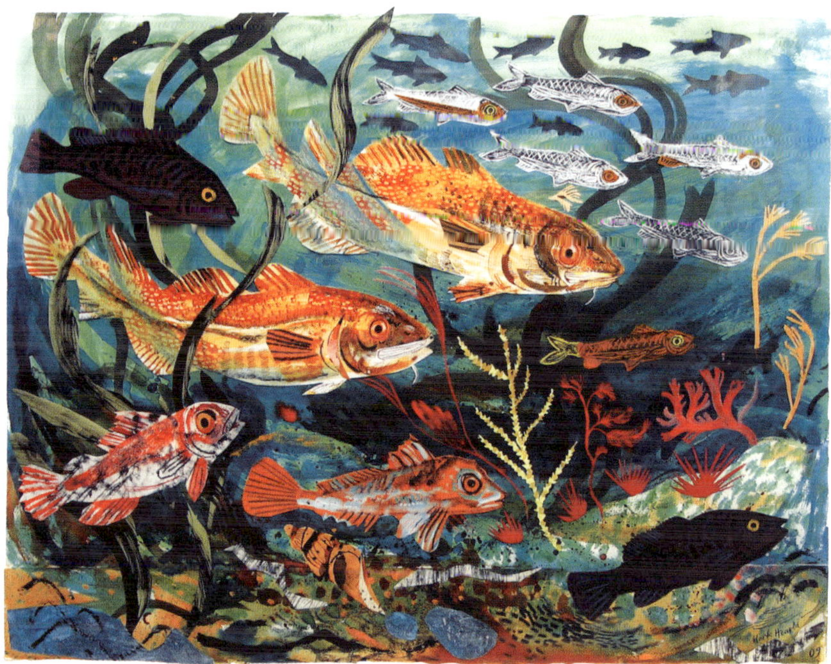

Marine Life (above) and Deep Sea (right)

I made *Marine Life* for *The Magpie Eye*, my exhibition at Scarborough Art Gallery (see page 14). At the same time, I came across the chromolithographic plates of sea creatures by the nineteenth-century zoologist Philip Gosse; one, entitled *The Ancient Wrasse* (1854; below), was particularly striking in colour and set the tone for my own image. I then had it in mind to explore the salty depths in further pieces, and finally got down to it with *Deep Sea*. There are many more to come.

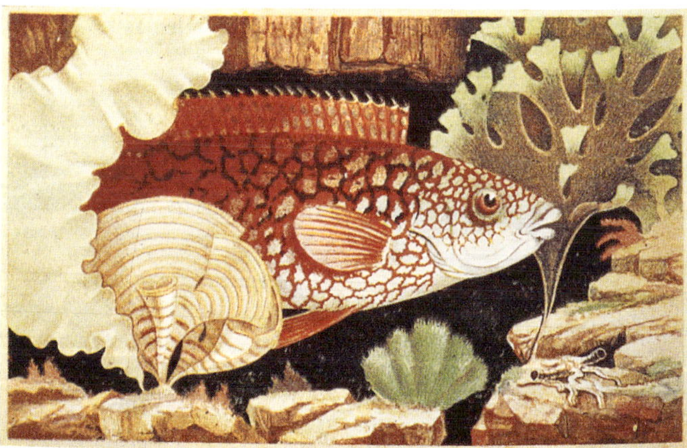

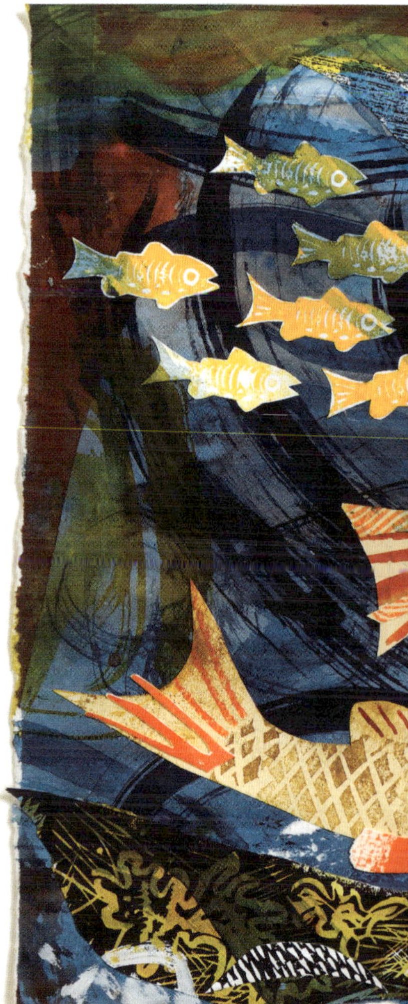

Marine Life

Making an image of the world under the sea feels playfully indulgent: it recalls the best aspects of art-and-craft afternoons at school, when we would work together on a display – somebody would make a crab, somebody else a starfish. Each time I depict fish underwater I revisit that childhood sense of wonder at the natural world. I begin by making a colour field in swirling blue and aqua; these colours then provide an excellent foil for the warm, patterned tones of the various fish.

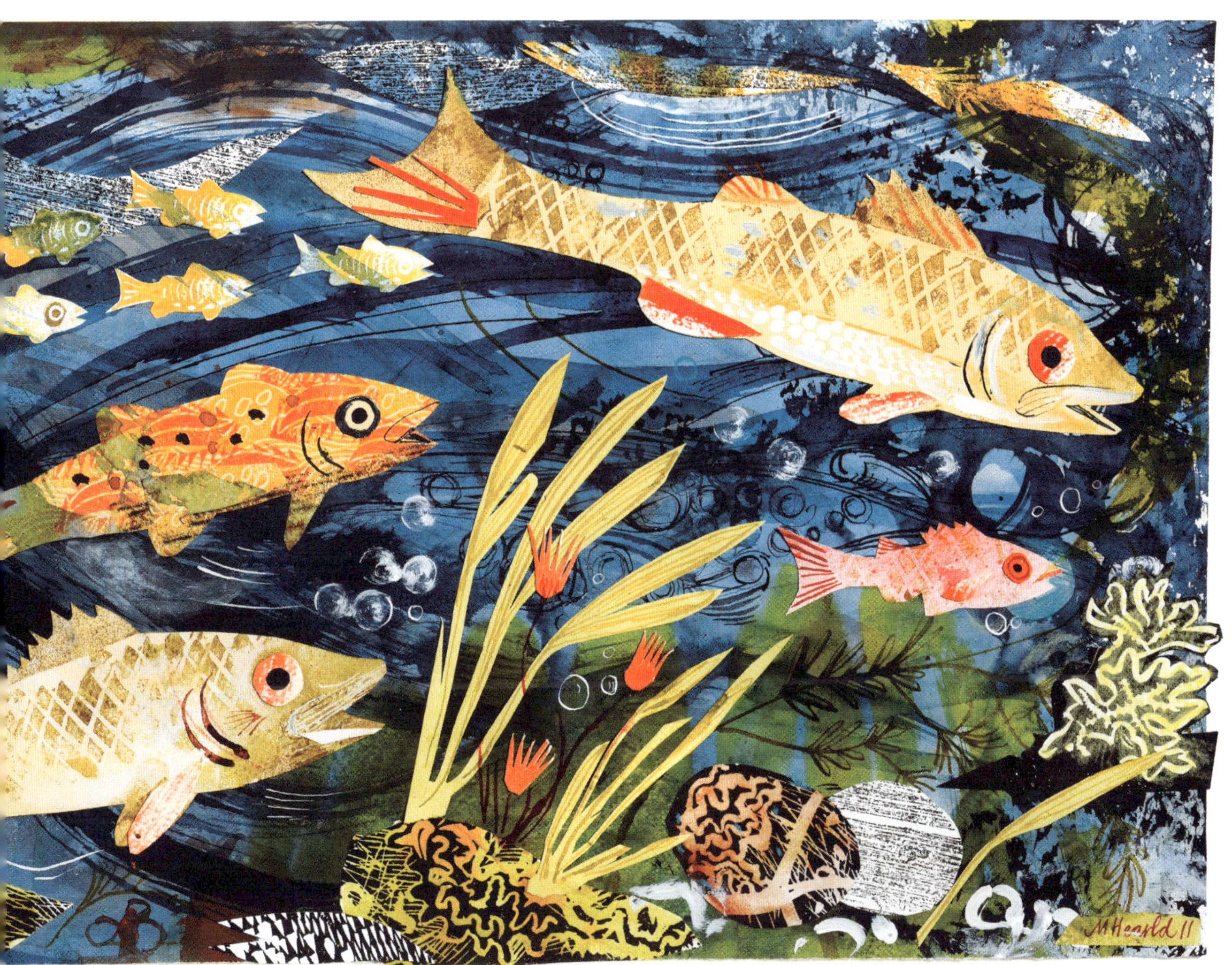

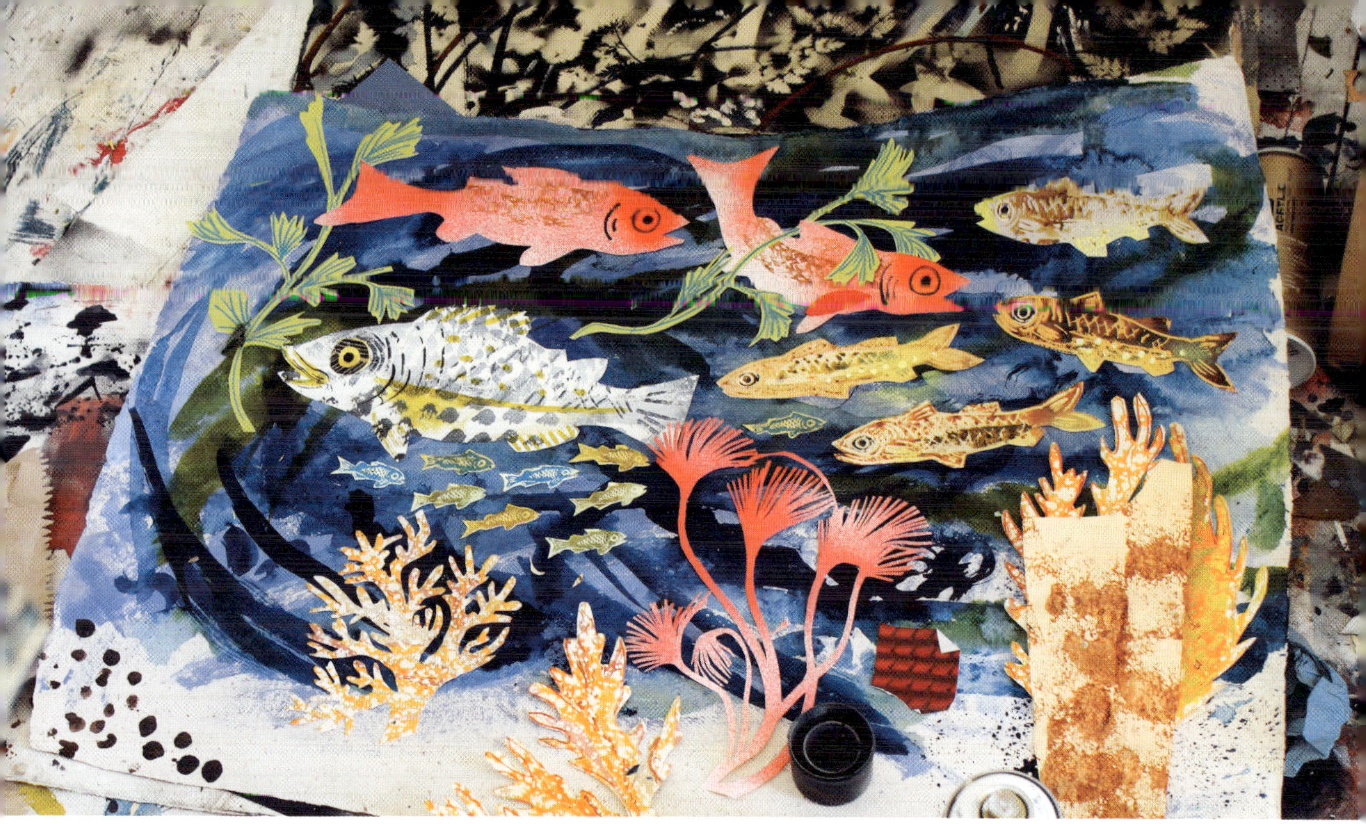

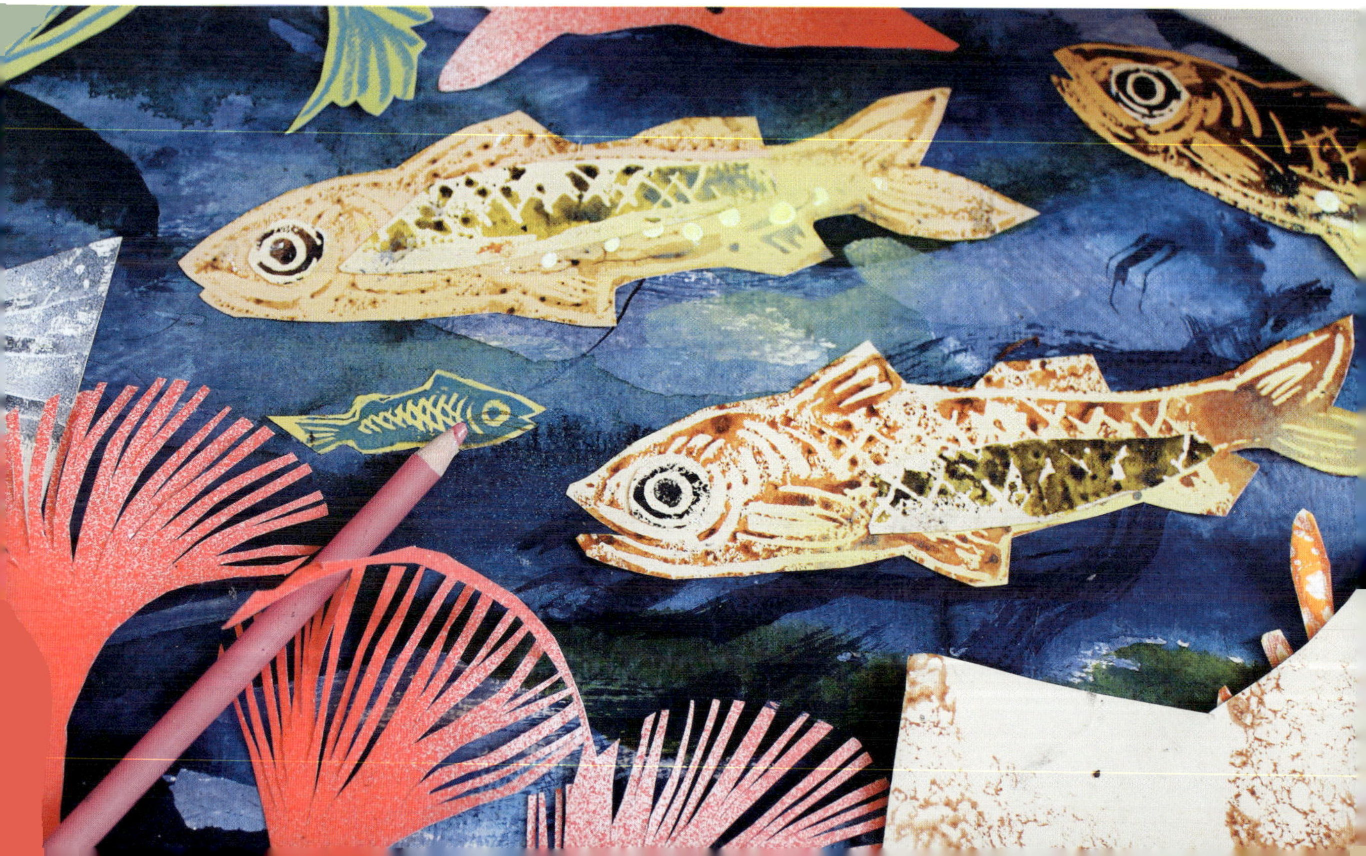

The Seabed

Despite my very best intentions,
I'm always left with about one
square foot of workspace on my
table. Large pieces, therefore, are
invariably made on the studio floor,
among the rich debris of collage
snippings – which are often picked
up and incorporated into the piece
of work on the go. Here, the coral
was cut out from a sheet of marbled
paper. Spray paints work well
to decrease definition and sit an
element firmly in the background.
The floor is accruing a spray-paint
patina of its own.

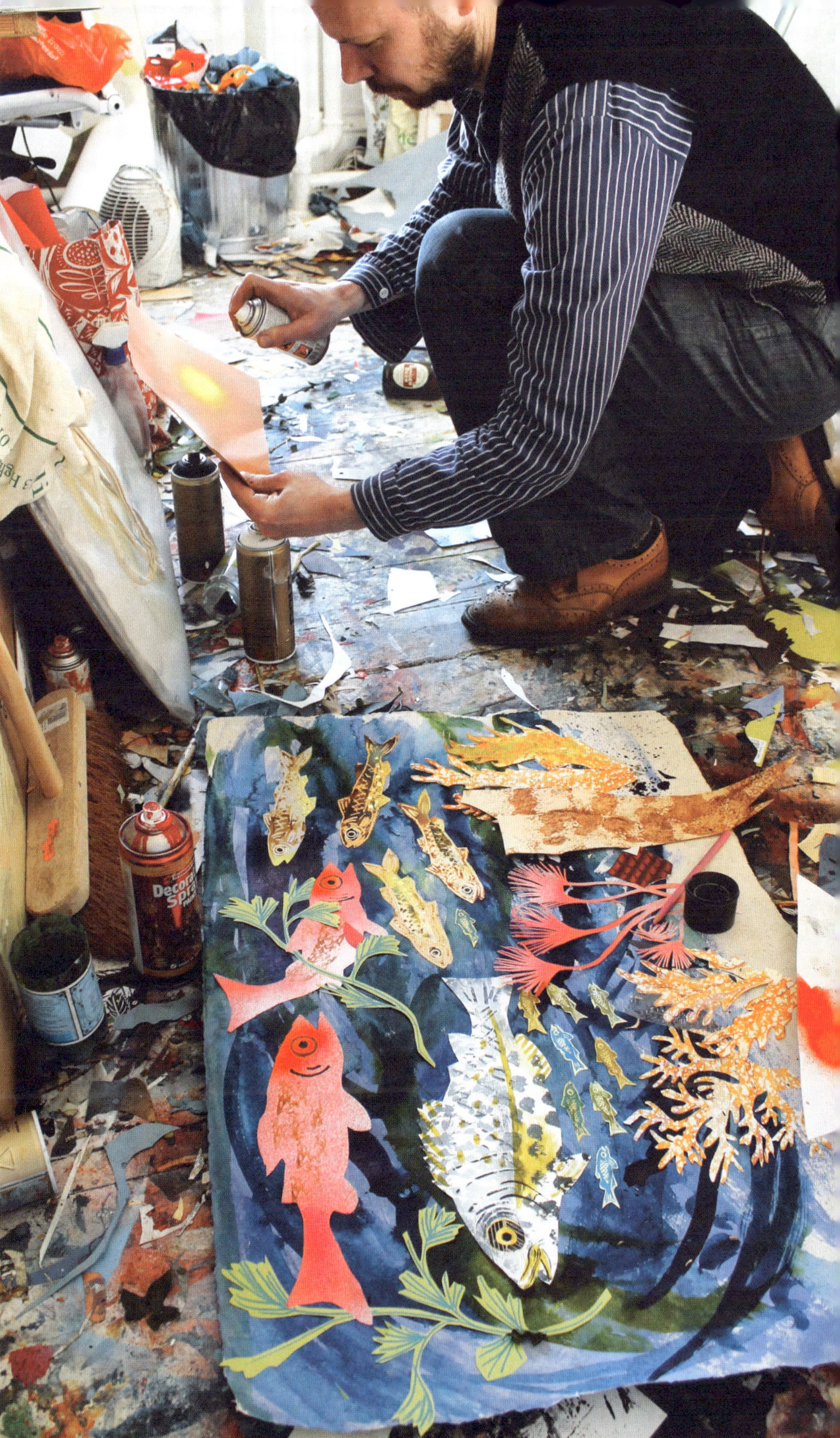

Fish Box (below)

With this piece, I was
interested in the abstraction
and compartmentalization
provided by the irregular format
of a cardboard envelope. Its shape
contains and frames the six fish
in a particularly satisfying way

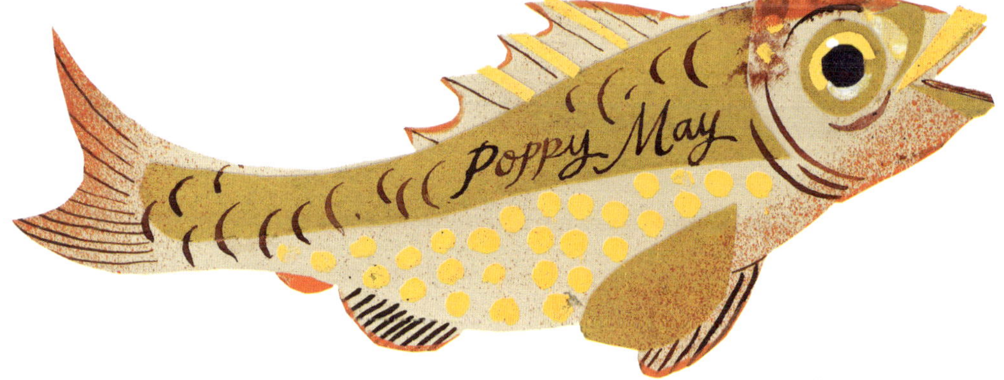

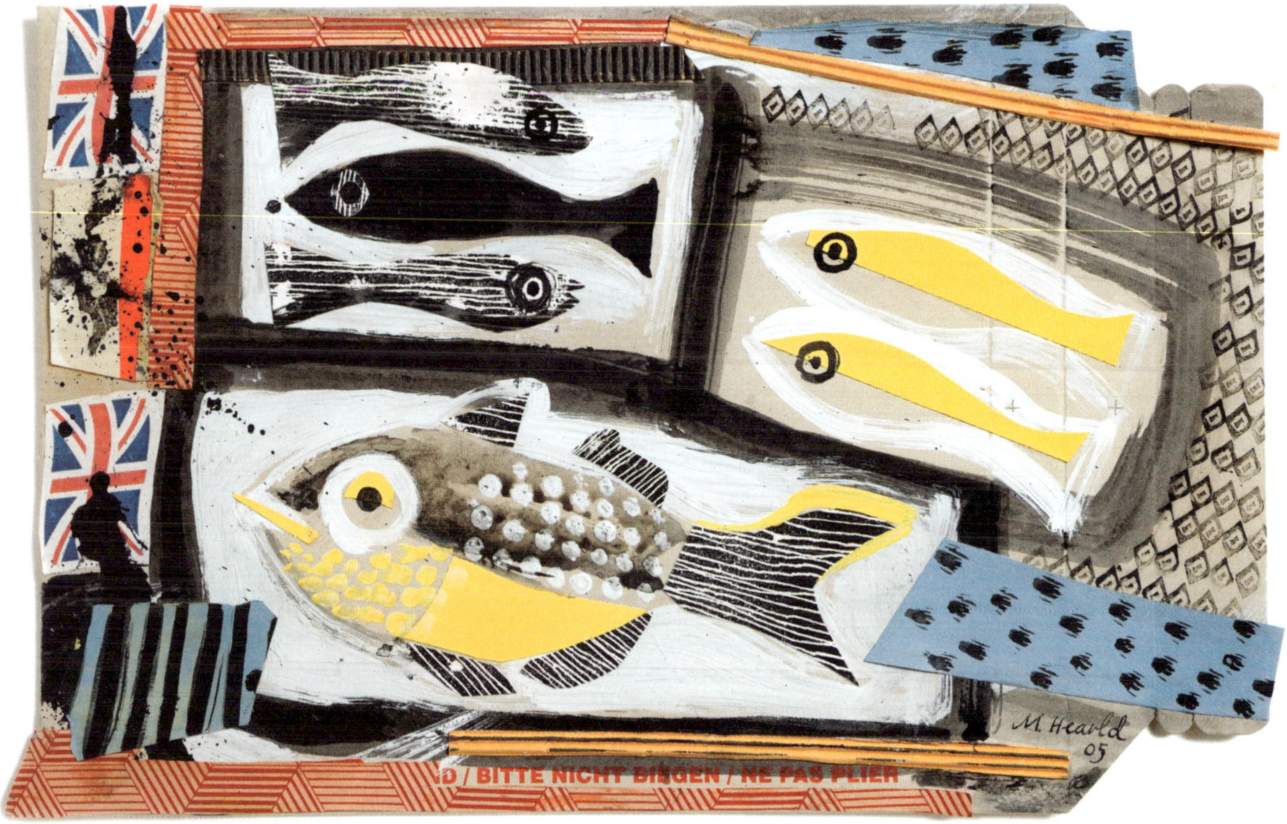

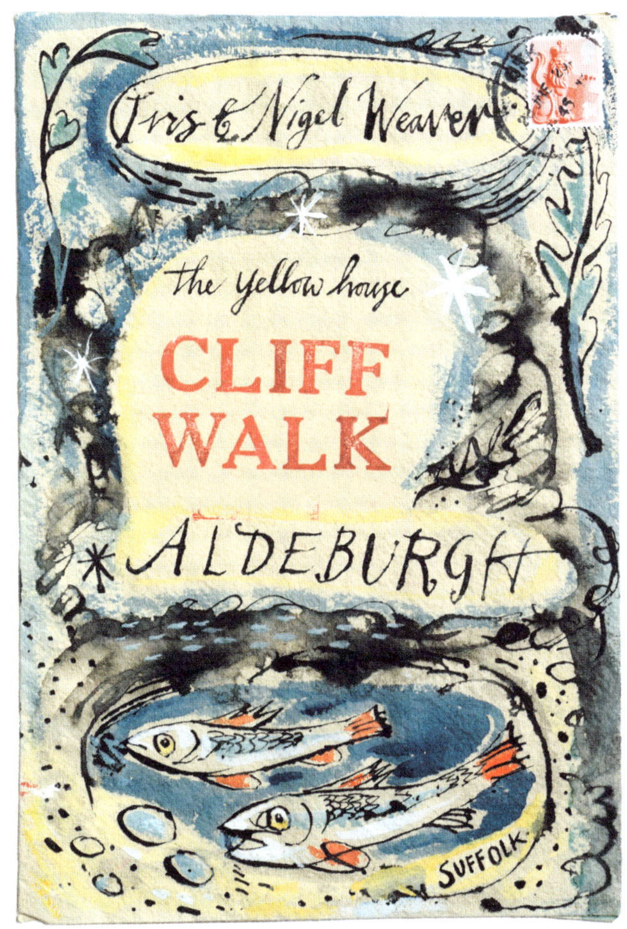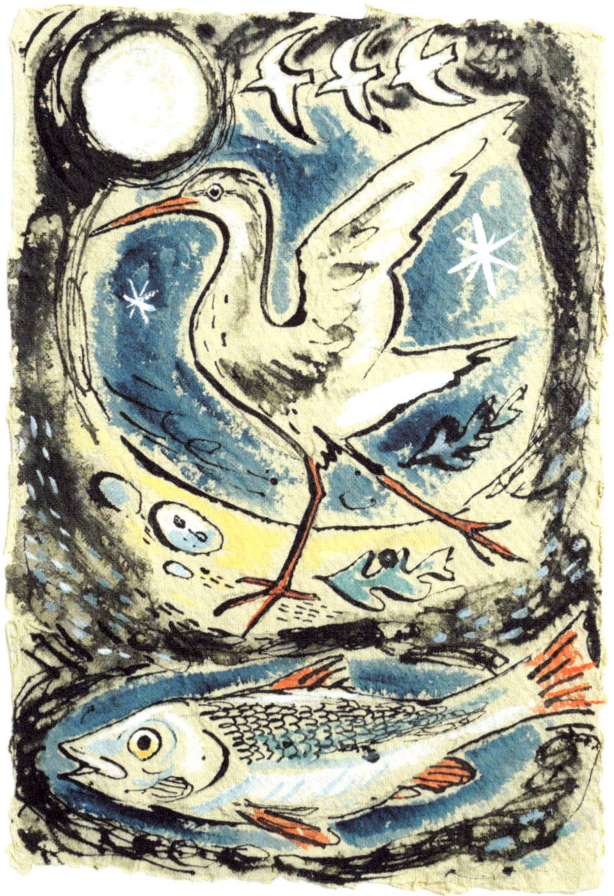

Wader and Fish (above)

In 2004, for Iris Weaver's summer exhibition in Aldeburgh, Suffolk, I created a large ink drawing titled *Waders and Fish*, which she particularly admired. It sold, so by means of a 'thank you', I posted her this miniature version in a drawn and stamped envelope.

Collaged Fish (right and opposite, top)

Venice

A holiday with Nigel and Iris Weaver, Chloë Cheese, Colin Wilkin and Emily in the most beautiful city in the world had all the ingredients for a creative experience. Little did I know that the discarded pages of a 1920s Italian fascist manifesto, discovered by Chloë beside a canal, would make the perfect visual equivalent for the stones of Venice. Initially, I was intimidated by both the beauty and the complexity of the architecture, but after a few days spent acclimatizing I felt brave enough to attempt some work. The pigeons in *Venetian Fantasy* (right) are made from some hand-pasted 1940s bookbinding paper that I found on a forgotten shelf in a paper shop. Often, a particular material provides the inspiration for an image.

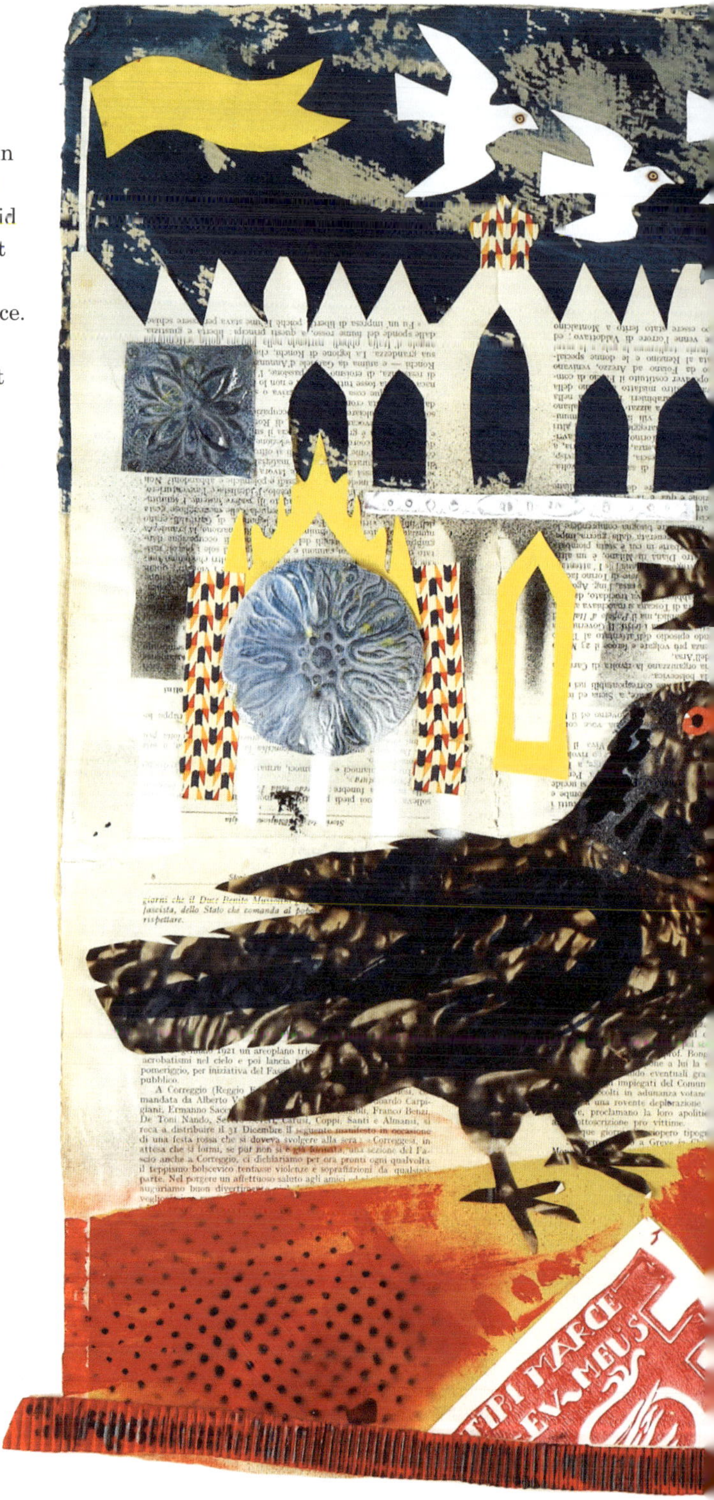

Venetian Fantasy

Begun in Venice, this collage was resolved in the studio, where roundels from an embossed wallpaper found their place as rose windows, and endpapers designed by Margaret Calkin James worked well as decorated pilasters. Doilies articulate the detailed carving above ogee windows, yellow flags flutter and a flight of white pigeons brings the scene to life.

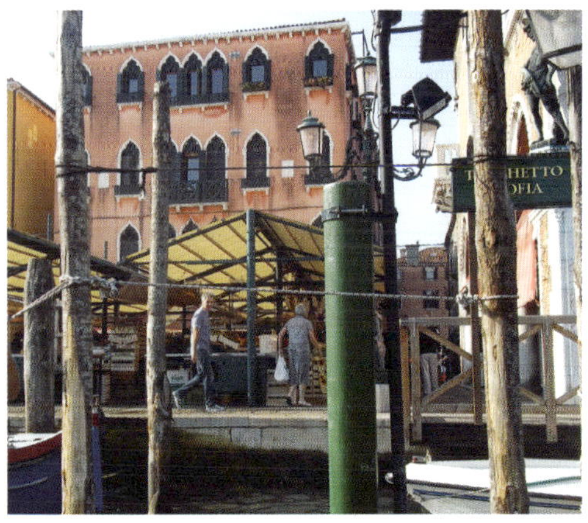

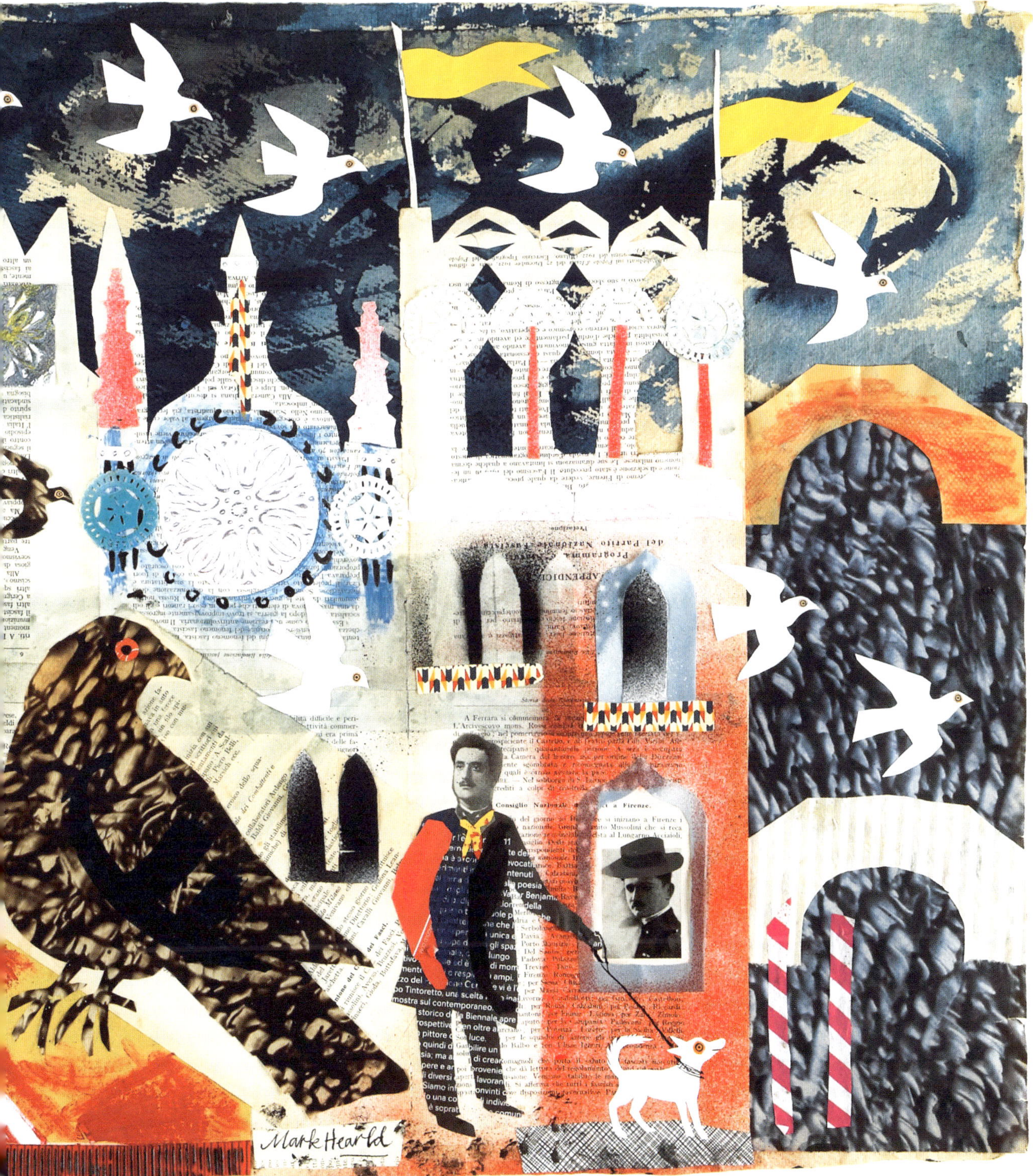
Mark Hearld

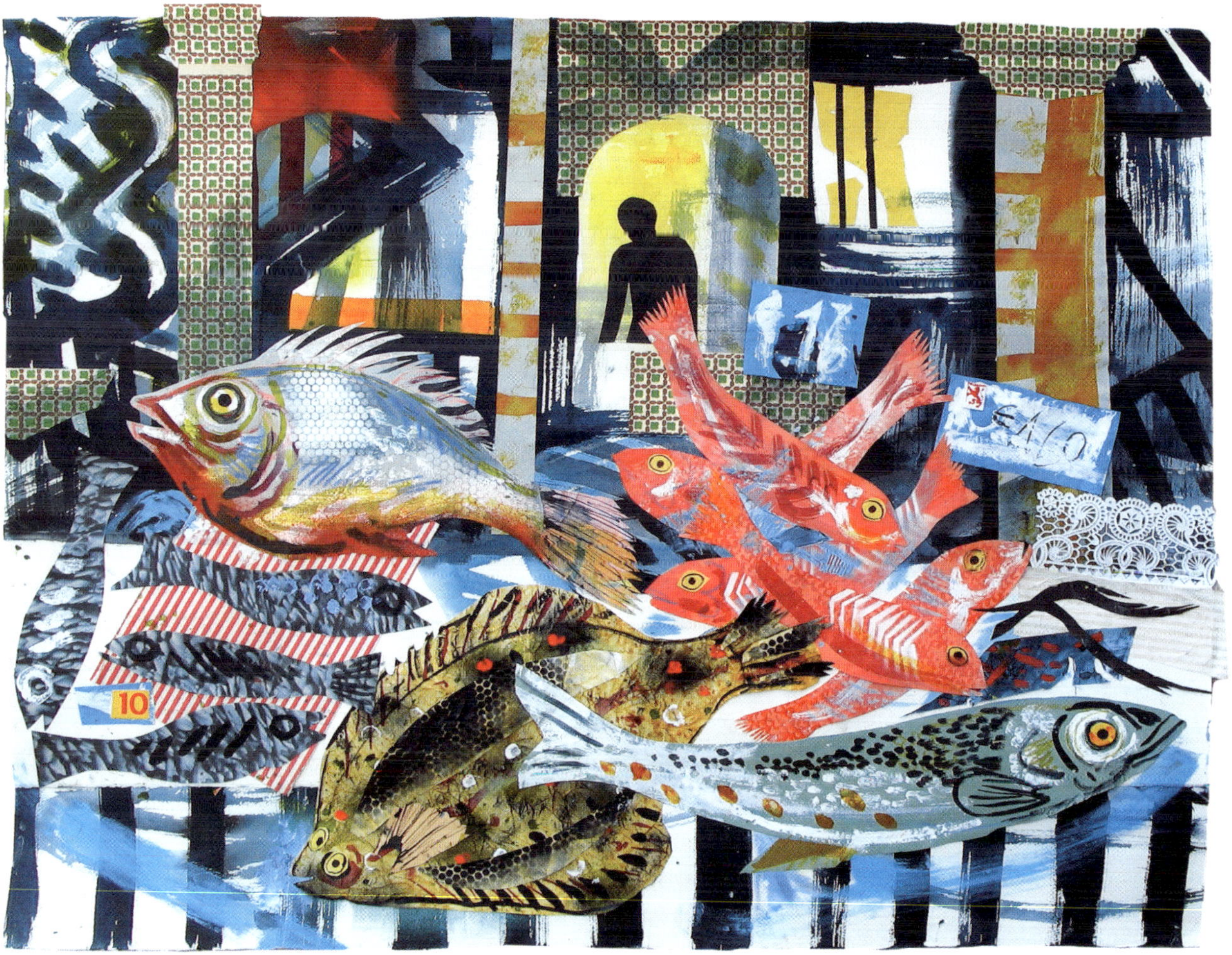

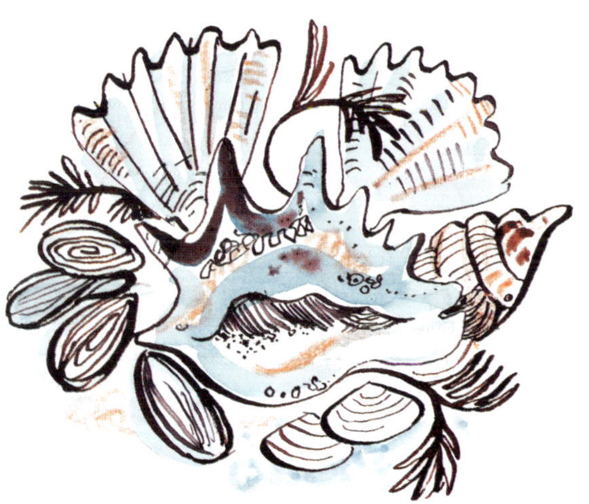

Venice Fish Market

When I visited the fish market in Venice each morning to buy food for the evening meal, I was reminded of the wonderfully descriptive passages about the market in an essay by Elizabeth David. I was also fascinated by the spectacle of the scene, the incredible displays of fish and the elegant Venetians striking a deal or sipping a macchiato in a neighbouring cafe. Each stall is like a seventeenth-century still-life: the sheer abundance and variety are a feast for the eyes.

The ritual of ordinary life in Venice is very appealing; shopping for a selection of fragrant grapes and a bag full of wild mushrooms, followed by coffee and people-watching, was a daily treat. All the characters in the Venetian collages with walk-on roles were taken from the pages of the found manifesto.

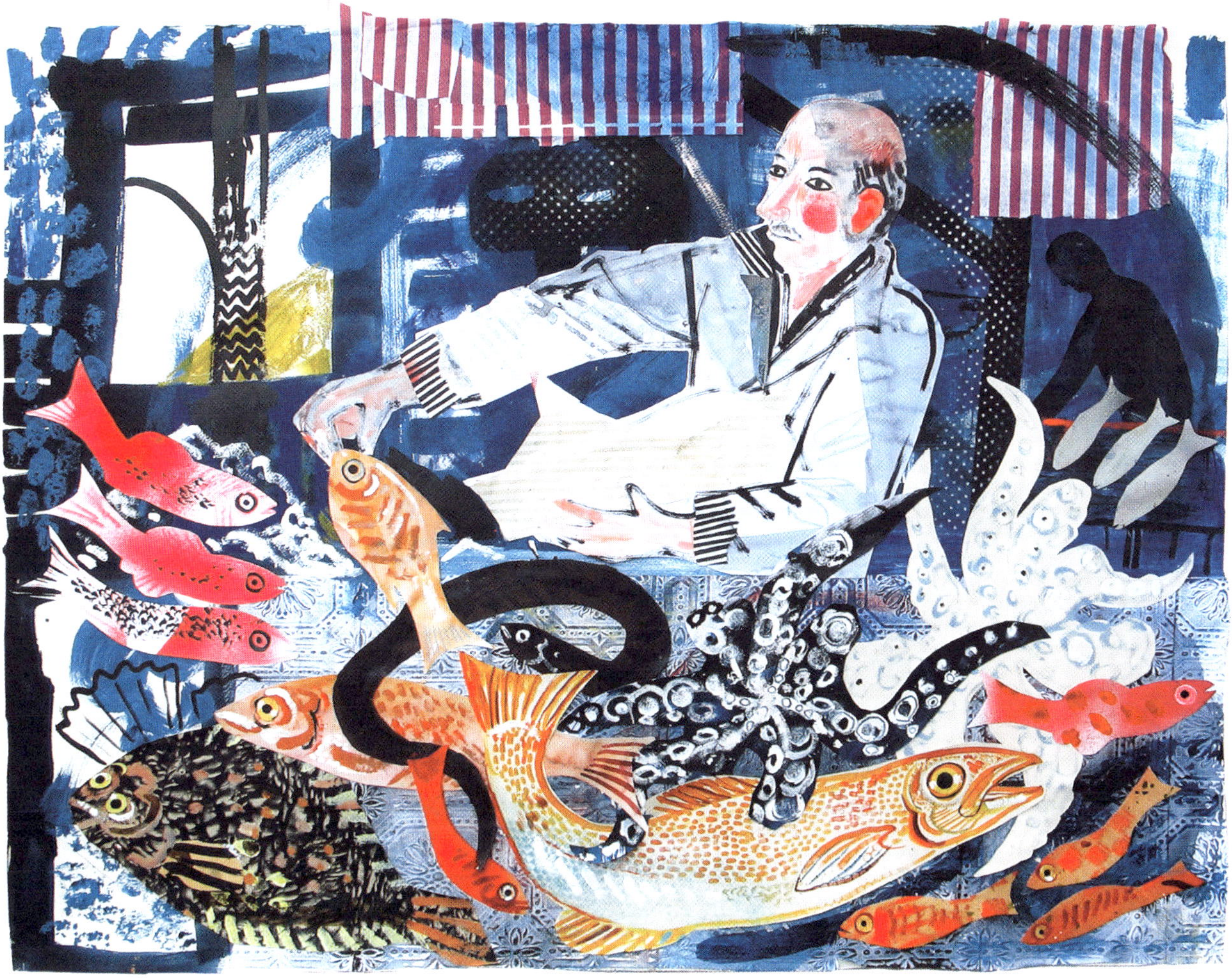

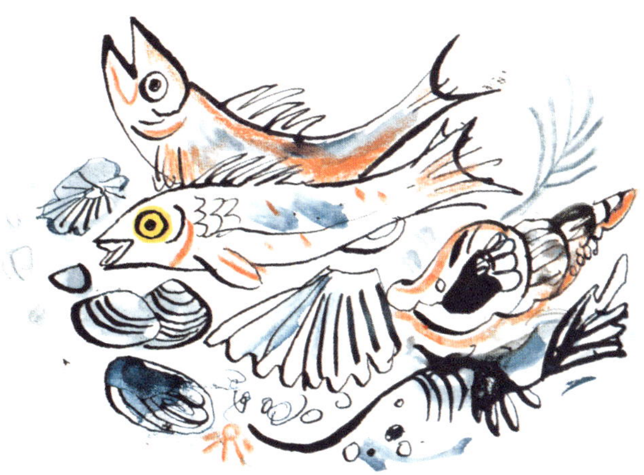

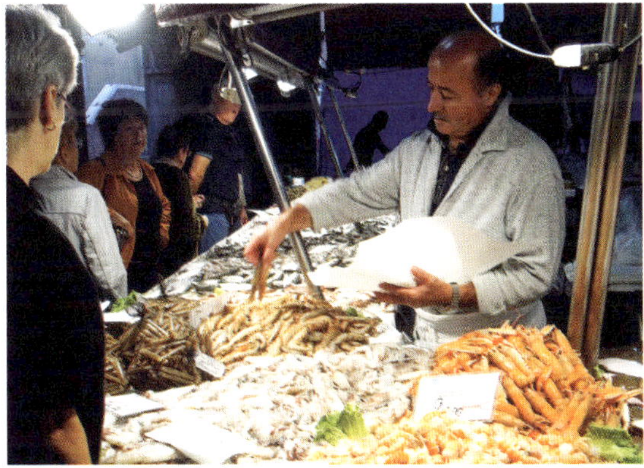

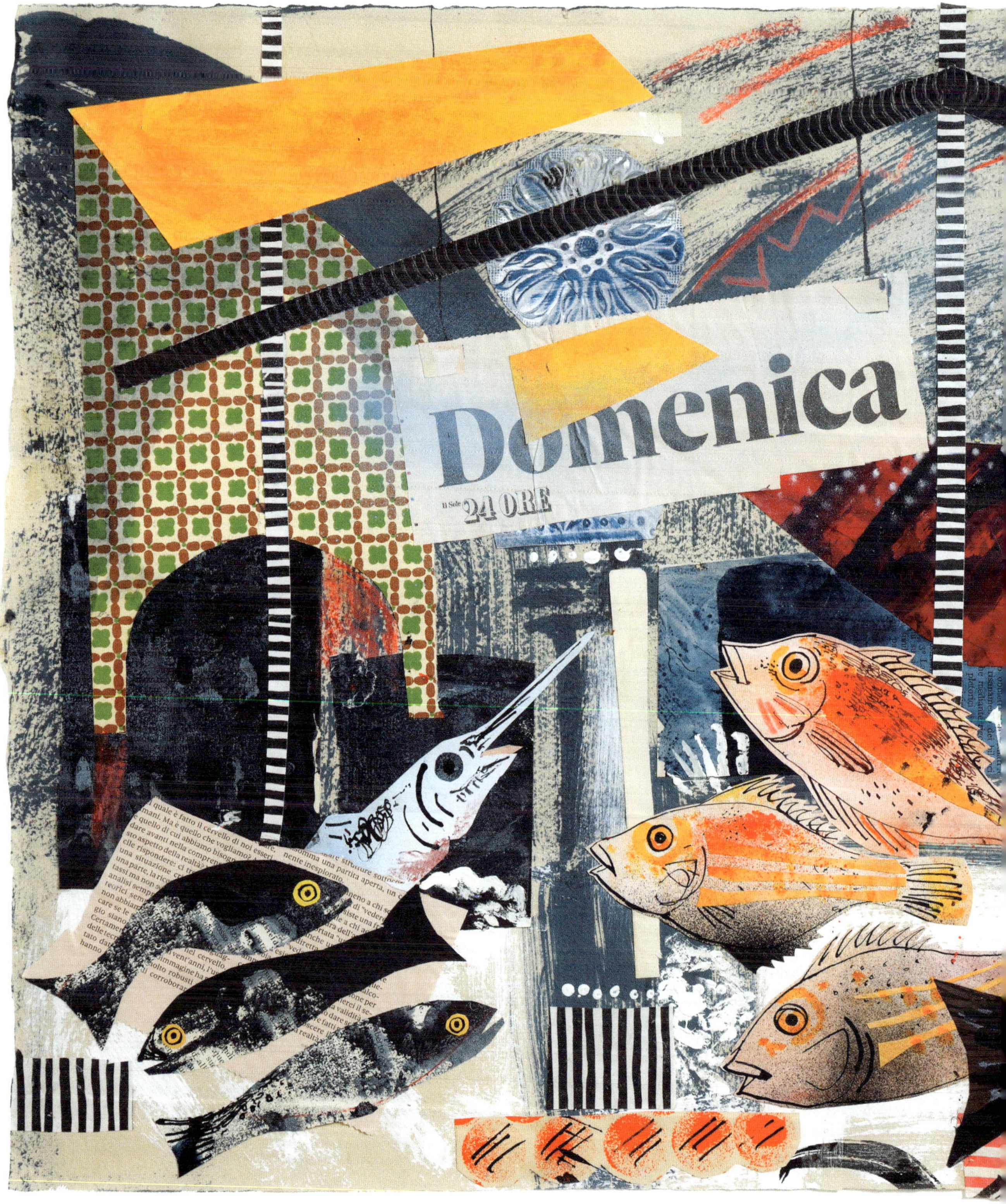

Domenica
Il Sole 24 ORE

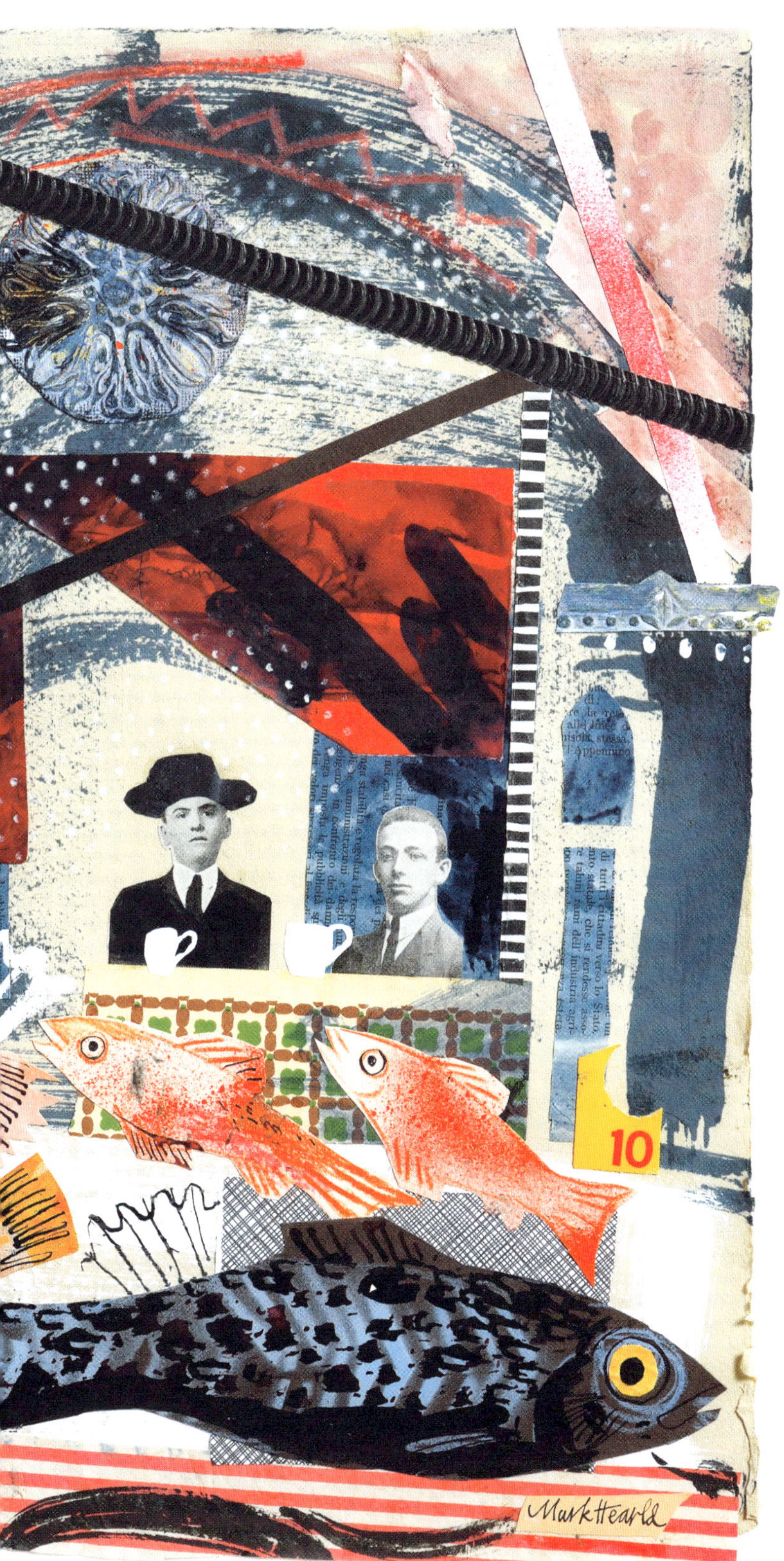

Domenica

I'm fairly certain that 'Domenica'
is the Italian for 'Sunday'; whether
or not there is a fish market on
a Sunday in Venice is immaterial.
What the image required was the
graphic abstract quality provided
by the bold lettering suspended
above the abundant pescatorial
offerings. A tiled wall is made
from Florentine patterned paper
bought in a forgotten bookbinder's
down an alley. A man under a
slightly absurd hat drinks coffee
with his companion; both men
were snipped out of the fascist
manifesto. Picasso said something
like: 'All the art is on the floor.' The
discarded remnants of one collage
are the starting point for the next.

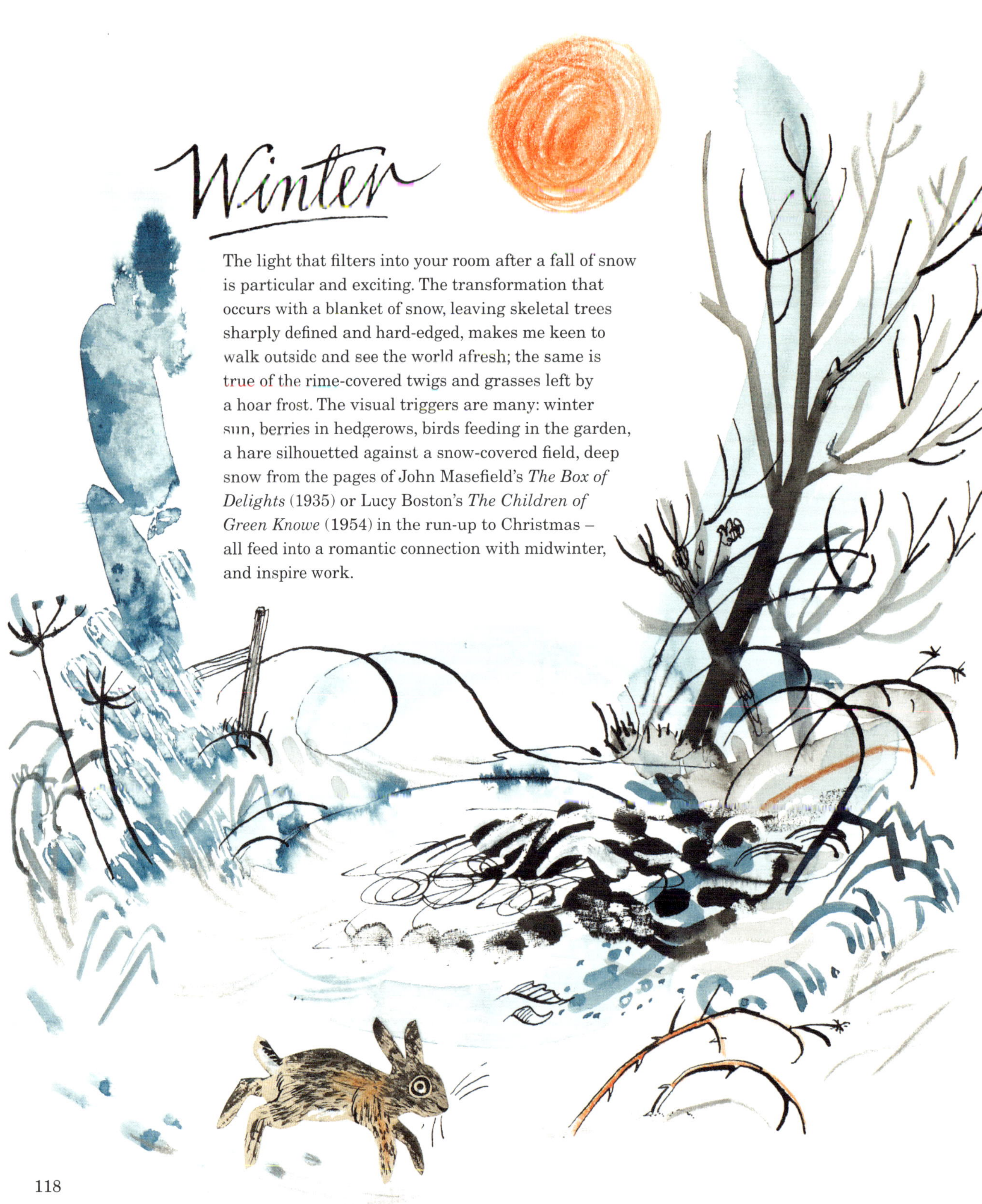

Winter

The light that filters into your room after a fall of snow is particular and exciting. The transformation that occurs with a blanket of snow, leaving skeletal trees sharply defined and hard-edged, makes me keen to walk outside and see the world afresh; the same is true of the rime-covered twigs and grasses left by a hoar frost. The visual triggers are many: winter sun, berries in hedgerows, birds feeding in the garden, a hare silhouetted against a snow-covered field, deep snow from the pages of John Masefield's *The Box of Delights* (1935) or Lucy Boston's *The Children of Green Knowe* (1954) in the run-up to Christmas – all feed into a romantic connection with midwinter, and inspire work.

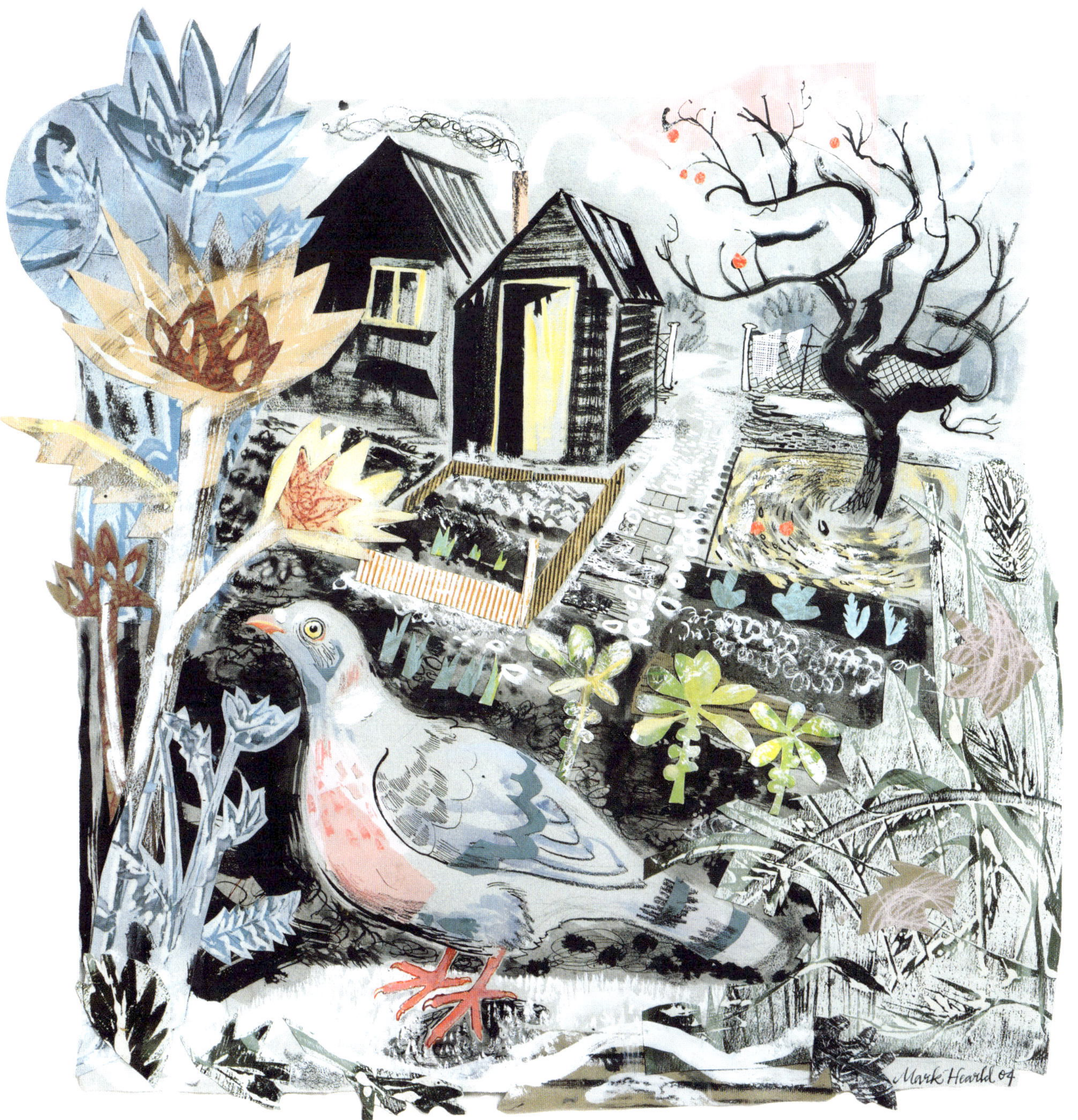

Wood Pigeon

Commissioned by neighbours in Heslington, this collage features a wood pigeon and a crop of Brussels sprouts. My neighbours were well aware, however, that the two don't always mix.

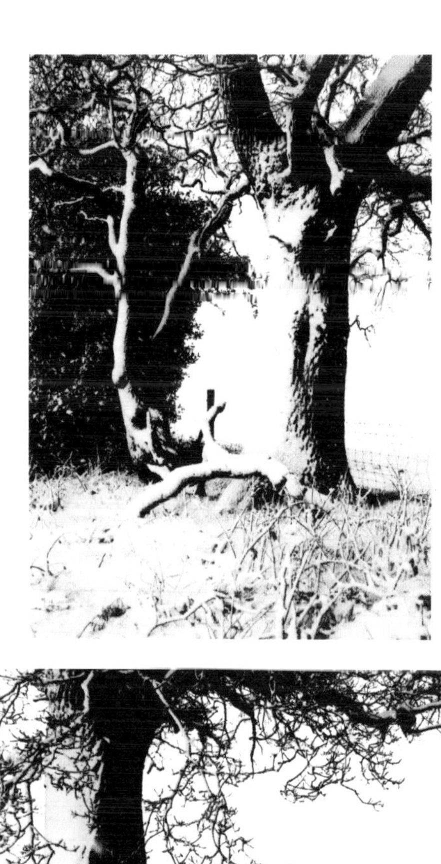

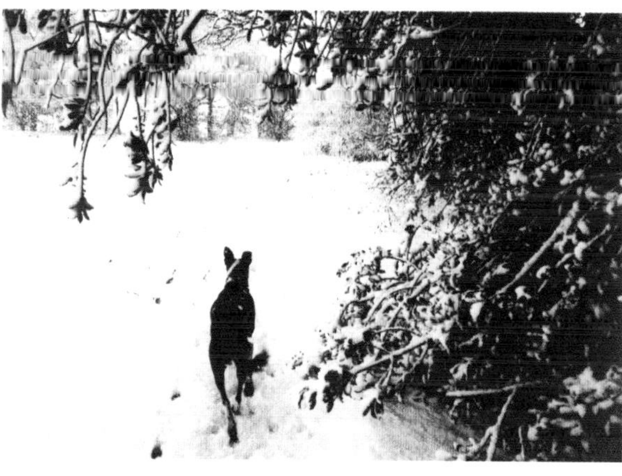

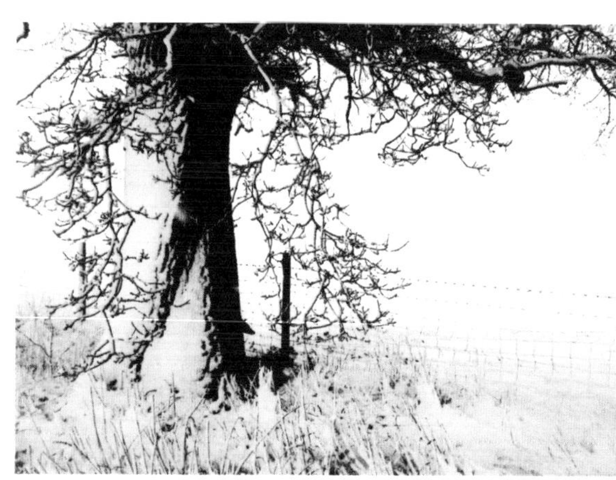

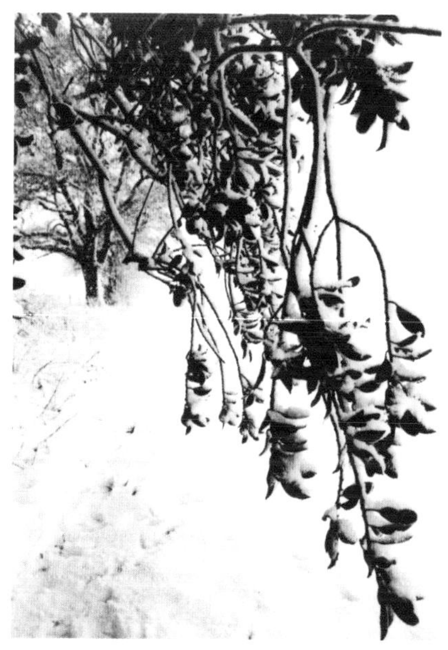

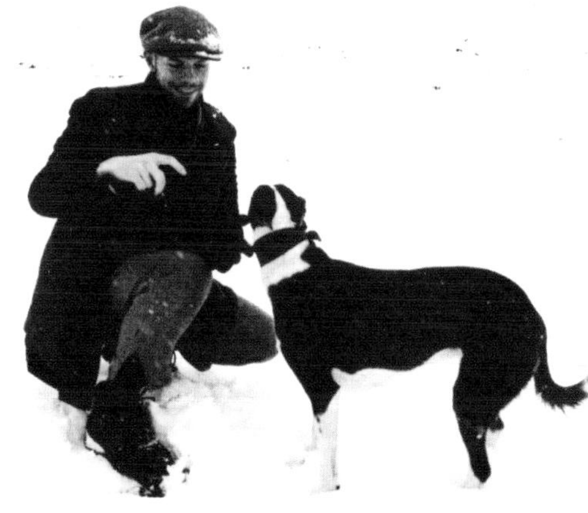

A set of photographs taken on a snowy morning in February 2005 during a walk with the dogs around Heslington.

The First Snow of Winter

On a walk in the snow, my parents'
whippet caught a hare that had
obviously been weakened by the
cold. It was upsetting, but, as a
tribute to the hare and the beauty
of the winter landscape, I decided to
make this lithograph. It uses some
photographic imagery (see right)
for the texture of the snow-covered
stubble and the winter branches, as
well as a range of drawn marks in
lithographic crayon.

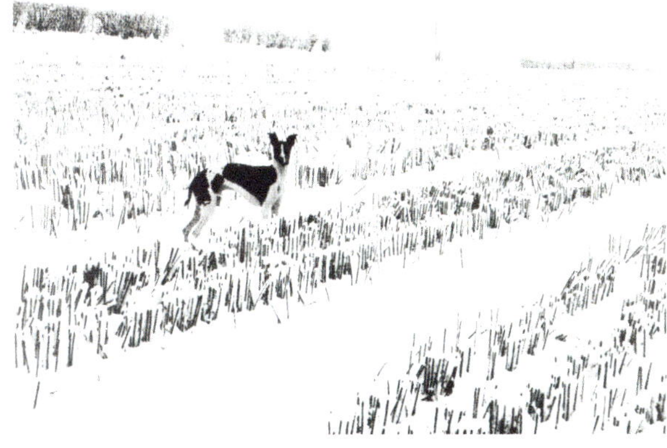

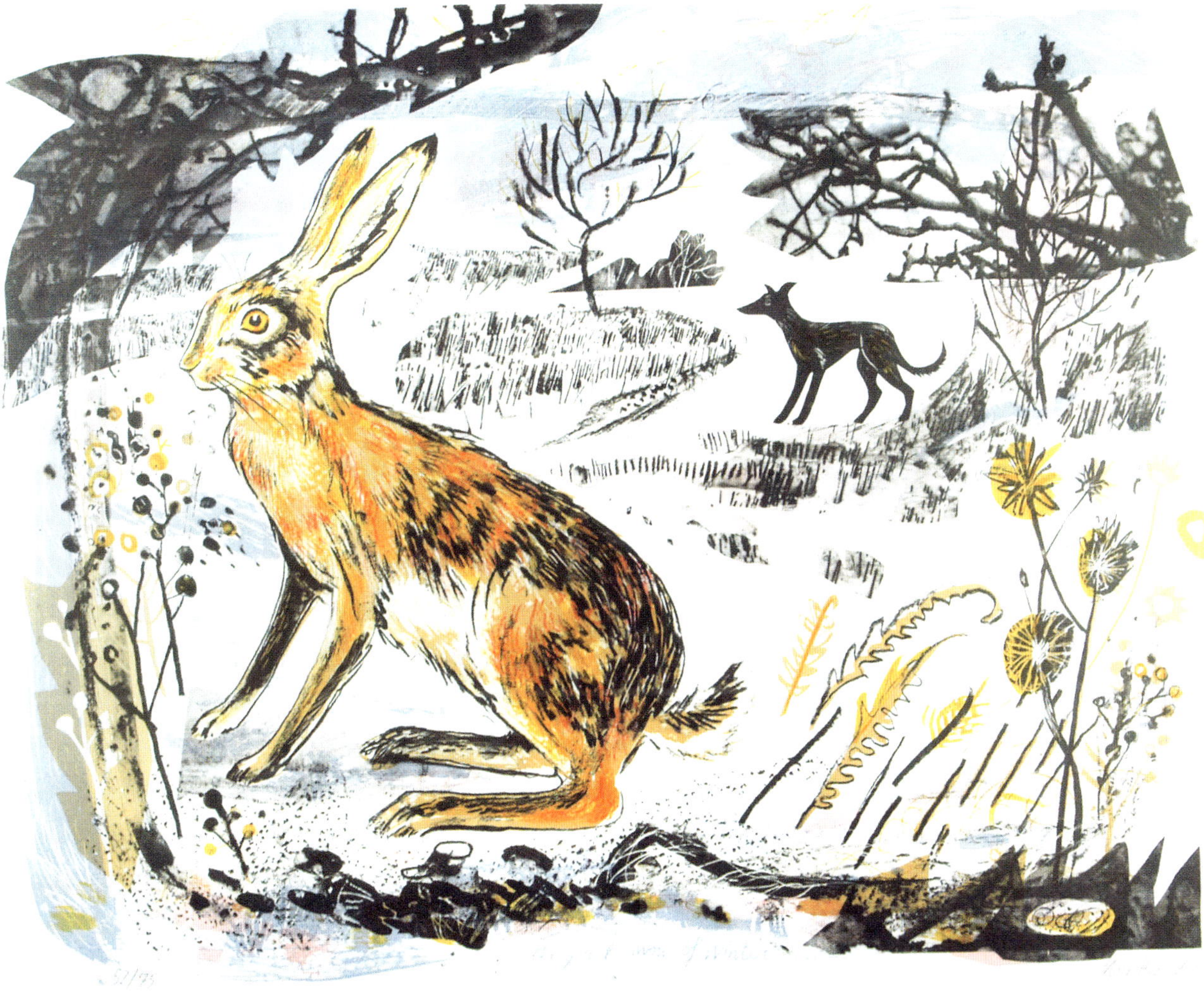

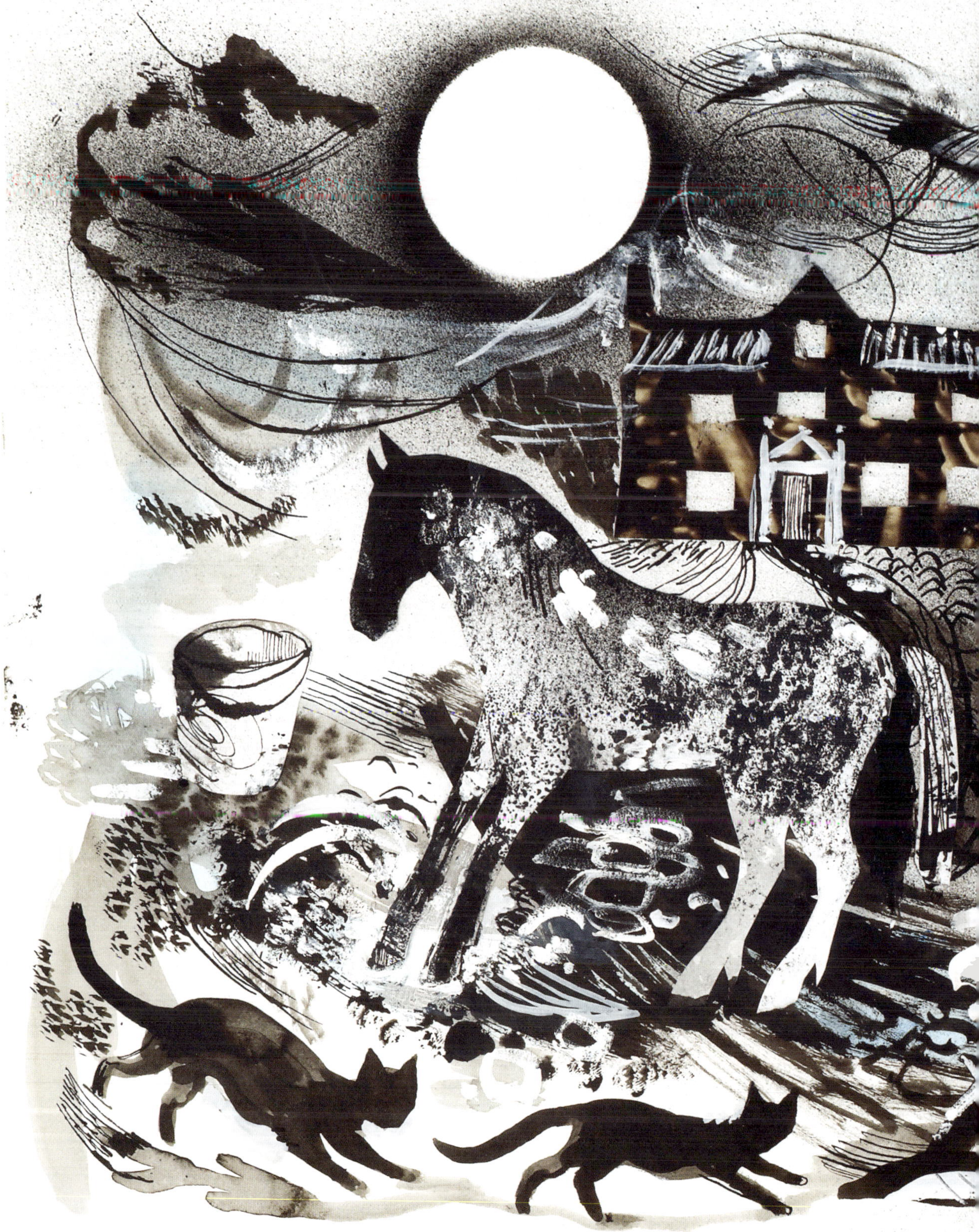

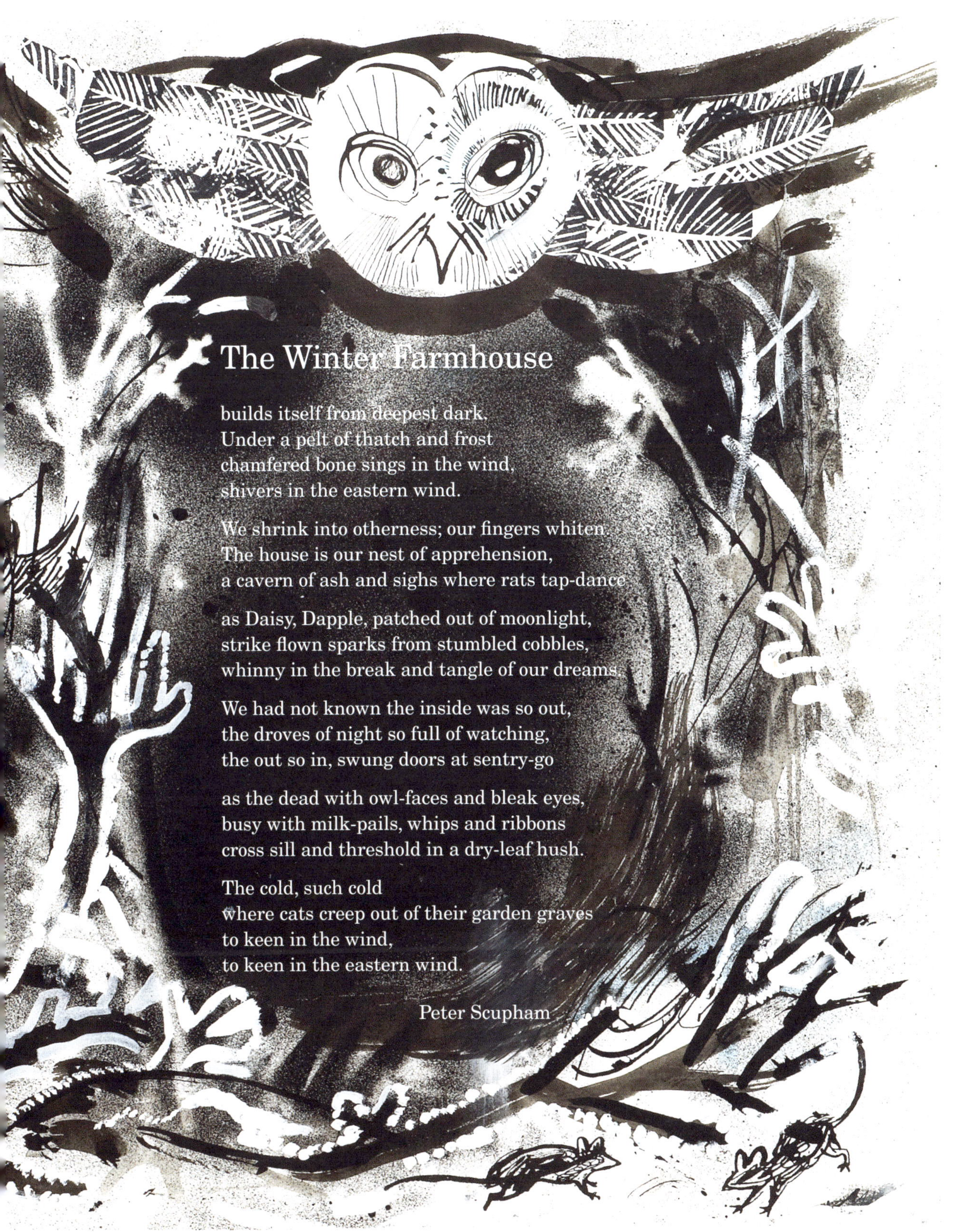

The Winter Farmhouse

builds itself from deepest dark,
Under a pelt of thatch and frost
chamfered bone sings in the wind,
shivers in the eastern wind.

We shrink into otherness; our fingers whiten.
The house is our nest of apprehension,
a cavern of ash and sighs where rats tap-dance

as Daisy, Dapple, patched out of moonlight,
strike flown sparks from stumbled cobbles,
whinny in the break and tangle of our dreams.

We had not known the inside was so out,
the droves of night so full of watching,
the out so in, swung doors at sentry-go

as the dead with owl-faces and bleak eyes,
busy with milk-pails, whips and ribbons
cross sill and threshold in a dry-leaf hush.

The cold, such cold
where cats creep out of their garden graves
to keen in the wind,
to keen in the eastern wind.

Peter Scupham

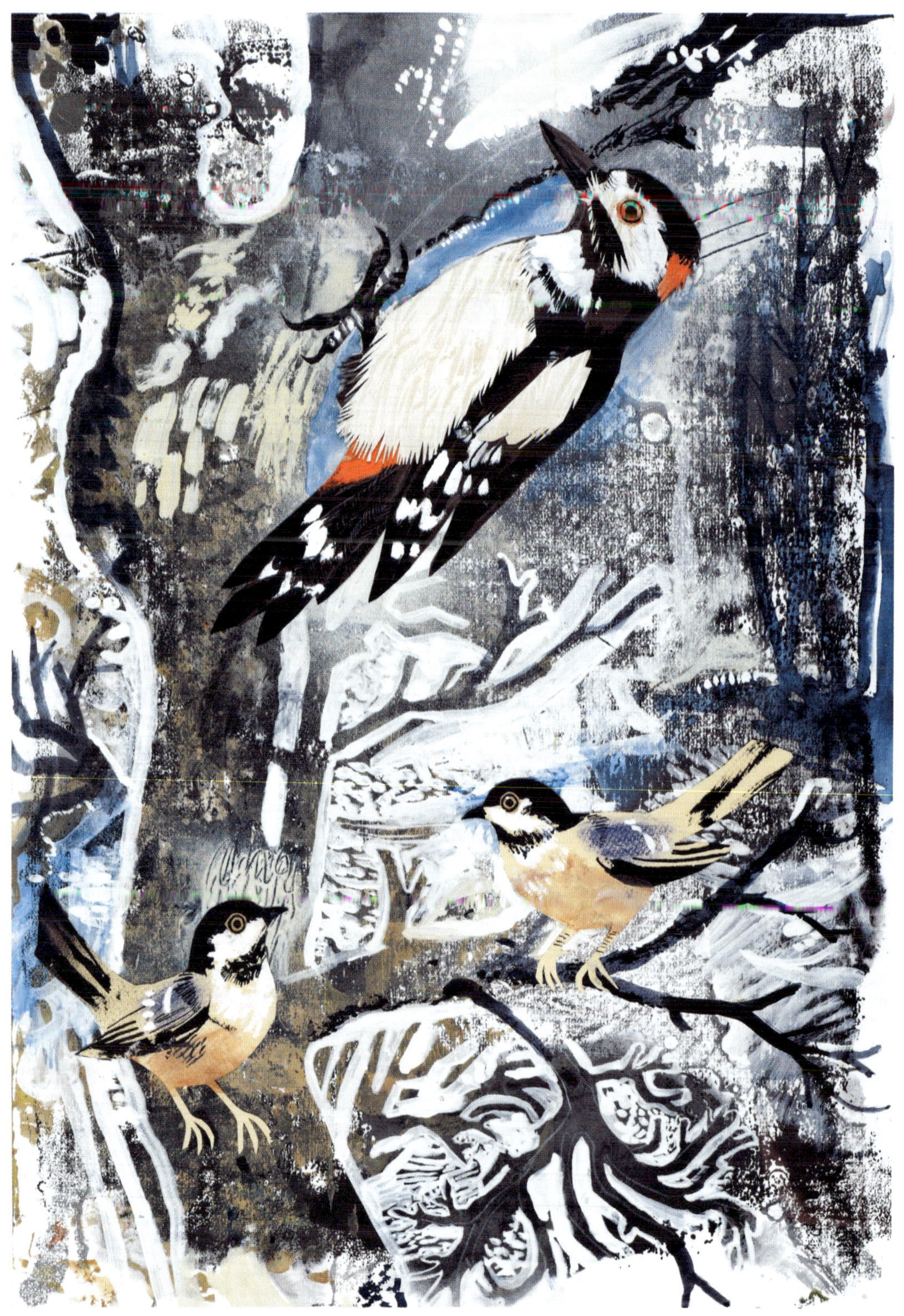

Recently, I've begun to work in series.
In this instance, the first significant
snow of winter required a creative
response. The snow had melted by
the time I came to make each piece
(see also pages 126 and 127, top), but
a collection of leftover monoprinted
papers provided the perfect
beginning. Each sheet of paper
had a range of marks to respond to:
abstract shapes and textures that
suggested the figurative forms of
a snowscape. It was my intention
from the outset to keep these images
pared back in colour; I'm continually
excited by the way in which snow
transforms the landscape. The birds
and animals in each scene bring
colour and life to the work.

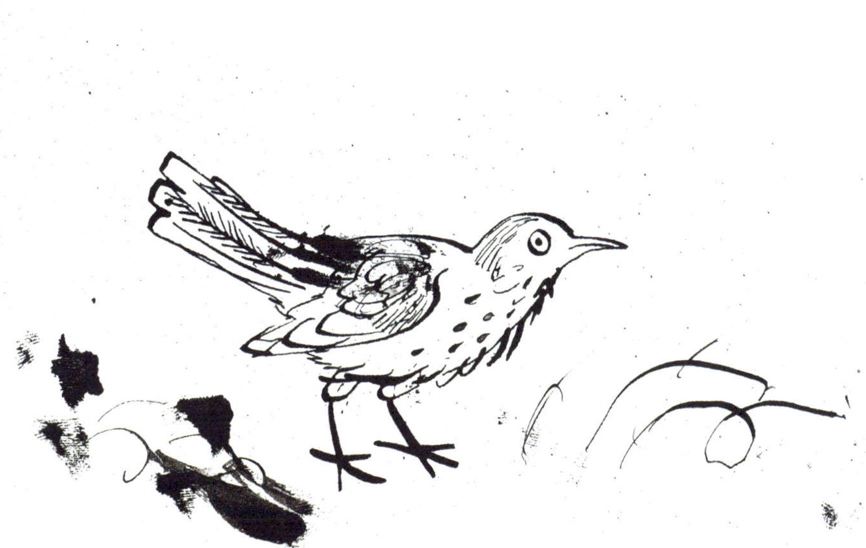

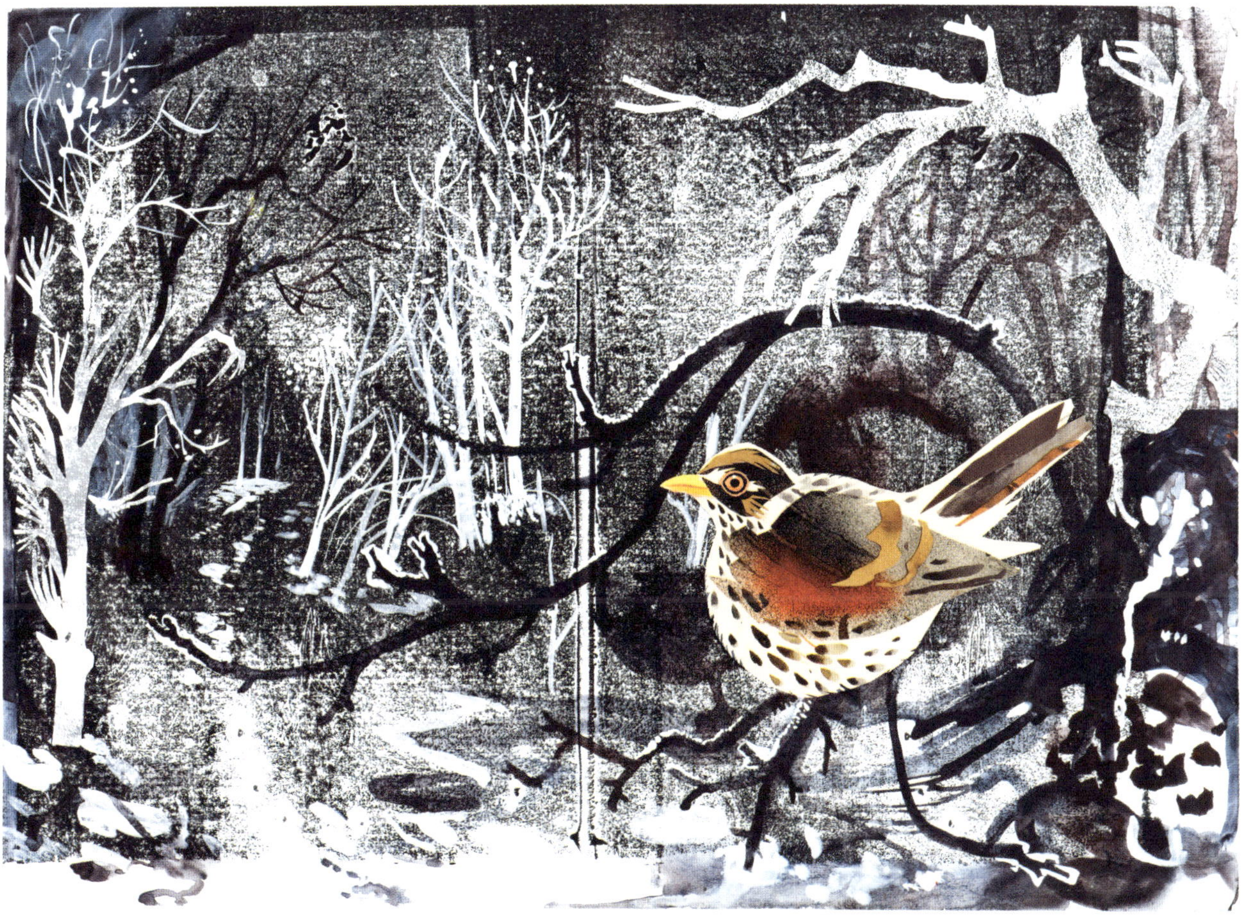

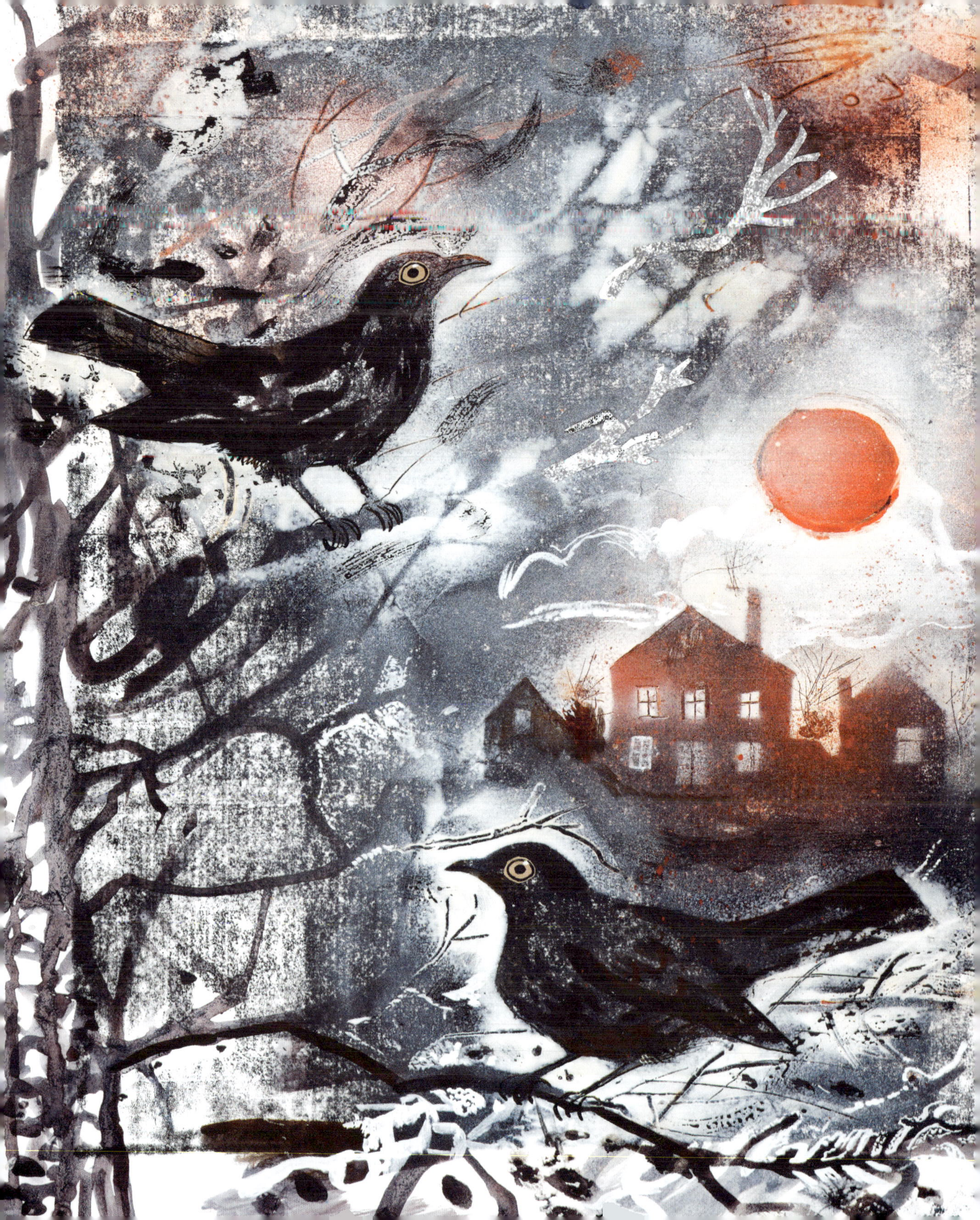

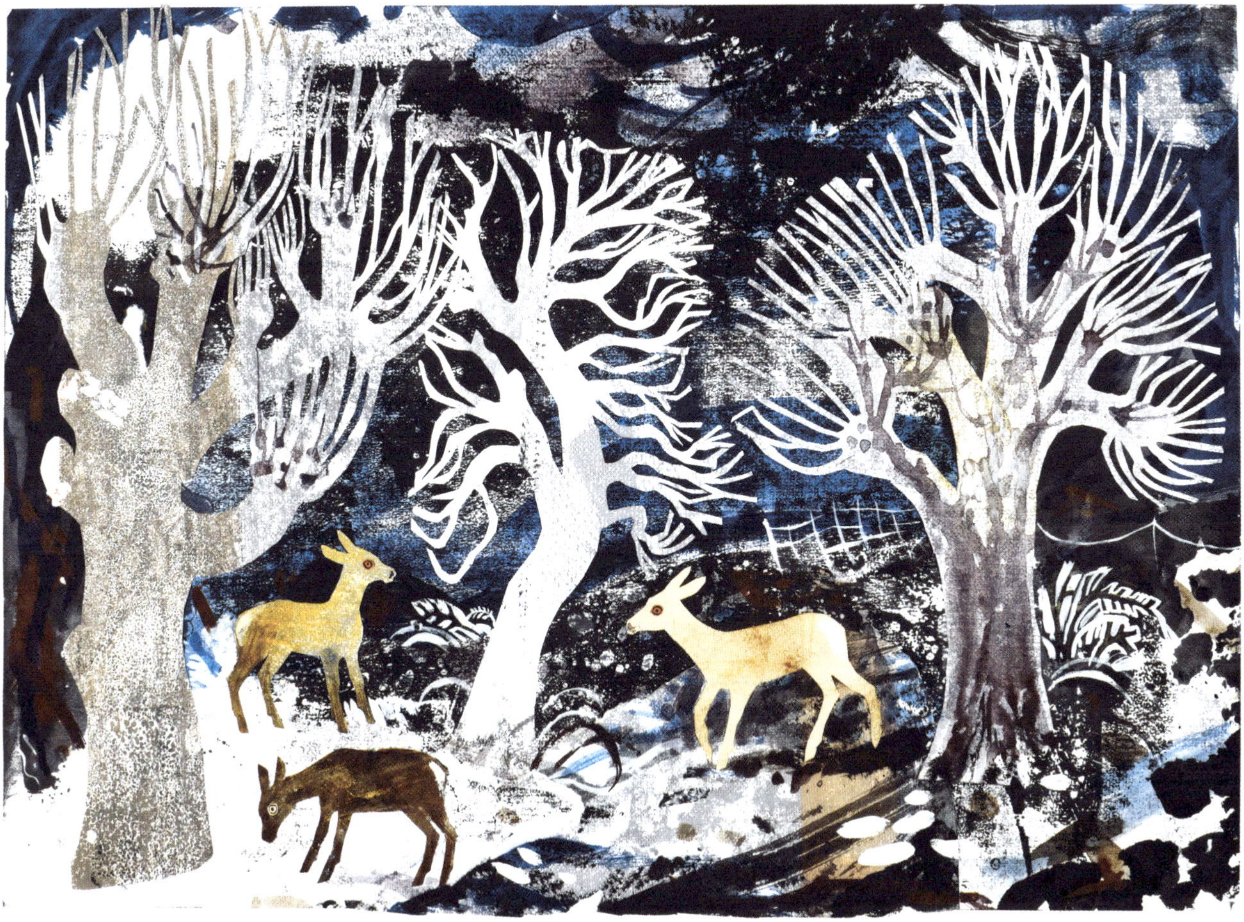

Deer at the Wood's Edge

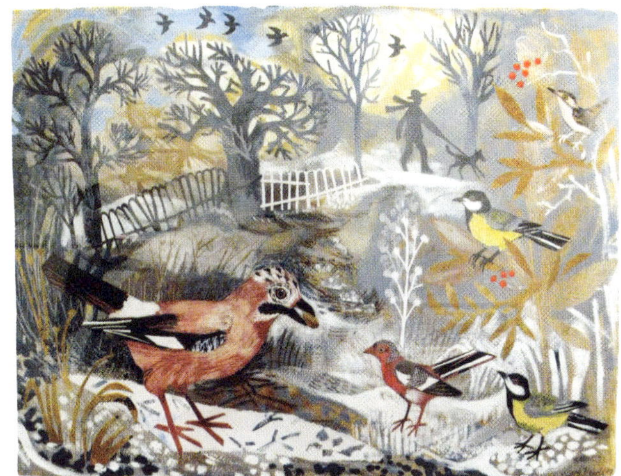

Blackbirds at Dawn

Jay on the Heath

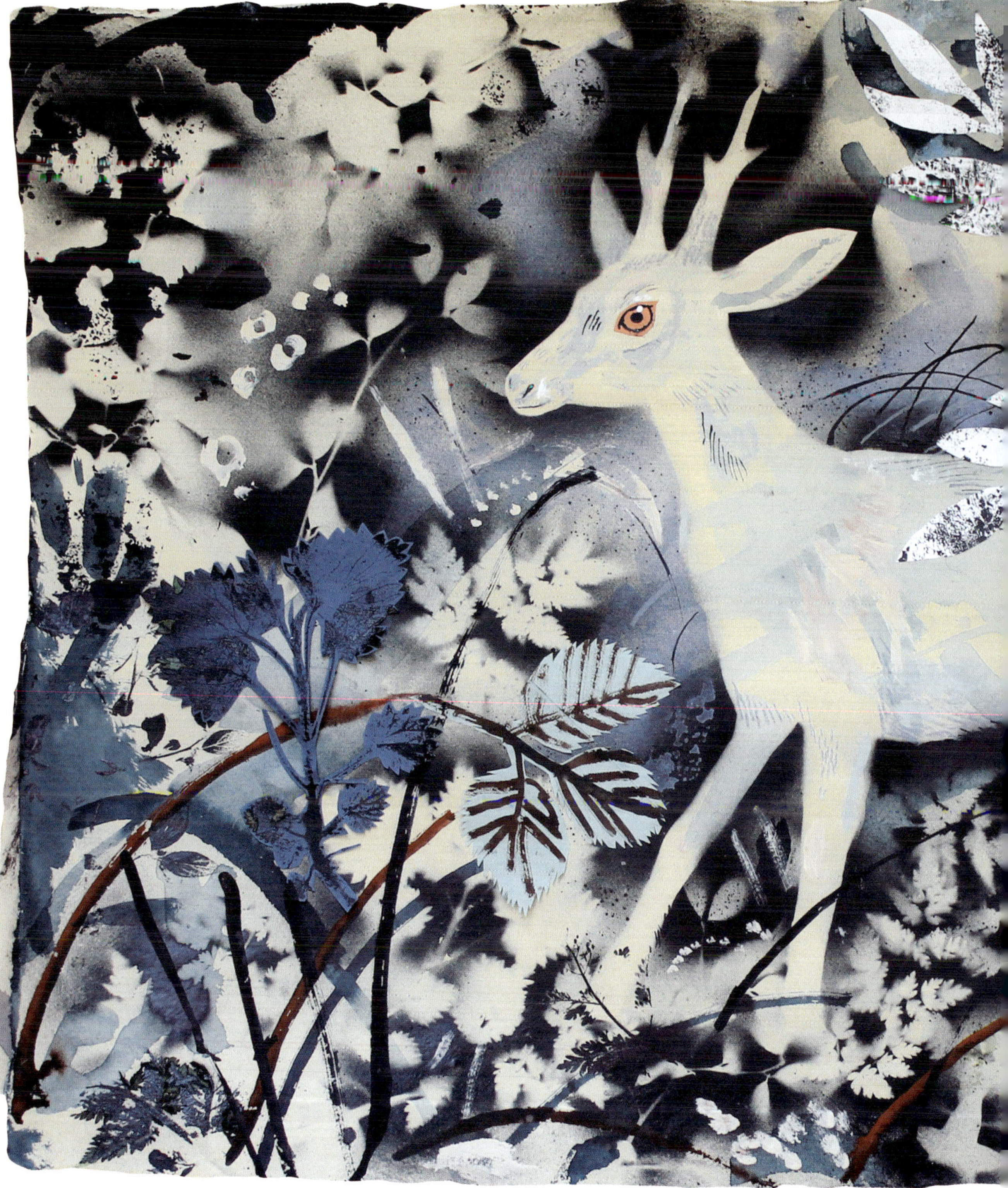

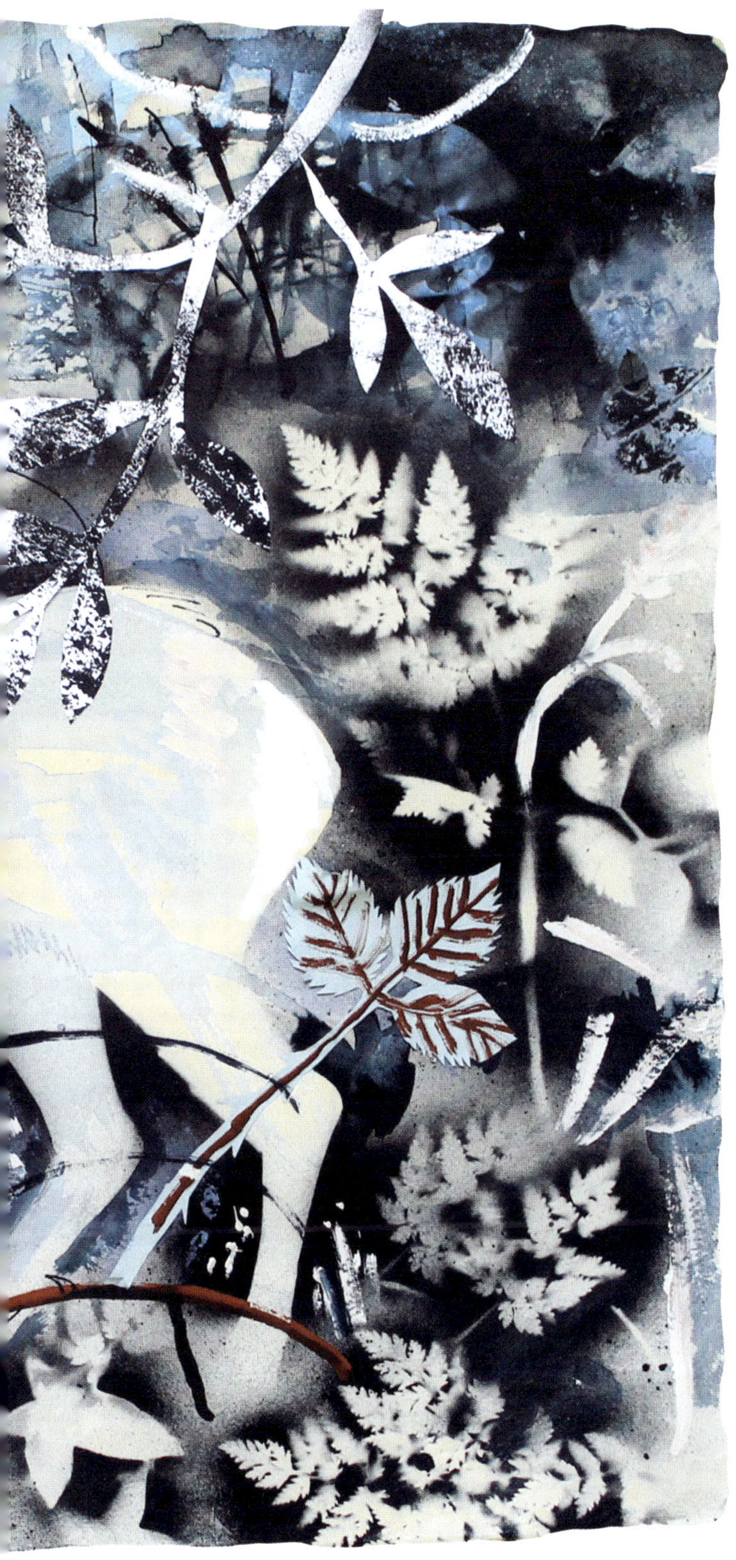

Roebuck

An encounter with a roebuck on
the edge of a wood as I drove round
a sharp bend presented me with a
fully formed image. The light was
beginning to fade, so the scene
was essentially monochromatic.
This did not diminish the intensity
of the deer's gaze; startled, it froze
momentarily before bounding into
the wood. I used underpainting,
a paper stencil, real leaves, collage
and black spray paint to create the
diffuse forms in the half-light.

The Artist as Designer

At the heart of Mark Hearld's work is a strong graphic quality and a feeling for composition and abstract pattern-making. A remarkably versatile artist, he has applied his graphic skills to a multitude of different projects, from designing fabrics, wallpaper and ceramics to decorating objects and furniture for the magical children's film *Nanny McPhee* (2005). 'As well as just making pictures to go on a wall,' he explains, 'I enjoy making and designing objects. The artists I most admire, such as John Piper and Edward Bawden, were also designers. It's about enjoying the visual quality of the objects that surround you. That's really the impetus behind everything I make. Also, there is something lovely about designing an object that people can afford to buy. They might not want to purchase a big painting, but they can buy just a cushion. To design something that's functional and domestic really appeals to me because I like creating a home. I like creating a wonderful space.'

As a designer, Hearld has decorated both handmade and factory-produced ceramics. Not having trained as a potter, he began by painting ready-made blanks in a ceramics cafe (see page 146), adorning plates, tiles and mugs with images of foxes, hens, cats and even the flowers from Bawden's garden. Many of these decorative but useful objects were given patterned edgings that recall the abstract motifs developed by the Bloomsbury artists for the ceramics in their kitchen at Charleston, East Sussex – a place Hearld especially admires (see page 12). By covering several tiles with a single image, he has also created decorative ceramic panels, such as *Bantam and Thistles* (2006), which recalls the tradition of painted ceramic fire surrounds. Hearld's inspirations are rooted in his enthusiasm for British ceramics and in his own collection. The shelves in his home are brimming with all kinds of pottery: English slipware, Sunderland lustre-ware jugs, mocha-ware mugs, sponge-ware bowls, creamers in the shape of cows, and factory-produced teacups and mugs with decorations by the artists Graham Sutherland and Eric Ravilious. In general, Hearld is not attracted to the refined sensibility of Meissen

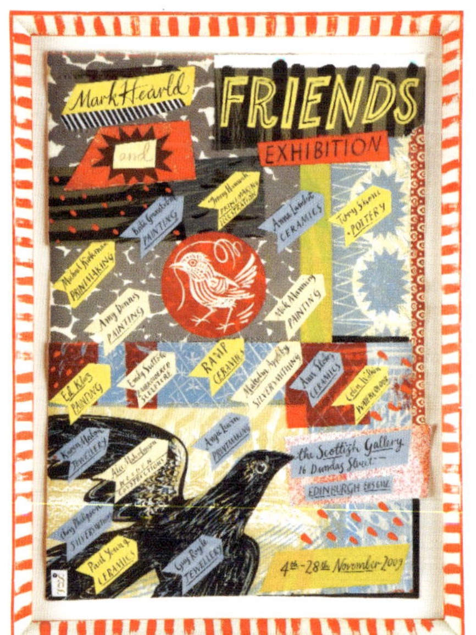

Exhibition poster, 2009, collage, 59 × 42 cm (23¼ × 16½ in.)

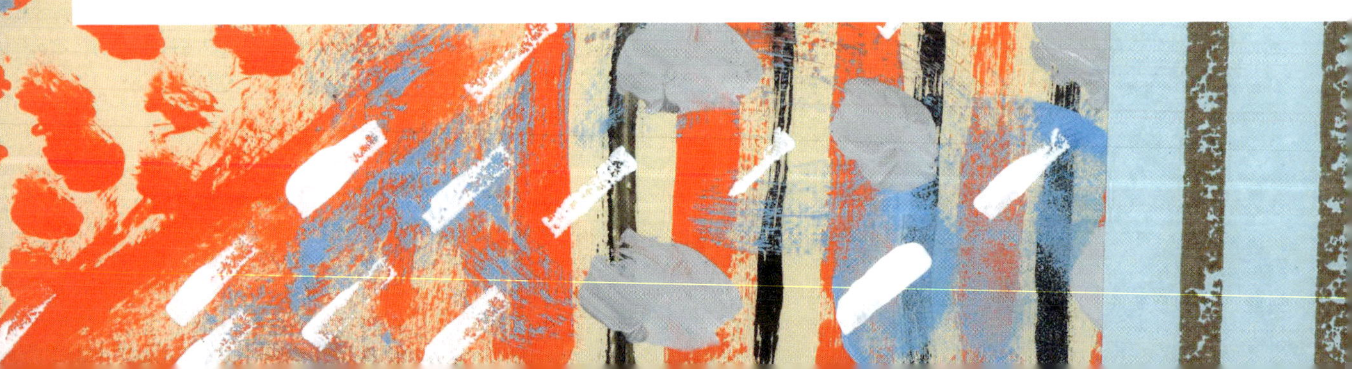

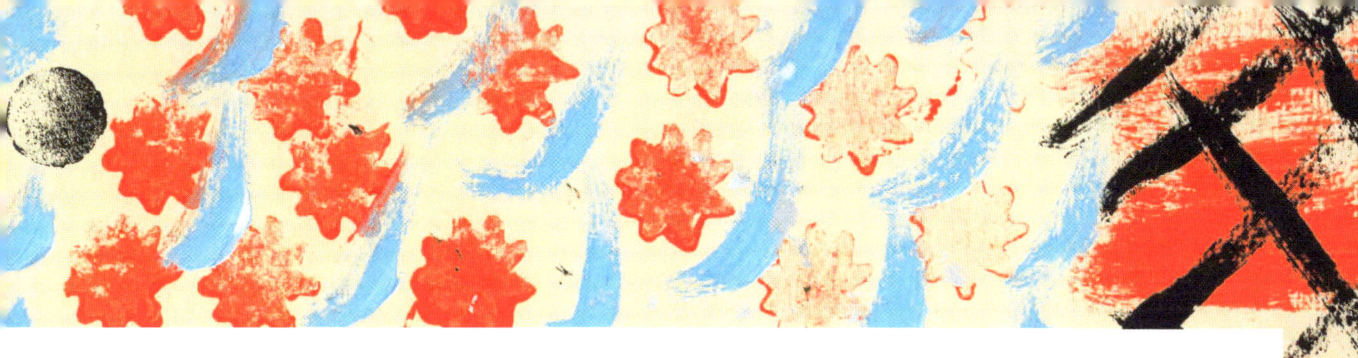

or Dresden ceramics, preferring the more earthy pottery that forms part of English folk heritage: seventeenth-century English Delft tiles, Nottingham salt-glazed flasks in the form of chained bears, and eighteenth- and nineteenth-century Staffordshire figure groups and the modern 'pew groups' that they have inspired, such as those by the potters Paul Young and Geoffrey Fuller. Hearld also enthuses about the vitality of Picasso's ceramics and the work of the 'Picasettes', a group of British ceramics artists of the 1950s, such as Richard and Susan Parkinson, who decorated porcelain birds and animals in a simplified, modern style.

Hearld has long been fascinated by artists' relationships with particular objects, such as the twentieth-century abstract artist Ben Nicholson's appreciation for the severity of Victorian mocha-ware mugs, with their blue and brown stripes. Hearld himself has a strong affinity for sgraffito-decorated North Devon harvest jugs and the slipware chargers decorated with mermaids, pelicans and unicorns by the seventeenth-century Staffordshire potters Thomas and Ralph Toft.

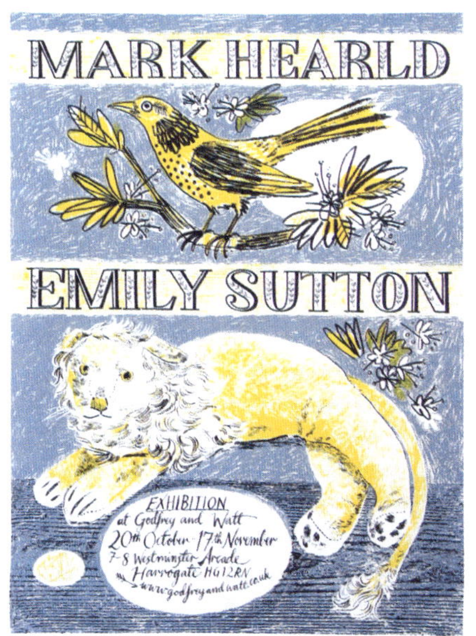

Exhibition poster, 2007, screen print, 59 × 42 cm (23¼ × 16½ in.)

Slipware is earthenware decorated with a mixture of coloured clay and water, and finished with a galena lead-oxide glaze, which gives it its characteristic yellow tinge. Working in collaboration with the potter Terry Shone at his harbourside pottery in Whitby, North Yorkshire, Hearld created his own modern slipware in response to that of the Tofts. To make the decorated platter *Slip-trailed Tumbler* (page 147, bottom left), for example, he cut out newspaper stencils to put down on the body of terracotta clay thrown by Shone. Then, after painting the clay with white clay slip, he removed the stencils and made some marks in the surface of the clay before overlaying some of these with a slip trailer similar to that used by the Tofts. This is just one example of how Hearld has applied his feeling for collage and decoration to other forms of creativity.

Although Hearld is the first to acknowledge that he is not a potter, as an artist he is drawn to collaborating with both individual potters and ceramics manufacturers in order to realize his creative ideas. His first foray into commercial design was the

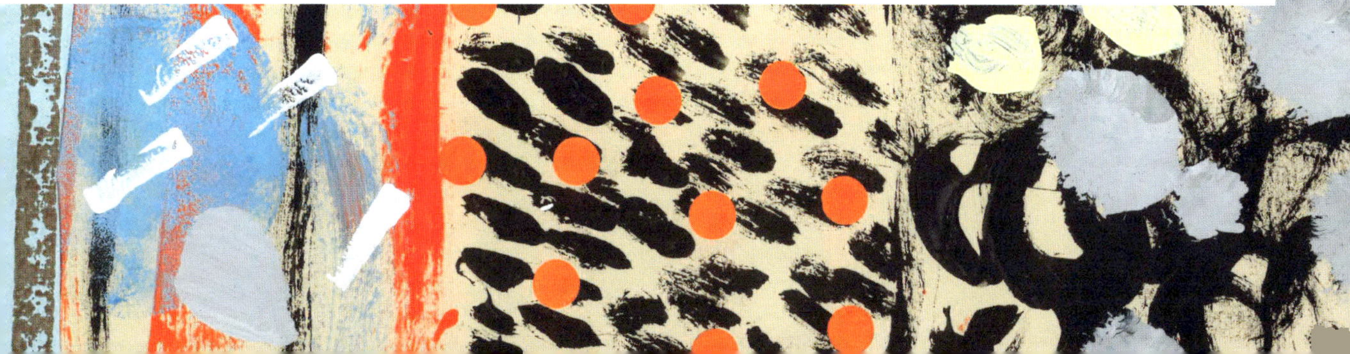

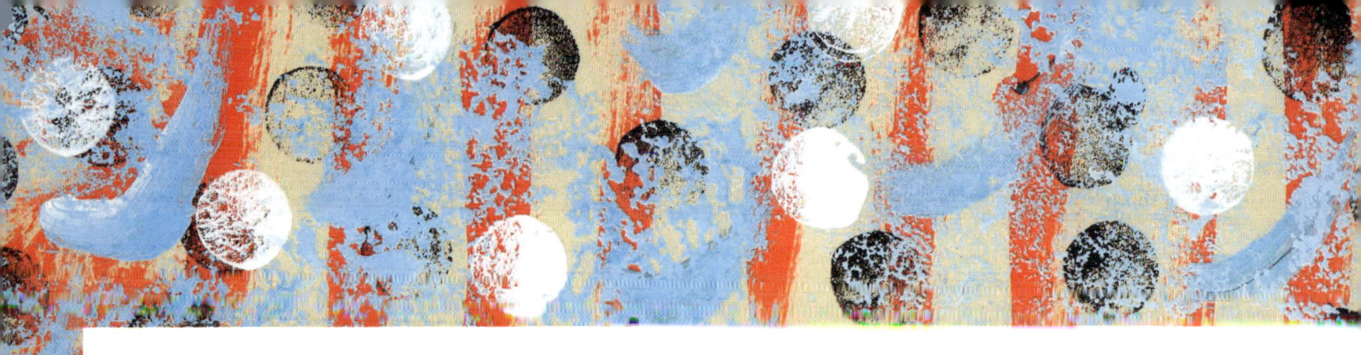

Blue and Red Animal range of sponge-ware pottery for Emma Bridgewater, the British ceramics manufacturer based in Stoke-on-Trent, Staffordshire. Sponge-ware is a type of pottery dating back to the late eighteenth century, and is described by Hearld as 'a classic bit of popular art'. Collected by John Piper, among others, it is named after the natural sponge that was used to decorate factory-made blanks with simple repeat patterns in bold colours. For the *Blue and Red Animal* series, Hearld's designs for a hen, goose, fox and hare were cut from synthetic sponge using his paper cut-outs as patterns. Although the pottery itself was factory-produced, Hearld was closely involved in its making, visiting Staffordshire to sample the results. The simple but distinctive range of mugs, plates and bowls featuring Hearld's cut-out animals and birds is thus a contemporary take on a historic tradition. In 2011 he was commissioned by the Tate to design a range of ceramic tableware. Named *On the Wing* (page 136), it was produced at the Burleigh Pottery in Staffordshire using transfer images designed by Hearld and printed with the help of a ceramics lithographer in Stoke-on-Trent. Hearld worked out his designs by cutting pieces of paper to size and wrapping them around blanks supplied by the pottery. Each of the three-colour designs, one of which features a central image of a starling and birds in flight, consists of three separate transfer images – one for each colour – applied to the pottery by hand. Whether handmade or not, Hearld's ceramics form an eye-catching addition to any kitchen.

Hearld has a particular interest in the versatility of such artists and designers as Enid Marx and Peggy Angus, who, in addition to producing prints and illustrations, created designs for furnishings, textiles and wallpaper. 'I was really excited by an exhibition at the Fine Art Society in London in 2003 called *Artists' Textiles in Britain*', he explains. 'I saw such people as Graham Sutherland and Henry Moore crossing over into design in the 1950s and thought, I'd like to do that.' He especially admires such design houses as Collier Campbell and its patterns of the 1980s, including *Liberty Bauhaus* and *Côte d'Azure*. Since 2006 Hearld has been creating screen-printed textiles and wallpapers in collaboration with

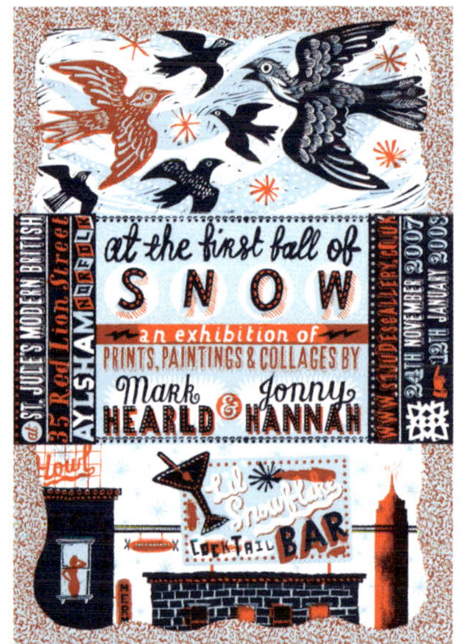

Exhibition poster (with Jonny Hannah), 2007, screen print, 59 × 42 cm (23¼ × 16½ in.)

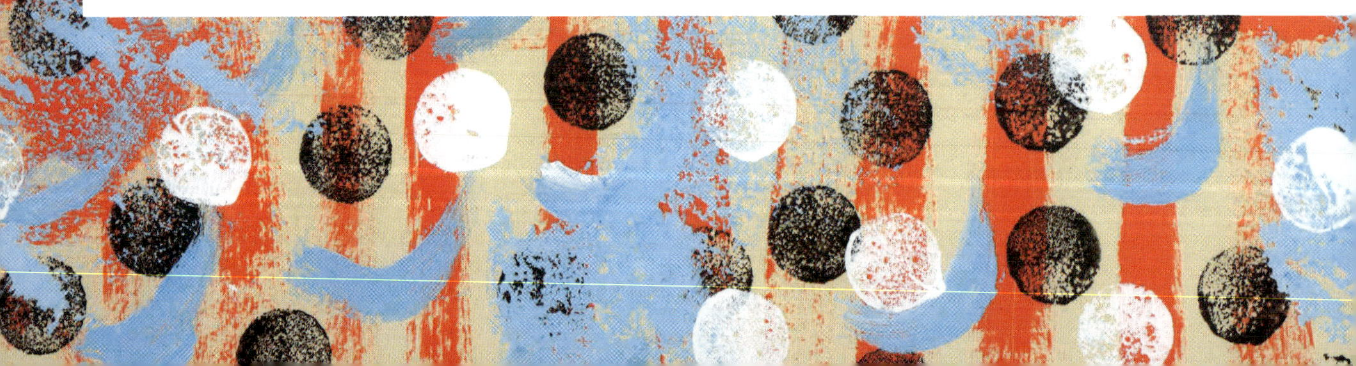

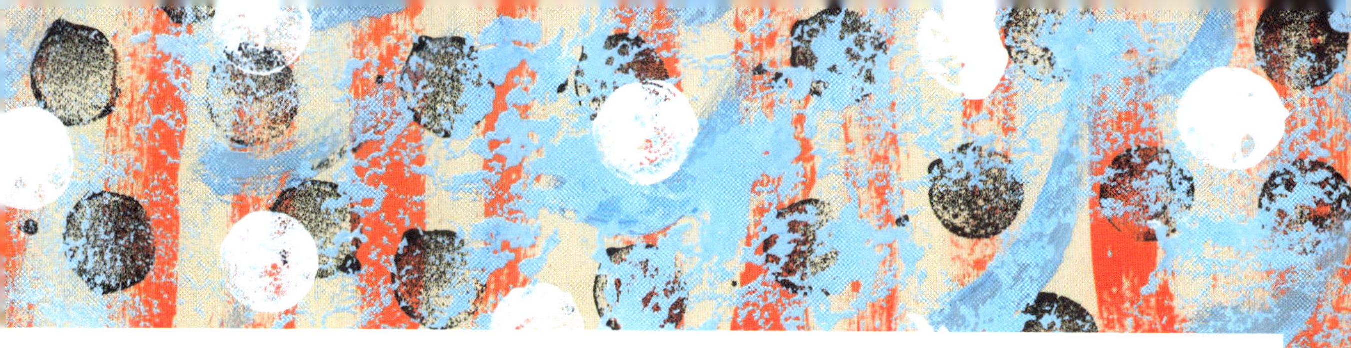

St Jude's, which produces artist-designed fabrics and papers ('in the tradition of David Whitehead Ltd in the 1950s and 1960s', says Hearld) by such artist–illustrators as Jonny Hannah, Ed Kluz and Emily Sutton.

Hearld's first fabric design was *Doveflight* (pages 134–35), a swirling pattern of blue and white doves set within curving tree branches. This formed a natural extension to his printmaking, since he created linocut blocks that were then used in the screen-printing process. 'I did it in the most complex way', he recalls. 'Normally, if you were going to do a repeat pattern you would use a half-drop [where the repeated pattern is positioned halfway down the side of the preceding area of pattern], but for *Doveflight* I used three blocks and two colours, with half-drop repeats that tessellate. I looked at various books on patterns and textiles to see how the patterns worked. It was a very steep learning curve as I didn't know any better, but, as a piece of design, I am still really proud of it.' Its success was confirmed when it was used for the cover of Drusilla Cole's *The Pattern Sourcebook: A Century of Surface Design* (2009), which features the fabrics of such artists as Duncan Grant, Lucienne Day and E.Q. Nicholson. Hearld has since designed *Bird Garden* (page 137), which consists of a dense network of abstract patterns, including zigzags, triangles and diamonds, broken up by nesting pigeons, serpentine plant forms and garden birds. It is a much simpler design than *Doveflight*: a one-block repeat with a half-drop, printed in three colourways.

Among Hearld's other creations are a Tate-commissioned cotton tote bag (pages 138–39), which reflects the patterns in *On the Wing*, and, to celebrate the fiftieth anniversary of the Curwen Studio, lithographed pattern papers (see, for example, the background to pages 22–23) in the tradition of such artists as Enid Marx, Edward Bawden, Eric Ravilious and Paul Nash, all of whom designed pattern or endpapers for the Curwen Press in the 1920s. Essentially, whether it be for paper or a textile, Hearld's approach to pattern design is the same. 'It is all surface-pattern design,' he says, 'although technically there is movement in a cloth. I have always been interested in applied art, such as wallpapers and textiles.' In 2011 he designed a single-colour wallpaper for St Jude's called *Harvest Hare* (pages 140–43), which features the joyous scene of a hare leaping through cornfields with birdlife all around. Consisting of a one-block repeat pattern in a half-drop format, it was inspired by Bawden's design for the dust jacket of Ambrose Heath's *Good Savouries* (1934).

Whether in the form of a textile or wallpaper print, or a decoration on a plate or mug, Hearld's designs bring nature into our lives, as though a hare were bounding out of the wall, or doves were flying across the curtains. Hearld has a remarkable talent for creating beautiful and thought-provoking objects for our homes, to be treasured and enjoyed every day.

SIMON MARTIN

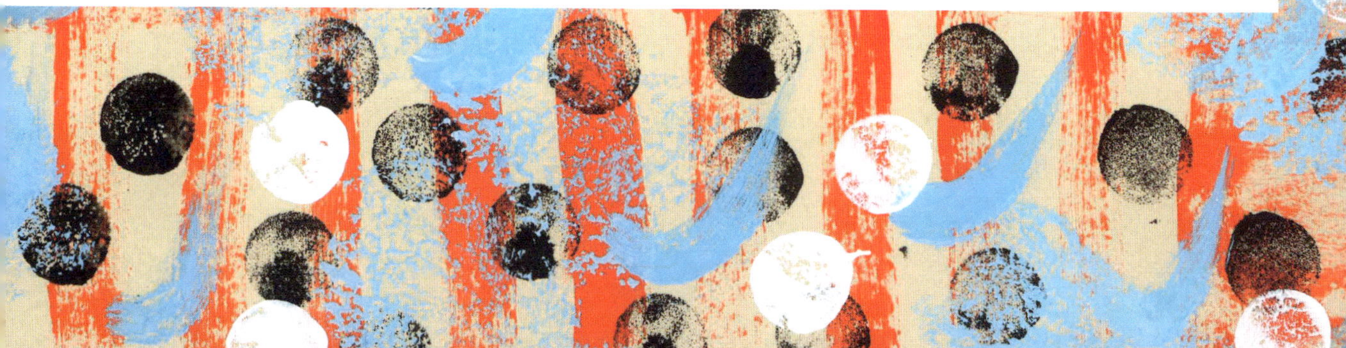

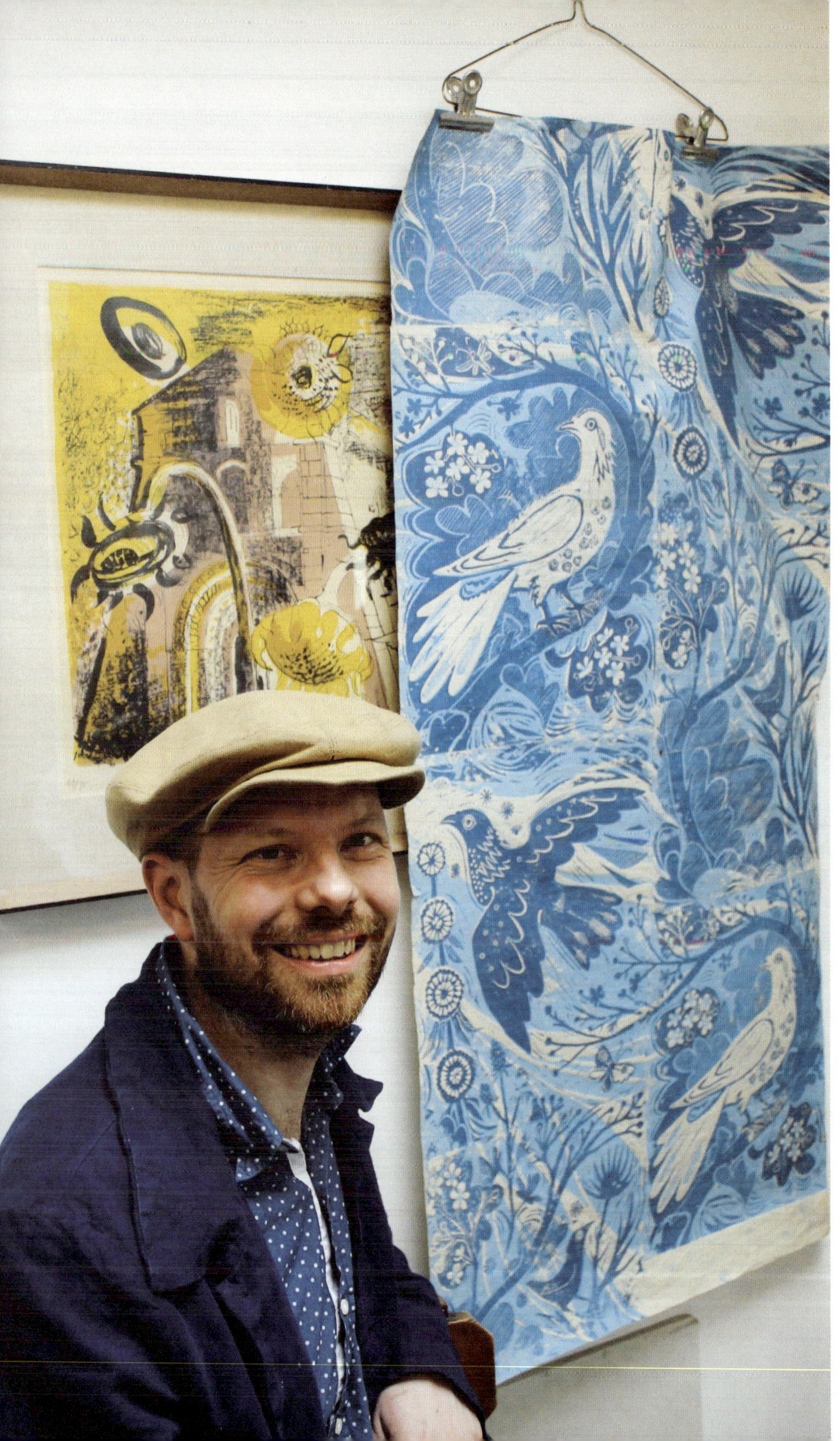

Doveflight

In the summer of 2006 I began collaborating with Simon and Angie Lewin of St Jude's on my first fabric for the company, *Doveflight*. I had long been interested in surface pattern and textile design, but, as an artist, felt it was somebody else's world. St Jude's offered me the opportunity to work as a designer, which I have embraced ever since. My approach to the everyday is visual, which means designing functional objects beautifully has become a creative imperative. William Morris and Barron & Larcher, as well as Martha Armitage and Josef Frank, are among the surface-pattern designers I admire the most, and their commitment to design shows me what's possible.

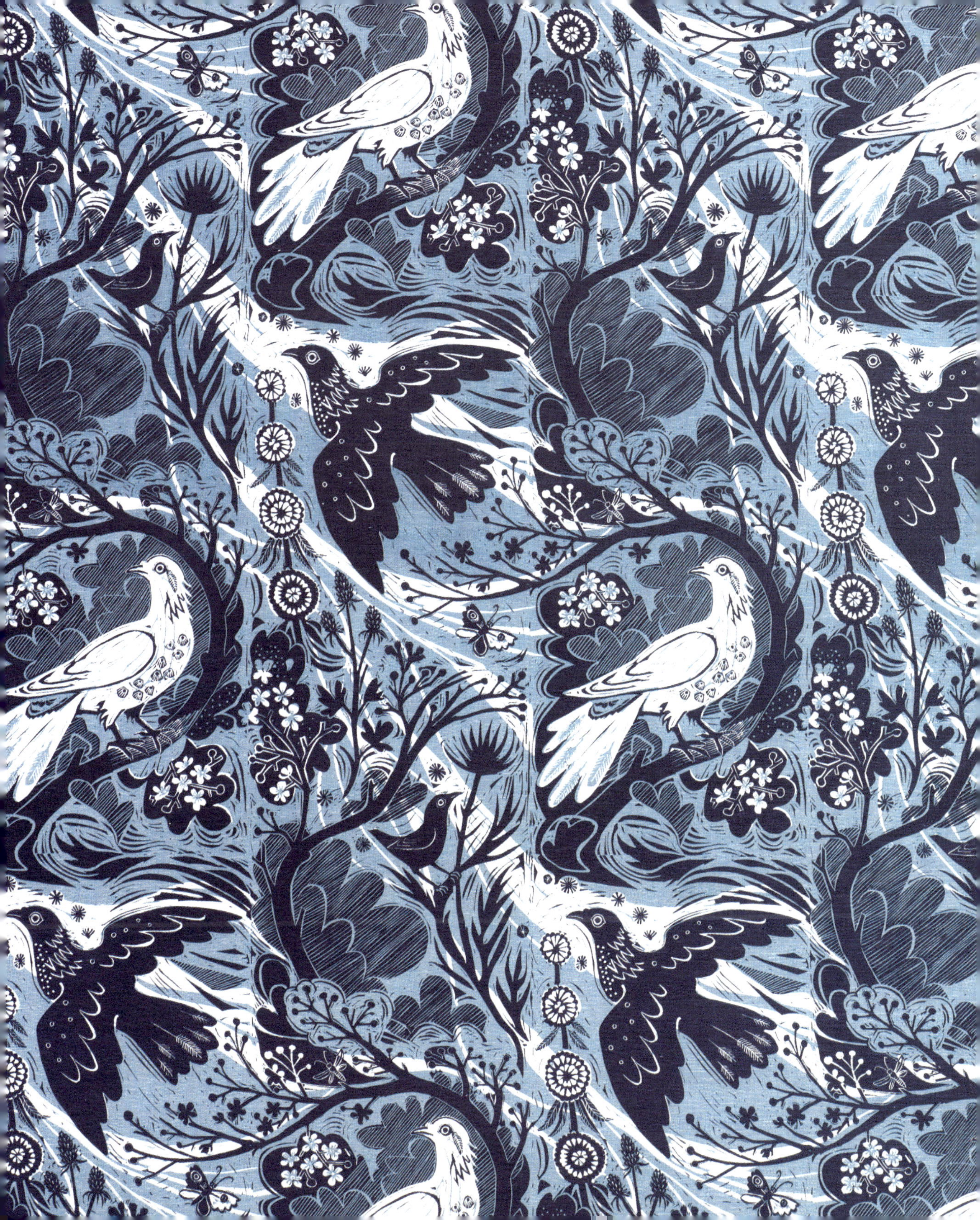

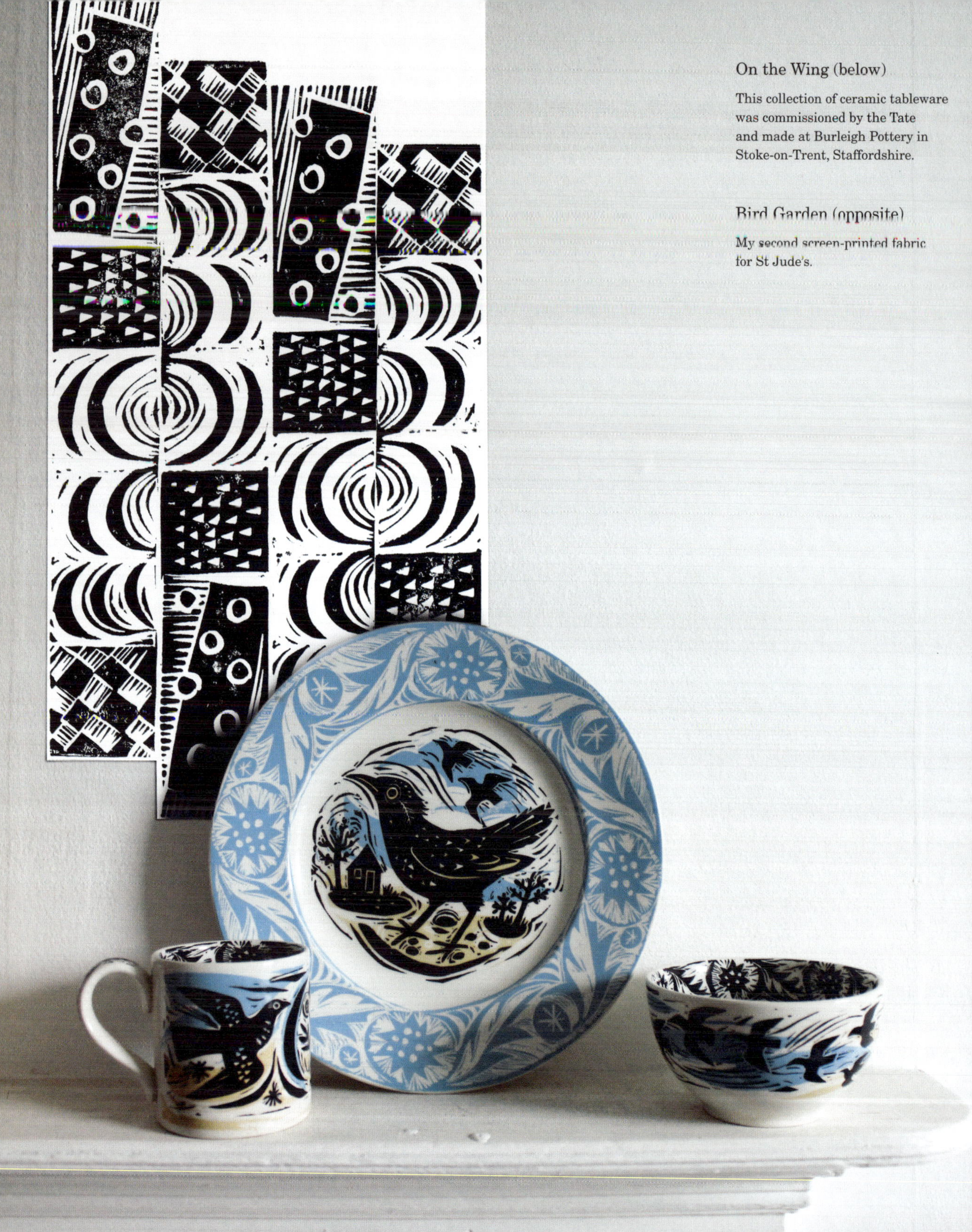

On the Wing (below)

This collection of ceramic tableware was commissioned by the Tate and made at Burleigh Pottery in Stoke-on-Trent, Staffordshire.

Bird Garden (opposite)

My second screen-printed fabric for St Jude's.

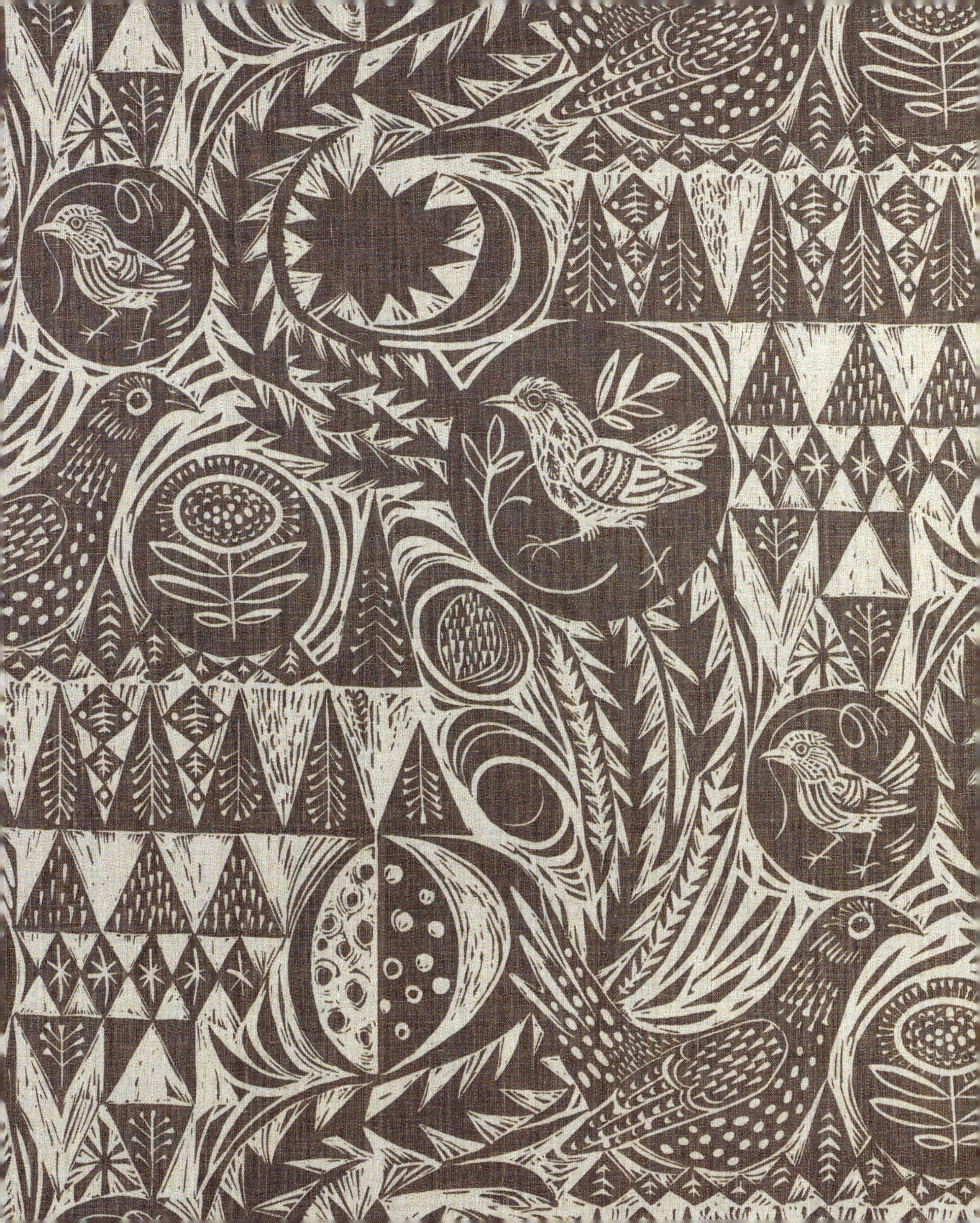

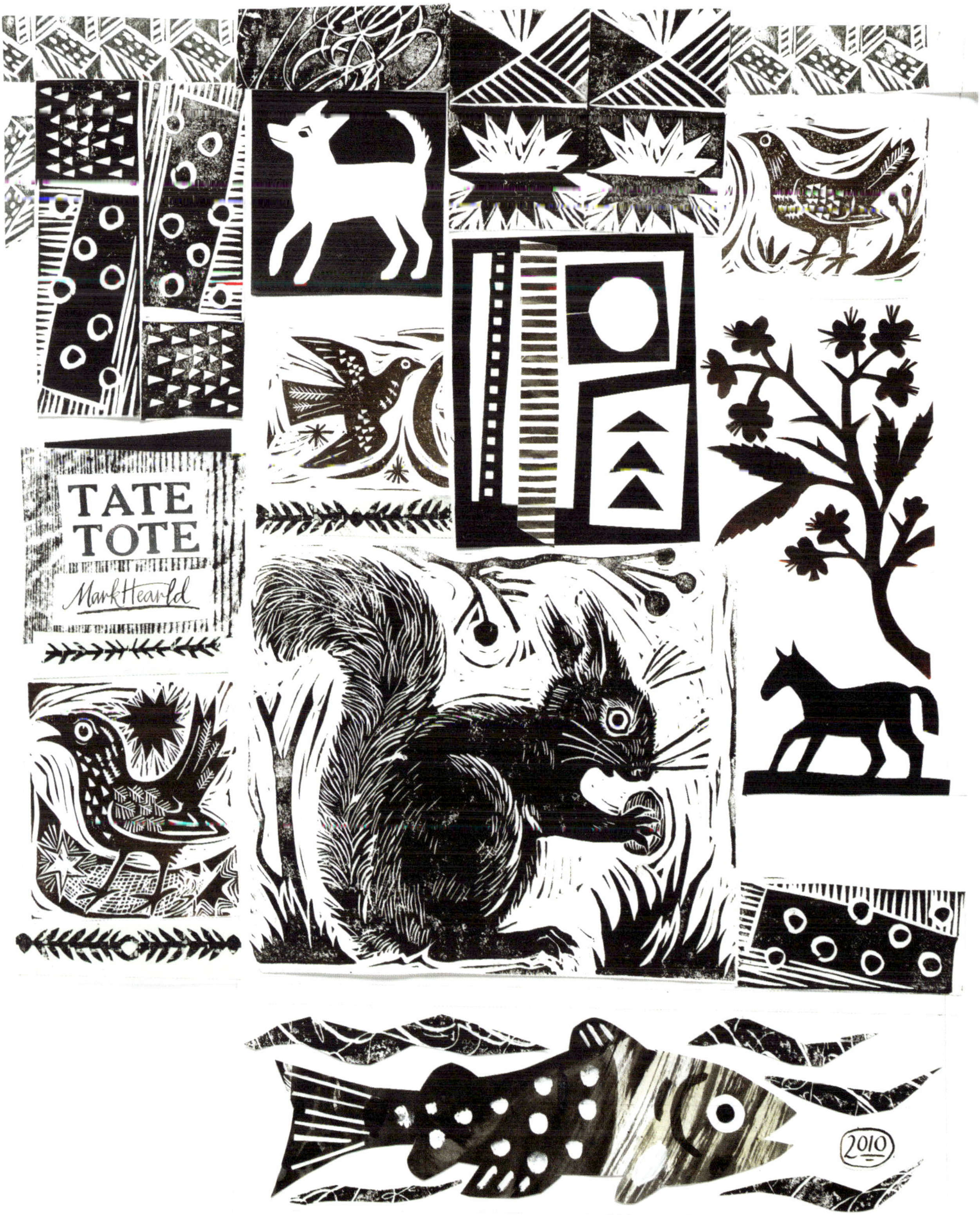

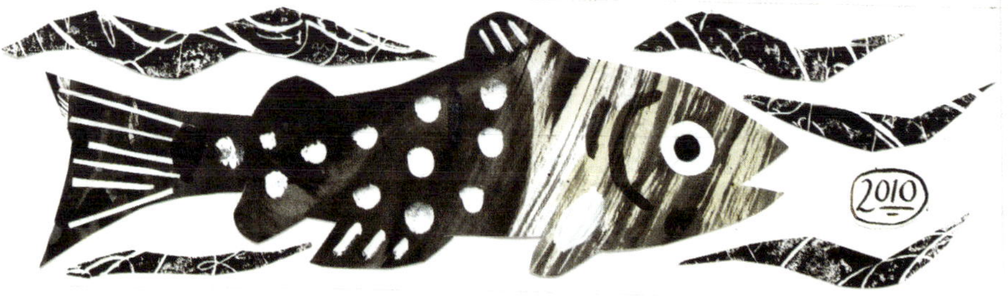

TATE
TOTE
Mark Hearld
2010

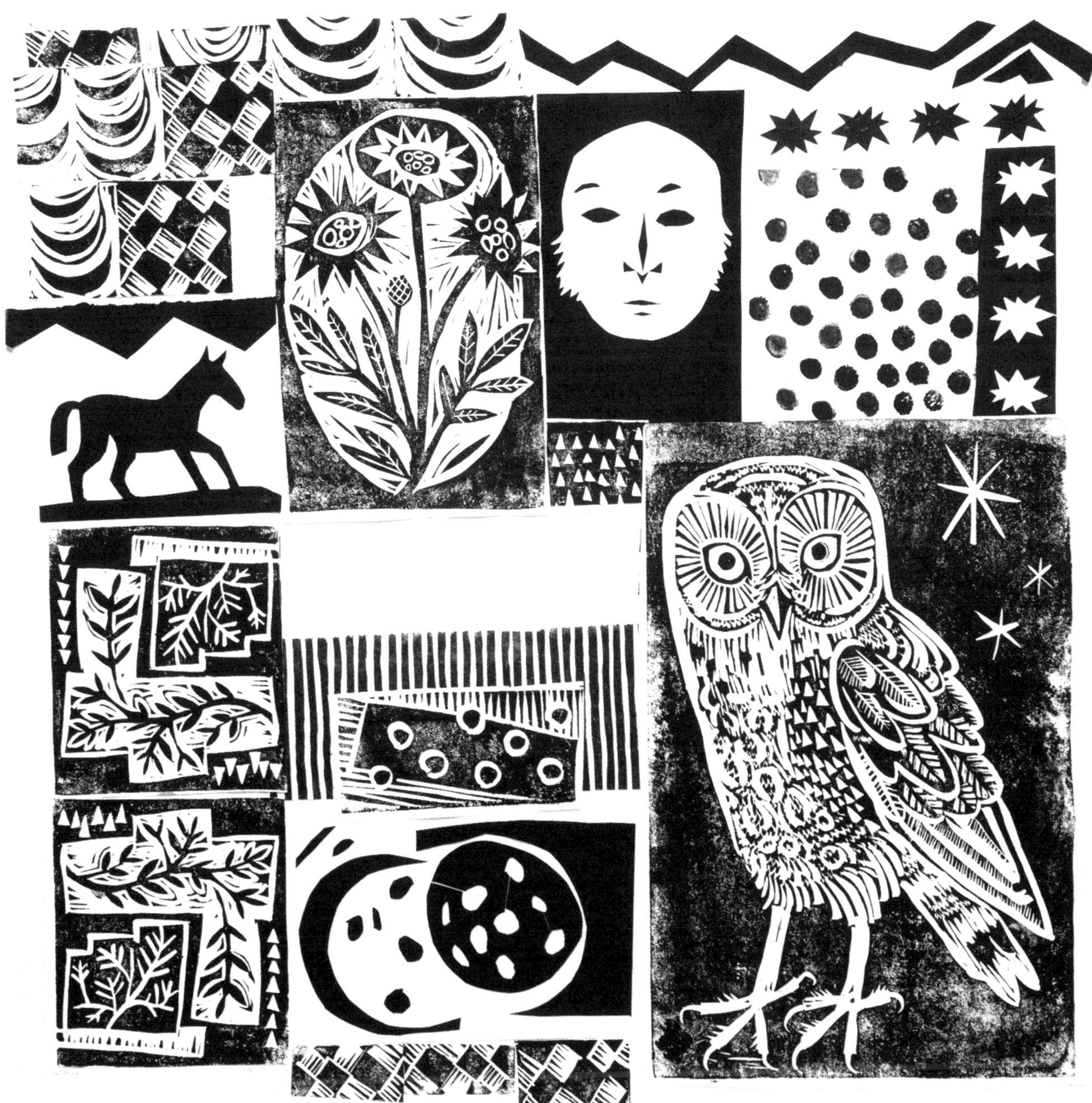

Tate Tote

A little owl and a squirrel are the focal points of the main panels of the tote bag that I designed for the Tate. This is one of three separations, the others being for a dove grey and a mustard yellow. The overall design is a collage of miscellaneous images and patterns in a bold, graphic style; the fish (opposite) is a surprise image on the base of the bag. The patterned artwork for the handle can be seen on page 136, behind the *On the Wing* tableware.

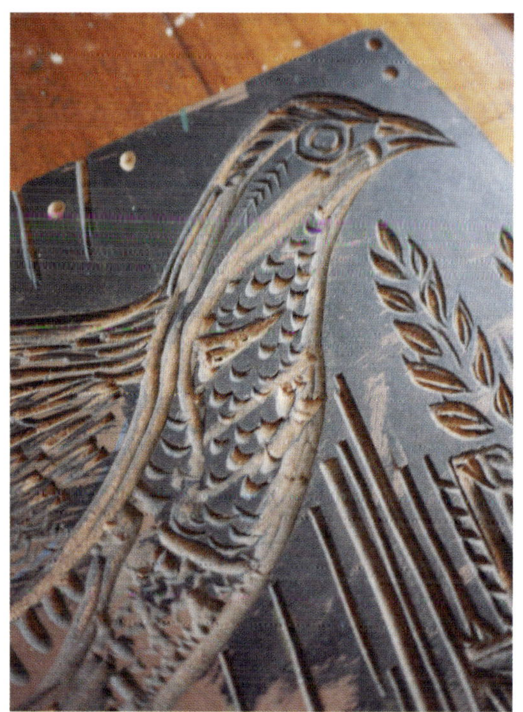

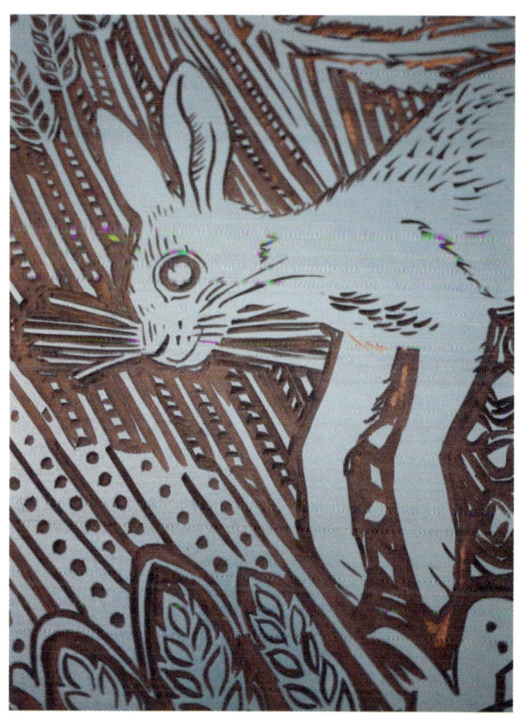

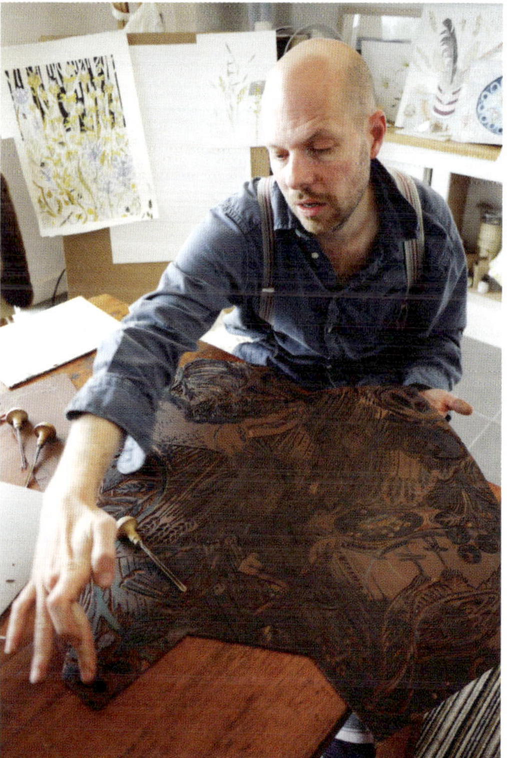

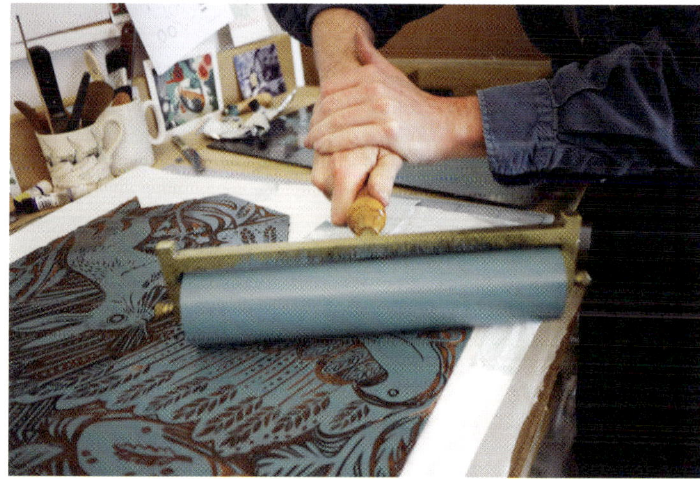

Harvest Hare

The colour of a ripening cornfield and the structural, repeating quality of ears of corn were the starting points for my first wallpaper design. Hares and sparrows animate the pattern, and a rank bramble brings linear movement. To create the pattern, I used a shaped piece of lino that tessellates using a half-drop repeat. The corn changes direction to give rhythm, and I play with tonal counterpoint, that is, dark against light, and light against dark. On page 143, a working rough, which establishes the key visual dynamic of the pattern, is shown with a finished section of the design.

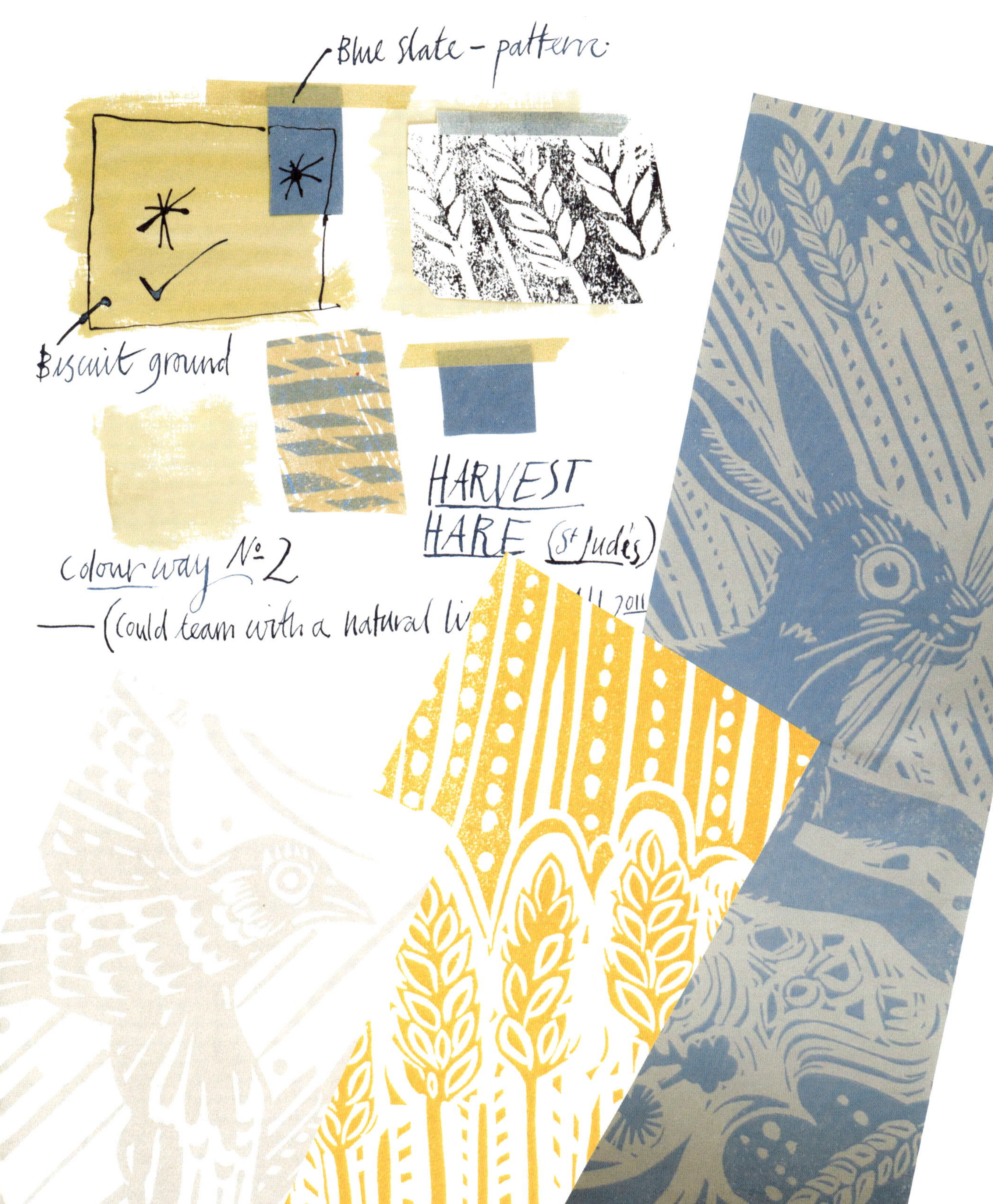

Blue slate - pattern:
Biscuit ground
HARVEST HARE (St Jude's)
colour way Nº 2
— (could team with a natural li...

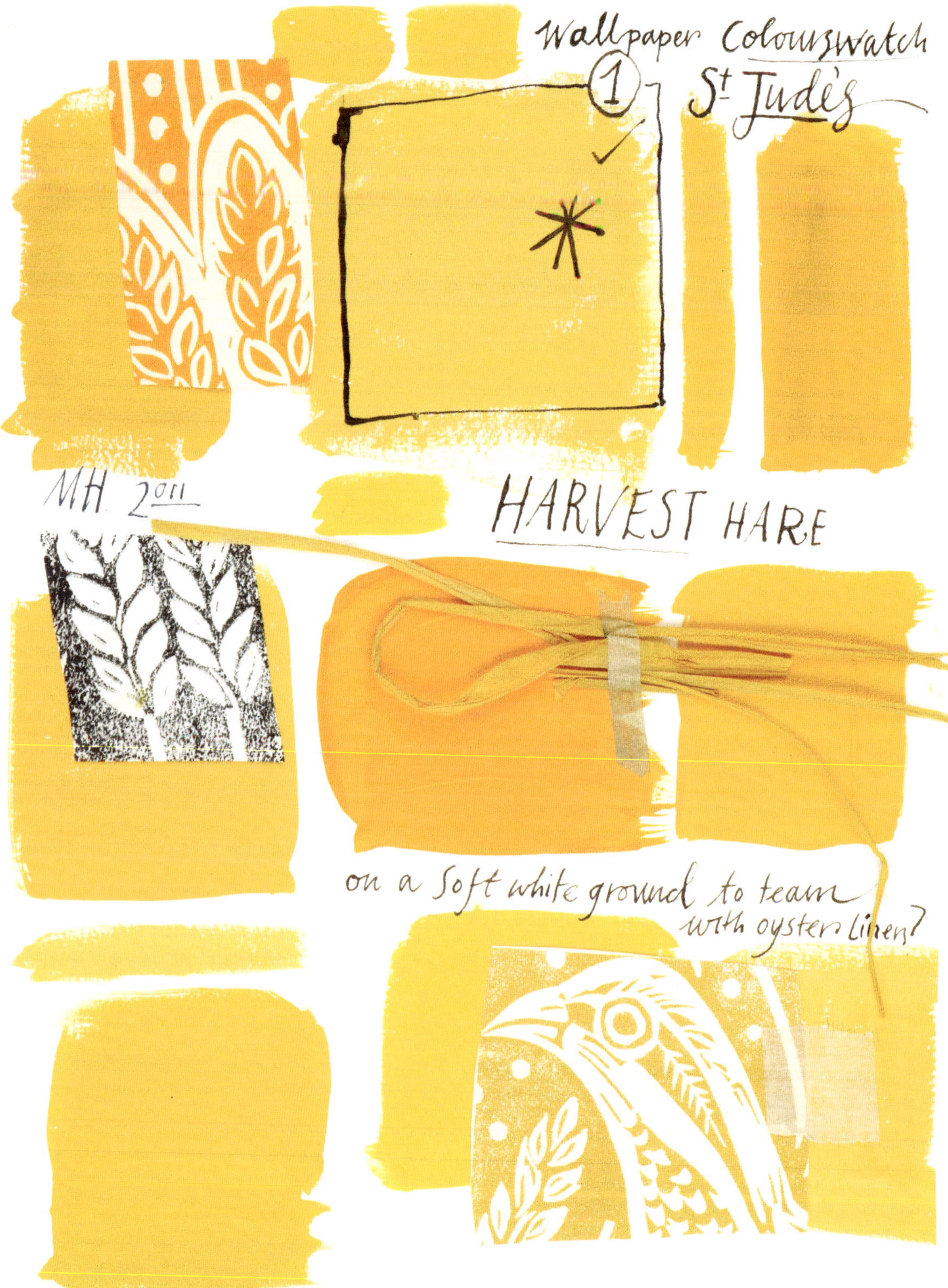

Wallpaper Colourswatch
1 St Jude's
HARVEST HARE
MH 2011
on a soft white ground to team
with oyster linen?

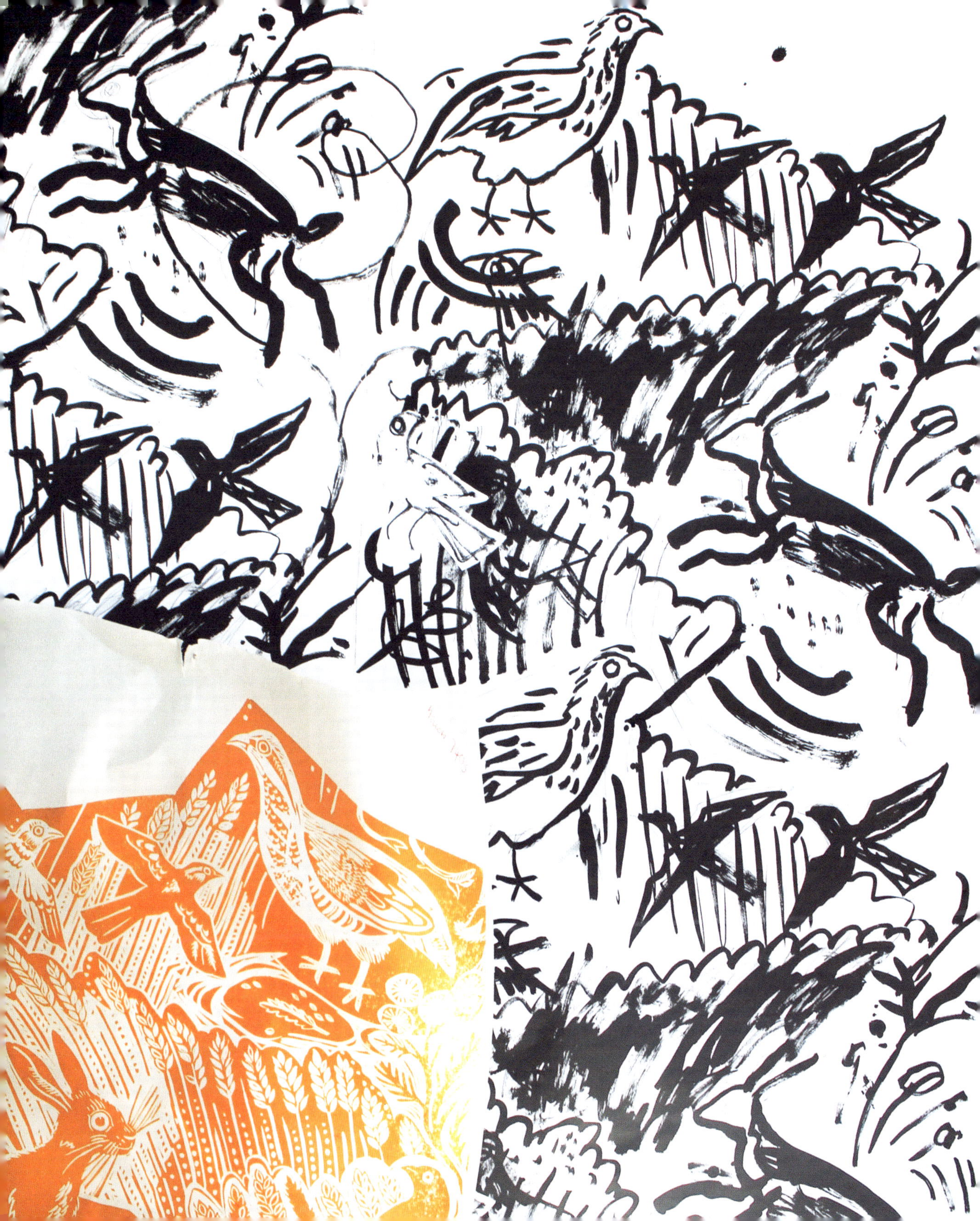

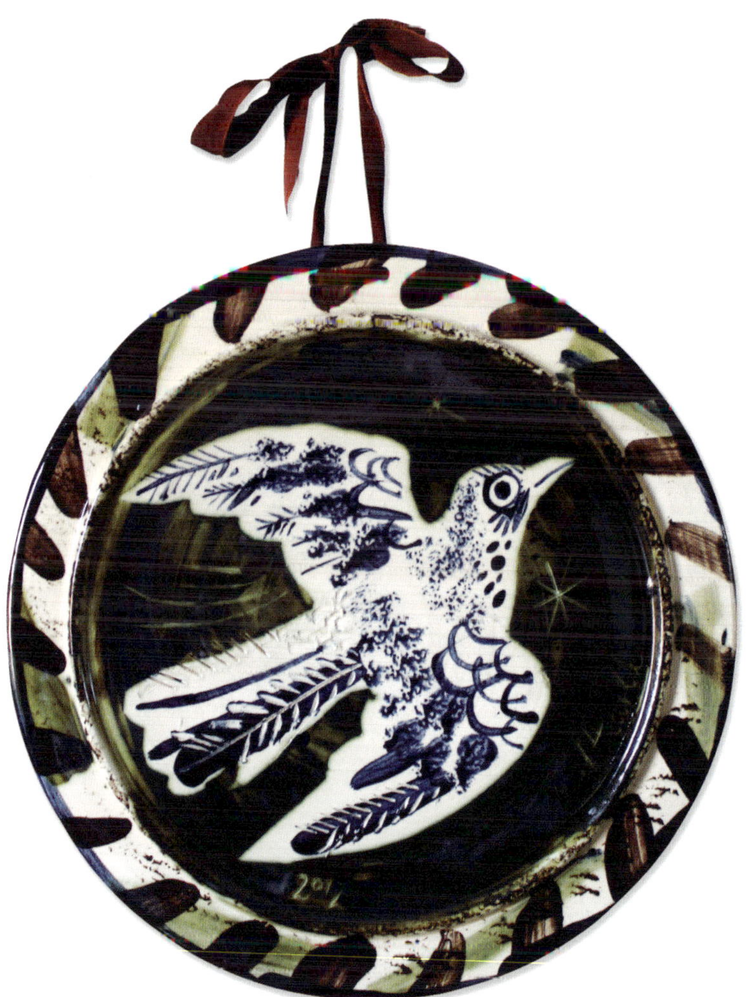

Ceramics

It is an absolute creative joy to pitch up at possibly the finest Georgian house in Whitby, with a 'bottle' window and a roof lantern with views out to sea, and be welcomed by master potter Terry Shone (pictured opposite), with whom I collaborate in his harbourside pottery. Platters, roundels or tiles are waiting under polythene to be decorated, and with folk music by Magpie Lane emanating on a loop from a dusty CD player in the corner, I set to work with scissors and newspaper stencils, fuelled by coffee and Danish pastries. I work continuously – often late into the night, perhaps stopping for a crab sandwich at lunch – until the batch is complete. Then the real potter takes over: once the pots are dry, Terry glazes, finishes and fires them.

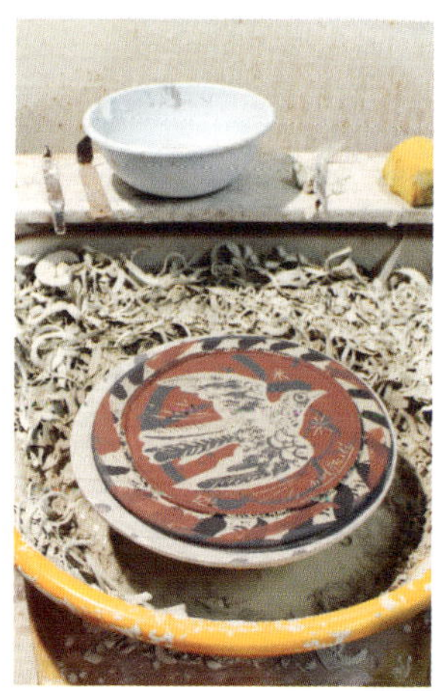

Thrush Roundel

To hang the completed *Thrush Roundel* (above), I use a piece of Petersham ribbon bought from a retired milliner at a car boot sale. It complements the rich olive-green and cobalt slip decorations, which start out deep red before firing (left). This piece belongs to a batch of work made with a full range of colours. More usually, however, I use white slip on a red body, as in the case of the platters and tiles shown on page 147. Iron in the glaze turns the white slip a wonderful mustard yellow, a finish known as 'honey glaze'.

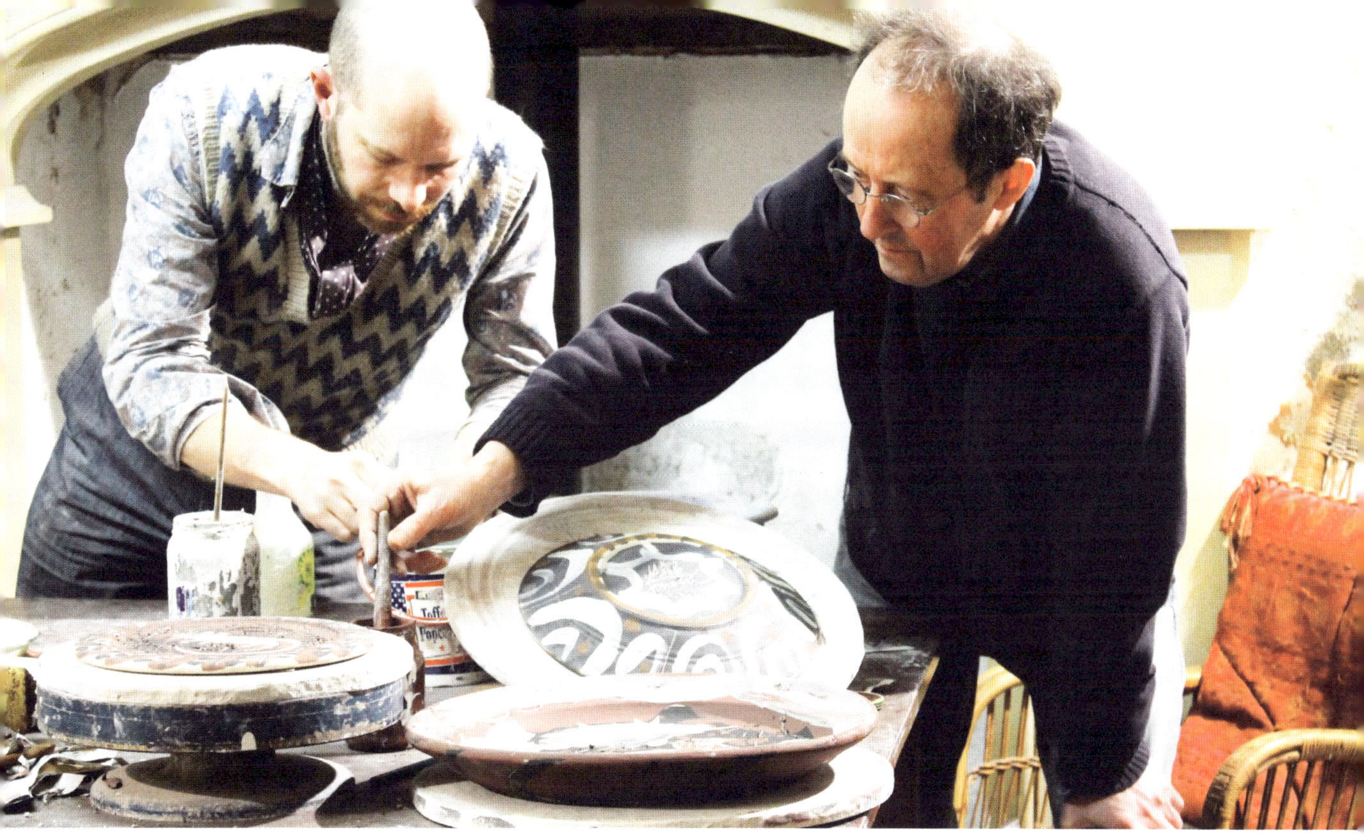

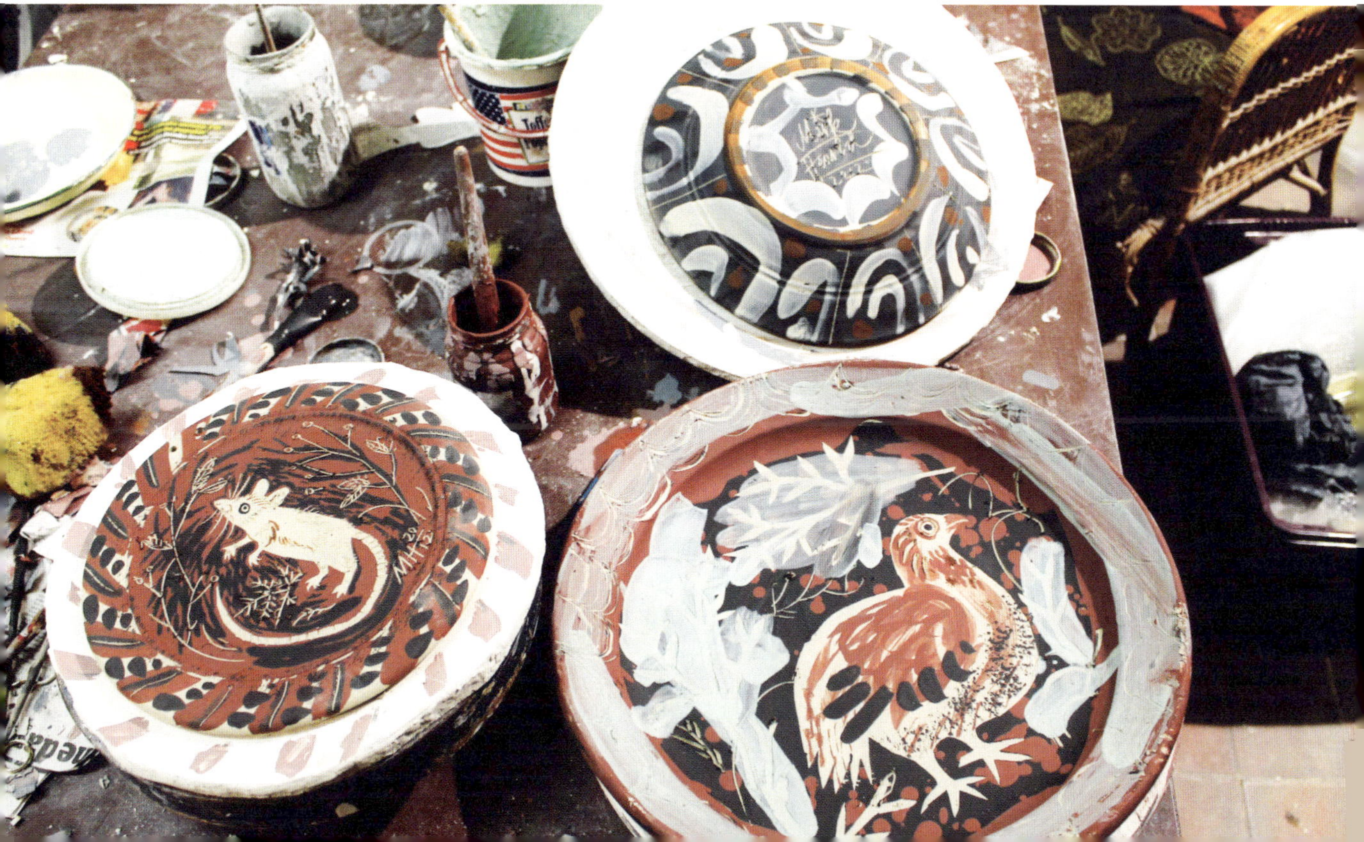

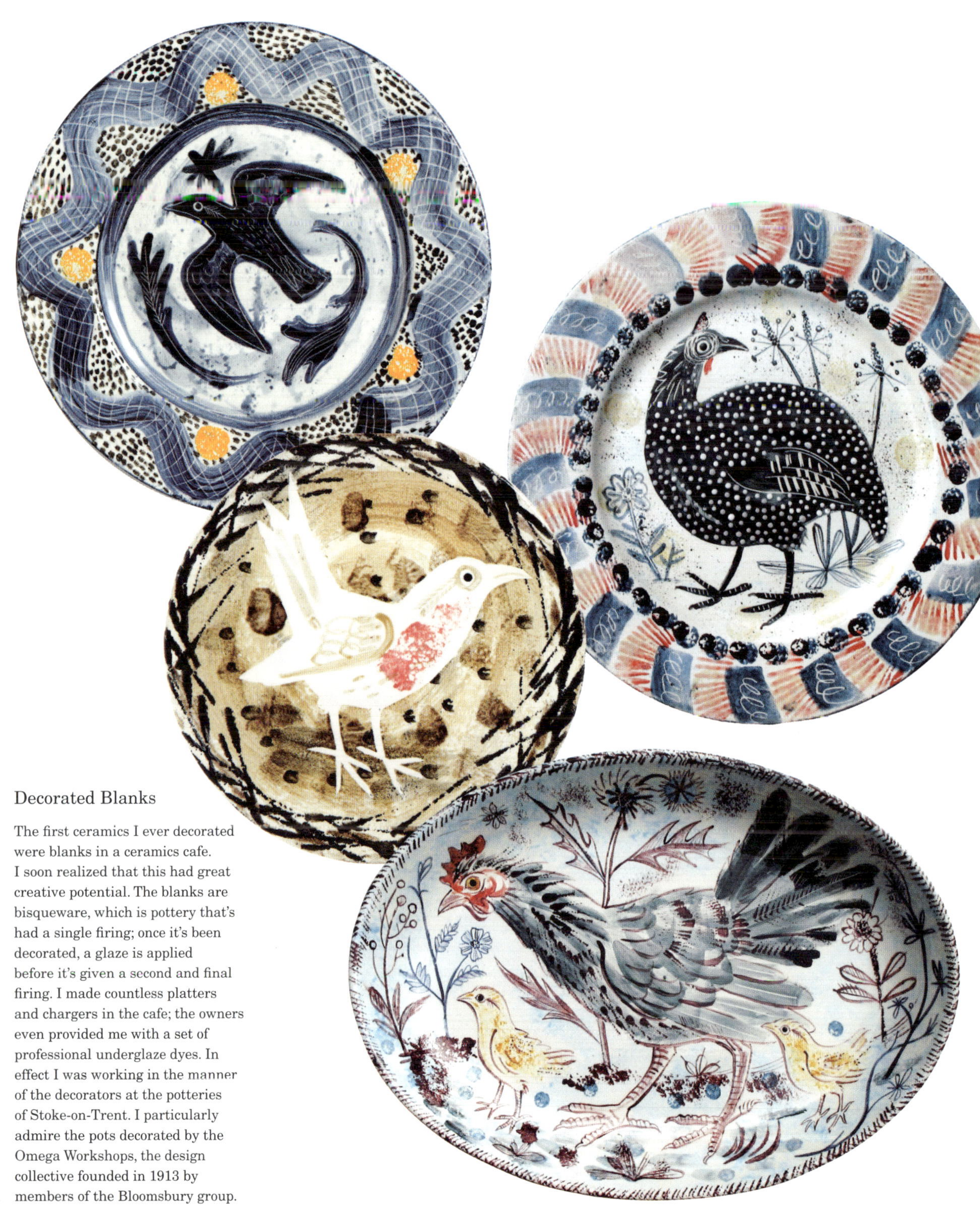

Decorated Blanks

The first ceramics I ever decorated were blanks in a ceramics cafe. I soon realized that this had great creative potential. The blanks are bisqueware, which is pottery that's had a single firing; once it's been decorated, a glaze is applied before it's given a second and final firing. I made countless platters and chargers in the cafe; the owners even provided me with a set of professional underglaze dyes. In effect I was working in the manner of the decorators at the potteries of Stoke-on-Trent. I particularly admire the pots decorated by the Omega Workshops, the design collective founded in 1913 by members of the Bloomsbury group.

146

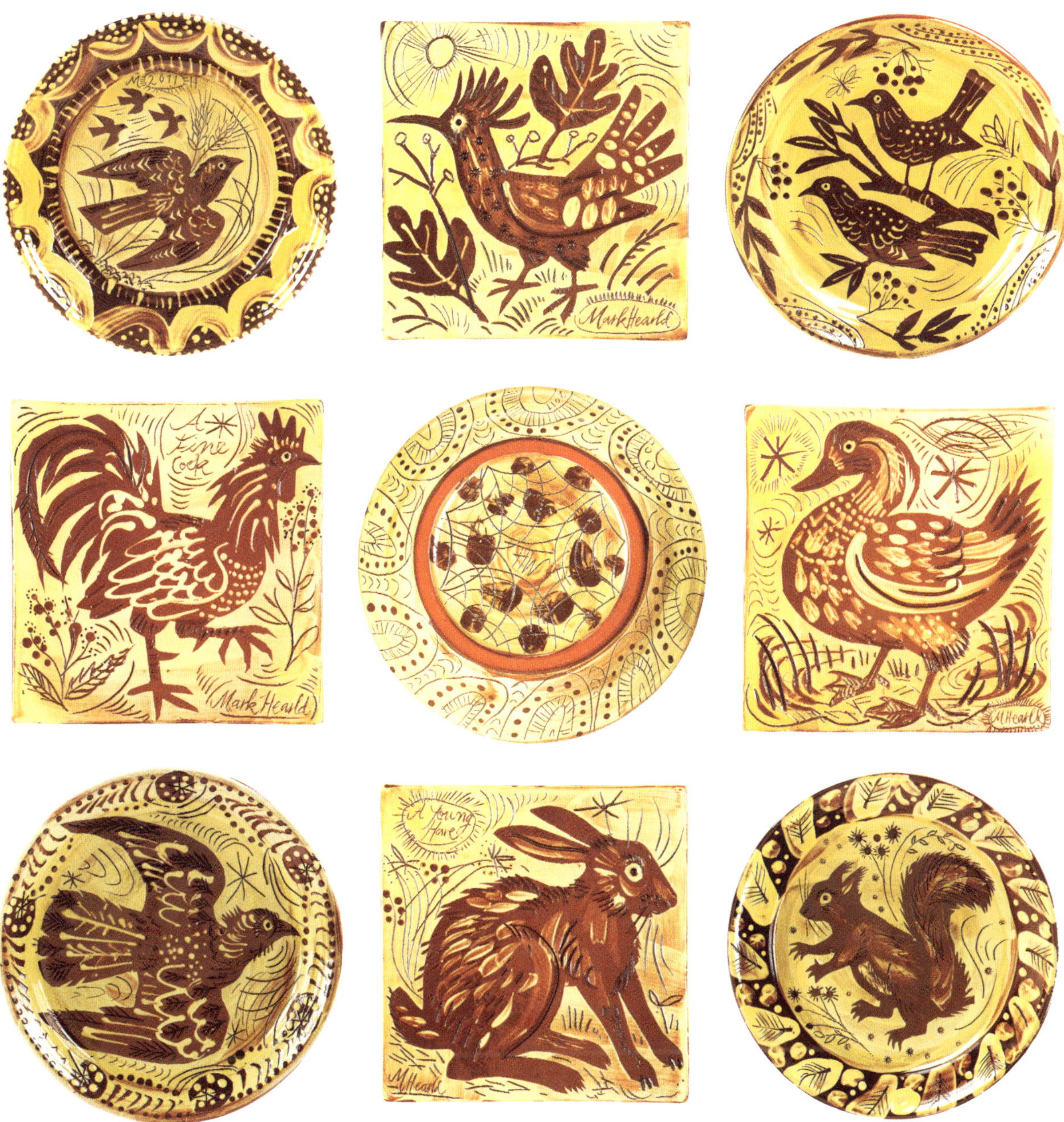

Honey-Glaze Tiles and Platters

Working with a potter on leather-dry clay followed the work I'd done on bisque-fired blanks (opposite), and once I'd got my hands on the clay itself it was hard to go back.

The capacity for a more physical approach and depth of surface achieved through sgraffitoed marks and slip-trailed flourishes took it all to a different level.

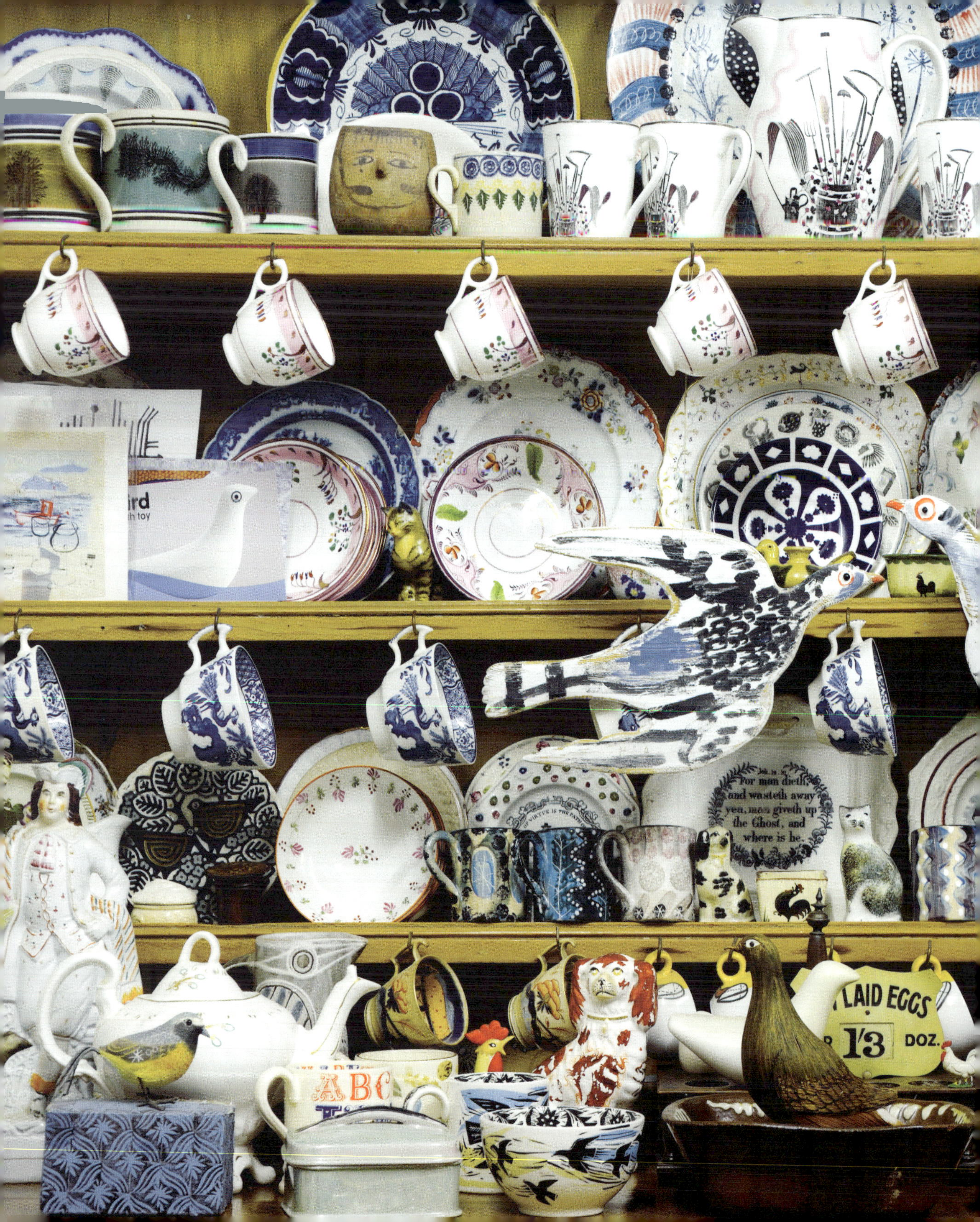

ird
h toy
For man dieth,
and wasteth away
yea, man giveth up
the Ghost, and
where is he.
VIRTUE IS THE
LAID EGGS
1/3 DOZ.
ABC

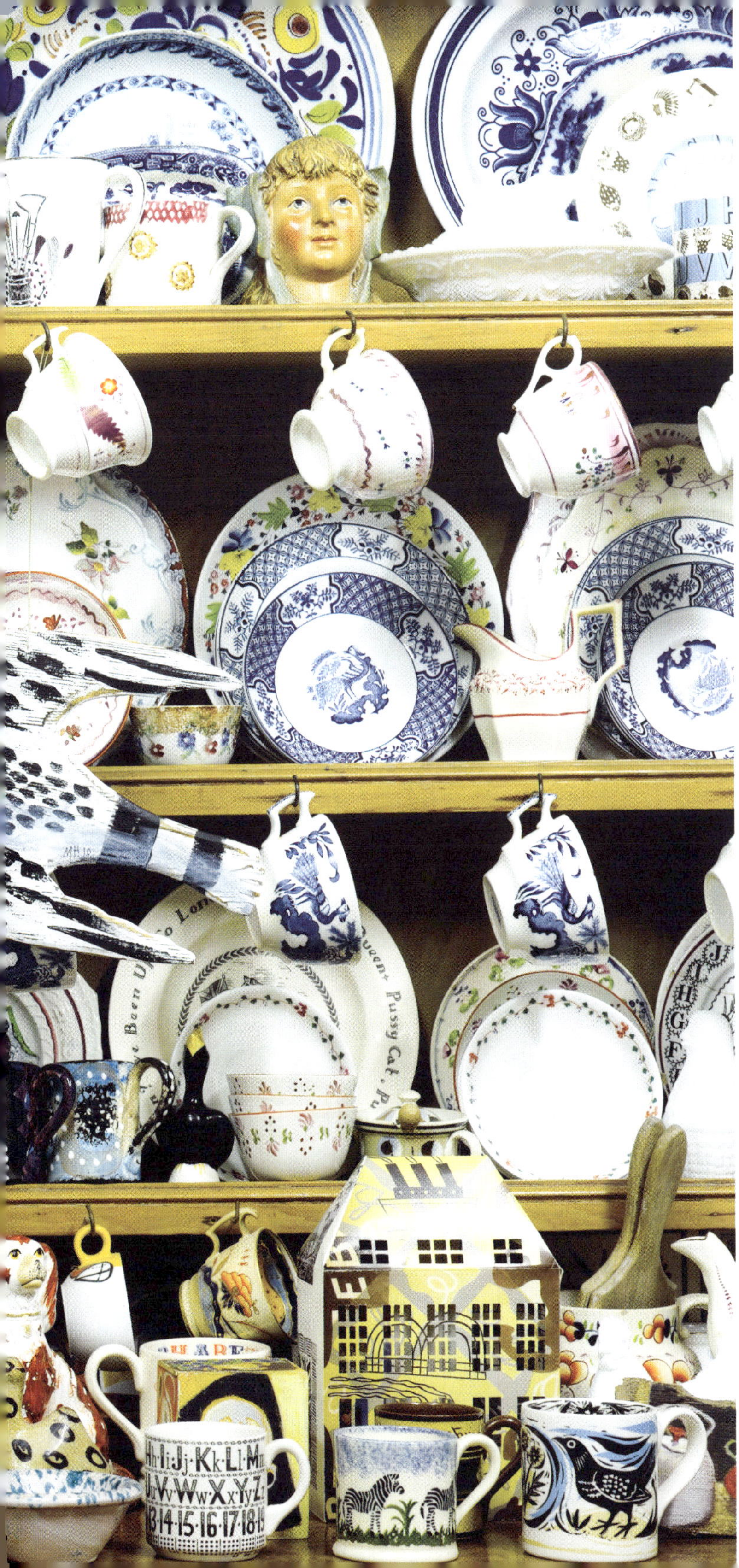

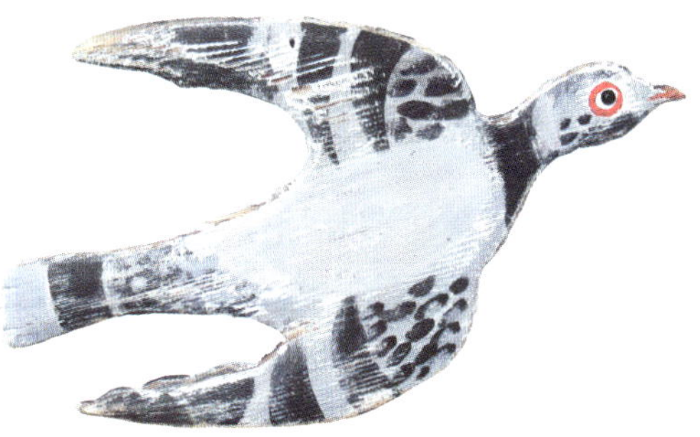

Wooden Pigeons, Iris's Dresser

The idea for the wooden pigeons came from a postcard, brought back from the Orkney Museum in Kirkwall, featuring a die-cut advertising card in the shape of a pigeon. The form was very satisfying, and led to a collaboration with Alex Godfrey, who cut out the pigeons in wood; I then decorated and finished each bird individually. I enjoyed thinking about the colour combinations and pattern elements of the birds, two of which can be seen here against the decorative ebullience of Iris Weaver's dresser. Also on display is a set of six 'coffee cans', or mugs, that I decorated for Iris (first shelf up), and my ceramics for the Tate (bottom; see page 136).

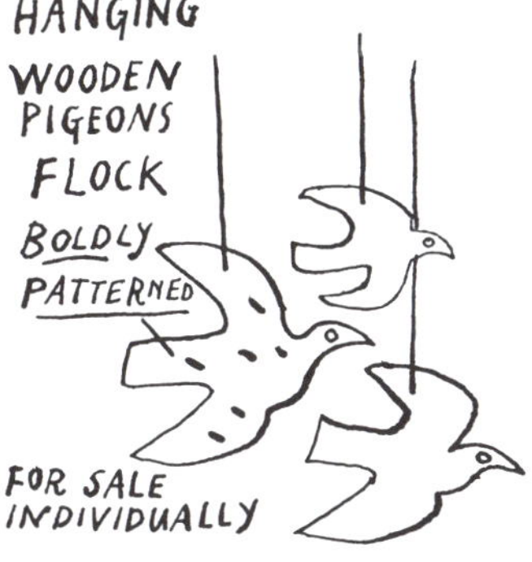

Cats

The pleasing stripes of a tabby appear on the wooden cat and in a collage, although the two works were made years apart. Creating the distinctive striped pattern has an enduring appeal, and the tabby feels like the archetypal cat.

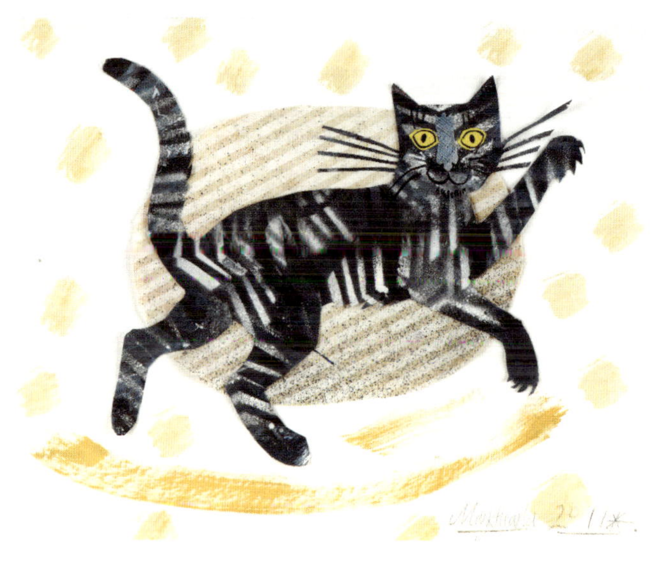

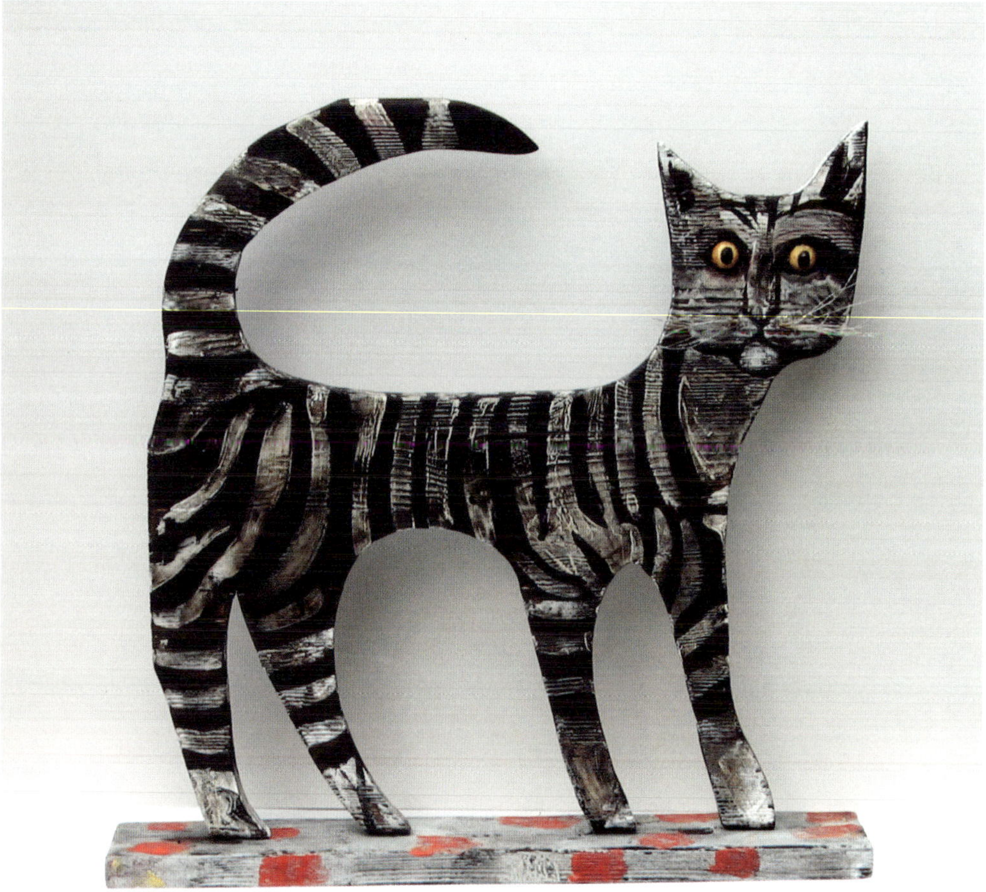

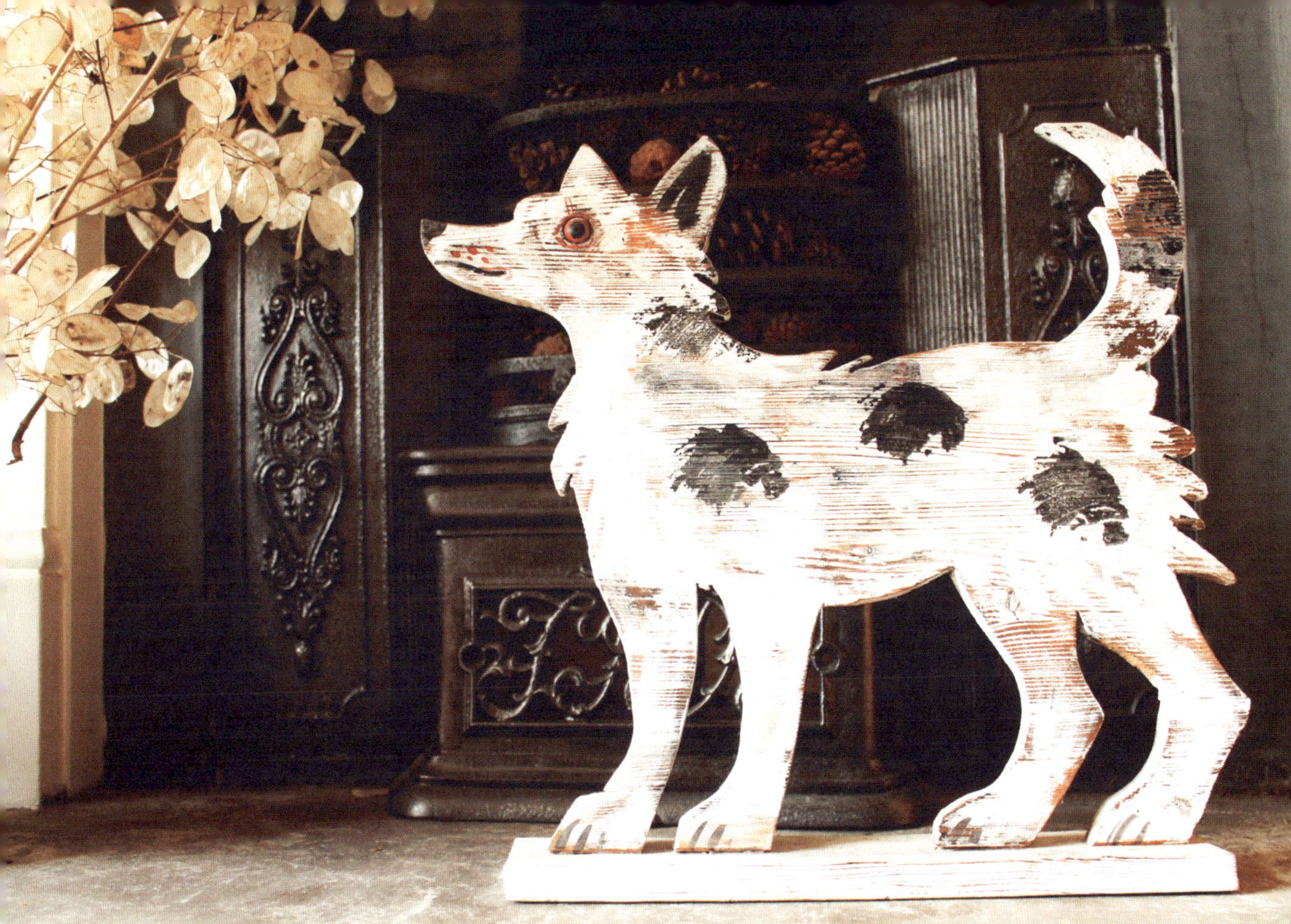

Objects

Dog

This wooden dog was inspired by the seventeenth- and eighteenth-century folk-art tradition of 'dummy boards', *trompe l'œil* cut-outs of people and animals often used as summer fireguards. I cut the dog out of pine, burnt it lightly to bring out the grain, then applied paint and rubbed it back. A wooden bead forms the eye. The importance of the silhouette relates to the shapes I use in collage. Here, the flat cut-out suddenly becomes a three-dimensional object.

Although my work is ordinarily two-dimensional, I'm a great collector of 'things'. I cannot pass an antique shop or miss a Saturday car boot fair on the Knavesmire in York for fear of some fantastic artefact passing me by. Finding a must-have object fulfils a similar impulse to creating it myself, but on returning from New York, say, with a head full of artefacts from the American Folk Art Museum, I feel the urge to make objects: decoy ducks, dummy boards, carved weathervanes, hand-decorated slipware chargers. In making such things, I often collaborate with other makers, which is a relief from the act of creating alone.

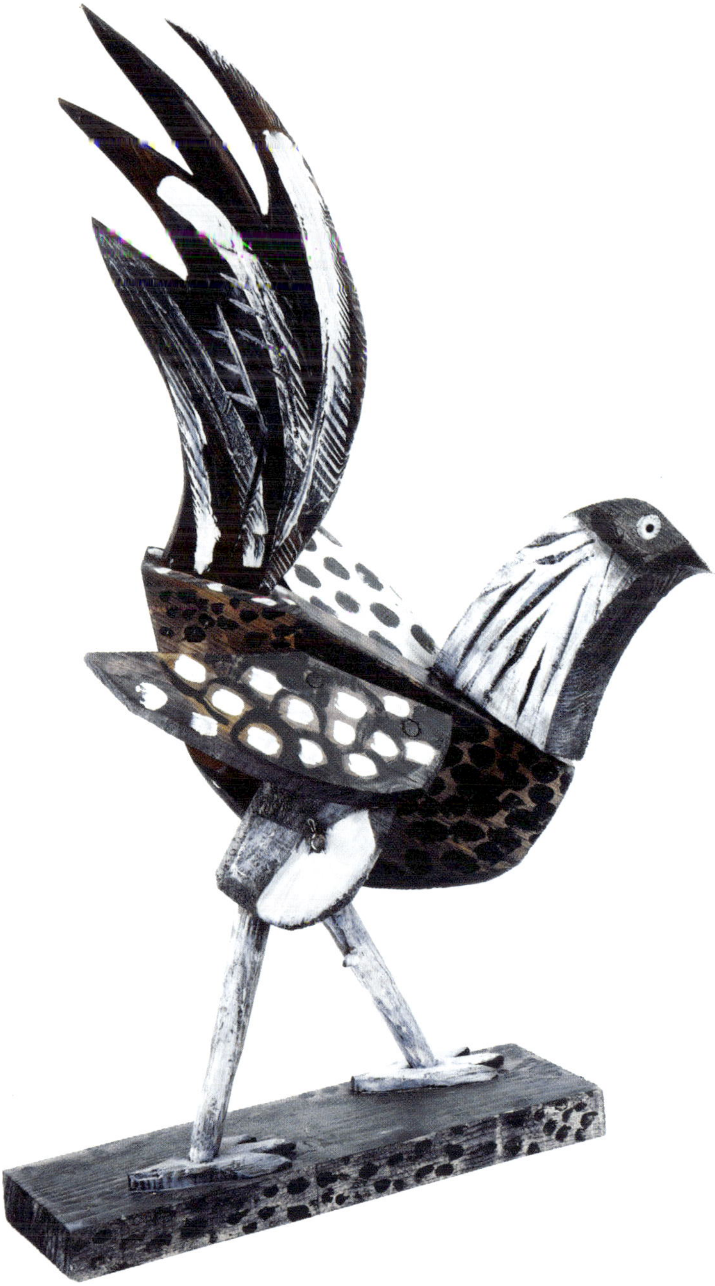

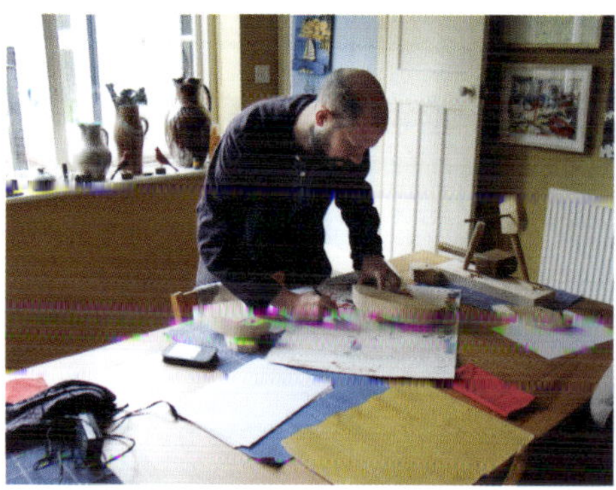

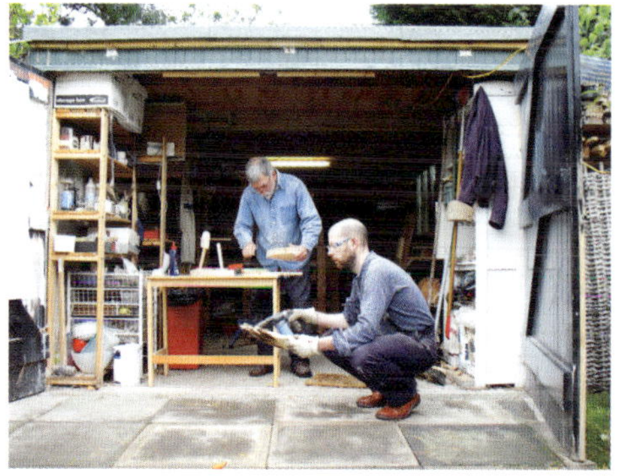

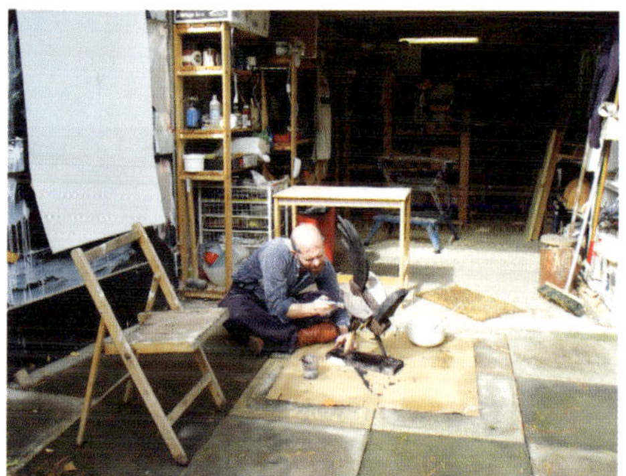

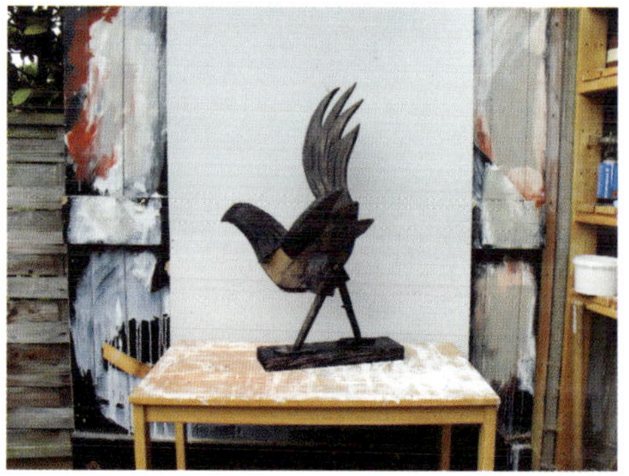

Cockerel

This piece definitely takes inspiration from Picasso's sculptures, as well as from his cubist collages. It's wonderful to create in three dimensions, and this work is about both form and pattern: the surface mark-making was of equal importance to the sculptural mass. The cockerel is articulated: its head and body can be moved to determine its stance. The process of making was exciting, and gave me another opportunity to work with Alex Godfrey (pictured second from top). He made sure it won't fall to bits.

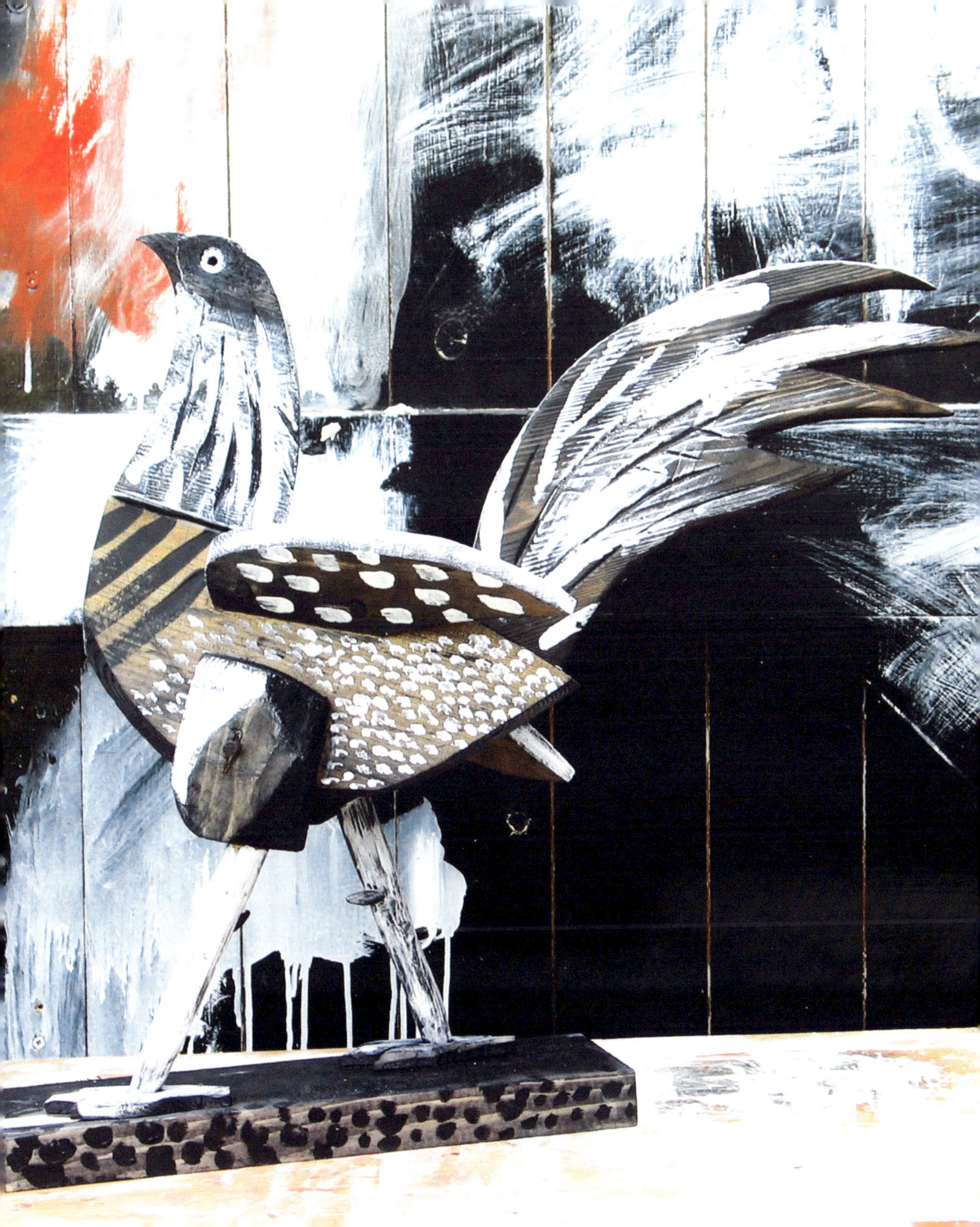

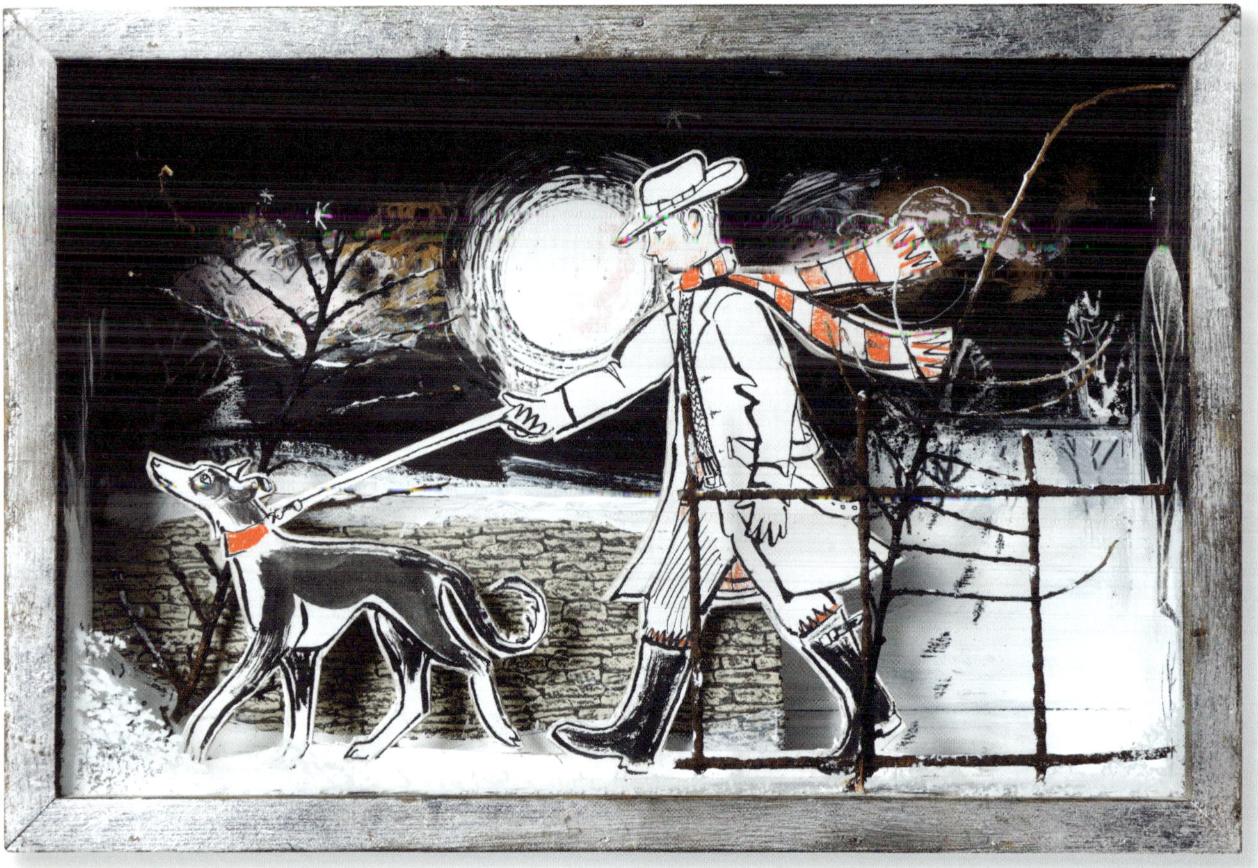

Boxes

A fascination with Victorian
dioramas, miniature butchers'
shops and boats in boxes inspired
me to make a series of box works.
I rarely draw figures, but as a
dog walker I sometimes appear in
my own pieces with some dog or
other. In *Dog Walker* (above), I'm
walking Mags, my parents' lurcher.
Margaret Steward commissioned
me to make a box work (opposite)
to celebrate the seventieth birthday
of her partner, Peter Scupham.
It features Old Hall, their
sixteenth-century house in Norfolk
complete with stucco mermaids,
wall paintings and a thatched roof.
I chose to set the house in a winter
forest, where wild creatures and
family pets animate the snowscape.

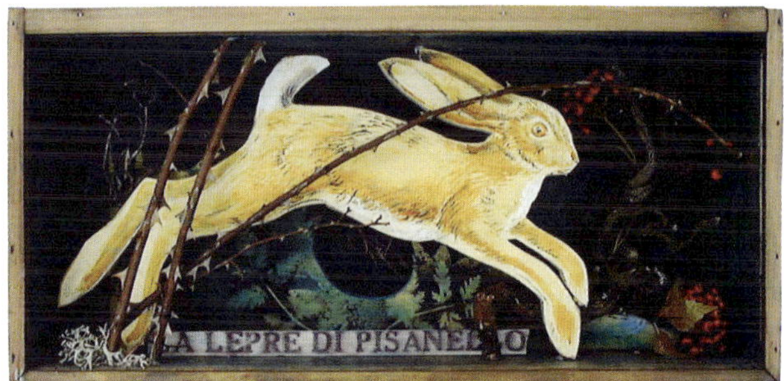

Pisanello's Hare (Box Work)

This box work, made inside an old
drawer found in a derelict hut on
Dungeness in Kent, was one of the
first pieces I exhibited at Godfrey
& Watt, the gallery in Harrogate,
North Yorkshire, co-founded by Alex
Godfrey. It also led to the lithograph
Pisanello's Hare (pages 26–27).

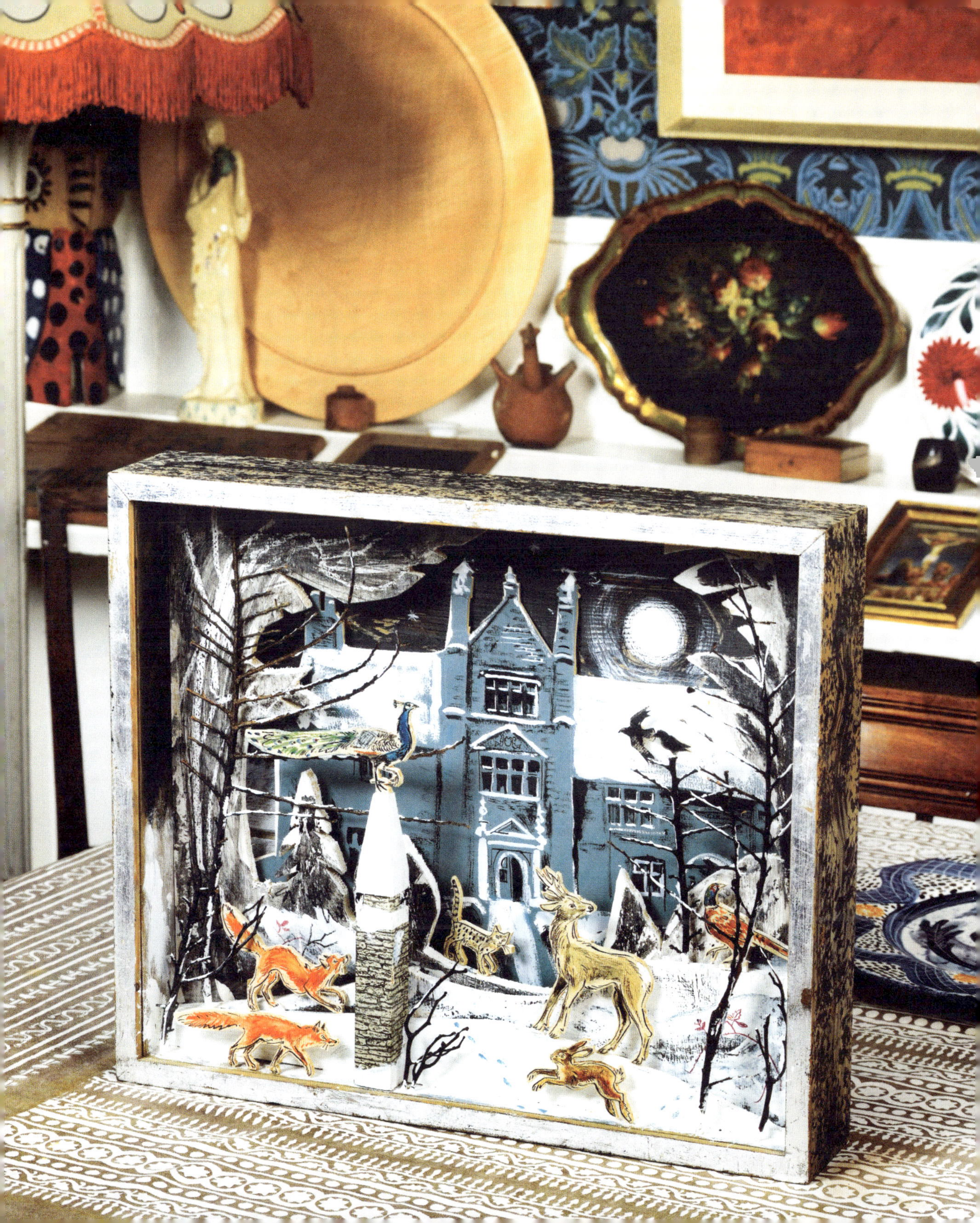

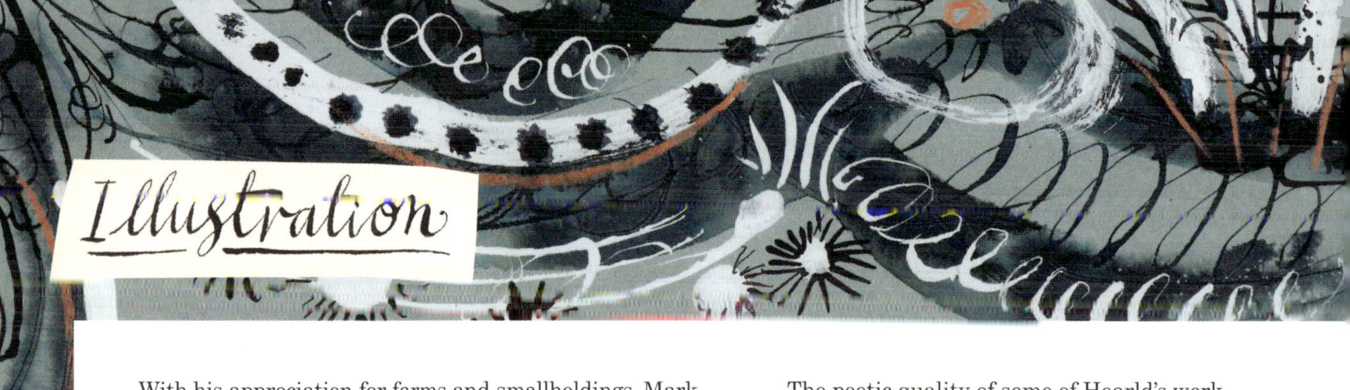

With his appreciation for farms and smallholdings, Mark Hearld was the ideal person to illustrate the cover of a recent edition of Stella Gibbons's cult novel *Cold Comfort Farm* (2011; first published 1932), in which the heroine, Flora Poste, arrives at a ramshackle farm owned by her eccentric relatives the Starkadders. Within the patterned-paper borders of Hearld's cover (page 162) is a collaged view of the farm, with the bull named Big Business – released from his pen by Flora – in the foreground. But Hearld's childlike view can also give way to a more brooding atmosphere. When asked by Penguin Books to produce a cover for the paperback edition of Ross Raisin's first novel, *God's Own Country* (2009; pages 162–63), Hearld created a linocut design that is at once lyrical and tinged with a sense of threat, reflecting the story of a marginalized and troubled adolescent growing up on a farm on the Yorkshire moors. Hearld's cover features a gnarled tree and several carrion crows silhouetted against the sky, recalling a wood engraving by the visionary artist–poet William Blake entitled *The Blasted Tree and Blighted Crops* (1821). A similar darkness is evident in Hearld's cover for a compilation of poetry by Ted Hughes (page 162), one of a series of hardback editions of twentieth-century poetry marking Faber & Faber's eightieth anniversary in 2009. The central image of a hawk, its talons curling around some text, suggests Hughes's poem 'Hawk Roosting' (1960), which includes the lines: 'Between my hooked head and hooked feet: / Or in sleep rehearse perfect kills and eat.'

The poetic quality of some of Hearld's work – specifically, those pieces in the tradition of such British pastoral artists as Samuel Palmer and John Minton – led his collage *Harvest Moon* (page 55) to be used as the cover for *Borrowed Landscapes* (2011), a book of poetry by Peter Scupham (whose poem 'The Winter Farmhouse' appears on page 123 of this book). Similarly, Hearld's nocturnal view of Christ Church Spitalfields in London, part of his series of illustrations for *Spitalfields Life* (2012; see pages 164–65), features a huge, poetic, Palmeresque moon, which lights up the rooftops. Other images in the book depict nature in the city: a fox foraging in rubbish bins, a Red Admiral butterfly in a graveyard, a cat chasing a rat past a market barrow.

This sense of looking at wildlife with fresh eyes equally characterizes Hearld's illustrations for *A First Book of Nature* by Nicola Davies (2012; see pages 166–69). The book is full of images of the kind of natural life that a child might encounter: nesting birds, newborn lambs, tadpoles in a pond, geese, caterpillars and butterflies, and even a lizard. The illustrations are a mixture of collage, painted and hand-drawn pieces, linocuts, pastel markings and spray-painted skies, giving the book a textured immediacy and vitality. 'Cut-out pigeons fly through the air and collaged fish swim in a rock pool', explains Hearld. 'This book was a joy to illustrate. Nicola's text is so observant and particular that its rich cast of creatures were a delight to bring to life.' Hearld's illustrations reflect his 'child's-eye view'

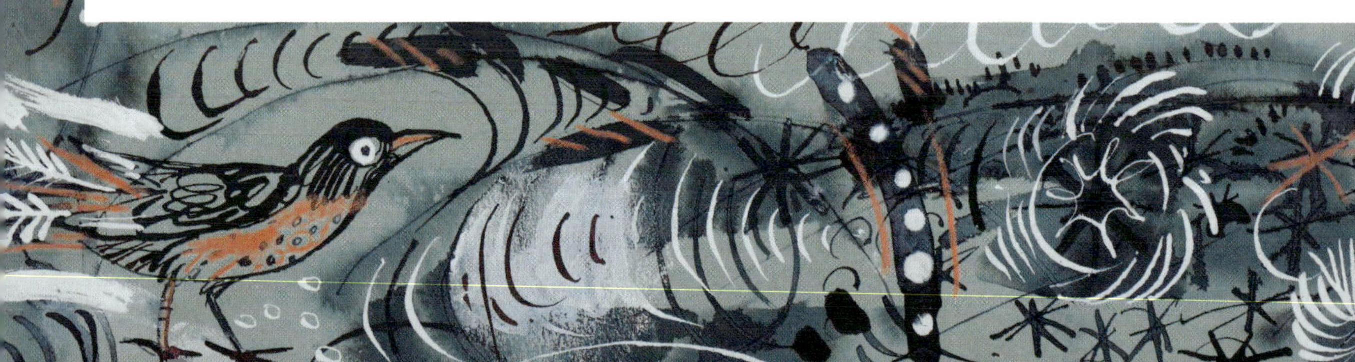

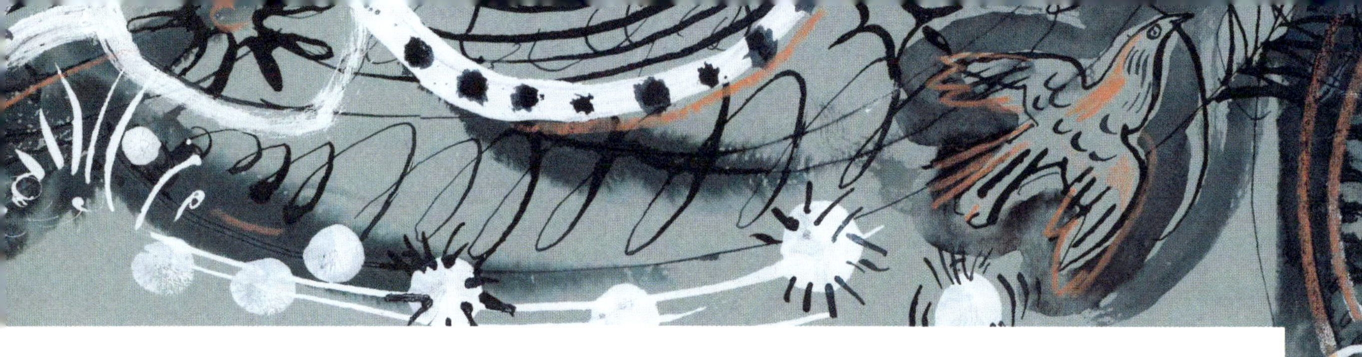

and his remarkable ability to impart to others his own
enthusiasm for nature. The book connects children to
nature in a simple and direct way: hand-drawn lists of
how to make compost are surrounded by collaged scrap
paper and a mischievous mouse, while a recipe for Berry
Crumble sits among curving brambles and a hungry
starling. There are also beautifully drawn objects
that might be found on a beachcombing expedition,
a thronging bird table with instructions on how to
make bird cake, and ideas for things to do in a den.

The hand of the artist is ever present in Hearld's
work. The line that characterizes his drawings is
equally fluid in his distinctive handwriting. He often
uses an ink pen for composing letters and texts, treating
the act of writing like drawing. He cites seeing Picasso's
handwritten letters in Paris and admiring their
flourishes and humorous graphic doodles in hand-
dipped ink, as well as nineteenth-century copperplate
pen-work, with its scrolls and cartouches. 'I love the
feeling of writing with a dip pen,' he explains, 'taking
off pressure on the upstroke and adding pressure on
the down-stroke.' In common with his illustrations, his
handwriting style connects with the artist–illustrator
tradition in British art, which stretches back to the
illustrated books of poetry by Blake, such as his *Songs
of Innocence and Experience* (1789); the piped frosting-
style lettering of Graham Sutherland's work for David
Gascoyne's *Poems 1937–1942* (1943); and John Minton's
illustrations for Elizabeth David's first two cookery

books (1950 and 1951). The relationship between
handwritten text and image is important to Hearld's
work, since he values the former's graphic quality. While
many artists would happily settle for a typed exhibition
checklist, Hearld's invariably feature his handwriting
in printed form. He has also received commissions
to produce flyers and ephemera in his scrolled text,
such as a map of North Norfolk for St Jude's Gallery,
invitations and flyers for the National Book Fair in York
(pages 160–61) and a mind map for his exhibition *The
Magpie Eye* at Scarborough Art Gallery (see page 14).

In the age of email and text-speak, the handwritten
letter possesses a unique quality, especially when it
is clear that the author has taken such pleasure in
the act of mark-making. The arrival of a letter from
Hearld is nothing short of an event, because the
envelope has often been embellished with decorative
details, sometimes even an illustration (see, for example,
pages 176, left, and 178–79). As part of his range for
the Tate, Hearld created *Pigeon Post* (pages 182–83), a
correspondence card reminiscent of an old airmail letter.
Inspired by his love of Enid Marx's wartime children's
book *The Pigeon Ace* (1943), as well as by seeing
some decorated General Post Office (GPO) greetings
telegrams from the 1930s and 1940s, Hearld decided
to produce his own piece of postal ephemera. Featuring
his distinctive pigeons and decorative papers, *Pigeon
Post* captures the spirit of a handmade item while
encouraging handwritten communication.

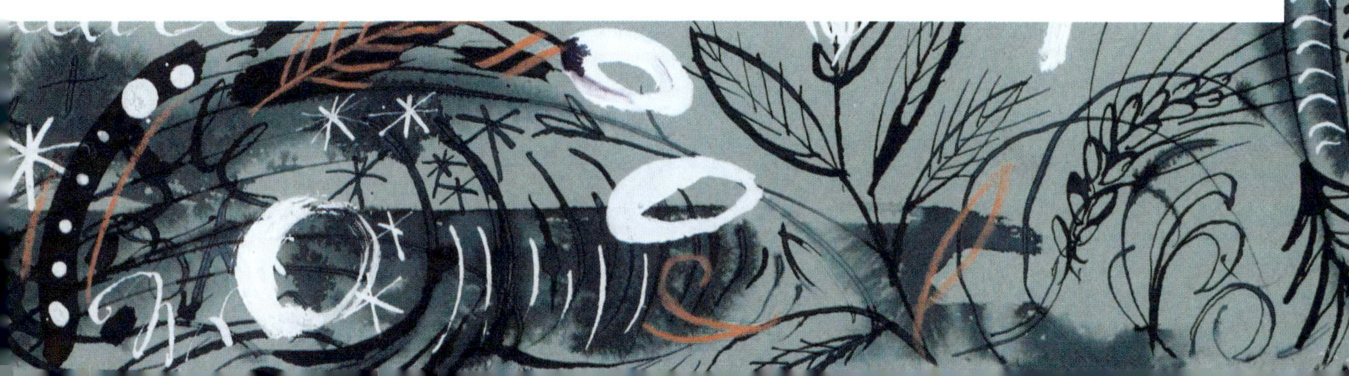

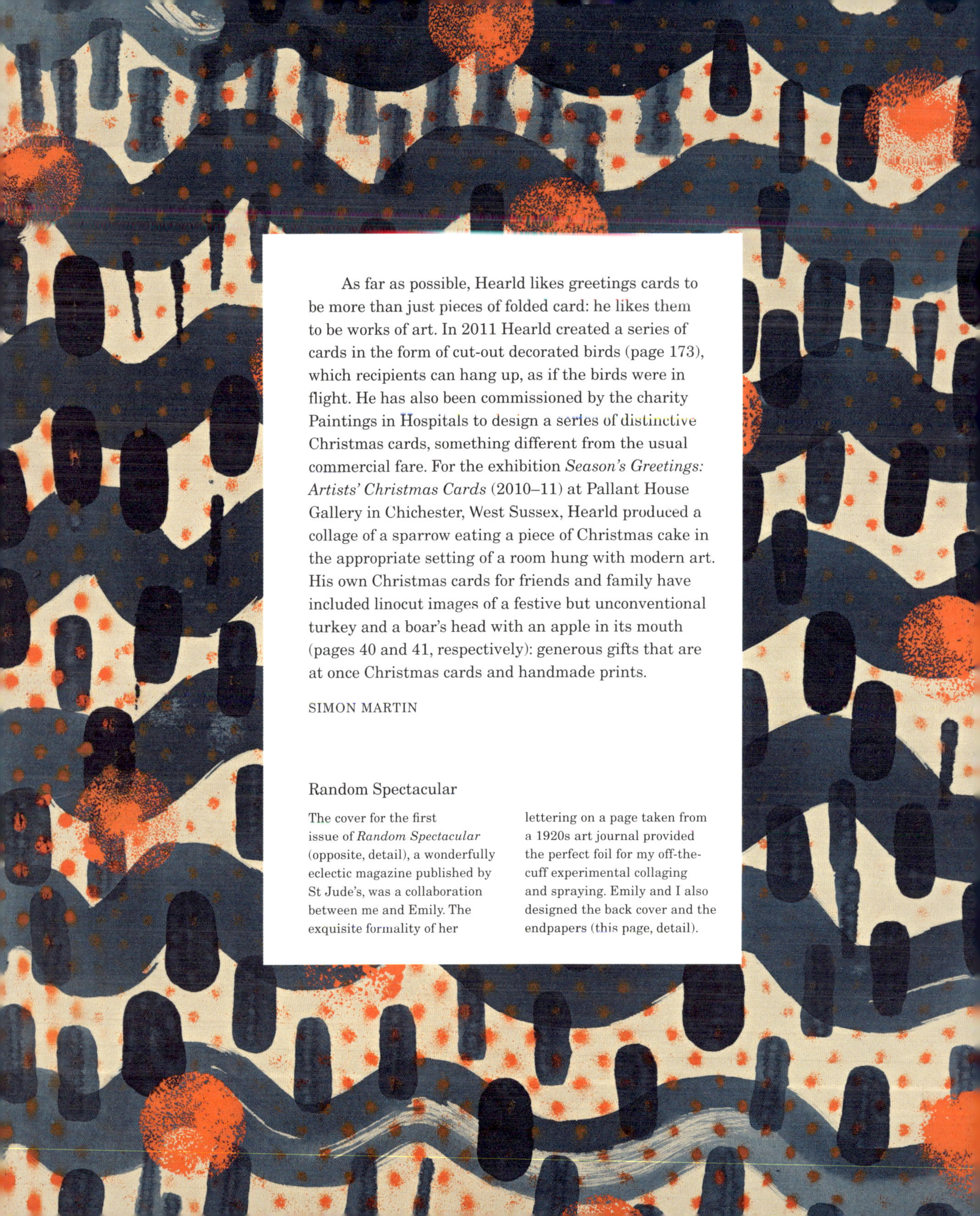

As far as possible, Hearld likes greetings cards to be more than just pieces of folded card: he likes them to be works of art. In 2011 Hearld created a series of cards in the form of cut-out decorated birds (page 173), which recipients can hang up, as if the birds were in flight. He has also been commissioned by the charity Paintings in Hospitals to design a series of distinctive Christmas cards, something different from the usual commercial fare. For the exhibition *Season's Greetings: Artists' Christmas Cards* (2010–11) at Pallant House Gallery in Chichester, West Sussex, Hearld produced a collage of a sparrow eating a piece of Christmas cake in the appropriate setting of a room hung with modern art. His own Christmas cards for friends and family have included linocut images of a festive but unconventional turkey and a boar's head with an apple in its mouth (pages 40 and 41, respectively): generous gifts that are at once Christmas cards and handmade prints.

SIMON MARTIN

Random Spectacular

The cover for the first issue of *Random Spectacular* (opposite, detail), a wonderfully eclectic magazine published by St Jude's, was a collaboration between me and Emily. The exquisite formality of her lettering on a page taken from a 1920s art journal provided the perfect foil for my off-the-cuff experimental collaging and spraying. Emily and I also designed the back cover and the endpapers (this page, detail).

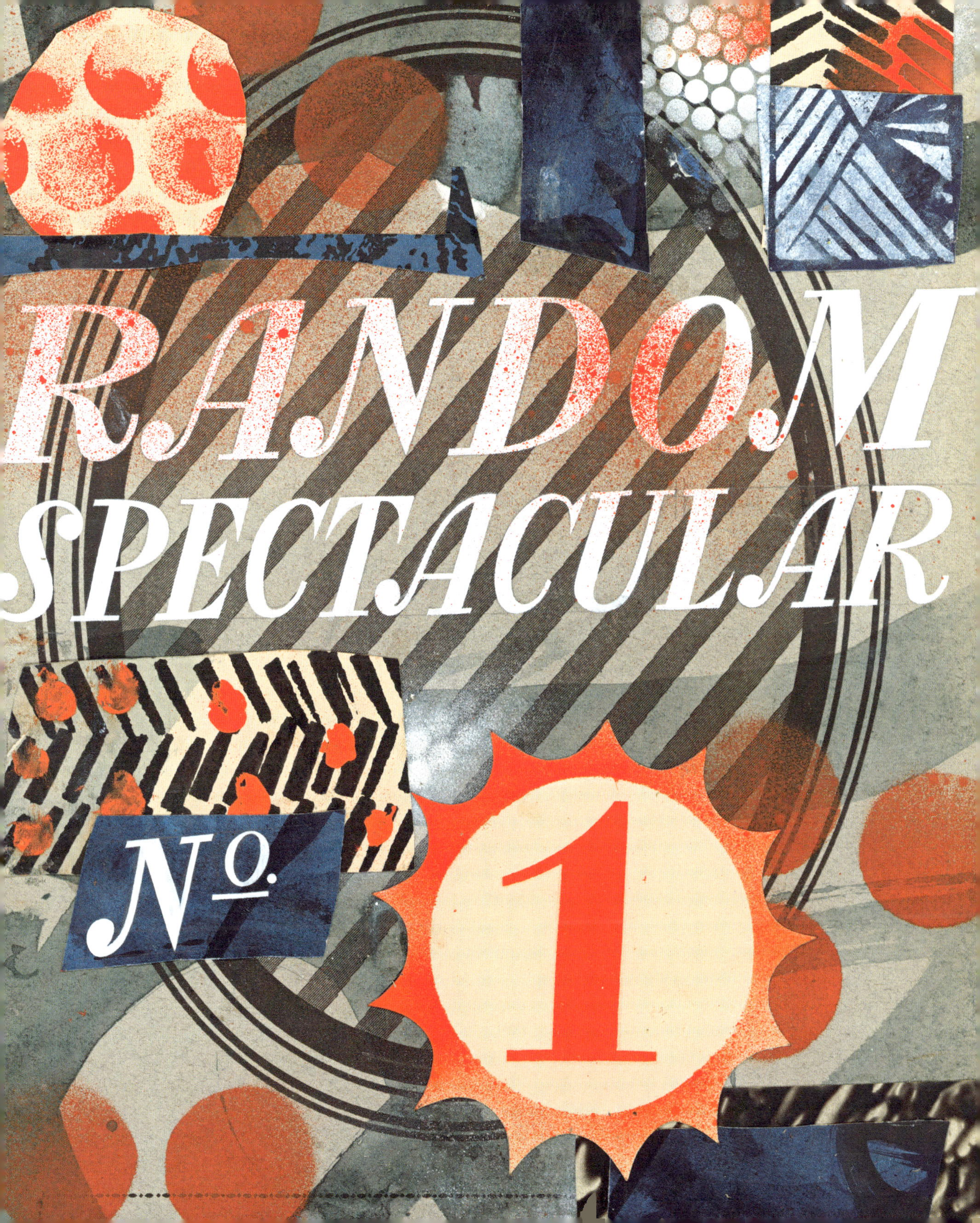

RANDOM
SPECTACULAR
Nº.
1

York Book Fair

I was approached by the organizers of York Book Fair and by the Provincial Booksellers Fairs Association (PBFA) to come up with promotional material for the fair and for book collecting in general. The existing PBFA logo had been designed by Edward Bawden, so I was keen to come up with a playful response. Cats carry piles of books, a mischievous mouse holds Bawden's cat logo on high, and a pigeon carries a banner in its beak. The whole project was great fun, and provided me with a lot of experience working with text and image. Ultimately, it led to the commission from the Tate to design a range of products (see, for example, pages 182–83).

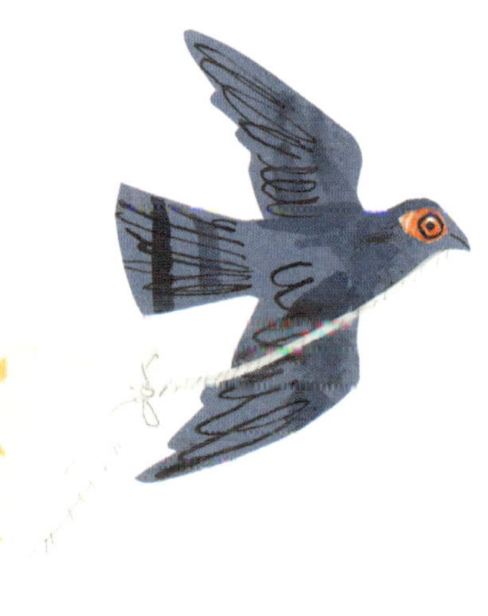

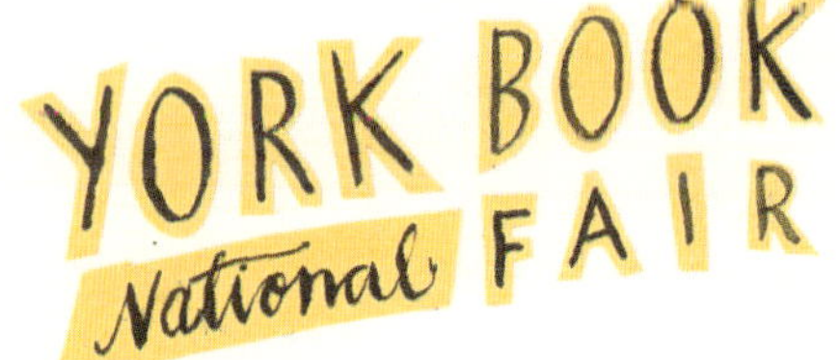

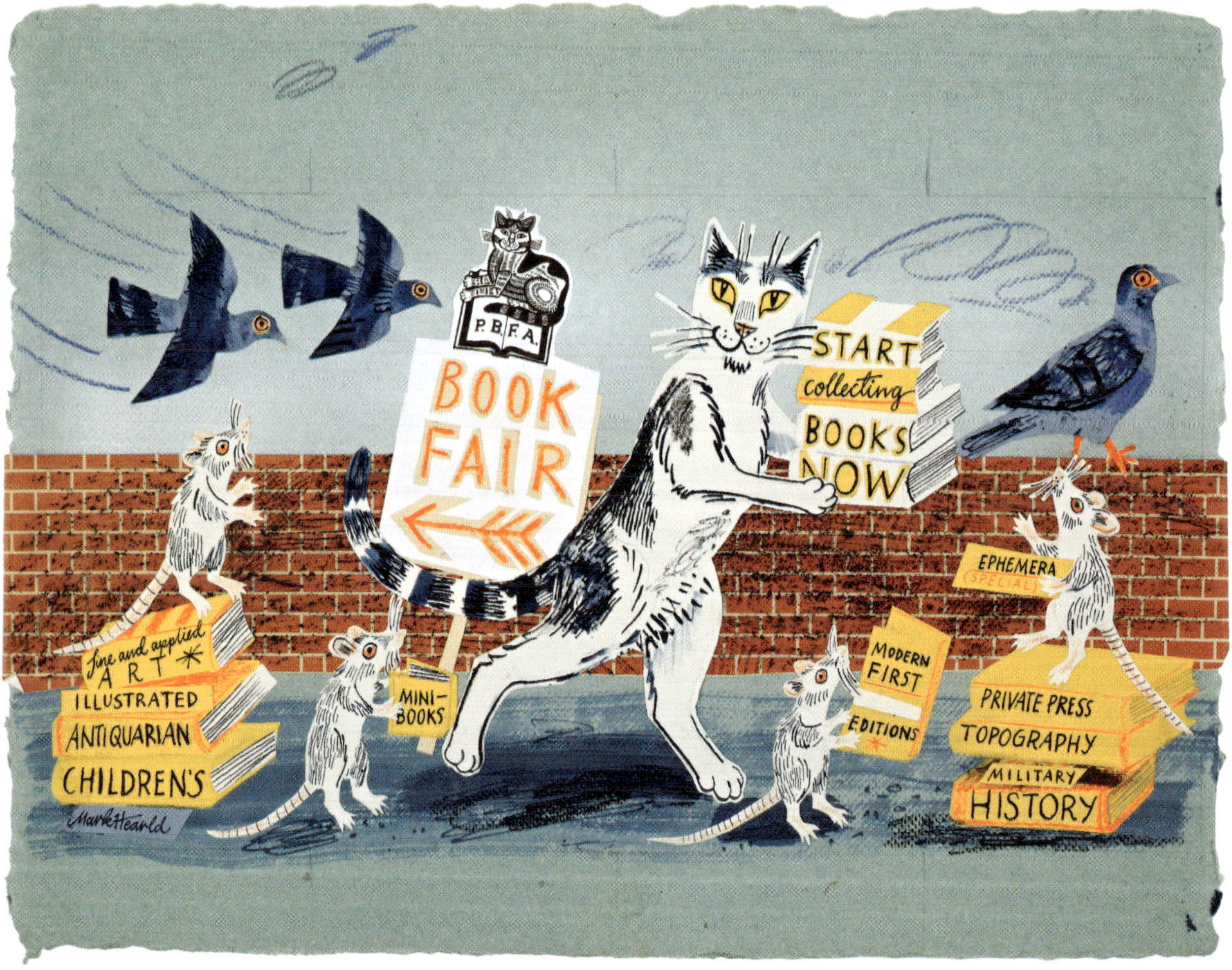

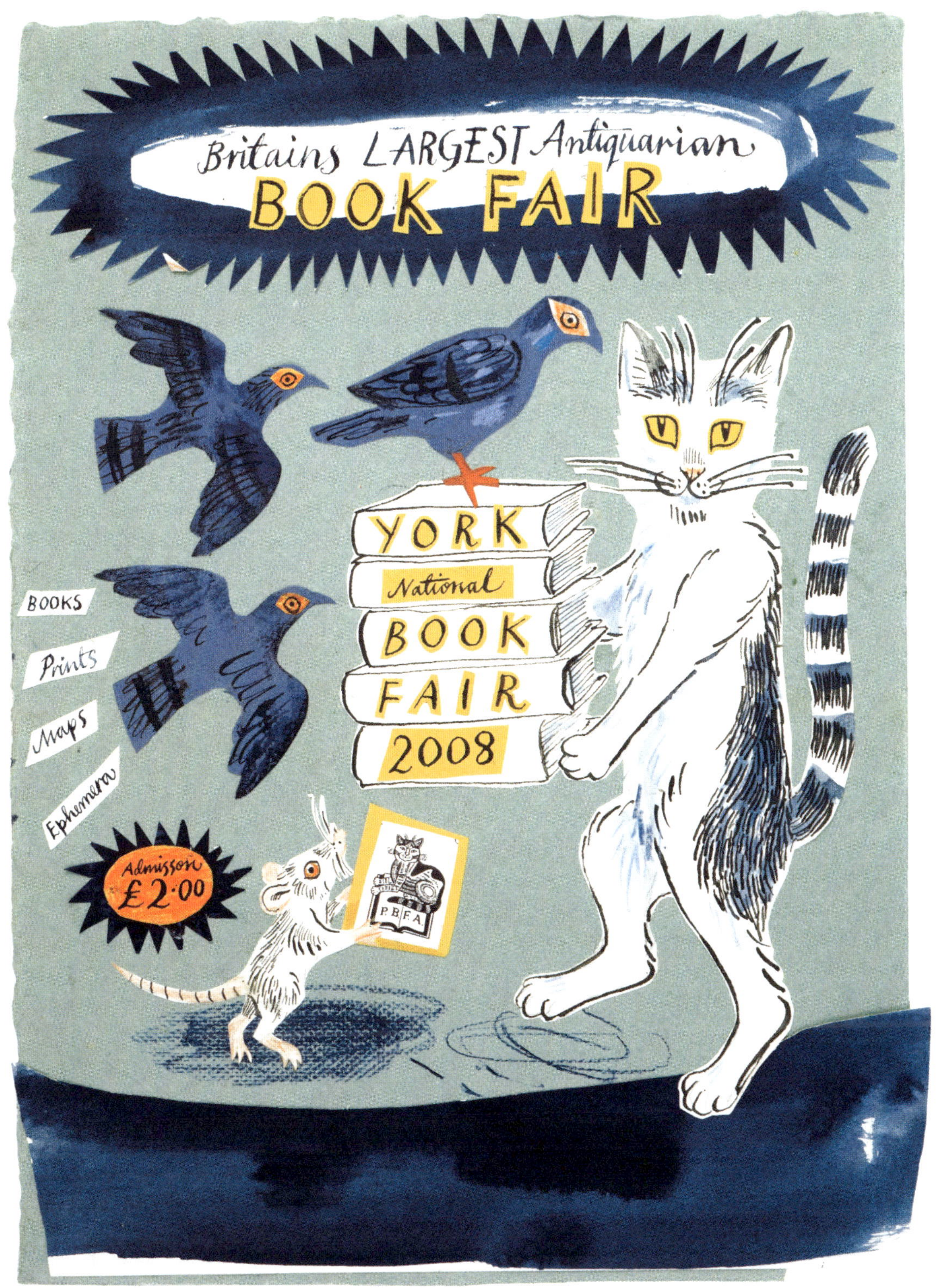

Britains LARGEST Antiquarian
BOOK FAIR
BOOKS
Prints
Maps
Ephemera
YORK
National
BOOK
FAIR
2008
Admission
£2·00
P.B.F.A

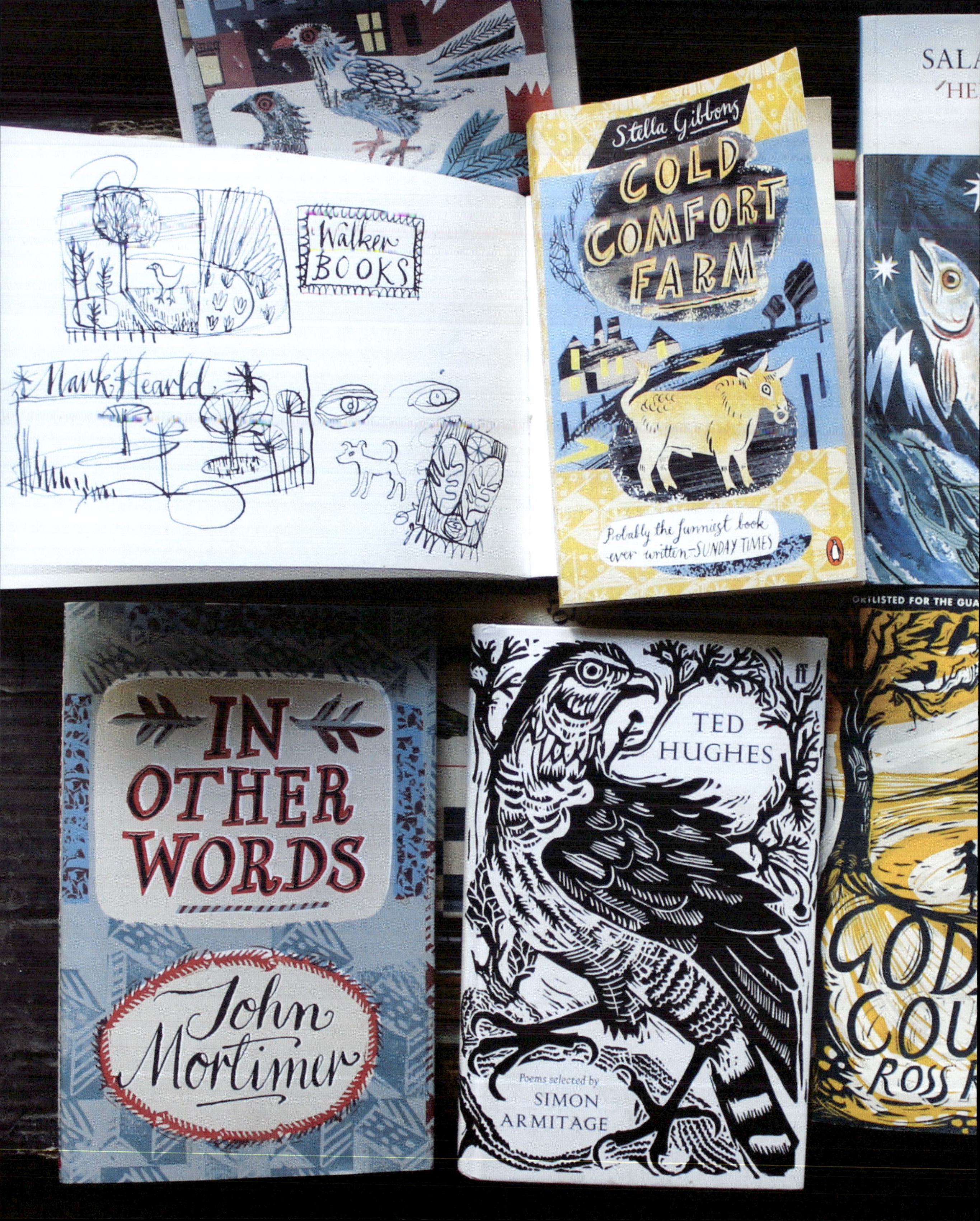

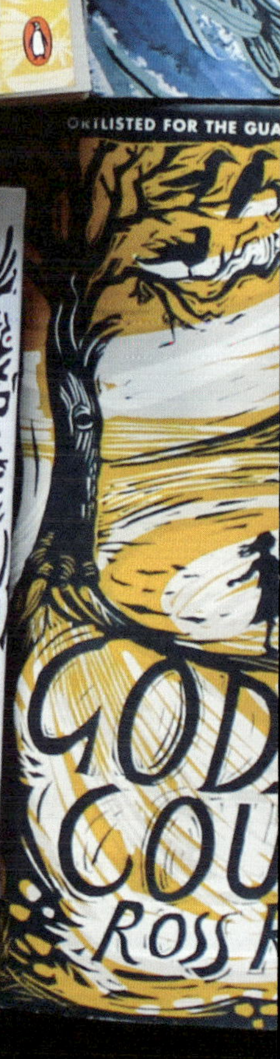
Walker
BOOKS
Mark Hearld
Stella Gibbons
COLD
COMFORT
FARM
Probably the funniest book
ever written—SUNDAY TIMES
SALA
HE
SHORTLISTED FOR THE GUA
IN
OTHER
WORDS
John
Mortimer
TED
HUGHES
Poems selected by
SIMON
ARMITAGE
GOD
COU
ROSS

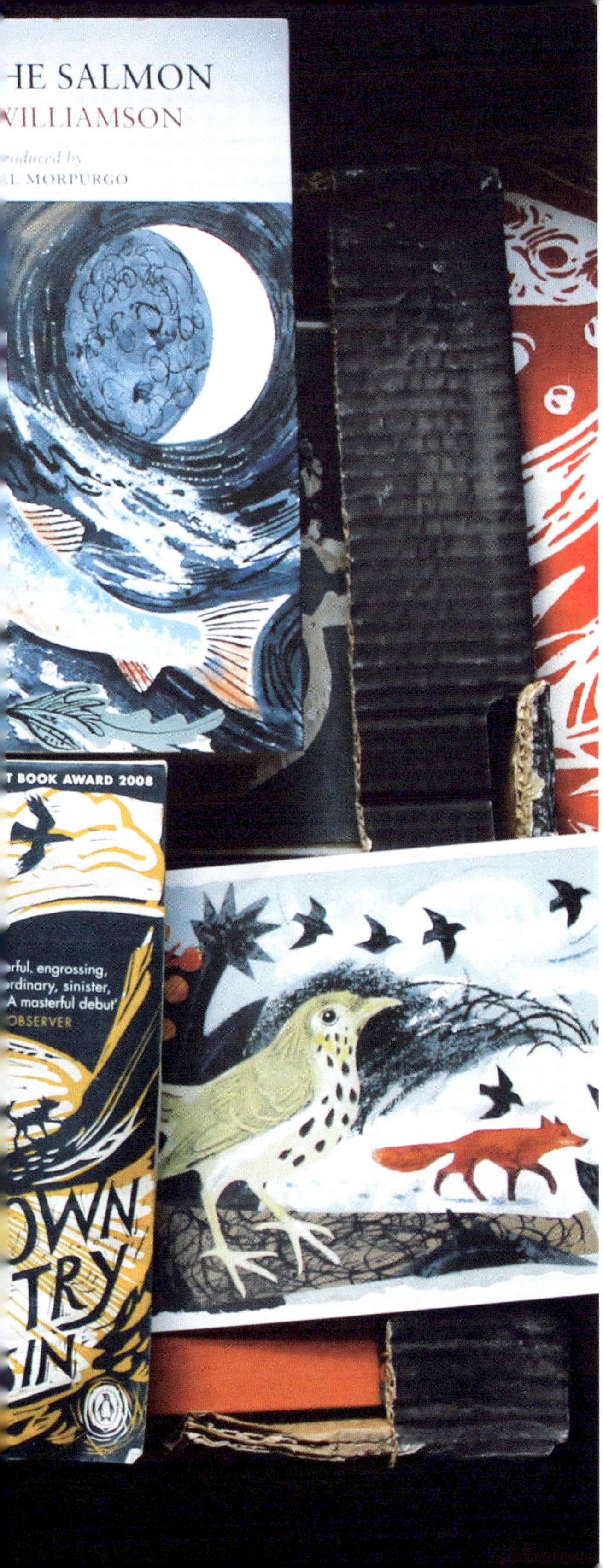

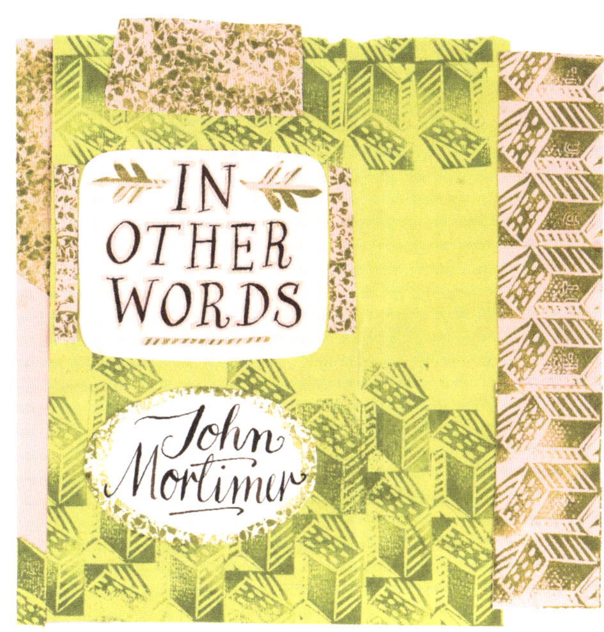

Book Covers

Book covers sell books. Whenever I design a cover, I try to ensure that it will catch the eye and stand out from the competition. I particularly enjoy having control of the entire design, making hand-lettering integral to the cover as a whole. Sometimes, as in the case of the Ted Hughes poetry collection, the formality of set type is just right. The pigeons and winter thrush peeking out from behind the books are Christmas cards that I designed for the charity Paintings in Hospitals.

163

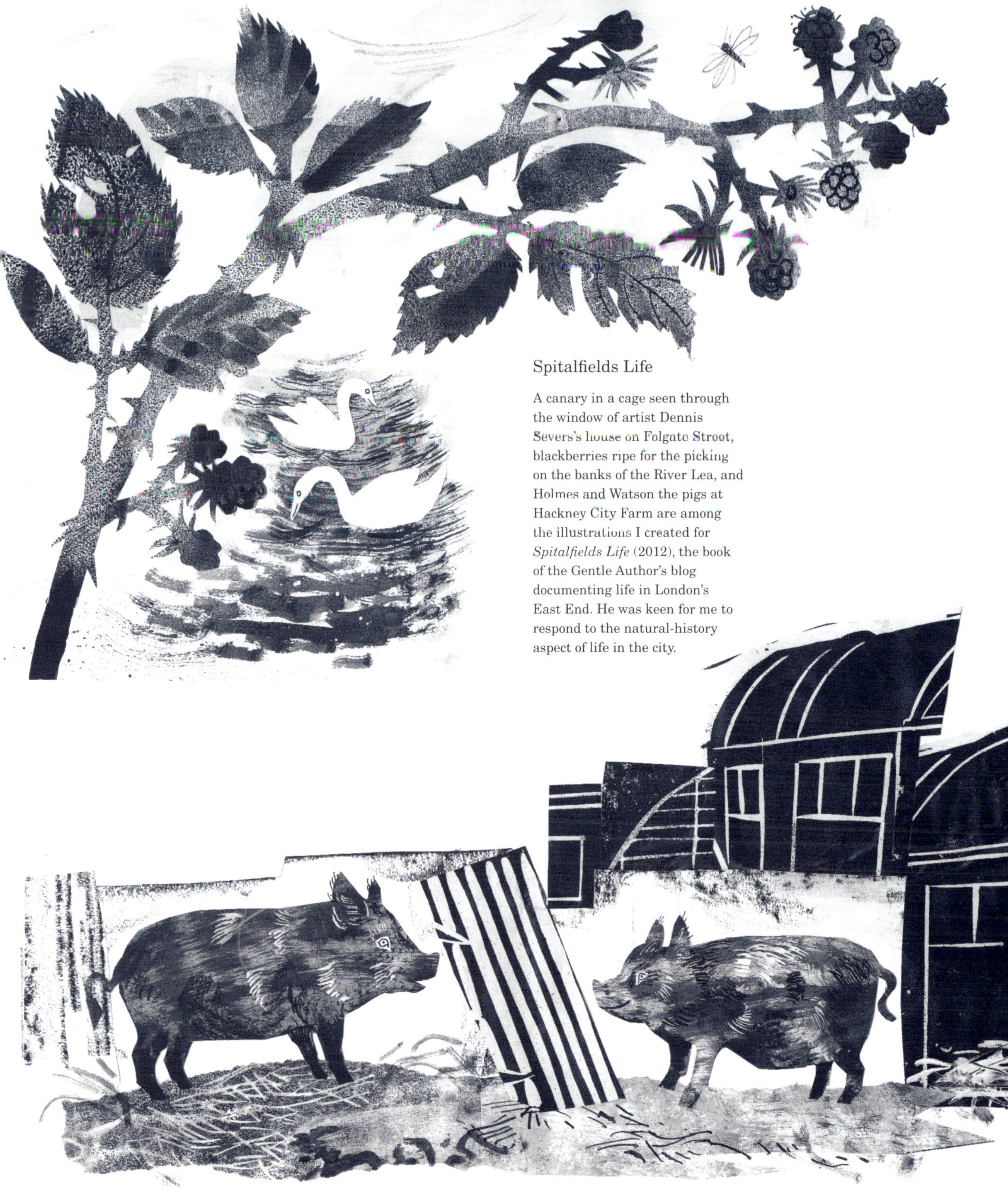

Spitalfields Life

A canary in a cage seen through the window of artist Dennis Severs's house on Folgate Street, blackberries ripe for the picking on the banks of the River Lea, and Holmes and Watson the pigs at Hackney City Farm are among the illustrations I created for *Spitalfields Life* (2012), the book of the Gentle Author's blog documenting life in London's East End. He was keen for me to respond to the natural-history aspect of life in the city.

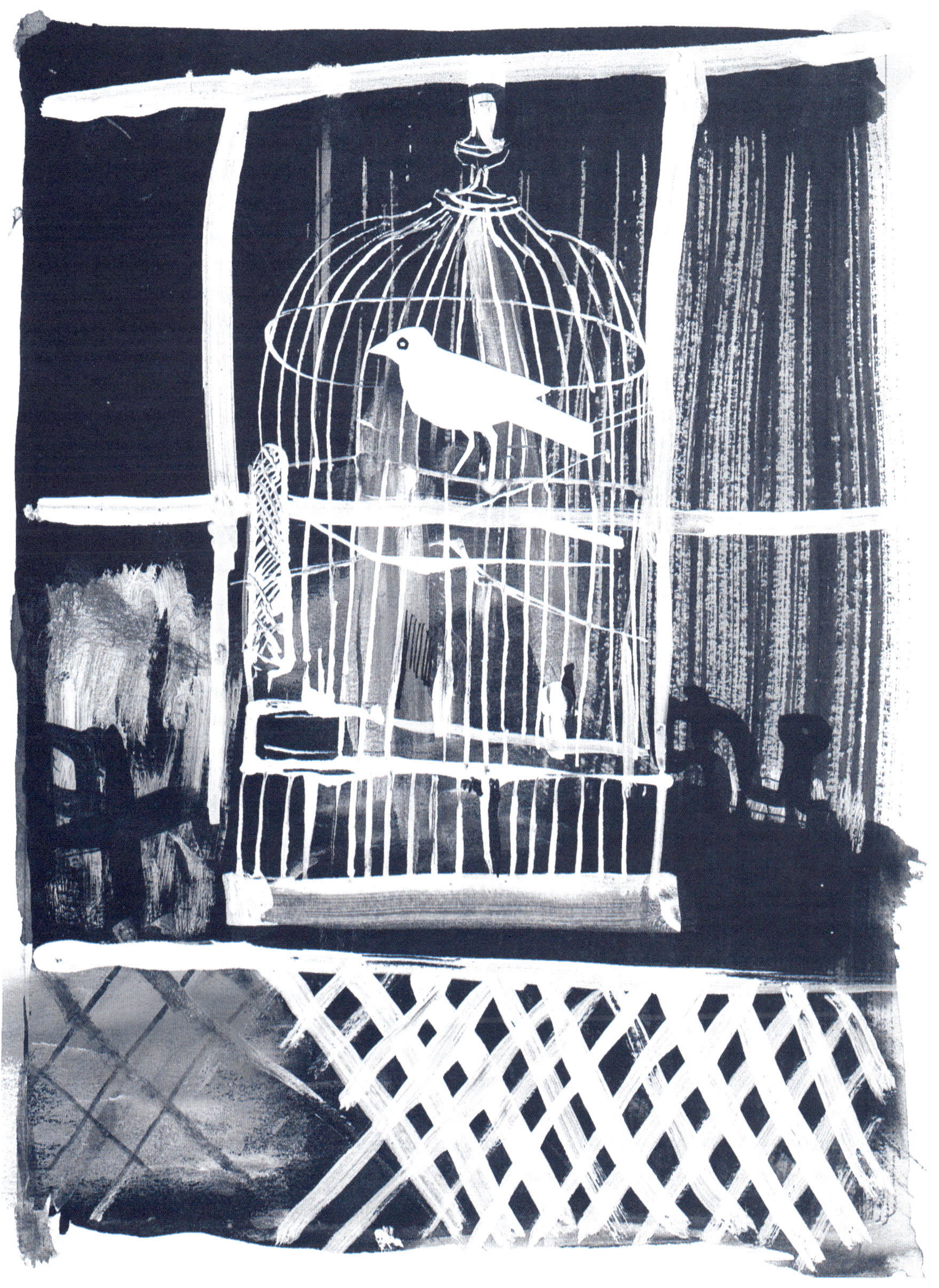

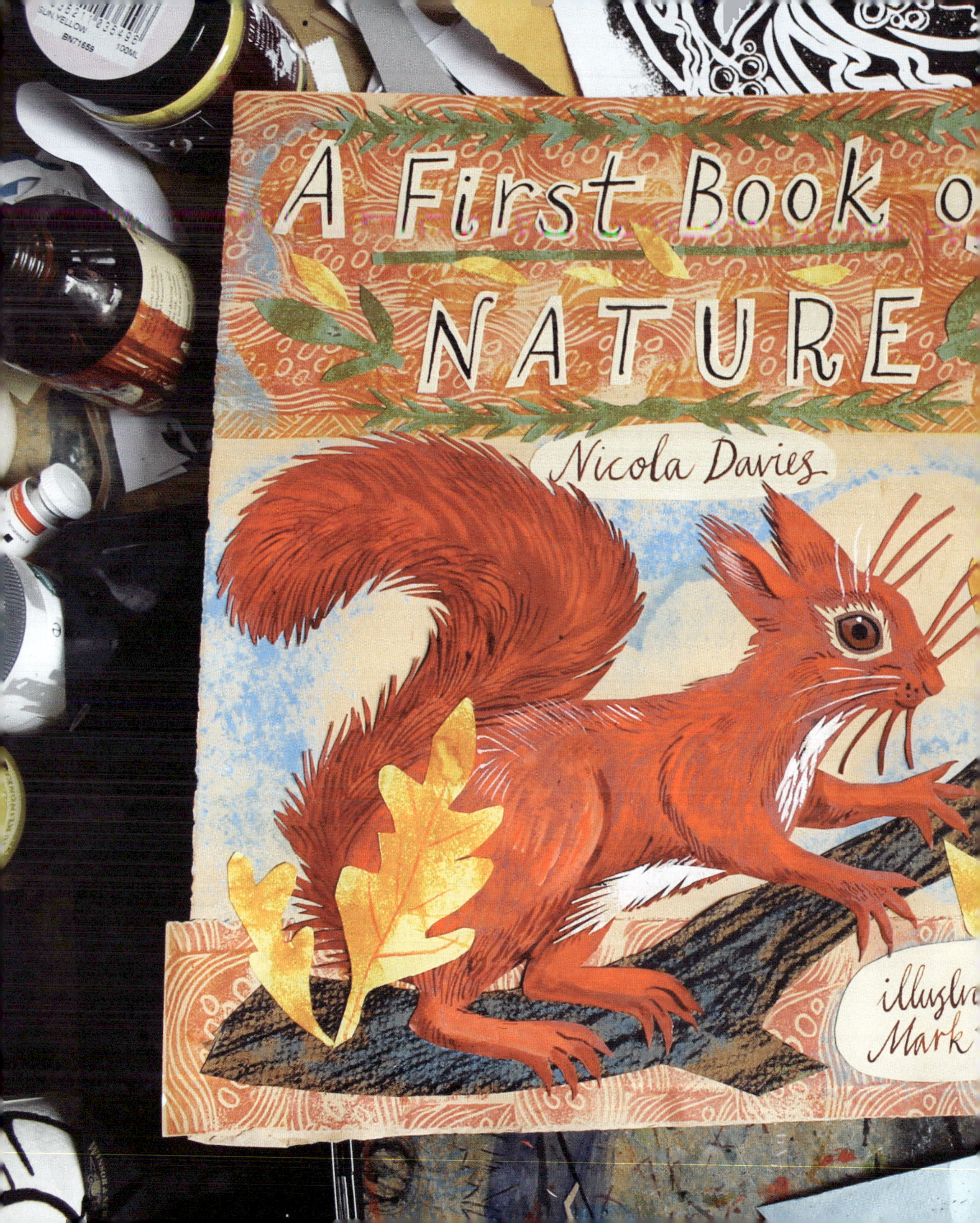
A First Book of NATURE
Nicola Davies
illustr
Mark

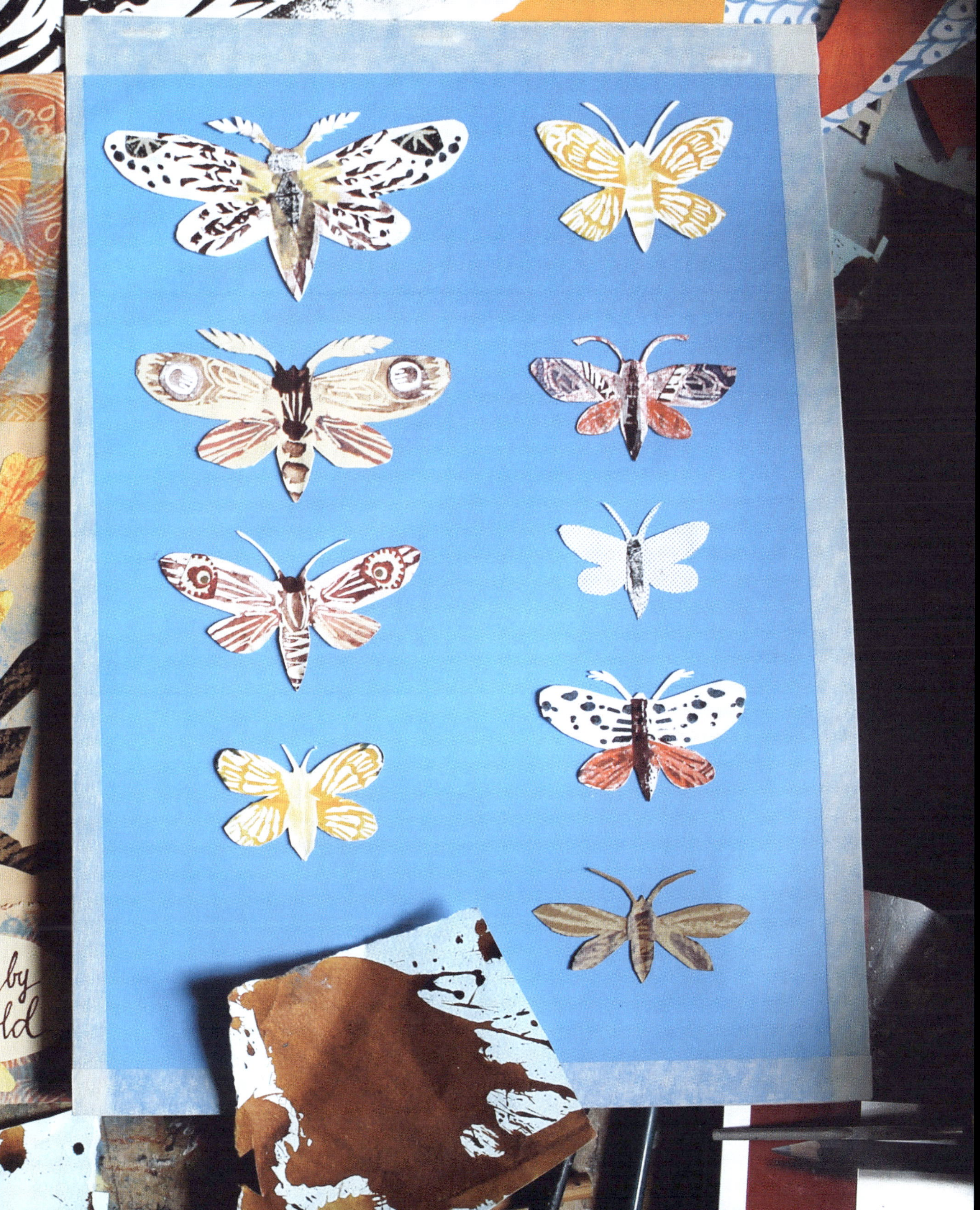

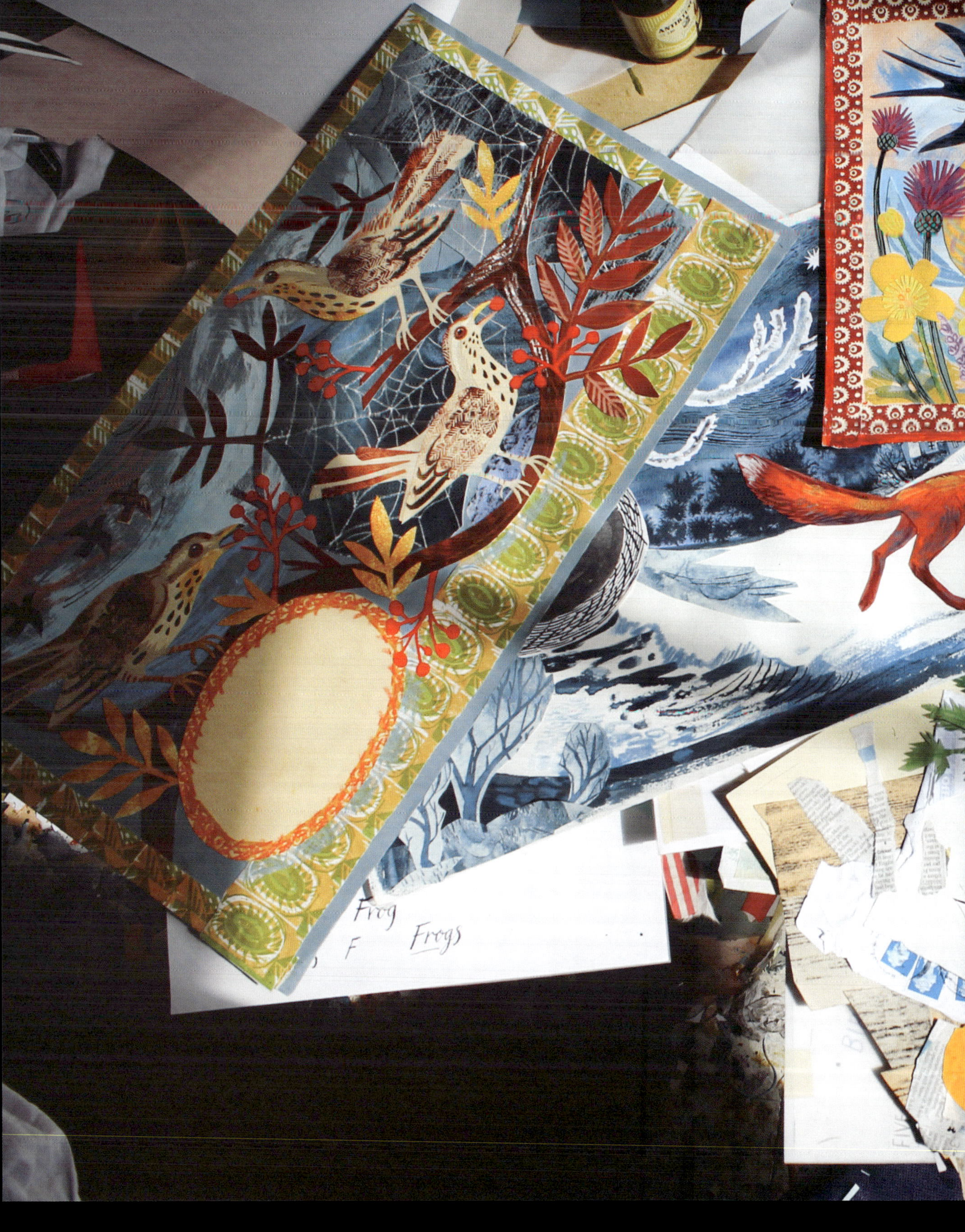
Frog
F   Frogs

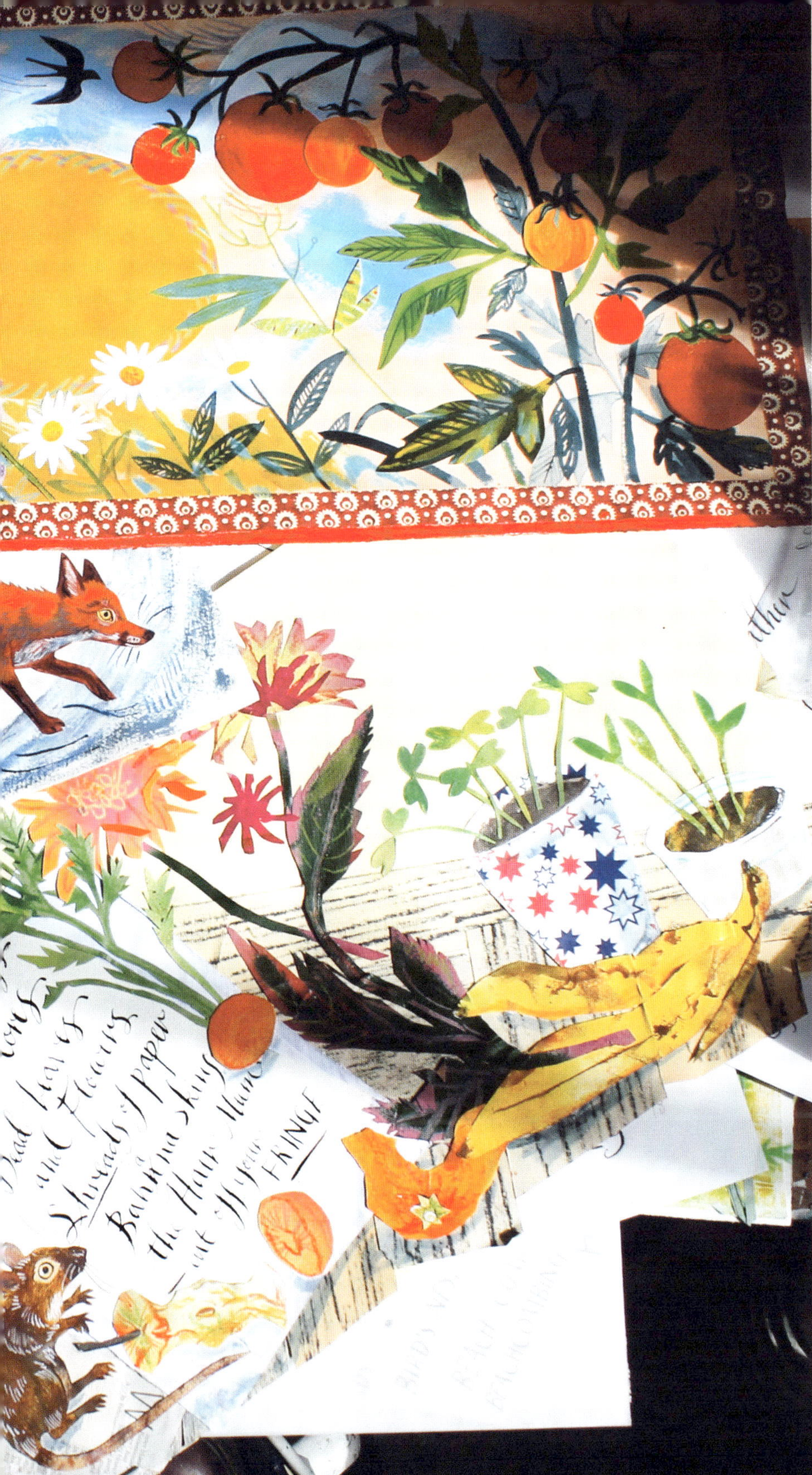

A First Book of Nature

Illustrating a 108-page book seemed a daunting proposition, but author Nicola Davies's text was so particular and observant, and right for me, that I had to give it a go. After a false start, I began working in earnest with Liz Wood at Walker Books. Her insight into the working approaches of individual artists gave me a huge amount of freedom to explore each spread fully. I felt in safe hands when she said that 'the book will triumph if it looks as though only your hands have touched it'. However, her input was invaluable. She had a constant struggle reining in my exuberance and ensuring that I left enough room for the text, but, most importantly, her acute visual sense gave direction and shape to the book as a whole. She would come up with a suggestion, which she knew I would ignore, but which would trigger an idea of my own and enable me to be ambitious. Working with the challenges posed by such a big book taught me a great deal about image-making.

It was hard to know which spreads to include here, but I've tried to provide a varied taster. The cover image (pages 166–67) shows the lettering as originally conceived, but it was decided, quite rightly, that something bolder was necessary, and so the lettering was changed. The squirrel was my first instinct for the cover, and really sets the tone for the book.

A Wedding in Tuscany

The brief to design a wedding
invitation for my friends Kate and
Tom was accompanied by a postcard
of the fourteenth-century fresco by
Ambrogio Lorenzetti in the Palazzo
Pubblico in Siena depicting a
Tuscan hill town, various figures
and a pig. Kate thought it would
make the ideal starting point. The
wedding itself was a delight.

A collage made in response to
a week's holiday in the Tuscan
countryside in July 2011.

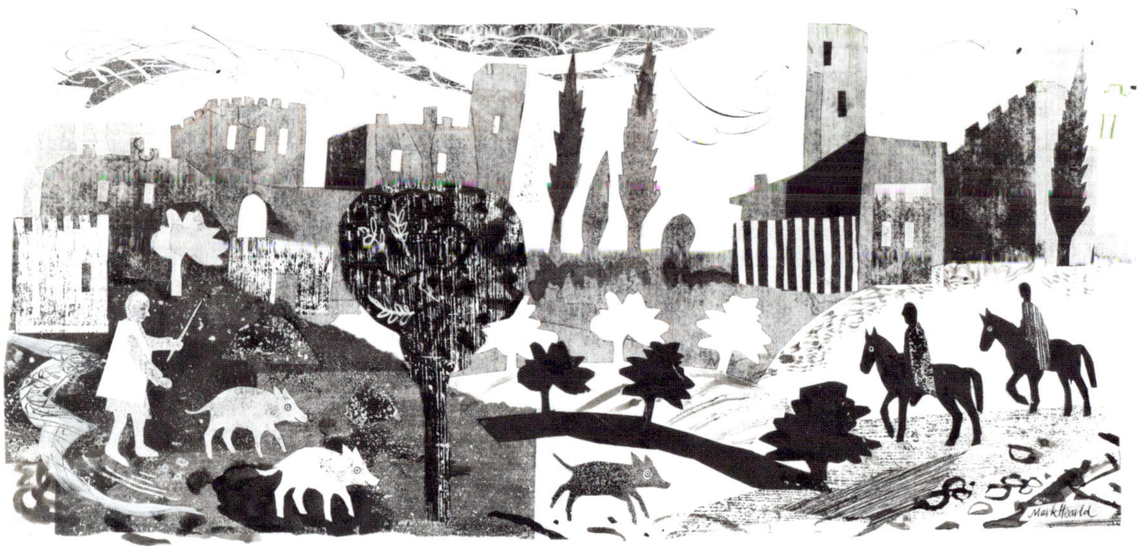

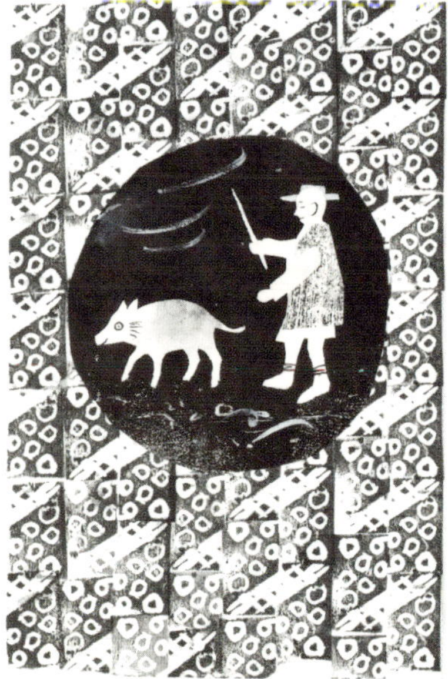

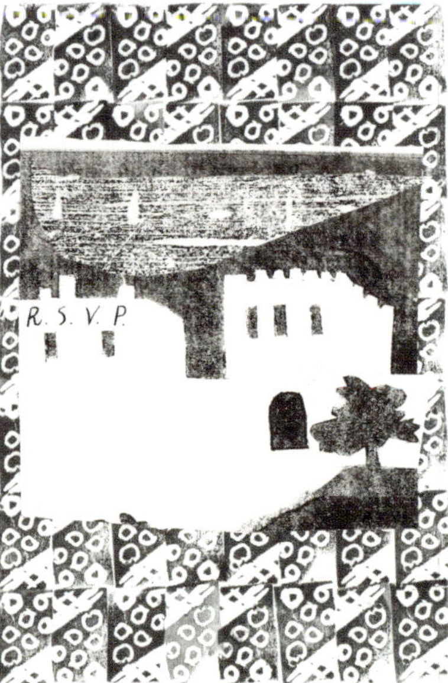

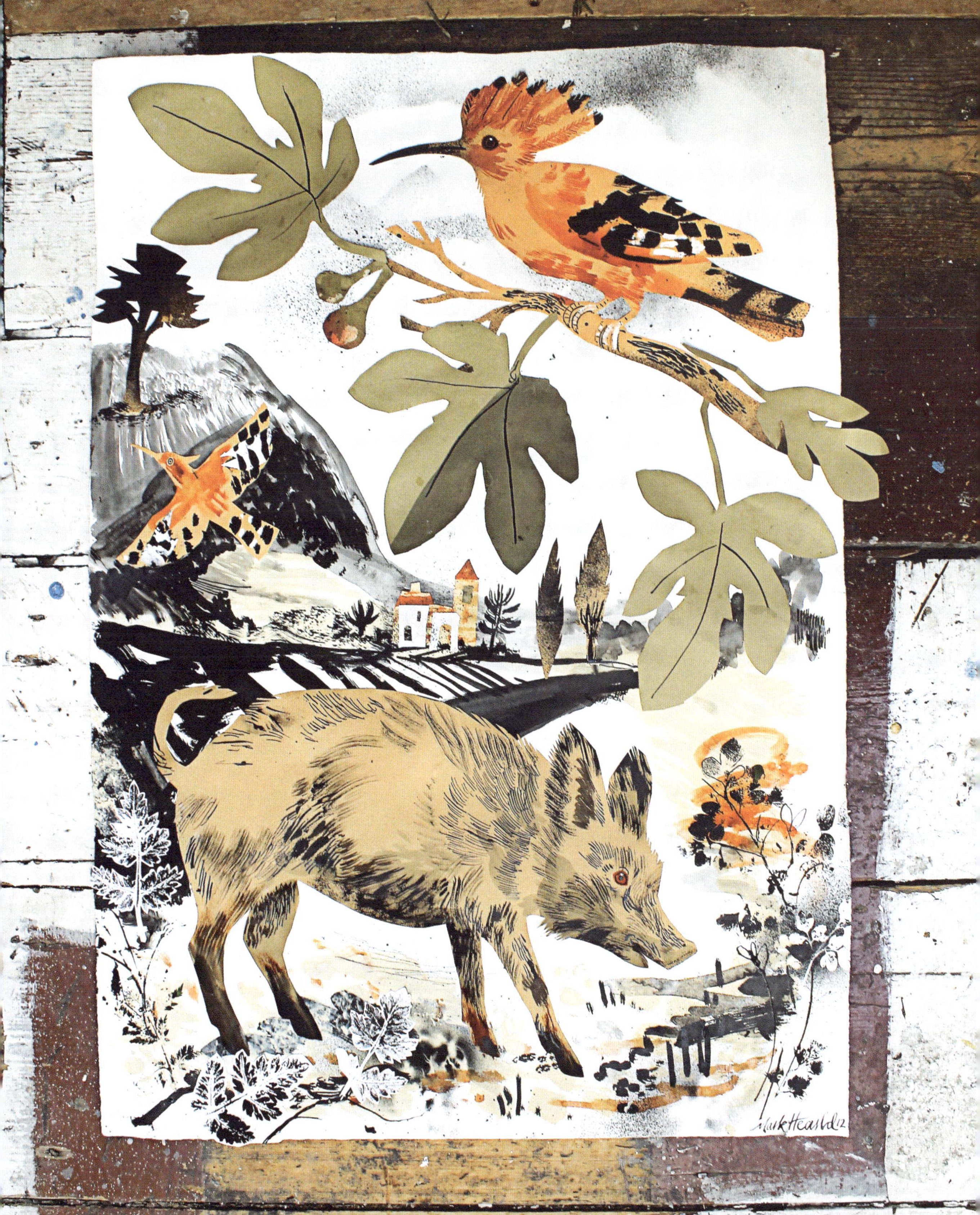

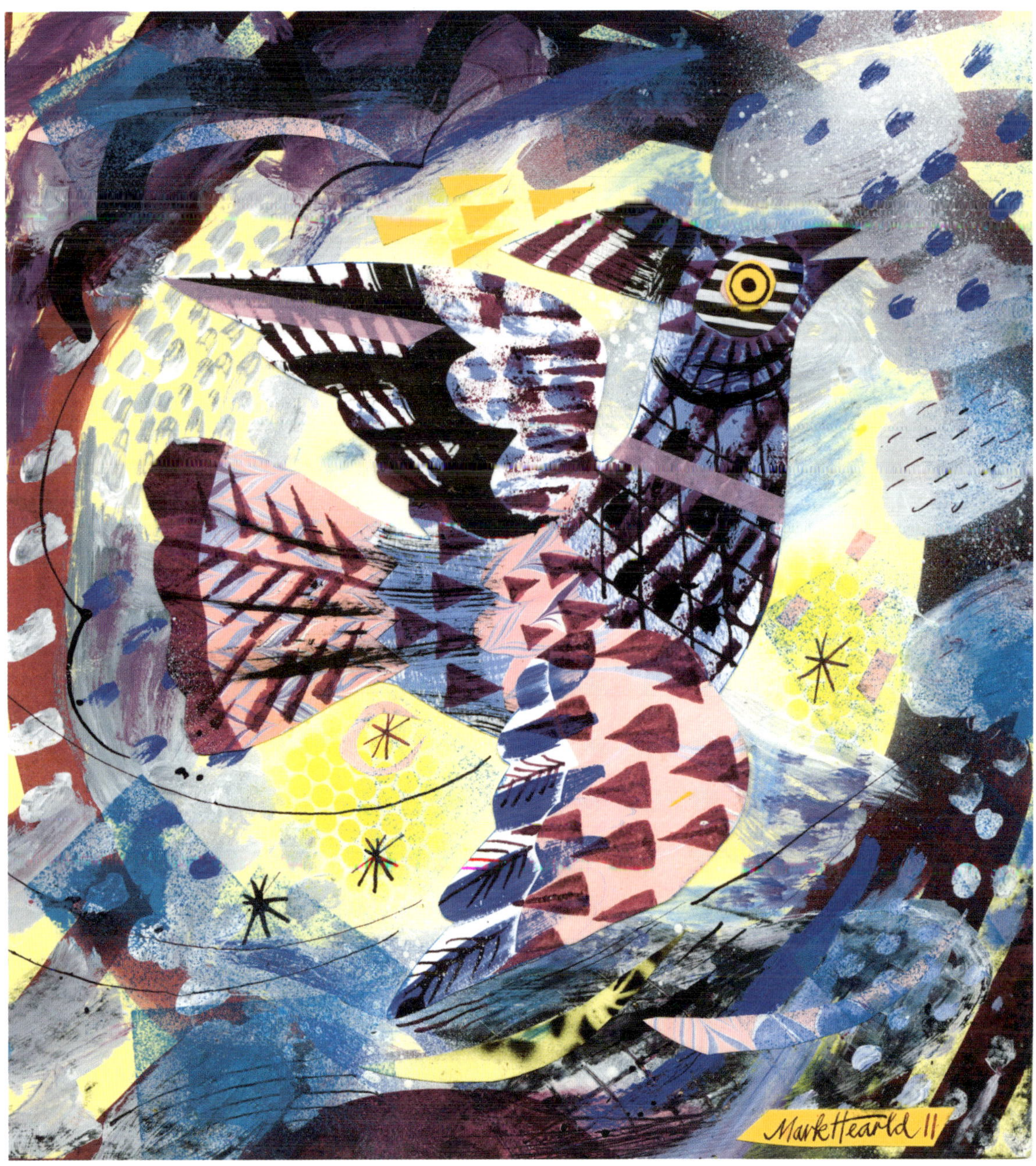

Flight

A cut-paper bird with fold-out wings – one of a number of such birds made as a take-home gift for friends who came to my thirtieth birthday party – had been propped in my front room for seven years. In 2011, however, it prompted a range of die-cut cards for Art Angels (opposite). I came up with a total of six patterned bird designs. The artwork for the birds was then used as the basis for a series of fourteen collages entitled *Flight*, which gave me the opportunity to explore abstract mark-making and colour; the tenth in the series, *Flight X*, is pictured above. It's satisfying to get the most from each creative idea.

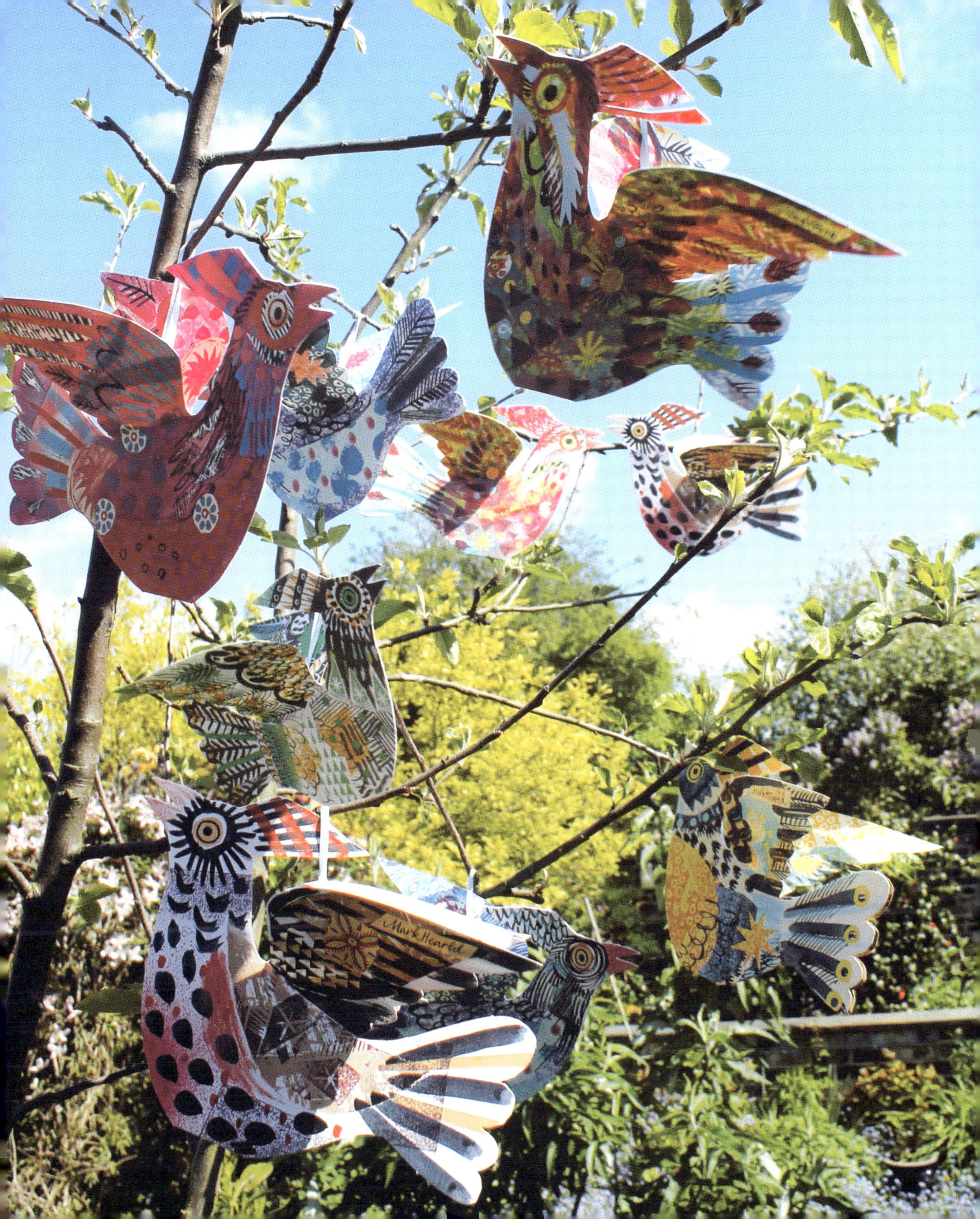
Mark Hearld

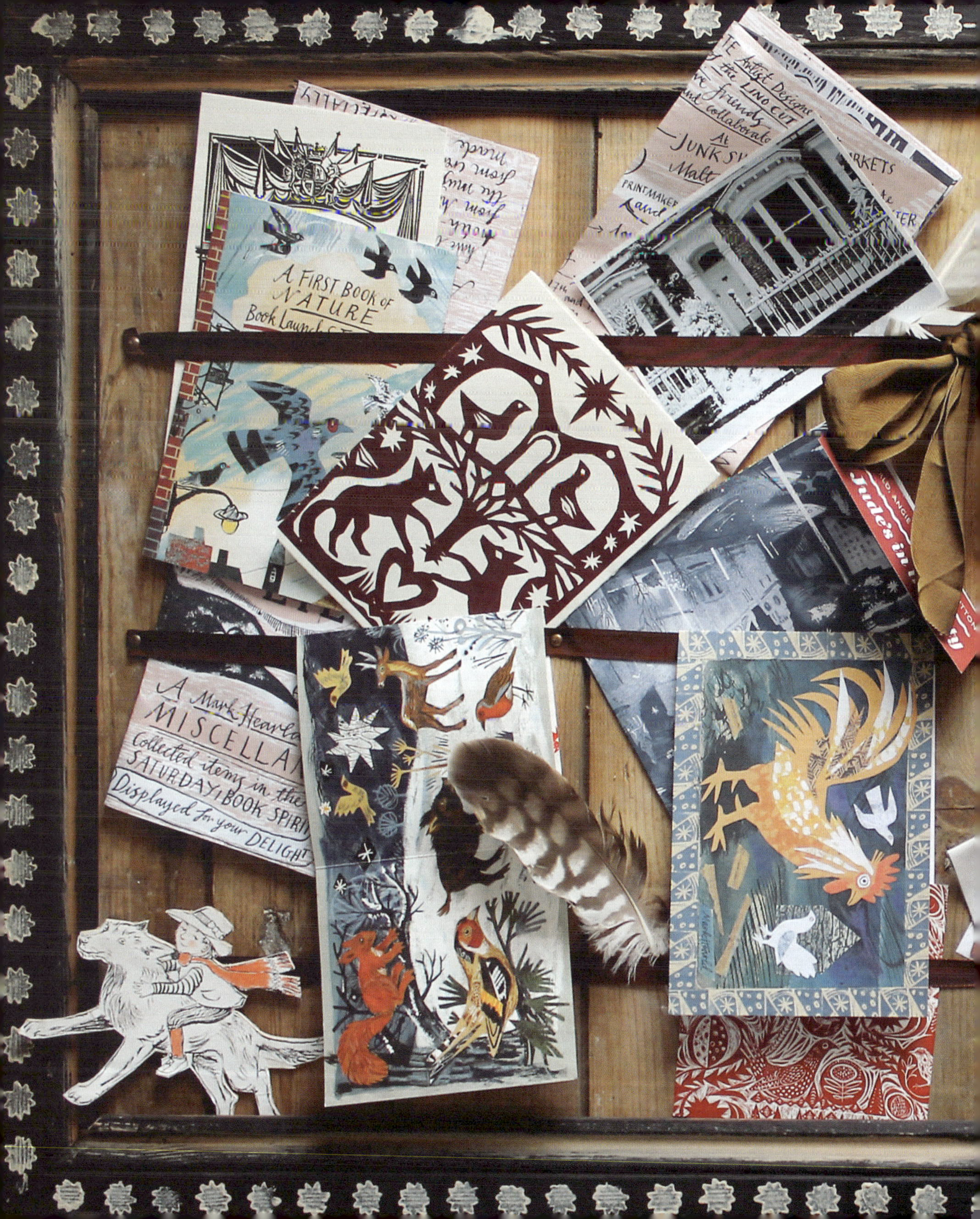
A FIRST BOOK OF
NATURE
Book Launch & T...
A Mark Hearld
MISCELLAN...
Collected items in the...
SATURDAY, BOOK SPIRI...
Displayed for your DELIGHT

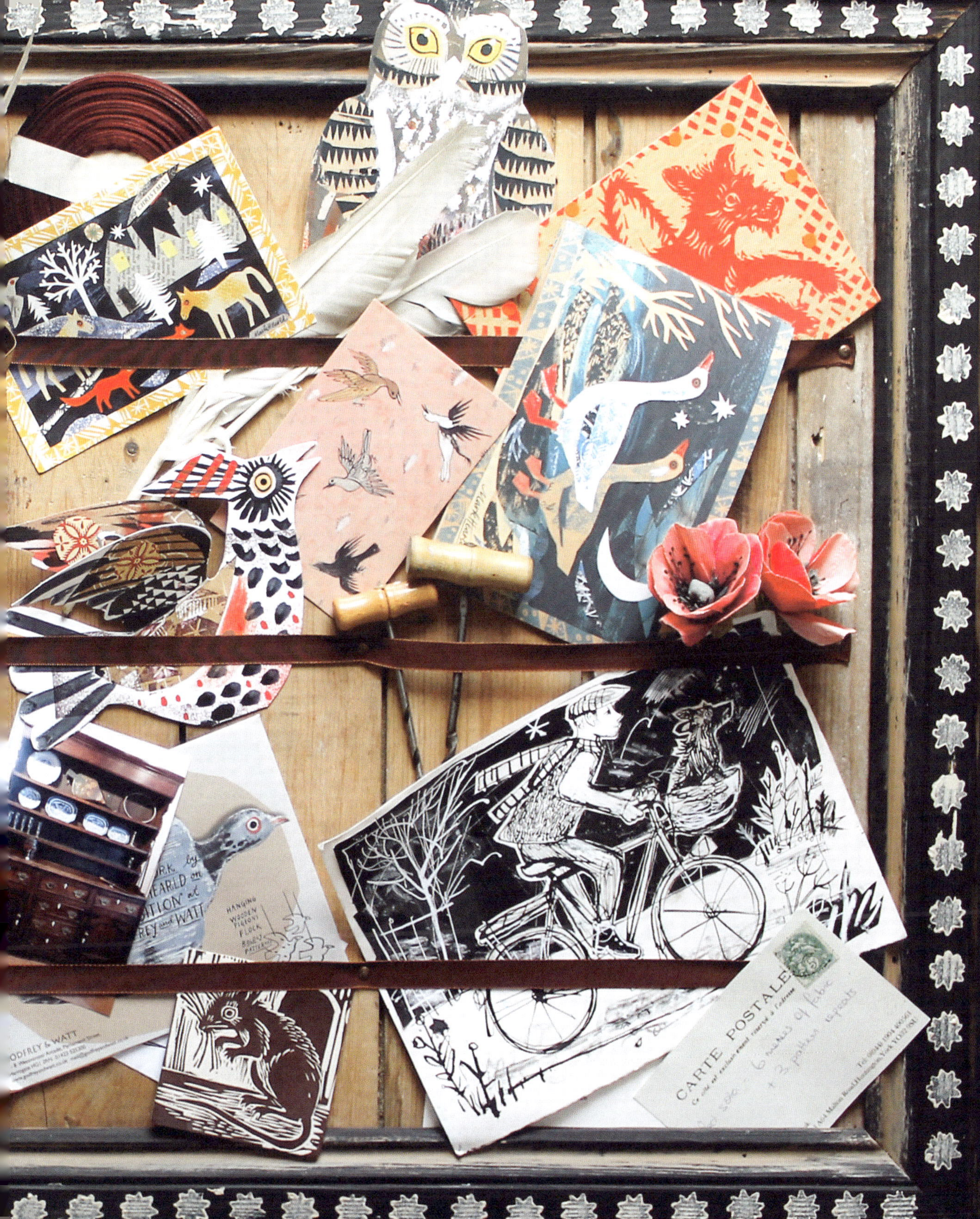
CARTE POSTALE
ODFREY & WATT

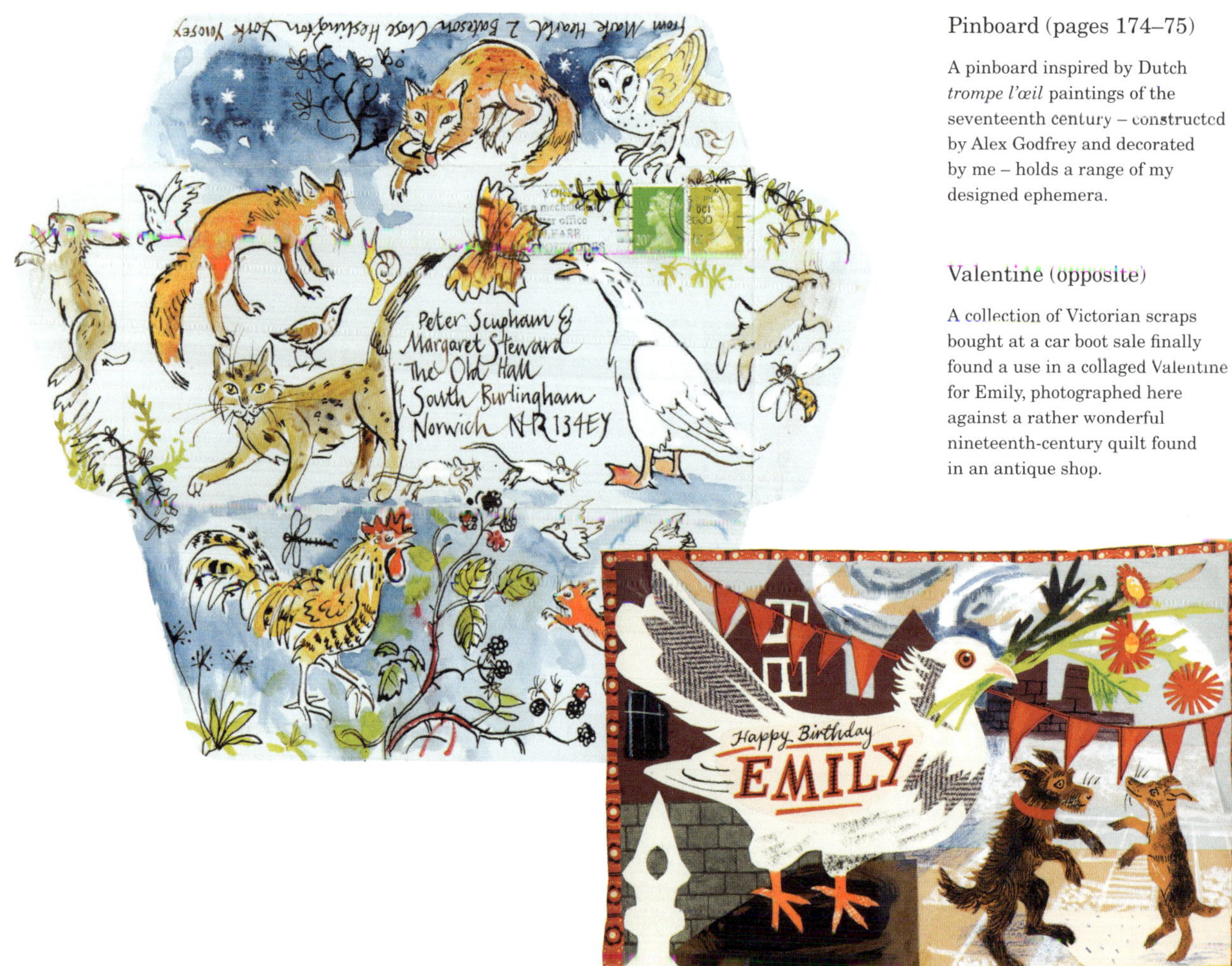

Pinboard (pages 174–75)

A pinboard inspired by Dutch *trompe l'œil* paintings of the seventeenth century – constructed by Alex Godfrey and decorated by me – holds a range of my designed ephemera.

Valentine (opposite)

A collection of Victorian scraps bought at a car boot sale finally found a use in a collaged Valentine for Emily, photographed here against a rather wonderful nineteenth-century quilt found in an antique shop.

Scrapbook Material

There's nothing more fun than creating an off-the-cuff design for an envelope or parcel that's about to be sent through the post. The fixed ingredients of stamps and an address provide a formal graphic structure to respond to. You can be as whimsical as you like; the important stuff is contained within. Birthday cards or collages, such as *Birthday Pigeon* (above, right) and *Em. S.* (pages 70–71), Christmas cards, invitations and decorated thank-you notes (above, left, and page 111, top) warrant special attention. The hope is that, at the very least, they will find their way into a cherished scrapbook.

Mail Art (overleaf)

Any envelope posted without decoration feels like a missed opportunity; script, spray paint and selected colour stamps are essential. Here, I had great fun before heading off to the Post Office, letting rip on large envelopes containing work for *A First Book of Nature* (see page 169).

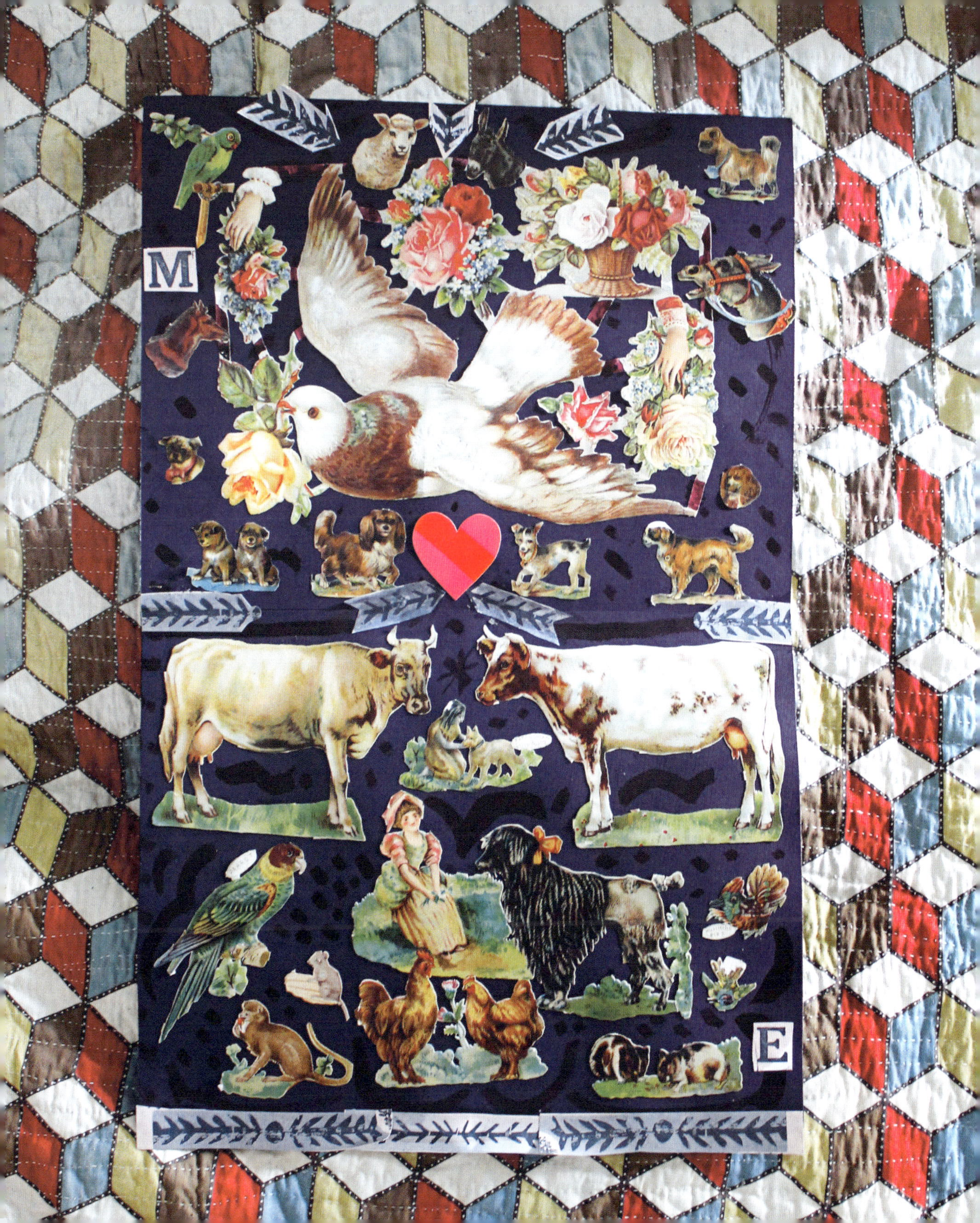

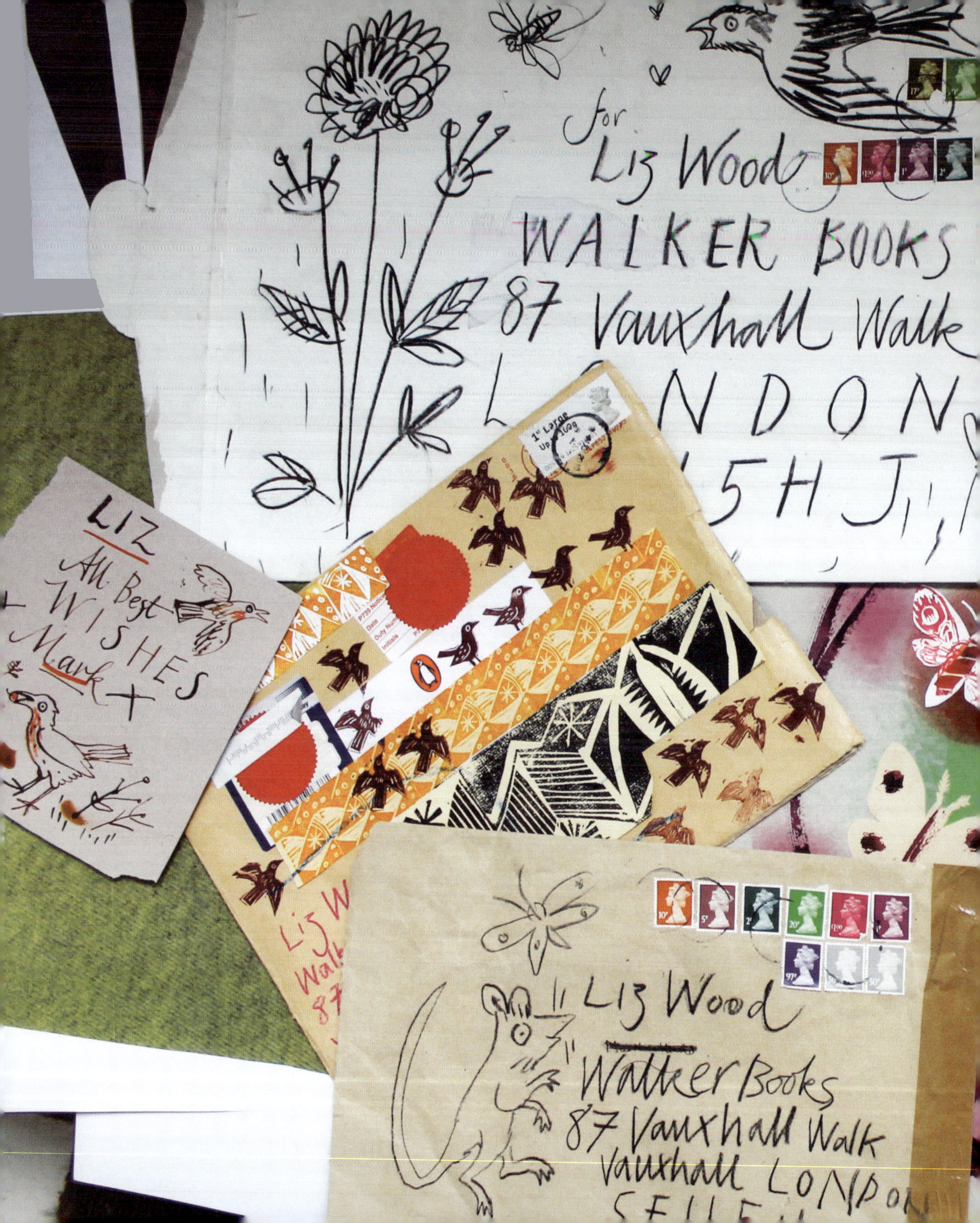
for
Liz Wood
WALKER BOOKS
87 Vauxhall Walk
LONDON
SE11 5HJ
LIZ
All Best
WISHES
Mark x
Liz Wood
Walker Books
87 Vauxhall Walk
Vauxhall LONDON
SE11 5HJ

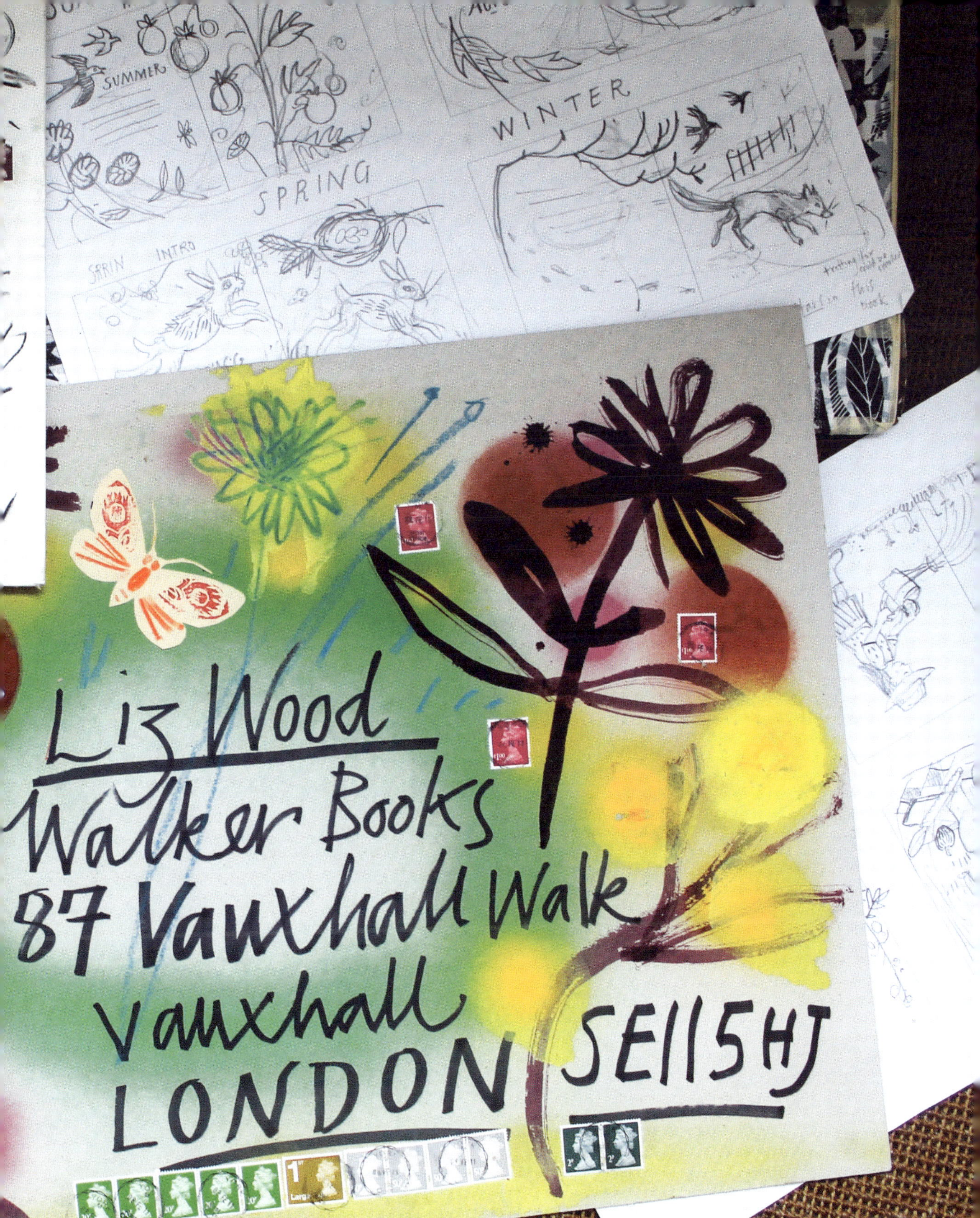

SUMMER
SPRING
WINTER
SPRIN INTRO
Liz Wood
Walker Books
87 Vauxhall Walk
Vauxhall
LONDON SE11 5HJ

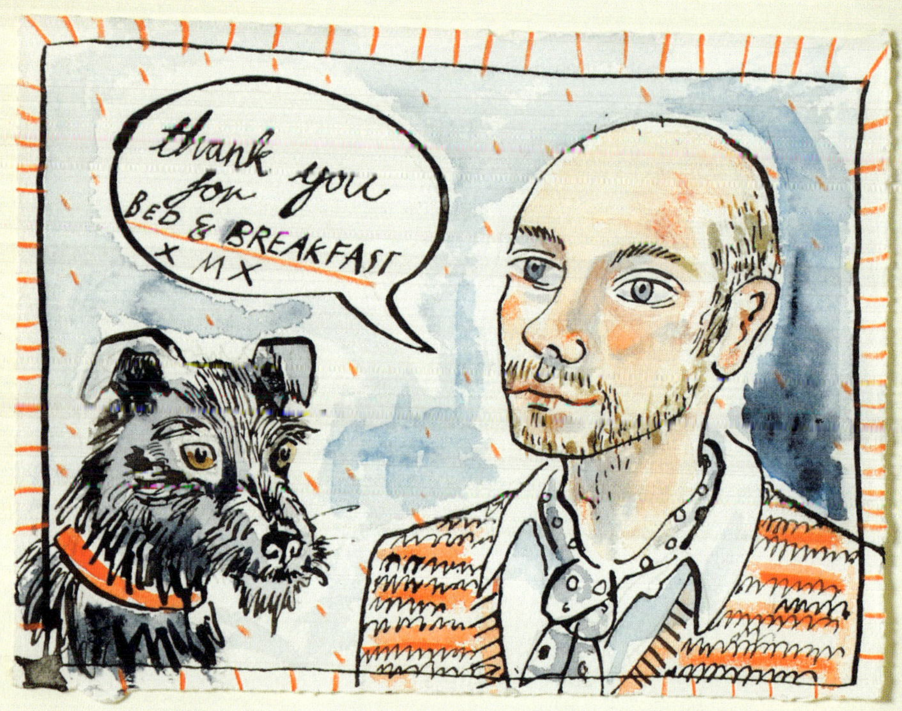

MARK HEARLD SELF PORTRAIT WITH FESTY

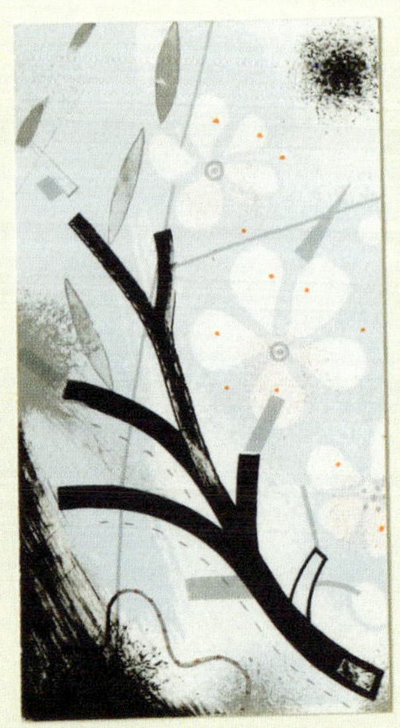

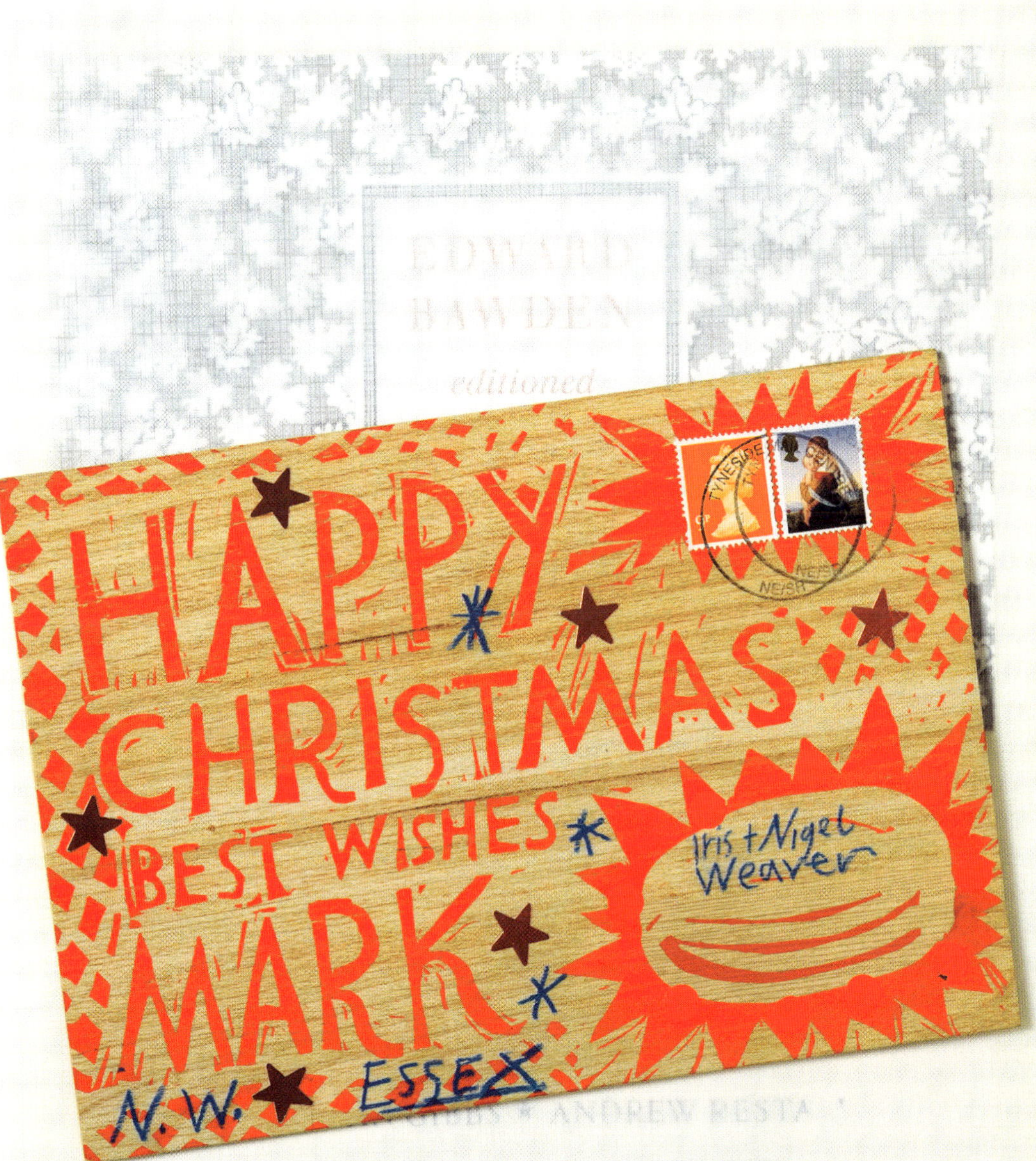

HAPPY CHRISTMAS
BEST WISHES
MARK
N.W. ESSEX
Iris + Nigel Weaver

Iris's Scrapbook
(pages 180–81)

There's a special incentive in designing ephemeral material if you know it will end up in a well-established scrapbook. Here, man and dog feature alongside a refined snippet by Colin Wilkin and a Bawden invitation card veiled enticingly by a leaf of tissue paper and a wooden Christmas greeting from me.

Pigeon Post

In the email age, I wanted to make a piece of postal ephemera in the mode of the GPO greetings telegrams that would remain on the recipient's mantelpiece long after they had read the contents. From a design point of view, it was fun working out how to create a letter and envelope in one, so that it was ready to write, address, stamp and post.

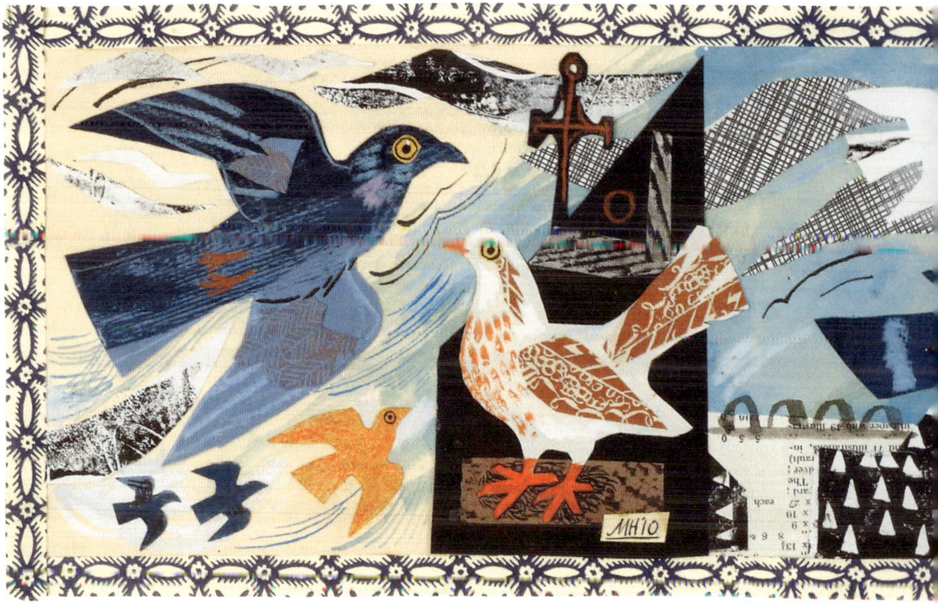

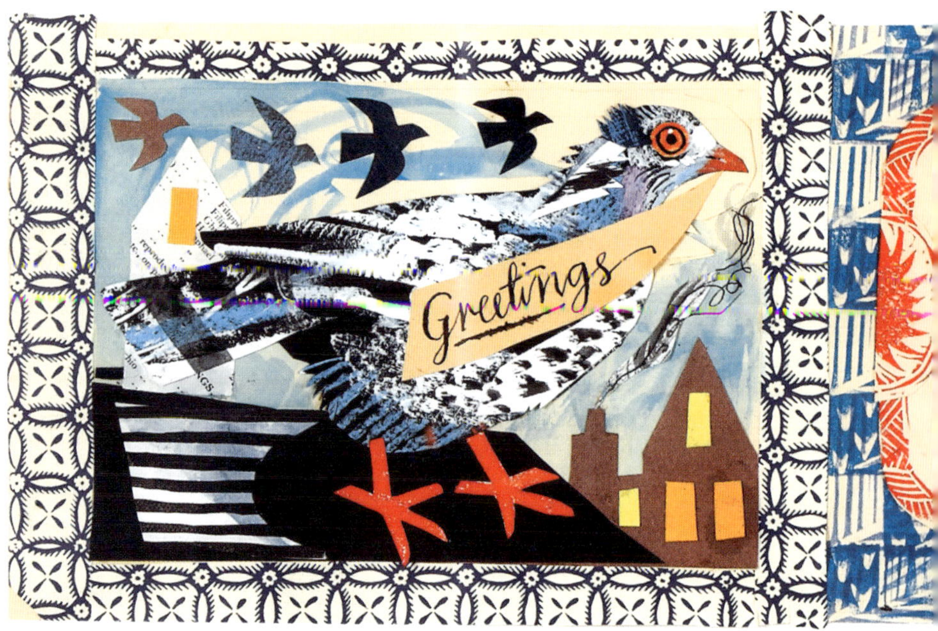

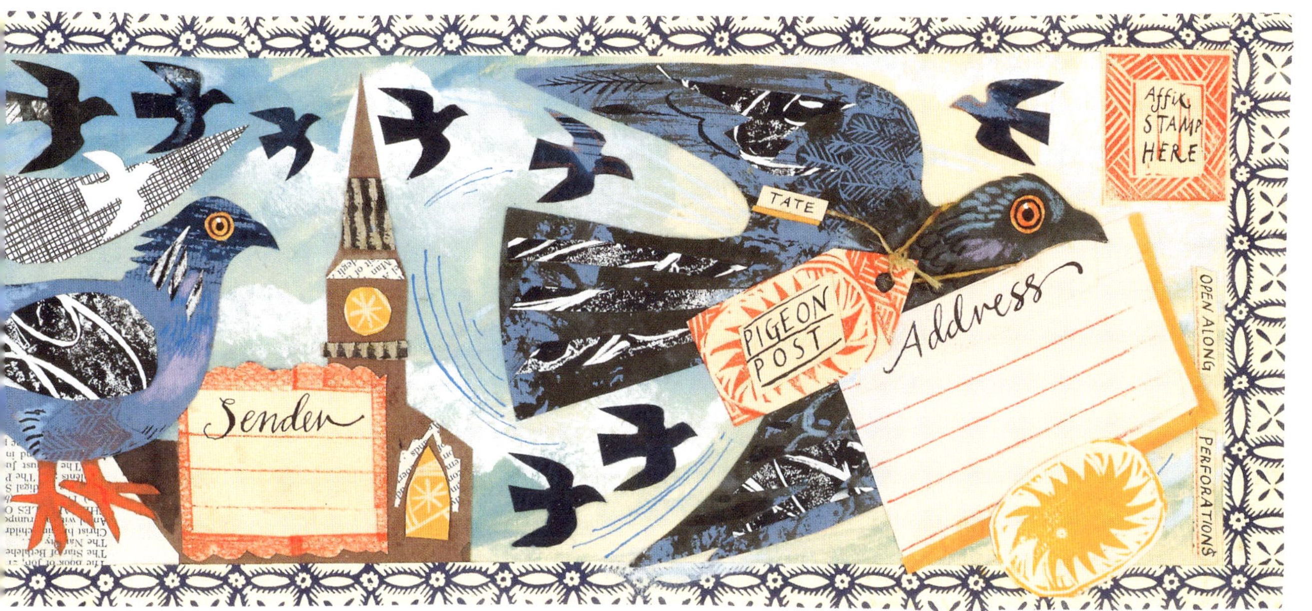

Affix
STAMP
HERE
TATE
PIGEON
POST
Address
Sender
OPEN ALONG
PERFORATIONS

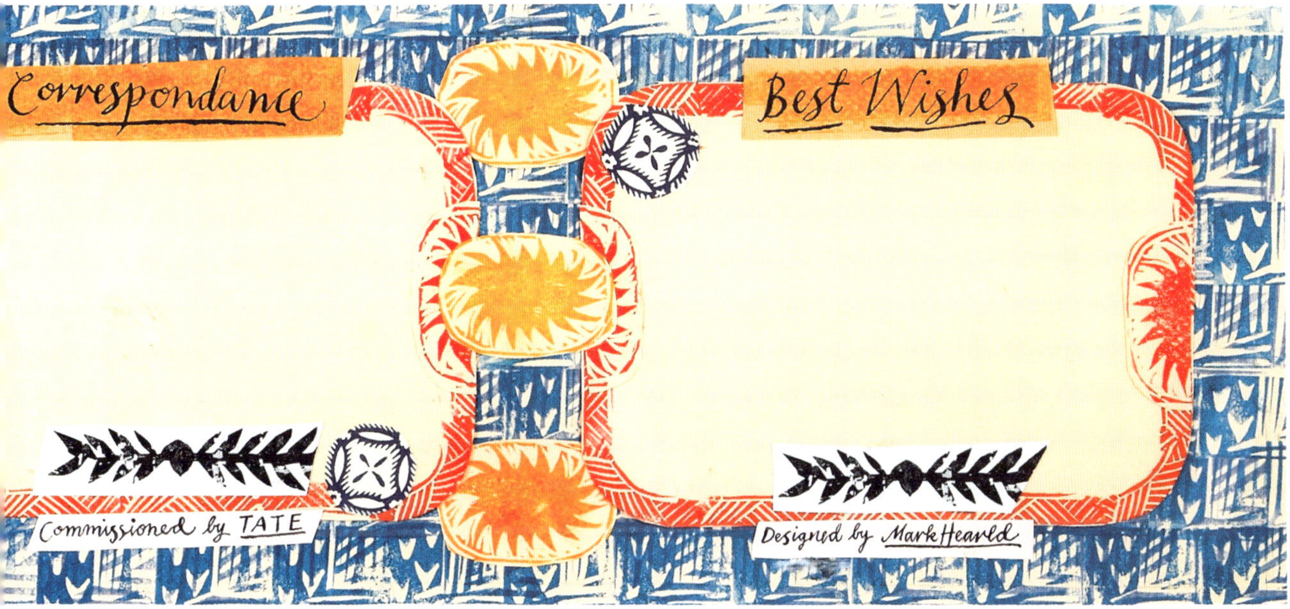

Correspondance
Best Wishes
Commissioned by TATE
Designed by Mark Hearld

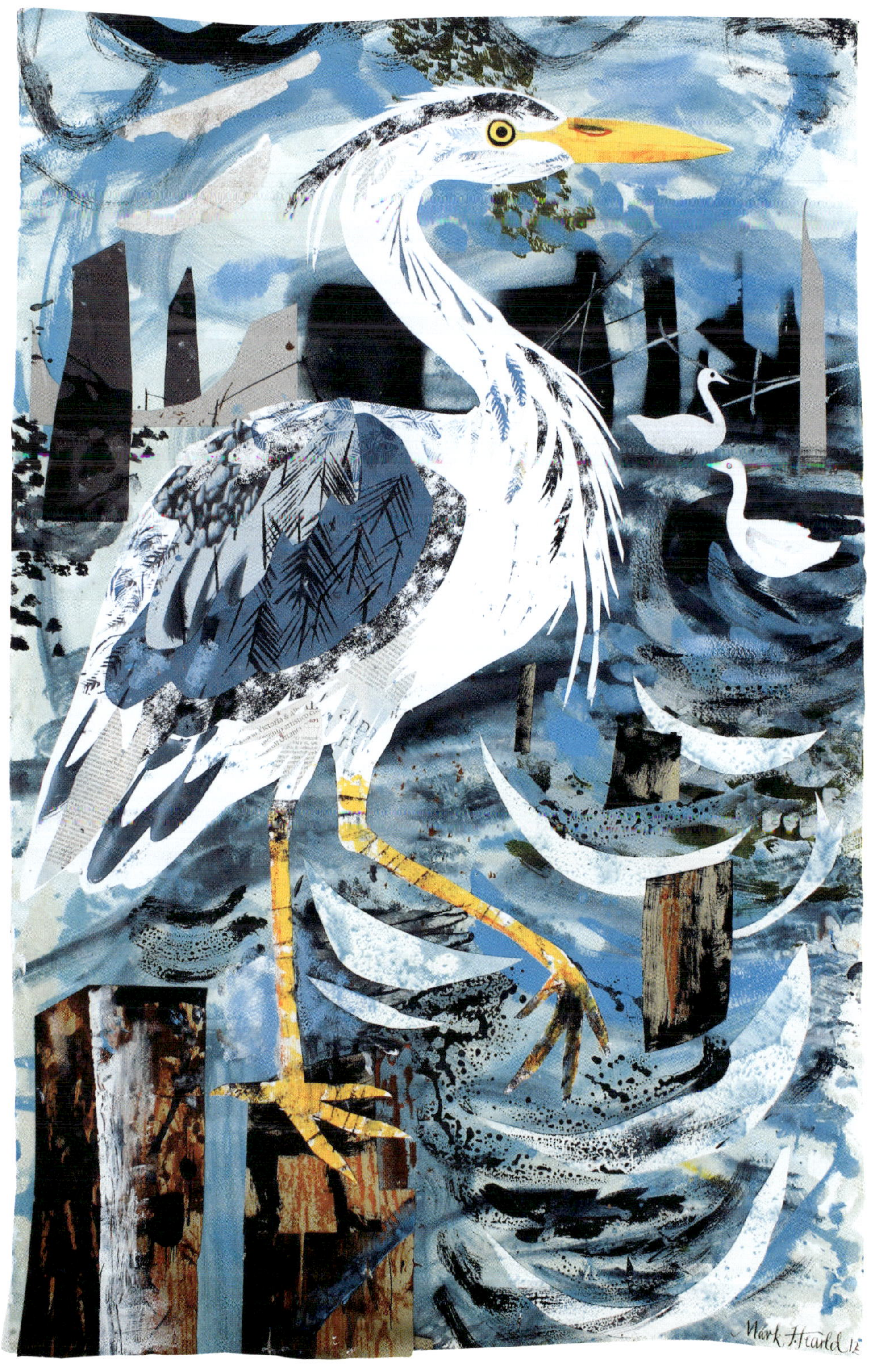

List of Works

Night Harbour (p. 71)
2010
Collage
50 × 75 cm (19⅝ × 29½ in.)

Lewis Lighthouse (p. 72)
2010
Collage
56 × 56 cm (22 × 22 in.)

The Yellow Boat (p. 73)
2010
Collage
80 × 60 cm (31½ × 23⅝ in.)

Salmon Return to the Thames
(pp. 74–75)
2010
Lithograph
73 × 96 cm (28¾ × 37¾ in.)

Thames Cormorant (pp. 76–77)
2012
Collage
56 × 75 cm (22 × 29½ in.)

Bird on the Shore (p. 78, bottom)
2009
Collage
15 × 21 cm (5⅝ × 8¼ in.)

Carrot Crop (pp. 80–81)
2007
Collage
56 × 75 cm (22 × 29½ in.)

The Quince Tree (pp. 82–83)
2011
Collage
47 × 105 cm (18½ × 41⅜ in.)

Allotment – Goat Husbandry
(pp. 84–85, top)
2007
Lithograph
35 × 102 cm (13¾ × 40⅛ in.)

Bramble and Apple Allotment
(pp. 84–85, bottom)
2007
Lithograph
35 × 102 cm (13¾ × 40⅛ in.)

Blue Shed (p. 86, top)
2005
Collage
38 × 58 cm (15 × 22⅞ in.)

Autumn Splendour (p. 86, bottom)
2005
Collage
51 × 106 cm (20⅛ × 41¾ in.)

Autumn Thrush (pp. 88–89)
2012
Collage
56 × 75 cm (22 × 29½ in.)

Brown Hare (p. 90)
2011
Collage
56 × 75 cm (22 × 29½ in.) unframed

Mountain Hare (p. 91)
2011
Collage
56 × 75 cm (22 × 29½ in.) unframed

Little Owls (p. 92, top)
2011
Collage
56 × 75 cm (22 × 29½ in.)

Donkey (p. 92, bottom)
c. 2006
Lithograph
19 × 22 cm (7½ × 8⅝ in.)

Fox (p. 93, top)
2011
Collage
56 × 75 cm (22 × 29½ in.)

Fox (p. 93, bottom)
c. 2006
Lithograph
22 × 15 cm (8⅝ × 5⅞ in.)

Macaque (p. 94)
2007
Collage
40 × 35 cm (15¾ × 13¾ in.)

Tiger (p. 95)
2007
Collage
34 × 32 cm (13⅜ × 12½ in.)

Tunnock's Mouse (p. 96, top)
2011
Collage
17 × 21 cm (6¾ × 8¼ in.)

Mouse on the Run (p. 96, bottom)
2011
Collage
17 × 21 cm (6¾ × 8¼ in.)

On the Pantry Shelf (p. 97)
2008
Collage
29 × 30 cm (11⅜ × 11¾ in.)

Jay (p. 98, top)
2009
Lithograph
36 × 48 cm (14⅛ × 18⅞ in.)

Bullfinch (p. 98, bottom left)
2009
Collage
15 × 21 cm (5⅞ × 8¼ in.)

Cock Sparrow (p. 98, bottom right)
2007
Collage
15 × 20 cm (5⅞ × 7⅞ in.)

Pick Your Own (p. 99, top)
2009
Lithograph
37 × 49 cm (14⅝ × 19¼ in.)

Wren (p. 99, bottom left)
2010
Collage
15 × 15 cm (5⅞ × 5⅞ in.)

Chaffinch (p. 99, bottom centre)
2006
Collage
15 × 19 cm (5⅞ × 7½ in.)

Goldfinch (p. 99, bottom right)
2006
Collage
15 × 21 cm (5⅞ × 8¼ in.)

Black Swan Charger (p. 100, top)
2005
Ceramic
35 × 49 cm (13¾ × 19¼ in.)

Mute Swan (p. 100, bottom)
2009
Collage
75 × 75 cm (29½ × 29½ in.)

Black Swan (p. 101)
2002
Collage
48 × 48 cm (18⅞ × 18⅞ in.)

Over the Rooftops (p. 102)
2009
Collage
56 × 112 cm (22 × 44⅛ in.)

St Paul's Pigeons (p. 103)
2009
Collage
15 × 21 cm (5⅞ × 8¼ in.)

Starlings (pp. 104–105)
2010
Collage
44 × 56 cm (17⅜ × 22 in.)

Marine Life (p. 106, top)
2009
Collage
76 × 100 cm (29⅞ × 39⅜ in.)

Deep Sea (pp. 106–107)
2011
Collage
40 × 60 cm (15¾ × 23⅝ in.)

The Seabed (pp. 108 and 109)
2012
Collage
56 × 75 cm (22 × 29½ in.)

Collaged Fish for Poppy May
(p. 110, top)
2012
Collage
16 cm (6¼ in.), length

Fish Box (p. 110, bottom)
2005
Collage
29 × 42 cm (11⅜ × 16½ in.)

Wader and Fish (p. 111, top right;
envelope shown top left)
2004
Ink and watercolour
21 × 15 cm (8¼ × 5⅞ in.)

Collaged Fish for Billy Jake
(p. 111, bottom)
2012
Collage
16 cm (6¼ in.), length

Venetian Fantasy (pp. 112–13)
2011
Collage
56 × 77 cm (22 × 30⅜ in.)

Frutti di Mare (p. 114, top)
2011
Collage
81 × 101 cm (31⅞ × 39¾ in.)

Venice Fish Market (p. 115, top)
2011
Collage
81 × 101 cm (31⅞ × 39¾ in.)

Domenica (pp. 116–17)
2011
Collage
46 × 63 cm (18⅛ × 24¾ in.)

Wood Pigeon (p. 119)
2004
Collage
56 × 56 cm (22 × 22 in.)

The First Snow of Winter (p. 121)
2005
Lithograph
63 × 81 cm (24¾ × 31⅞ in.)

Winter Woodpecker (p. 124)
2012
Collage and monoprint
58 × 42 cm (22⅞ × 16½ in.)

Redwing (p. 125, bottom)
2012
Collage and monoprint
42 × 58 cm (16½ × 22⅞ in.)

Blackbirds at Dawn (p. 126)
2012
Collage and monoprint
58 × 42 cm (22⅞ × 16½ in.)

Deer at the Wood's Edge (p. 127, top)
2012
Collage and monoprint
42 × 58 cm (16½ × 22⅞ in.)

Jay on the Heath (p. 127, bottom)
2009
Collage
55 × 76 cm (21⅝ × 29⅞ in.)

Roebuck (pp. 128–29)
2012
Collage
56 × 75 cm (22 × 29½ in.)

Doveflight (p. 135)
2006
Screen-printed fabric in three
colourways
Printed width: 138.8 cm (54⅝ in.)

On the Wing (p. 136, bottom)
2011
Ceramic tableware
Mug: 8 cm (3⅛ in.), height
Plate: 25 cm (9⅞ in.), diameter
Bowl: 12 cm (4¾ in.), diameter

Bird Garden (p. 137)
2009
Screen-printed fabric in three
colourways
Printed width: 137 cm (53⅞ in.)

Tate Tote *(pp. 138–39; single
separation shown)*
2010
Cotton canvas tote bag
40.5 × 34.5 × 10 cm
(16 × 13½ × 3⅞ in.)

Harvest Hare *(p. 141)*
2012
Single-colour wallpaper in three
colourways

Thrush Roundel *(p. 144)*
2012
Ceramic
30 cm (11¾ in.), diameter

Bird Platter *(p. 146, top)*
2005
Ceramic
34 cm (13⅜ in.), diameter

Birthday Plate for J.H. *(p. 146,
centre left)*
2006
Ceramic
22 cm (8⅝ in.), diameter

Guineafowl and Plantain *(p. 146,
centre right)*
2005
Ceramic plate
34 cm (13⅜ in.), diameter

Hen and Chicks *(p. 146, bottom)*
2005
Ceramic charger
41 cm (16⅛ in.), width

Birds and Barley *(p. 147,
top row, left)*
2011
Slipware
31 cm (12¼ in.), diameter

Tuscan Hoopoe *(p. 147,
top row, centre)*
2011
Slipware
22 × 22 cm (8⅝ × 8⅝ in.)

Slip-trailed Songsters *(p. 147,
top row, right)*
2011
Slipware
35 cm (13¾ in.), diameter

A Fine Cock *(p. 147, middle
row, left)*
2011
Slipware
22 × 22 cm (8⅝ × 8⅝ in.)

Slipware platter, underside
(p. 147, middle row, centre)
2011
Slipware
35 cm (13¾ in.), diameter

Duck and Star *(p. 147, middle
row, right)*
2011
Slipware
22 × 22 cm (8⅝ × 8⅝ in.)

Slip-trailed Tumbler *(p. 147,
bottom row, left)*
2011
Slipware
31 cm (12¼ in.), diameter

A Young Hare *(p. 147, bottom
row, centre)*
2011
Slipware
22 × 22 cm (8⅝ × 8⅝ in.)

Red Squirrel *(p. 147, bottom
row, right)*
2011
Slipware
31 cm (12¼ in.), diameter

Wooden Pigeons *(pp. 148–49)*
2009
Painted wood
Each pigeon: 33 cm (13 in.), length

Decorated Coffee Cans *(pp. 148–49,
centre of first shelf up from bottom)*
Date unknown
Ceramic
Six coffee cans, each 9 cm (3½ in.),
height

Tabby Cat *(p. 150, top)*
2011
Collage
26 × 30 cm (10¼ × 11¾ in.)

Cat *(p. 150, bottom)*
2005
Painted wood
40 × 45 cm (15¾ × 17¾ in.)

Dog *(p. 151)*
2005
Painted wood
45 × 50 cm (17¾ × 19⅝ in.)

Cockerel *(pp. 152 and 153)*
2011
Painted wood
56 × 56 × 20 cm (22 × 22 × 7⅞ in.)

Dog Walker *(p. 154, top)*
2003
Box construction
23 × 32 × 10 cm (9 × 12⅝ × 3⅞ in.)

Pisanello's Hare (Box Work)
(p. 154, bottom)
2002
Box construction
39 × 56 × 25 cm (15⅜ × 22 × 9⅞ in.)

Old Hall *(p. 155)*
2003
Box construction
45 × 54 × 12 cm
(17¾ × 21¼ × 4¾ in.)

Original artwork for PBFA
booklet 'Start Collecting
Books Now' *(p. 160)*
2008
Collage
21 × 34 cm (8¼ × 13⅜ in.)

Original artwork for York Book
Fair catalogue *(p. 161)*
2008
Collage
35.5 × 26.5 cm (14 × 10⅜ in.)

Selection of book cover designs
(pp. 162–63)
Clockwise from top left: Stella
Gibbons, *Cold Comfort Farm*
(Penguin, 2011); Henry Williamson,
Salar the Salmon (Little Toller
Books, 2010); John Mortimer,
In Other Words (Viking, 2008),
initial artwork; Ross Raisin, *God's
Own Country* (Penguin, 2009);
Ted Hughes, *Ted Hughes* (Faber
& Faber, 2009); John Mortimer,
In Other Words (as above),
final design

Illustrations for *Spitalfields Life*
(2012) *(pp. 164–65)*
2011
Ink and collage

Original artwork for front cover of
A First Book of Nature (2012)
(pp. 166–67)
2010
Collage
28.5 × 26 cm (11¼ × 10¼ in.)

Original artwork for *A First Book
of Nature* (2012) *(p. 167)*
2010
Cut paper
Nine moths, each 3–5 cm
(1⅛–2 in.), width

Selection of original artwork for
A First Book of Nature (2012)
(pp. 168–69)
2010–11
Collage
Each spread: 28.5 × 52 cm
(11¼ × 20½ in.)

A Wedding in Tuscany *(p. 170;
front and reverse shown)*
2011
Monoprint and collage
21 × 45 cm (8¼ × 17¾ in.)

Boar and Hoopoe *(p. 171)*
2012
Collage
75 × 56 cm (29½ × 22 in.)

Flight X *(p. 172)*
2011
Collage
22 × 21 cm (8⅝ × 8¼ in.)

Flight *(p. 173)*
2011
Die-cut card
Set of six cards, each
18.5 × 22.5 cm (7¼ × 8⅞ in.)

Menagerie Envelope *(p. 176, top)*
2000
Ink and watercolour
25 × 30 cm (9⅞ × 11¾ in.)

Birthday Pigeon *(p. 176, bottom)*
2009
Collage
28 × 38 cm (11 × 15 in.)

Valentine *(p. 177)*
2009
Collage
45 × 29 cm (17¾ × 11⅜ in.)

Original artwork for Pigeon Post
correspondence card *(pp. 182–83)*
2010
Collage
Two parts, each 15 × 61 cm
(5⅞ × 24 in.)

Heron *(p. 184)*
2012
Collage
101 × 66 cm (39¾ × 26 in.)

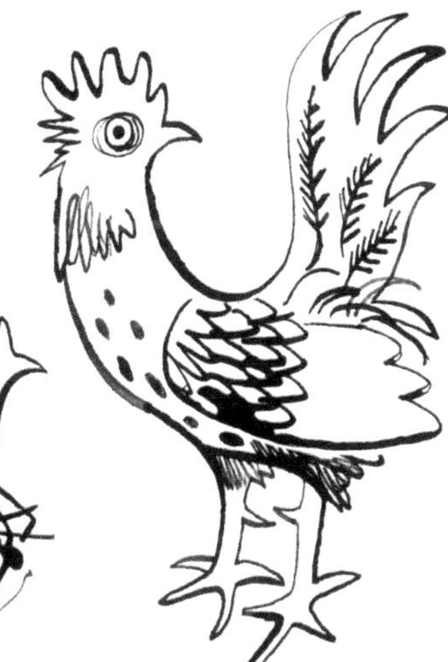

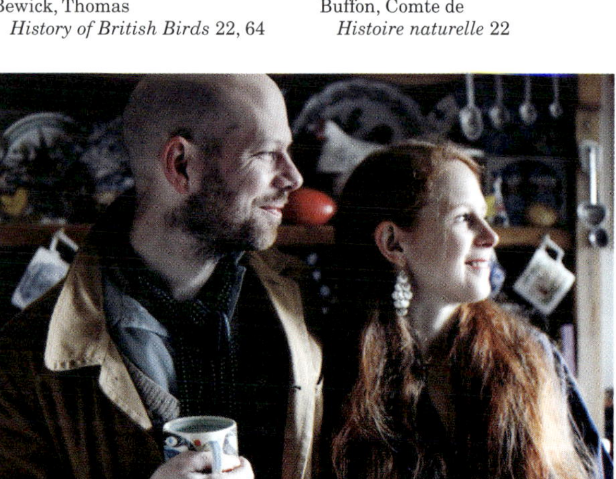

Acknowledgements

I would like to thank the publishing team at Merrell for making this book happen ESPECIALLY Nicola Bailey, with whom it has been an absolute pleasure to collaborate on its design. Simon Martin for his informed texts and contributions to its structure, Everyone who lent work to be photographed. Nigel & Iris Weaver for hosting a photo shoot, Colin Wilkin for coming up with a title for the book at their kitchen table, and so too every one who has supported my creative endeavours over the years. Alex and Mary Godfrey for giving me the first exhibition, Simon and Angie Lewin for giving me the chance to try my hand as a designer. Dan Bugg for editioning my linocuts so beautifully. Jenny Roland and the wonderful printers at the Curwen Studio for publishing my lithographs. Les Prince for his superb framing and his persistent wise words. Jerry Shone for welcoming me into his pottery. Amy Husband for enduring the creative squalor in our studio and of course all my friends and family and

Em and Feste who make life SPECIAL

Published by Merrell Publishers,
London and New York

Merrell Publishers Limited
70 Cowcross Street
London EC1M 6EJ

merrellpublishers.com

First published 2012
Compact hardback edition first published 2022

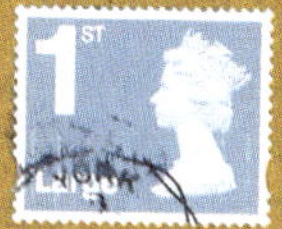
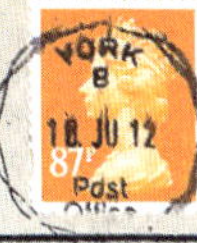
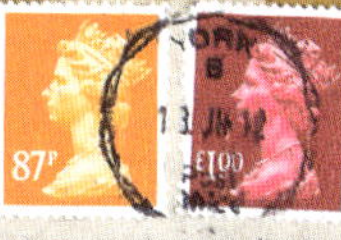
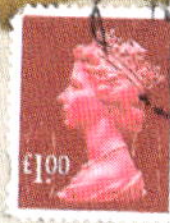
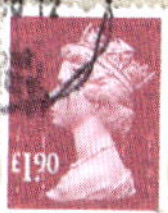

ISBN 978-1-8589-4709-9

Produced by Merrell Publishers Limited
Designed by Nicola Bailey
Project-managed by Mark Ralph
Indexed by Hilary Bird

Printed and bound in China

Page 7: Mark Hearld moving out of his flat
in Portland Street, York, spring 2012.
Pages 16–17: Portland Street pigeon holes.

Picture Credits
© Doug Atfield: pages 11, 14, 15 (top), 20, 34–35,
40, 44–45, 46, 47, 54, 72, 73, 76–77, 99 (bottom
right), 101, 110 (bottom), 111 (top), 116–17, 119,
138, 139, 146 (top left), 148–49, 154 (top), 155, 176
(top), 180–81; © The Estate of Edward Bawden.
Photo: The Fry Art Gallery: page 9 (right); The
Fitzwilliam Museum, University of Cambridge,
UK/The Bridgeman Art Library: page 8 (left);
from *Fleamarket Chic: The Thrifty Way to Create
a Stylish Home* (2012) published by CICO Books/
Simon Brown: pages 16–17; © Julian Trevelyan
Estate. Photo: Tate Images: page 9 (left); Ian
Macdonald: pages 10, 12; Joanna Mazzotta: page 31;
© The Trustees of the Piper Estate: page 8 (right)

MARK HEARLD studied at Glasgow School of
Art and the Royal College of Art, London. He is
a highly versatile artist, using a wide range of
media and design projects to explore his love of
nature, his interest in English popular art and
his belief in the importance of living life visually.
His book *Raucous Invention: The Joy of Making*
was published in 2022.

SIMON MARTIN is the Director of Pallant House
Gallery in Chichester, West Sussex. A specialist in
modern British art, he is the author of numerous
monographs and exhibition catalogues on such
artists as John Piper, John Minton, Edward Burra,
Colin Self and John Tunnard.

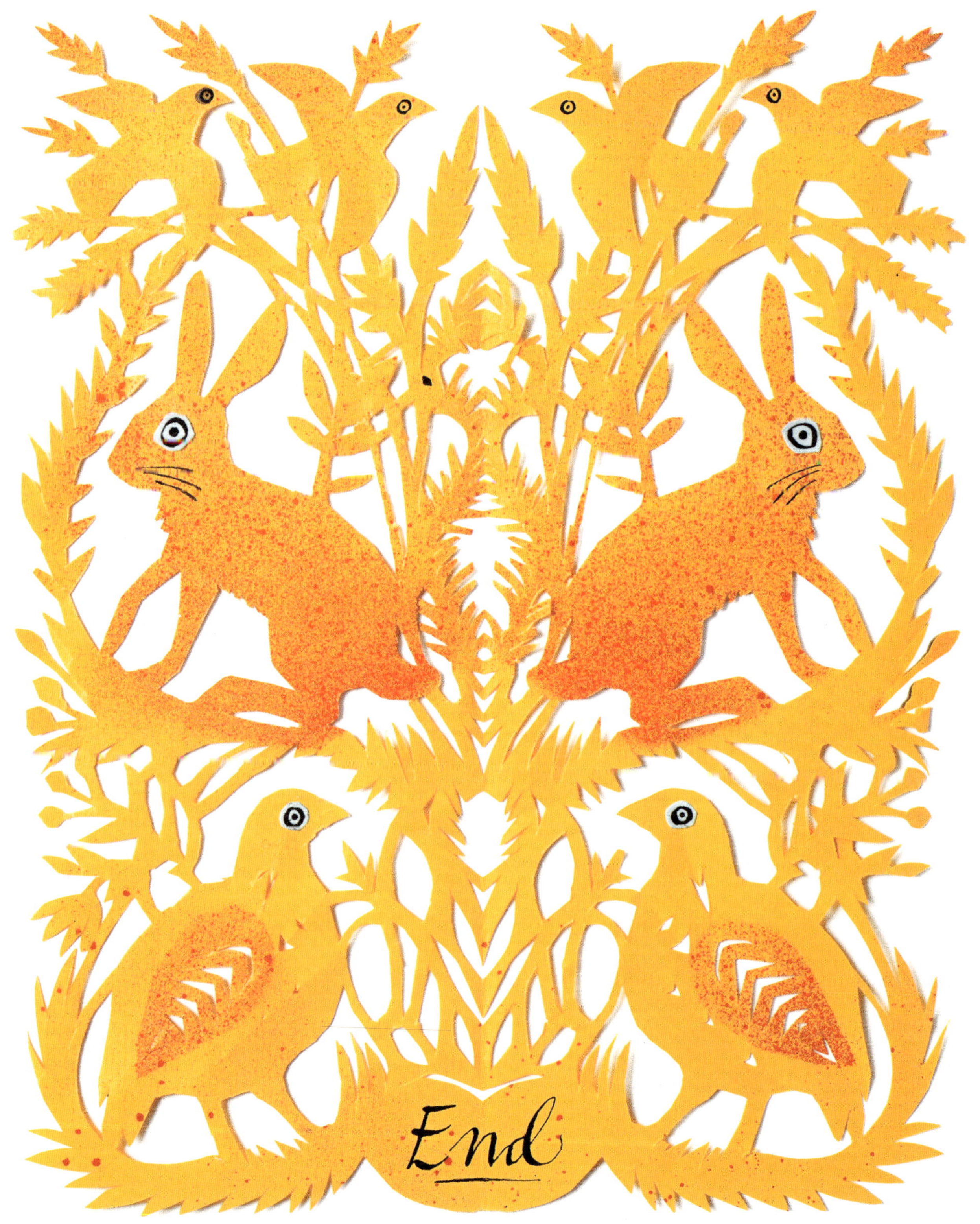

End

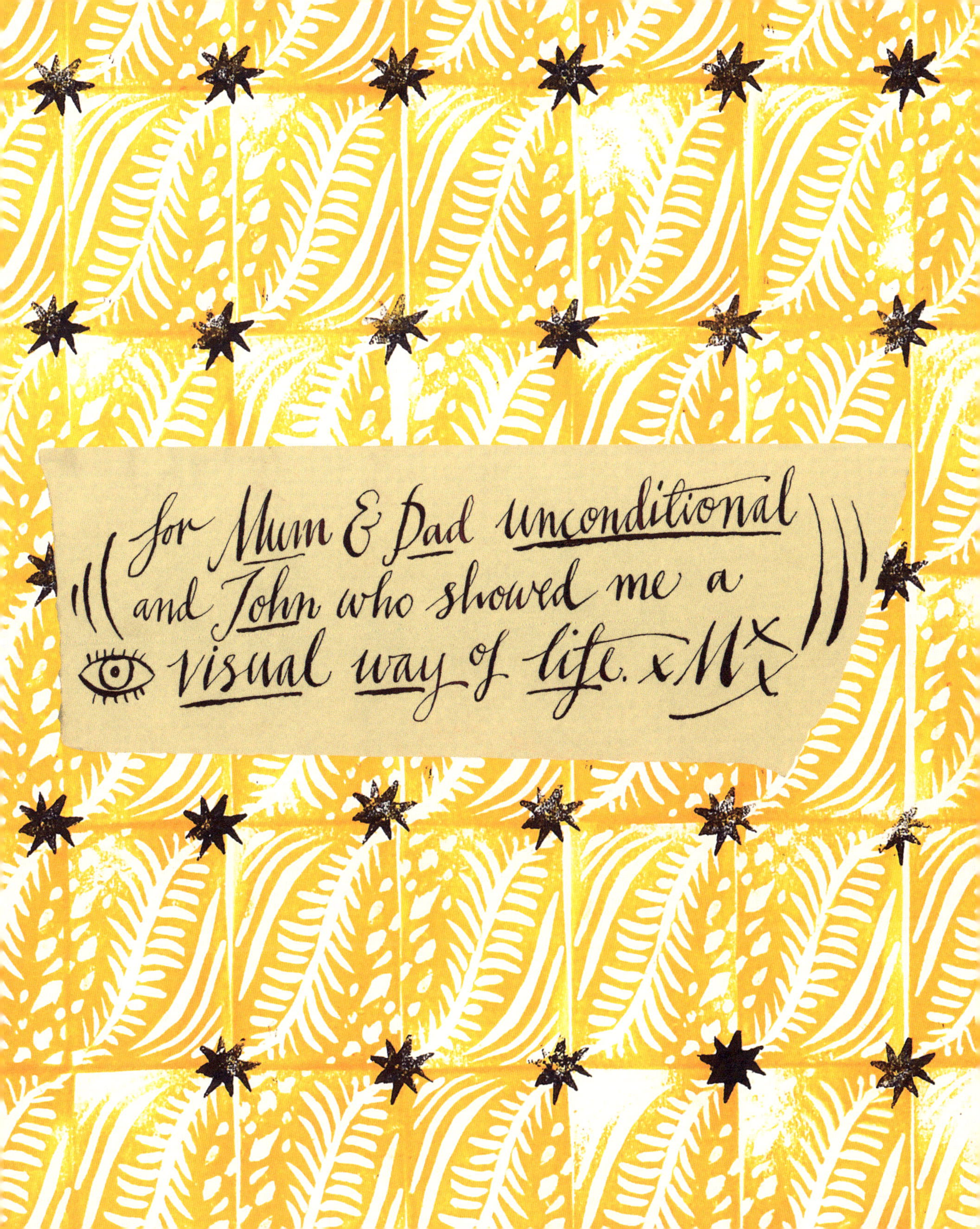

for Mum & Dad unconditional
and John who showed me a
visual way of life. xMx

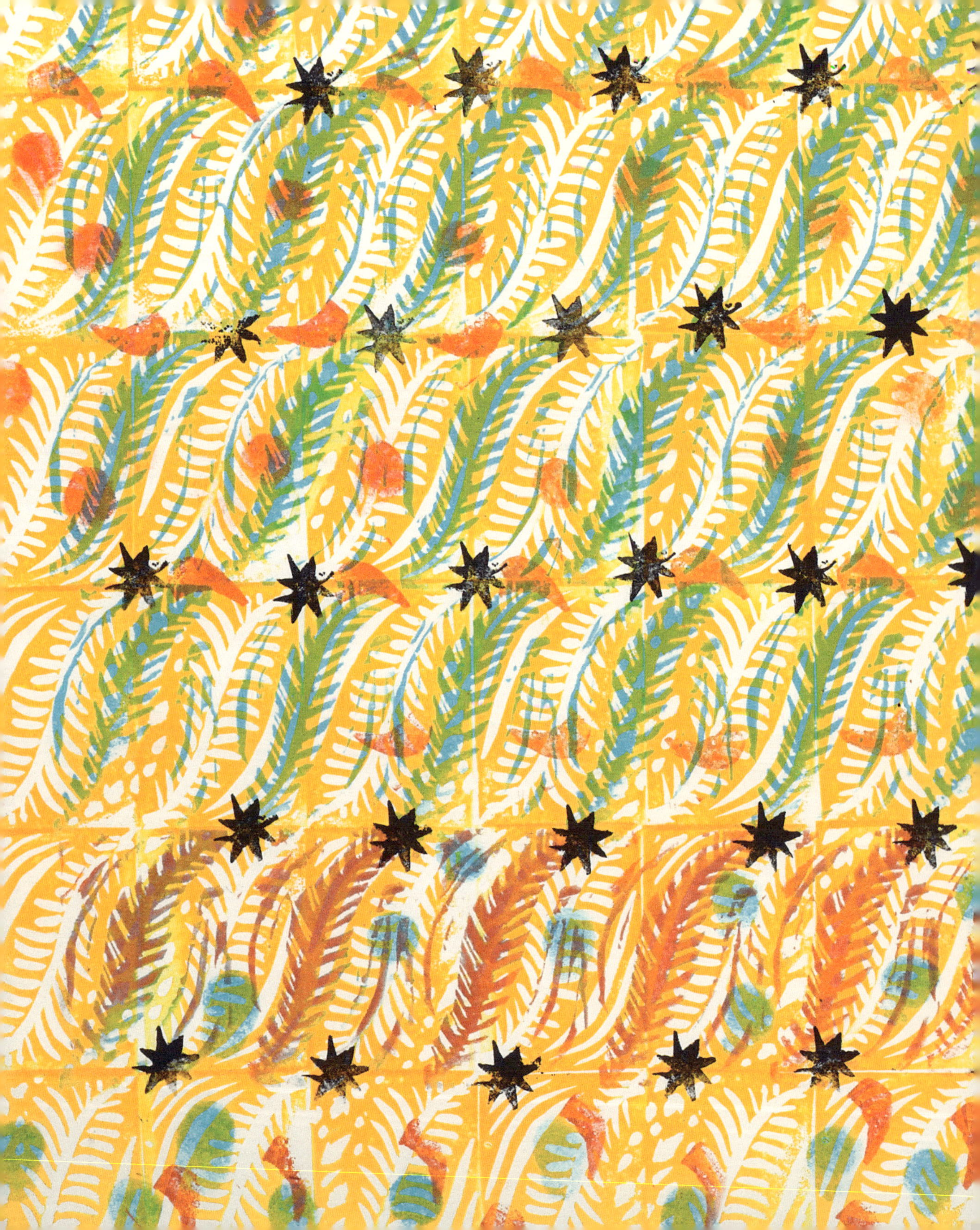